1982

Theatrical Set Design

Set for *Once Upon a Mattress*, East Carolina University. Designed by Robert T. Williams. Directed by Edgar R. Loessin.

SECOND EDITION

Theatrical Set Design

the basic techniques

DAVID WELKER

Designer and Professor of Theater Arts
Wake Forest University
Winston-Salem, North Carolina

ALLYN AND BACON, INC.
BOSTON, LONDON, SYDNEY

Library of Congress Cataloging in Publication Data

Welker, David Harold.
  Theatrical set design.

  Includes index.
  1. Theaters—Stage-setting and scenery. I. Title.
PN2091.S8W38 1979   792'.025   78–20987
ISBN 0-205-06451-5

Production Editor: Rowena Dores
Design Editor: Paula Carroll
Manufacturing Buyer: Linda Card

Printed in the United States of America.

In dedicating this book, I would like first to express my appreciation to my wife,

Dorothy Welker

for her constant encouragement and advice.

It would be fitting also to mention all of the outstanding teachers and students, from whom I have learned much, but the list would be impossibly long. They must be represented by five names, each one standing for dozens of others:

Dr. Frank M. Whiting
Mr. Whitney Ballantine
Mr. John Figlmiller
Mrs. Paula Starks Wilson
Mrs. Kathy Olsen Tyler

CONTENTS

Preface

There is a story about a man who, over a period of two decades, taught his wife to cook superbly without knowing how to cook, himself. He did it by announcing, after having tried each dish, "No good," or "A little better," or "That's a good one—keep it." It is possible to teach any art, including set design, in the same way, except that twenty years are never available in the hurried and harried quadrennium set aside for a college education. Pedagogical efficiency requires that the study of an art be organized in a comprehensive and consistent theory.

Theory is an inflammatory word, for many artists. One old text remarks that there are, fortunately, no rules for set design; and one new text repeatedly gives long introductions to various aspects of design and then closes each discussion with the statement that the particular item cannot be taught. Such nihilistic commentators view theories as restrictive (notice the pejorative use of the word "rules"). This text is expressive of the belief that theory—that is, an organized explanation and understanding of the factors operating in an art—is liberating rather than restricting. The major factor in a work of art is undoubtedly the artist's taste, imagination, and intelligence, a complex that comes from his or her basic nature and cannot be supplied by any text or teacher. But even this group of qualities may be educated and sharpened by example and discussion, and the methods by which such elements may be applied and expressed in design can be taught, provided an adequate theory is developed to describe them. It is the purpose of this book to present such a theory.

Without a theory, there is very little to say about an art. Previous books about set design, when they were not simply collections of examples, have contained little actual discussion of the subject. Even the titles have usually combined design with some other topic, the major part of the book being concerned with the added subject. Thus, one is entitled *Scene Painting and Design,* another *Stage Scenery and Lighting,* a third *Stagecraft and Scene Design.* This book is not an *and* book; it deals with set design alone, in its two aspects of art and craft. It is intended to give the student the basic techniques—what he needs to master the art of design—and nothing else.

A major practical problem in the preparation of the book, in fact, was determining what might safely be omitted; an exhaustive discussion would have extended to thousands of pages. One omission should be especially noted. No attempt was made to give a history of set design; rather, history was used only as the source of isolated illustrations intended to clarify points of theory and practice for the student.

All set designers are concerned with providing a set that helps the director plan the arrangement and movements of the actors, that helps the actors express their interrelationships and emotions, and that expressively underlines the mood of the play: these and similar elements of design must be considered by any artist. The specific techniques and methods by which such goals are attained, however, are so diverse that probably no two designers operate in exactly the same way. Obviously, no text could describe all, or even a small percentage, of the various patterns of practice. Each designer develops methods of attacking the problems of design that are precisely adjusted to his or her own tastes and habits of thinking. In their first study of the art, however, students need instructions that will provide them with a clear-cut procedure, even though they may alter it or replace it with a different one in later years. This text attempts to supply such a procedure. It should be emphasized, however, that this procedure is intended only to guide students through their first exploration of the art of set design; as they become more experienced they will almost certainly discover a somewhat different path that will be more congenial to them. This qualification applies to all of the technical and procedural discussions in the book, even though it is not always directly stated.

It can be expected that an individual instructor's methods and techniques will also differ from those described in the book. The methods described are those that seem to be most effective for the beginning student. An experienced artist often handles design problems automatically or unconsciously; the student can solve such problems only by consciously focusing on them. It is hoped that the methods described in the text will be helpful to both students and instructors, if they care to follow them, but that instructors will find it easy to alter them or substitute other techniques that they find more congenial.

This book is planned as the text for a course in set design on the college level, although it is hoped that it might also be useful for students who prefer to work independently, without enrollment in a formal class. It assumes that the students are intelligent, that they have attended plays, and that they are interested in learning to design scenery. No other special knowledge is presumed.

The organization of the book is intended to be psychological; that is, the various topics are discussed in the order in which it seems likely that students will need them, and the steps in design are arranged to match the order in which accomplished artists turn their attention to them.

In revising the text, I have been assisted by the comments of teachers who have been using it through the years, but even more valuable have been the suggestions of the hundreds of students in my own classes. This new edition incorporates many of their recommendations, especially in the discussion of the difficulties sometimes encountered in the director-designer relationship and in the expanded discussion of esthetics.

For brevity, I have used masculine pronouns when referring to "the set designer" or "the director" in general. This is not meant to exclude the many excellent female set designers and directors.

Set design is of course only one of the arts of the theater, and not the most important; but the theater, as the greatest and most complex (even if least perfect) of all the arts, is so near the center of human thought and experience that even this single aspect of it is at least potentially a great and significant art. It is hoped that this book will help clarify and facilitate the practice of that art for the designers of the future.

DAVID WELKER

PART I

INTRODUCTION

1

THE ROLE of THE DESIGNER

A bell rings in the lobby to remind latecomers that they must hurry to their seats in the theater. Even as they enter, the lights at the back of the auditorium have begun to fade, and the stage curtain begins to glow as the *curtain-warmers* (spotlights pointed at the curtain from above the ceiling of the auditorium) are slowly brought up by the light crew. As the double fading is completed, down for the house lights and up for the stage lights, the curtains part.

The room revealed on stage is obviously expensively decorated and obviously in bad taste—in fact, a burlesque of decorative fads of the early fifties. (See *Figures 1-1* and *1-2*.) At the front of the stage, on each side, is a counter. The one at the left has a fancy bar stool next to it; the one at the right holds a telephone. At the back, four steps of polished grey-green tile lead to an entrance hall, with a door at the back directly facing the audience and a door at the side leading to the bedroom. Opposite the bedroom door are a hall tree and a console table. The second step is broad, forming a landing on which rests a fireplace with a raised opening and a brass hood extending up to the ceiling.

Starting near the fireplace is a shelf that runs along the back wall to the corner and then continues along the right wall to where it disappears behind the right bar. The section of the shelf against the back wall is wider

Figure 1-1. Set for Neil Simon's *Come, Blow Your Horn.*

Figure 1-2. The *Come, Blow Your Horn* set in use.

Figure 1-3. The little peasant persuades the cowherd to take his calf to pasture (Paul Sills' *Story Theater*).

than the rest and serves as a desk. The walls are green, with white woodwork, but little of them is visible, since each one is draped with black-and-white zebra cloth. The floor is covered wall to wall with a mottled, rather drab, green rug. The kitchen is visible through an opening in the left wall, but the view is obscured by a curtain of beads arranged in broad stripes of green alternating with narrow stripes of crystal. The curtains are repeated at the front of the hall.

The room is a mess. A shirt has been carelessly thrown over a tall potted plant in one corner of the room, a coat lies across the arm of a sofa, and papers and other articles of clothing are strewn about on the floor and other furniture.

What we are seeing is not a living room in a suburban home. The impersonal, cliché décor could be found nowhere except in an apartment house for singles, and the general mess, the liquor bottles filling the bar at the left, and the four-foot-by-six-foot op-art nude hanging over the desk identify the setting unmistakably as a bachelor apartment—occupied by a young man trying hard to play the role of swinger, somewhat self-consciously and without complete success.

Through the hall door, Alan Baker enters, just behind Peggy Evans, his date for the evening, and *Come Blow Your Horn,* Neil Simon's first play to reach Broadway, has begun. The play is hardly great drama, but it is

Figure 1-4.   The four animals of "The Bremen Town Musicians" serenade the night as they look out the window of the robber's cottage *(Story Theater).*

good fun. At the end, the would-be swinger has turned square and is engaged to be married, and his conventional younger brother has reversed his role to try a bit of swinging for himself.

Across town, another play is in progress, with a totally different kind of setting. It has the appearance of an illustration for a child's book. (See

Figures 1-3, 1-4, and *1-5.*) At the left of the stage is a four-foot-high platform painted in a naive technique to indicate that it is made of stone. Hung above it on invisible wires is a three-dimensional roof covered with large, bright-red shingles, topped by a chimney made of oversize bricks. The walls of the house are missing, but thin slashes of yellow curve up at each corner to mark their edges.

Leading up to the platform is a flight of steps, each one shaped like a crescent moon, and a similar flight at the other end of the platform runs up to a high landing and then back down to the floor of the stage— a flight of stairs going nowhere. A bush stands near the platform that forms the foundation of the house, and twelve-foot-high trees frame the stage picture. They too are obviously pretend trees: the trunks and branches are twisted grotesquely like ropes, and each branch ends in a clutching three-fingered hand. Each tree and bush has been split vertically in the center, and the two halves have been swung back at right angles to suggest the pop-up pictures that appear in children's books. The entire set is surrounded at the back and sides by a rail fence, with a stile at each side enabling the actors to step over it. The stage floor is stippled in green to suggest grass, and a broad yellow path winds along the front of the stage from one stile to another.

The play is Paul Sills's *Story Theater,* which is made up of ten separate episodes, each one based on a familiar folk tale. Since all are enacted on the same set, with a few changes of properties, the audience is asked to help out with its imagination. In "Two Crows," based on a story by Aesop, one crow finds an oyster on the beach, but cannot open it. The yellow path then becomes a sandy beach. A second crow advises the first to fly high up and break the oyster open by dropping it down on the sand. The high flight of stairs leading up to nowhere becomes the path up which the actor flies, and he pauses on the landing to drop the oyster down to the beach.

In another episode, "The Robber Bridegroom" *(Figure 1-5),* the space under the stairs becomes the basement of the house, in which the beautiful heroine searches for her fiancé. *Story Theater* is unusual in that it is enjoyed almost equally by people of all ages: this audience is made up of children from the first grade through high school, college students, college professors, and townspeople.

In still another theater, the stage set is made up of a series of platforms of various heights, painted in bright colors and arranged to form a maze with unexpected turns, odd openings, and dead-end paths *(Figure 1-6).* Hidden in one of the platforms are three barrels, which appear magically during a momentary blackout. Out of these, numerous actors climb— more people than the barrels will hold. The floor of the stage is painted in glowing rectangles. Occasionally, the audience is asked to imagine that the platform areas represent specific locales—the deck of a ship, the throne room of a palace—but most of the time they represent nothing at all, serving simply as guides for the actors' movements, levels to separate

Figure 1-5. The little old woman in the basement of the murderers' cottage warns the miller's daughter that she must flee for her life ("The Robber Bridegroom," *Story Theater*).

the actors and raise them for emphasis, and occasionally cul-de-sacs in which they are trapped. The play is Tom Stoppard's *Rosencrantz and Guildenstern Are Dead.*

Figure 1-6. Rosencrantz and Guildenstern watch the enactment of a tragic scene by Hamlet and members of the court (Tom Stoppard's *Rosencrantz and Guildenstern Are Dead*).

A thousand further examples might be described, but these three suggest something of the range of scenery, from the realism of the set for *Come Blow Your Horn,* through the let's-pretend game of *Story Theater,* to the essentially abstract architectural pattern of *Rosencrantz and Guildenstern Are Dead.* To a large extent, each play creates its own style. Indeed, different productions of the same play are likely to display different styles. For example, the set for the professional production of *Story Theater* was little more than a wide, six-sided platform with a slanted top, two short flights of stairs leading down from the platform, and some neutral-colored walls and drapes to hide the sides and back of the stage.

But no matter what style of scenery is used, or what type of play is presented, all sets share one purpose—they are designed to create some kind of experience for the audience. The range of possible experiences is of course enormous. Some plays are intended just to be fun—for example, *Come Blow Your Horn,* Shakespeare's *The Merry Wives of Windsor,* and the musical comedy *A Funny Thing Happened on the Way to the Forum.* Other plays are intended to make us more vividly aware of some aspect of life to which the playwright believes we pay too little attention—for example, Arthur Kopit's *Indians* and Joseph Heller's antiwar play, *We Bombed in New Haven.* Other plays are intended to make us think about problems of life that have not yet been solved and that the playwright feels are important—for example, Ken Kesey's *One Flew Over the Cuckoo's Nest,* all the plays of Bertolt Brecht, most of Shaw, Ibsen's *An Enemy of the People* (as well as many of his other plays), and all of Pirandello.

Other playwrights may try to persuade the audience to accept their own views of life or solutions to current problems. Wilder's *Our Town* and *The Skin of Our Teeth* are clearly of this type, as are many of the plays of Tennessee Williams. It is arguable that all of the plays of Aristophanes, Aeschylus, and Euripides are of this type, as are (somewhat less clearly) those of Sophocles. Most of Sartre's plays are of this persuasive type. So are nineteenth-century melodramas like *The Drunkard* and *Our American Cousin.*

This kind of listing is excessively simplistic. It would be more accurate to say that each play is intended by the playwright to serve its own unique purpose, and that there should be as many categories as there are plays. Certainly, there might well be disagreement about the examples given—and they were chosen in an attempt to exclude borderline plays. As just one illustration, it has been seriously argued that *The Bald Soprano* is (1) a comedy, (2) not a comedy but a tragedy, (3) absurd, (4) entirely sensible, (5) simply an amusing experience, and (6) conventionally didactic. The same kind of disagreements could be discovered in commentaries on Giraudoux's *The Madwoman of Chaillot,* Beckett's *Waiting for Godot,* and Shakespeare's *The Merchant of Venice* and *Hamlet,* as well as hundreds of other plays of varying quality.

Let us accept, then, (1) that each play is intended to provide an experience for the audience; (2) that the experience the author hopes will be created is in some degree unlike that intended for any other play; and (3) that, as a corollary to the first two assumptions, the primary function of all the members of the staff who have creative assignments (excluding those who are to serve as ushers, ticket-sellers, and the like) is to *communicate* with the audience in such a way that the author's intention will be achieved.

UNITY IN PRODUCTION

It is of the greatest importance to remember that drama is a cooperative art, each production involving a large number of people. The program of one university production, chosen almost at random, lists the following staff members as contributing to the experience of the audience (omitting those responsible for the box office, publicity, ushering, cleaning, etc.):

	Number of People
Director	1
Assistant to the Director	1
Cast	39
Speech Director	1
Set Designer	1
Shop Foreman	1
Shop Assistant	1
Construction Crew	14
Lighting Designer	1
Lighting Crew	11
Properties Master	1
Properties Crew	6
Costume Designer	1
Costume Crew	10
Makeup Designer	1
Makeup Crew	6
Sound Engineer	1
Sound Crew	4
Production Manager	1
Assistant Production Manager	1
Stage Manager	1
Assistant Stage Manager	1

All of these 105 people bring their individual interests, enthusiasms, skills, knowledge, prejudices, limitations, perceptions, experiences, and attitudes, as well as the human possibility of occasional error and bad judgment, to their work on the play. On the simplest level of efficiency, the activities of such a group of workers must be coordinated; on the more important level of achieving a unified work of art, all of the work of all the members of the staff must be fitted together harmoniously. As a simple example, there must be some means of preventing the set designer from choosing a vivid green for the walls of the set while the properties crew puts purple-and-orange slip covers on the sofa, the costume crew dresses the heroine in a brick-red evening gown, and the lighting designer chooses spotlight filters that flood the scene with mauve light. Throughout the more than two thousand years that make up the history of drama, various methods have been used to prevent esthetic chaos and to produce a unity of effect. The method currently in use is very recent, in terms of history. In fact, it was only about a hundred years ago that such great artists as the Duke of Saxe-Meiningen and Constantin Stanislavski developed the concept of a tight organizational pattern for the theatrical production staff, with a clear path of responsibility and authority leading to a single person whose primary function is making sure that the resulting production will create for the audience a unified esthetic experience.

In practice, a production usually starts with the script of the play. In addition to giving the words the actors are to speak, the script provides other information: the locale of the play, an indication of how the actors are to move about the stage, and the objects they will need (paper for writing a letter, a telephone, a window shade that can be raised, etc.). With a new play, especially in the professional theater, the playwright may be asked to revise scenes or acts, sometimes slightly, sometimes radically. Even with an established play, whether classic or modern, it may be necessary to make some script alterations to fit local conditions. For example, in the musical comedy *Once Upon a Mattress* an actress costumed to represent a bird is swung on stage suspended in an oversized birdcage. It is possible that a particular theater might lack facilities for flying such a unit, and the director would decide to sacrifice the effect out of simple necessity. After all revisions have been completed, however, the script constitutes the major body of information about the experience that it is hoped will be created for the audience.

Once Upon a Mattress is a delightful bit of froth; it is difficult to imagine anyone misinterpreting it as expressing an important philosophical analysis of human relationships. Most plays, however, contain a larger area of ambiguity, and some are open to significantly differing interpretations. Which of the various possibilities is chosen as a guide for the work of the staff may make a great deal of difference in what they do. If Giraudoux's *The Madwoman of Chaillot* is simply a light farce, it should be set, costumed, propertied, and lit in one way; if it is in fact a savage denunciation of twentieth-century European life (which it at least pretends to be), then all decisions about the set, costumes, properties, and lighting should be quite different. Obviously, one of these interpretations (or a third interpretation) must be chosen as a guide for the production, and someone must have authority to make such a choice. In the modern theater, that is the director.

THE DIRECTOR'S FUNCTION

We tend to think of directors as spending most of their time rehearsing the actors; in fact, less than half their working hours are spent in rehearsal, and training the actors is second in importance among their responsibilities. Here we are concerned with a director's most important responsibility—interpreting the script, defining the experience that is to be created for the audience, and then guiding the entire production staff (actors as well as technicians) so as to make sure that the work of each person harmonizes with that of all the others and that the work of the entire staff harmonizes with the director's interpretation of the play, making it maximally probable that the experience of the audience will be what the director intends.

DESIGN CONFERENCES

In this text we are of course concerned primarily with the relationship between the director and the set designer. After analyzing the play script, the director typically calls a meeting of the design staff (set designer, costume designer, lighting designer, and the heads of the properties and sound crews) to describe the director's conception of the production, focusing on the experience that is to be communicated to, or created for, the audience. At this meeting, it is the designers' responsibility to absorb fully and accurately the director's point of view and intentions; they are likely to ask questions about points they do not understand.

After the initial meeting, each designer engages in a complicated and more-or-less long and difficult process, beginning with a careful study of the script from the viewpoint that the director has prescribed. Next, the designer explores the resources available, selects those that he or she believes will contribute most to achieving the director's intention, works them into a tightly integrated pattern, and records the decisions in a communicable form. The chief of the sound crew will prepare a list of sound effects and musical recordings. Most of the other designers (especially the costume and set designers) will prepare a series of drawings, either rough sketches or finished plans.

At this point, each designer usually has an individual conference with the director to discuss and evaluate the designs. The director will be primarily concerned with making sure (1) that the design proposals are in harmony with the director's picture of the experience to be created for the audience, (2) that they are in harmony with the work of the rest of the staff (this of course can only be judged as the series of conferences with different designers proceeds), and (3) that the designs as submitted will contribute maximally to producing the desired effect.

If the designs as first proposed pass these three tests, the director will accept them and, ideally, will certify approval by signing or initialling the sheets that have been submitted. If the designs fail any of the three tests, the director will indicate that fact. Almost never is a director likely to say simply, "Those designs are terrible; go back and start over again." At worst, he or she will indicate the specific aspects of the designs that are unsatisfactory. For example: "Wilde describes Lady Bracknell as ringing the doorbell in a 'Wagnerian' manner; our regular doorbell, which you plan to use, won't produce exactly the right effect, so you'd better scratch that and try to find another one." More often, the director is likely to suggest an alternative: "Why can't we use a set of chimes, and actually play a phrase from Wagner—perhaps the call of the Valkyries? At least try it out and see what you think."

If the designs have been only partially approved, the designer makes a renewed attack on the problems that have been pointed out by the director. When the designer has discovered what seems to be the best solution, the director and designer have a second conference, focusing on the special problems identified in the first. Most often, the director accepts the new proposals; if not, the entire process is repeated until the designs are finally approved.

THE DESIGNER-DIRECTOR RELATIONSHIP

The procedure described in the preceding section is the way the director-designer relationship is supposed to work, and that's the way it does work in well-run theaters. Unfortunately, sometimes the design process does not move in this orderly and effective way, but breaks down, making it impossible to achieve effective designs; then design decisions that are second rate or worse are built into the production.

What goes wrong, and who is at fault? Of course, the problem might be that the designer is inexperienced or simply incompetent. Sometimes, however, the breakdown is the result of mistakes of the director. Directors, because of the position of authority conferred on them, necessarily establish and maintain the tone of the relationship between themselves and the designers. Designers must follow their directors' instructions, since it is the directors who will accept or reject their designs. This authority, however recently it was developed, has become so firmly established that unthinking or inexperienced theater people erroneously transform it into an assumption of infallibility: "Because the director is in charge, he can do no wrong." But directors vary enormously in their skill and in the soundness of their judgment, and like other human beings they sometimes make mistakes.

There is no reason why the same person cannot both direct a play and prepare designs for it—if that person has mastered the art of set design as well as the art of directing. Problems arise when directors who do not meet the necessary standards attempt to impose decisions on their designers, interfering in the proper design process.

It is a joy to work with good directors who know their job and do it, who know the proper function of designers and allow them to carry it out. Such directors occur frequently, but too often designers must work with the other type.

What can the designer do in such a situation? The most desirable action is to resign, but that may be impractical. As a second choice, it may be possible to educate the director. In one case, the designer drew up four different sets, one conforming to the director's specifications and three alternatives. In that case, the director was able to see that his demands were impractical and chose one of the alternative designs.

In lieu of either of those solutions, a designer can accept the unfortunate specifications and then attempt to work around them, at least introducing architectural or decorative elements that will distract the audience's attention from the director's intrusions. But this may involve a great deal of work, and it is almost certain to result in a set that is less effective than if the designer had been free to work soundly.

THE DIRECTOR'S EVALUATIONS

Nothing in this discussion is intended to imply that directors should not evaluate the designs submitted to them. The designers themselves will have developed, analyzed, and evaluated perhaps dozens of designs before choosing the best ones to submit, and it is proper and necessary that the directors should continue this evaluative process. What is objected to is the director's bypassing evaluation, preventing evaluation, and forcing adoption of untried, unevaluated, inspirations.

Furthermore, this discussion is not intended to suggest that directors should not point out unsatisfactory details or make suggestions of their own regarding the designs submitted to them. A director may say to the designer: "This is fine for most of the play, but there is one scene in which the maid has to exit on the left side of the stage, do an instantaneous costume change, run around behind the scenery, and make a surprise entrance from the right. Her costume will have an especially bouffant skirt, and the hall masking is too close to the back wall of the stage for her to run past as quickly as she has to. You'll have to fix that somehow."

A director doing Strindberg's *Easter* might say: "Several times we must see the ominous shadow of one of the actors on the window shade as he walks past outside the house, and each time the shadow must seem more threatening. You have placed the window in the side wall, so that the shadow that should dominate the scene will be almost unnoticeable. I realize the door is in the middle of the back wall, but why can't we move it left, and then right of it insert a bay window, which will face the audience more directly, and which will have the result of prolonging the shadow effect as we see the shadow move across three blinds instead of just one?'' No designer would resent comments and suggestions like those, which are genuinely helpful. They are likely to improve the final set rather than make it worse.

The timing, then, is of genuine importance. Suggestions made in advance of the designer's study hamper; those made after, help, if they are sensible and are based on a careful analysis of the designer's work. Furthermore, it is simply sound practice for all staff members to carry out their own responsibilities. Directors who try to half-design without doing the necessary analytical work not only make the resulting sets less effective, but also find they don't have enough time for their own responsibilities. The result is a bad set matched by bad directing and bad acting.

It is desirable that an easy working relationship be established between a director and designer, especially if they must work together on many productions. Some directors prefer to give designers great freedom and, especially when they are familiar with the designers' work, may approve sketches at a very early stage. They may even welcome suggestions from the designers with regard to the staging of the play. Other directors may make numerous suggestions for changes as the sketches and drawings are submitted to them. Obviously, some designer-director teams work together more smoothly than others, and when severe conflict develops it may even be preferable to dissolve the partnership. Ultimately, however, the tone of the relationship and the final authority in all decisions with regard to the designs must rest with the director.

THE WORK OF THE DESIGNER

In the early half of the nineteenth century, scenery was regarded as a separate theatrical element that had little relation to the action of the play. It was designed to be admired for its own sake. The present-day attitude is diametrically opposed. It has been said that the audience should not notice the scenery at all; if they should be so impressed with a set that they applaud it when the curtain first rises, the designer has failed! That is a somewhat exaggerated position; however, the basic principle is universally recognized as sound in the theater today.

In the professional theater, the designer is responsible only for preparing a series of paintings and drawings that include all the information necessary for building the scenery. Those drawings are then given to construction specialists, who do the actual building. Even in New York, however, the designer may serve as consultant for the builders and may supervise the painting, erection, and lighting of the set. In the nonprofessional theater (including educational, community, and summer theaters), it is far more common for the designer to serve in other capacities, in addition to planning the scenery and preparing the working drawings.

Each theater develops its own pattern of responsibilities and work assignments, so that no organizational chart will apply precisely to more than one or two theaters. However, the chart given in *Figure 1-7* illustrates a generalized pattern, which should be close to the organization of most theaters. The chain of command in which the designer is a link has been indicated by shading. The designer is immediately responsible to the director, who works under the general supervision of the administrator or administrative board of the theater. The designer oversees the work of the construction, shifting, and lighting crews, as well as that of the crew responsible for collecting or building stage properties.

The term *properties* is used in two ways in the theater and is often abbreviated to *props*. Hand props are objects handled by actors during performance. Most often, they include such small artifacts as trays, dishes, cigarette lighters, and telephones. At one edge of the classification, hand props join costumes. A handkerchief worn in the pocket as a decoration is part of the costume; if it is taken out and used to dust the furniture, or even to wipe the face, it becomes a hand prop. At the other edge, hand props merge with stage props.

Stage properties are variously defined in different theaters. Often the elements of a stage set can be analyzed so as to form two categories: (1) the flats, platforms, and stairs that constitute the basic structure and (2) the various detachable decorative elements (such as cornices, pilasters, pictures hung on the walls, window shades, and drapes) that are added after the basic structure has been assembled. The term *stage props* is normally used to describe the added decorative elements, which are the last things to be fastened in place when the set is erected and the first to be removed when it is torn down. In addition, all of the furniture is universally included under the term, and in some theaters *stage properties* is used to apply only to the furniture.

As in the case of costumes, some objects might be classified as either hand or stage props. A wastebasket that functions only as decoration and is never touched is clearly a stage property; if an actor were to use it to hide a gun, it would become a hand property. Fine logical distinctions have little value in deciding whether a particular item should be classified as a hand prop, a stage prop, or a costume; in practical theater production, however, the responsibility for supplying each item must be assigned to a specific crew, and the assignment is made on the basis of simplicity of work rather than on abstract definitions.

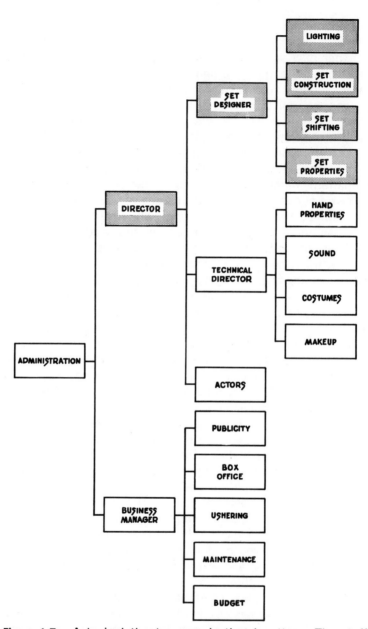

Figure 1-7. A typical theater organizational pattern. The staff members with whom the designer most often works closely are indicated by shading. In some theaters, one person may handle two or more allied assignments. If the combined positions are close together on the chart (for example, set design and lighting), the staff may consider them to be essentially a single activity.

Of the four crews operating under the supervision of the set designer, set properties is most integral to the designer's work, since the furniture and set decorations are an important element in the stage picture, for which the designer is responsible. At the least, designers will be asked to evaluate pictures, furniture, and similar stage properties; more often, they will prepare designs and working drawings that can be used in constructing stage properties that will harmonize with their basic scenic design. Closely related to their own work is lighting, which is also an important factor in the stage picture. Set construction and shifting are less essentially their concern. However, since their designs must provide for the efficient handling of both functions, designers are likely to serve as consultants, even when others may be in charge of the crews, and if a theater has a small staff, the designer may well supervise their work directly. Hand properties, costumes, and makeup all affect the stage picture, and directors may ask set designers to assist in evaluating them; often a designer will be included in conferences held by the director with the staff members in charge of those crews, but the designer is less frequently asked to assume direct responsibility for that work.

2

THE FUNCTIONS
of SCENERY

Fifty years ago, many small amateur groups, including high schools and some colleges, presented plays against a neutral background of dark-colored drapes, making no attempt to fit the visual environment to the mood or action of the play, beyond perhaps inserting a door frame or two to provide entrances and exits. Today, even amateur groups use specially designed settings that serve for a single production and are replaced for the next play. But performances are still sometimes presented in outdoor settings, or in buildings not designed to be used as theaters, with no attempt to provide an individual background suited to the particular play shown.

Some modern productions require only minimal and symbolic scenery: *The Fantasticks* is an example. These are frequently described as being "without scenery." Nevertheless, theater workers, including directors, actors, and set designers, cannot ignore the visual effect of the background, for it constitutes the environment within which the play is performed. It must be taken into account in planning any production. In most productions, the scenery is especially designed for the play, and in proscenium theaters it most often stands behind the proscenium. In Jacques Copeau's Théâtre du Vieux Colombier, a complex of architectural features was built solidly as permanent parts of the stage area, including

21

flights of stairs of various dimensions, entrance doors, a large inner arch, and platforms or landings. This architectural pattern was varied from play to play by the addition of furniture, drapes, platforms, and other familiar scenic elements. Sometimes the alteration was very slight; at other times it was so extreme as to conceal most of the basic architecture of the stage. Something of the same type of treatment appears in productions at the theater at Stratford in Ontario, as well as in many open-stage theaters throughout the United States.

Analogs may be found throughout theater history. At least in their later development, ancient Greek theaters provided a permanent architectural background for theatrical production, with entrance doors and other structures for use by the actors. In the Elizabethan theater, a very different architectural pattern appeared, and properties and decorations were used to adapt its appearance to a particular play more freely than in ancient Greece, although in comparison with modern practice the visual change was minimal.

The treatment of the visual environment of actors, then, has been extremely varied during the history of the theater, and even today productions appear at both extremes: one where the environment is totally designed for a particular production and one where the environment is not adapted at all to the play being shown. Instead of dividing the range of possible treatment into a series of groups, it seems simpler, for purposes of this discussion, to consider it as a single element of production, varying along a continuum; consequently, the terms *scenery* and *stage set* will be used here to apply to whatever the audience sees beyond and around the actors, whether its relationship is accidental or whether it is partially adapted to the production or totally specified by the designer.

THE FOUR FUNCTIONS

Scenery may serve four functions in the theater:

1. It may constitute a machine for organizing the arrangement and movement of the actors.
2. It may express the mood of the play.
3. It may give information about the locale and time of the play.
4. It may be visually interesting in itself.

Most scenery performs all these functions, although seldom with equal emphasis. (See *Figures 2-1* through *2-18,* which are scattered

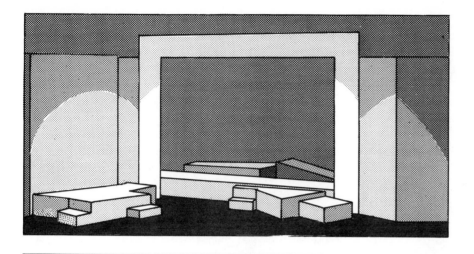

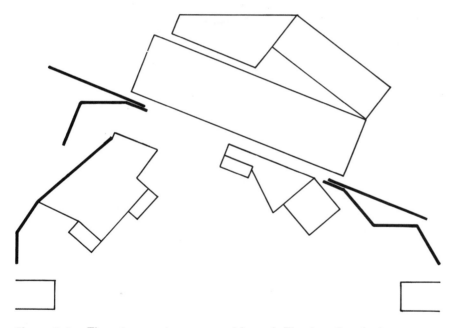

Figure 2-1. The stage set as a machine: *A Thurber Carnival.* The play is made up of short sketches. The set shown is essentially a series of platforms, cut in two by an inner proscenium that can be closed by two sliding panels (shown in the ground plan, but pulled out of sight in the top picture). While action is proceeding at the front of the stage, properties for the next scene can be set up behind the panels. Platforms can be spotlighted separately or together, and some scene changes need only an alteration in the lighting.

Figure 2-2. The *Thurber Carnival* set in use ("Gentlemen Shoppers"). [Photograph by Norm Burlingame.]

throughout this chapter.) The degrees to which the four functions are emphasized in the design for a particular play must be determined by an analysis of the script. If the design is a sound one, it will match as closely as possible the pattern of emphasis intended by the playwright. For a relatively static play like Maeterlinck's *Pelléas et Mélisande,* expressing the mood of the play may be of major importance; Rostand's *Cyrano de Bergerac,* with its highly localized settings, may require that major emphasis in design should be placed on giving information about locale; Millay's slight *Aria da Capo* could be treated so as to focus on the esthetic effect of the set—although all of those suggestions might well be rejected by a particular designer.

It is possible to describe the pattern that is generally applicable to most plays, and that pattern has been suggested by the order in which the functions are listed above. For most plays, the first function (organizing actors' arrangement and movement) is overwhelmingly the most important. Expressing the mood of the play is clearly secondary, but of great importance. Giving information about locale is very much less important, and creating an interesting visual pattern, while not negligible, is much less significant than any of the other three functions.

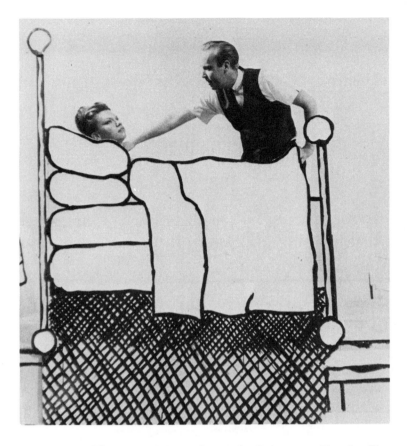

Figure 2-3. The expression of mood: Set properties in *The Thurber Carnival* imitate Thurber's cartoon style. ("The Unicorn in the Garden"). [Photograph by Norm Burlingame.]

THE HISTORIC NORM

The pattern of emphasis given to the different functions has varied greatly from period to period. Inigo Jones, who designed scenery for court masques during the reign of James I, strongly emphasized the spectacular interest of his sets, and the same pattern of emphasis was followed during most of the nineteenth century. Throughout most of the history of the theater, however, the first function—organizing the arrangement and movement of the actors—was emphasized almost to the exclusion of the other functions. In ancient Greece, for instance, the permanent architectural setting functioned superbly in assisting in the placement and movement of the players, but it gave almost no information about locale, was

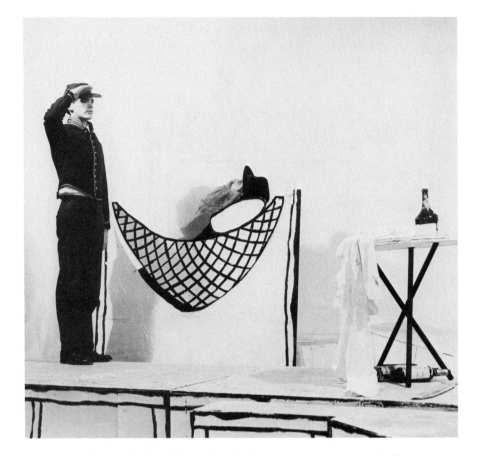

Figure 2-4. For this scene of *The Thurber Carnival* ("If Grant Had Been Drinking at Appomattox"), the hammock was constructed in silhouette. The hammock itself, separated from the masking section below it, was hung so it would swing. It was designed so that the actor representing Grant, sitting on a chair placed on the platform behind the unit, seemed to be lying in the hammock, with his head resting on the pillow. [Photograph by Norm Burlingame.]

relatively neutral visually, and expressed the mood of the plays so little that the most somber tragedies and the most hilarious comedies were acted in front of the same background. Very much the same pattern was followed in the public theaters in Elizabethan times (as contrasted with the masques, which were presented for private, invited audiences): tragedies and comedies were presented in essentially the same setting, and the background gave so little information about locale that playwrights found it necessary to insert frequent phrases into actors' speeches, identifying or describing the setting for the audience.

Figure 2-5. The expression of mood: Beckett's *Waiting for Godot.* The script describes the setting only as "A country road. A tree." The play's mood is one of dreary desolation. The set shown makes use of additional trees, with stylized, angular branches tangled overhead and dry weeds struggling out of the crevices of rocks.

Figure 2-6. The expression of mood and locale: The stone walls and floor not only indicate a medieval castle, but also suggest the coldness of what is in fact a prison *(The Lion in Winter).*

Figure 2-7. Gothic arches and the arrangment of actors in a single plane suggest a stained glass window, harmonious with the period and ecclesiastical feeling of *The Lark.*

THE DESIGN REVOLUTION

When the theater fell into decay in the early nineteenth century, set design became largely divorced from the other arts of the theater; stage sets became in effect enormous easel paintings, intended to be admired as self-contained works of art. Frequently they were commented on in reviews of the plays as if they were isolated from the other aspects of production. In the late 1800s, touring reached its height; professional touring companies crisscrossed the nation, stopping for a night or two to give performances at what were called opera houses in large and small cities throughout the United States. Sometimes such companies traveled with full casts and complete scenery. Other companies included only the stars, and shipped only costumes and properties; minor parts were played by

Figure 2-8. The farcical mood of Shakespeare's *Comedy of Errors* is reinforced by the director's decision to set the play in a circus ring and to transform the characters into circus performers.

local townspeople, and the theaters were expected to furnish the scenery. Often, a small group of sets was purchased, representing perhaps a living room, a kitchen, and an outdoors scene, usually a garden. Such sets were used over and over again, serving for whatever plays might be produced and consequently having no organic relation to any of them.

The shift of set design in the direction of easel painting to the point where some sets were frank copies of such paintings, and the spreading use of scenery that had little esthetic relation to other production elements, produced a reaction late in the nineteenth century. The development of gas lighting, including the limelight, and later electricity, may have been a factor in this reaction, since the more brilliant lighting revealed the artificiality and esthetic deficiencies of the traditional scenery with new clarity.

In any case, toward the end of the nineteenth century, a Swiss artist named Adolphe Appia produced a series of set designs and discussions of

Figure 2-9. One of the Dromios, a comic servant, is transformed into a circus clown (*The Comedy of Errors*).

Figure 2-10. Townspeople in *The Comedy of Errors* become circus acrobats.

Figure 2-11. The indication of locale: The monument shop in *Look Homeward, Angel.*

design theory that initiated a revolution in the art. Almost equally influential in the development of the new approach to scenery was Gordon Craig. Both of these men, however, were primarily theoreticians; the impact of their work on the practical theater came largely through the application of their philosophies throughout Europe by directors and designers engaged in continuing programs of production. The new concepts of design were demonstrated and popularized in the United States by many artists during the first third of the twentieth century, but one of the most influential was Robert Edmond Jones, who designed first for the Provincetown Playhouse and then became a notably successful Broadway designer.

The revolution in set design created by these artists has resulted in an approach to the art that is now nearly universal throughout the western world. Perhaps their greatest achievement was the establishment of the modern pattern of emphasis on the four functions of scenery. The advantage and justification of this pattern is that it matches the demands of most playscripts more precisely than any other pattern, although, as we have seen, particular plays may deviate from the pattern. In any case, it constitutes a useful basic operating formula, defining the best point of view from which the art may be studied.

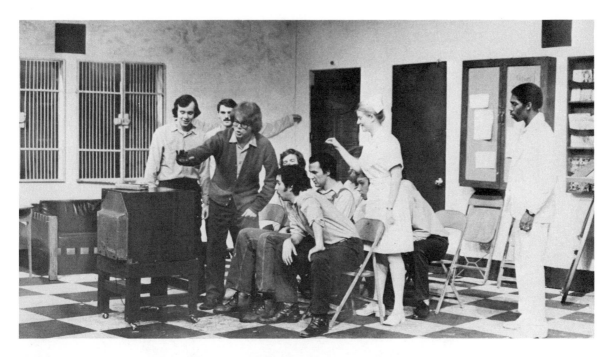

Figure 2-12. Both locale and mood are suggested by the barred windows of a lounge in a mental institution, the permanently soiled tile floor, the stained walls, and the loudspeakers and signal lights *(One Flew Over the Cuckoo's Nest)*.

Figure 2-13. The expression of locale: A relatively realistic upper-middle-class living room is created as a setting for Noel Coward's *Blithe Spirit.*

REALITY AND ILLUSION

Set design, like all the other arts, is constantly swept by fashions and fads. Such fashions are usually expressed most extremely in the work of second- and third-rate designers; great designers operate on the basis of fundamental principles, not passing fads. However, it seems desirable to mention one at the beginning of our study.

During the first quarter of the present century, before the full impact of the Appian revolution had been felt, a short-lived fashion dominated the theater. This movement was characterized by a desire for the precise reproduction of locales outside the theater. In terms of the four functions of scenery, major emphasis was placed on the third function (giving infor-

Figure 2-14. Free curves are used to suggest natural shapes and to create an esthetic pattern harmonious with the outdoor feeling of Shakespeare's *The Tempest.*

Figure 2-15. The frothy nonsense of Oscar Wilde's *The Importance of Being Earnest* is matched by a set suggestive of a series of Victorian picture frames. (See *Figures 2-18, 6-14, and 6-15* for a different treatment of this play by the same designer.)

mation about the locale of the play), but the designers went beyond that in an attempt to produce a kind of hypnotic *trompe le sens* that would, it was hoped, lead the members of the audience to forget that they were in a theater and believe that they were watching real events taking place in a real setting. The most extreme examples of such design have become subjects for ridicule. For a play set in a tenement room, David Belasco searched the slums of New York until he found a room that seemed suitable, bought it, and had it torn apart and reassembled on stage to serve as scenery for the play. For a play set in a butcher shop, another designer borrowed real sides of beef to hang behind the counter. This desire for total similitude also affected the treatment of lighting. When spotlights were used, a great deal of time was spent in diffusing the edges so as to conceal them from the audience; light was carefully adjusted so that its sources were apparently explained in naturalistic fashion: if a pool of light was needed in a certain area of the stage, a chandelier was hung above it to persuade the audience that that was the source of the light they saw.

Figure 2-16. Half circles on two levels form a geometric whole to produce an esthetically unified design for Chekhov's *The Three Sisters.* For this scene, a table and an elaborately carved screen on the upper level define a dining area. (See *Figure 16-19* for a ground plan of this set.)

It is perhaps not immediately evident why such a purpose is unsound, and to analyze it in full detail would require an exploration of esthetic theory beyond the scope of this text. The most forceful arguments against it are that it has always been unsuccessful and that it mistakes the purpose of art. No sane members of the audience are unaware that they are in a theater, watching a theatrical performance, and if it were possible to make them believe even momentarily that they were actually watching a scene in a real living room, perhaps by peering through a picture window, the illusion would be immediately dispelled by the presence of all the other people in the audience. It is not the function of theater, or of set design, to brainwash audiences into believing that they are engaged in two hours of window-peeping.

Yet a kind of realism lies at the base of all art. The function of a work of art is to provide the viewer with a genuine and significant experience that is itself real. *The Diary of Anne Frank, The Death of a Salesman,* even *Waiting for Godot,* heighten the audience's awareness of human heroism and despair, which are part of their experience outside the theater. But that awareness does not depend on their belief that what occurs on stage is actually occurring off stage—that a stage set is an actual room. Indeed,

Figure 2-17.   The addition of patio furniture pulls emphasis forward in the *Three Sisters* set, with the upper level bounded by two-fold screens symbolically decorated with outline pictures of birches.

Jo Mielziner's fine set design for *The Death of a Salesman* was unmistakably a new creation, frankly unrealistic, and not a copy of ordinary structures to be found outside the theater.

Art, indeed, must essentially deviate from ordinary experience—from reality. The theater presents actors, not ordinary people; set designs, if they are effective, are an abstraction, rearrangement, and interpretation of experience, not simply a copy. As a matter of fact, the unaltered copying of the world outside is so alien to theater art that ordinary clothing, furniture, and decoration must all be transformed for theatrical use. Often, a beginning designer will attempt to use such things on stage without alteration, but seeing them in place immediately demonstrates their ineffectiveness. Furthermore, they are ineffective in a way that at first seems startling: they look unreal.

The purpose of drama is to create a real experience for the audience. Many design styles and techniques may be chosen for that purpose, but the unanalytical imitation of objects and locales outside the theater is not one of them. Even as a style of design, naturalism is only one of many, and seldom the most effective. (The methods of achieving conviction and effectiveness in scenery are described in later chapters.) The designer's

Figure 2-18.   Designing for esthetics: Wilde's *The Importance of Being Earnest*. This design attempts to burlesque Victorian decoration. The use of a large number of decorative motifs produces an unusually busy pattern. The sets for Acts II and III are shown in *Figures 6-14* and *6-15.* [Photograph by Austin Studio.]

purpose is to create scenery that will fit into the total pattern of the play (as determined by the director's analysis of the script) and that will fulfill the four functions of scenery so as to make the most effective contribution to the production as a whole.

3

Scenic Resources: Scenery and Properties

Throughout recent centuries, special methods, materials, and techniques have been developed for building scenery. Familiarity with scenic construction is an advantage to a designer, and students who want to master the art of design should learn all they can about the related craft of construction. However, it is more important for them to learn what can be done by stagecraft workers than to acquire the necessary construction skills themselves. If designers know what can be done, they can make maximal use of their resources, without making unrealistic demands on the equipment, abilities, or available time of the construction crew. It is highly desirable that a designer work as a member of the construction crew for a few productions. A course in stagecraft would be even more effective.

A full description of set construction would require a separate book. Fortunately, good books on stagecraft are available. The most useful for the advanced designer is *Scenery for the Theatre,* 2nd rev. ed., by Harold Burris-Meyer and Edward C. Cole (Boston: Little, Brown and Co., 1972).

Many other books present the fundamentals of set construction in more elementary and readable fashion, including my *Stagecraft: A Handbook for Organization, Construction, and Management,* published by Allyn and Bacon, Inc. Although such books are of less value for the experienced artist, the beginning student of set design may well find them more immediately comprehensible and usable.

Design and construction are different activities, which require very different skills and points of view. In many American theaters, particularly in small college and community theaters, the two assignments of designing and supervising construction are combined and handled by a single craftsman-artist. To fill such a position, the theater worker must of course have mastered both areas, which can best be done only by following two separate courses of study. Although both activities are concerned with scenery, there is much less overlap between them than might be expected. It is possible to be a superb craftsman and be quite unable to design effectively, just as it is possible to be a great designer and yet be unable to construct an accurate miter joint or handle power tools skillfully. Since this text is limited to the work of designers, only those aspects of construction that are necessary for their planning will be discussed.

In the main, designers need to know what materials are available for use in building scenery, what they can reasonably expect a construction crew to do, and what conditions are necessary for the various types of work. As designers, they are not themselves required to develop the skills necessary for construction, and they will be able to function effectively even though they are unfamiliar with many techniques that are necessary for the actual building. For example, designers need to know what types of flats can be built and how to design them most economically. They do not have to be familiar with the methods of ensuring square corners, with the technique for stretching canvas across the frames, with the formula for the glue used in fastening the canvas to the frames, or with the rules for the placement of the grain of plywood in corner blocks. Designers should also become familiar with various types of wood joints, including the halved joint, and they should know that they cannot realistically ask a crew to make halved joints unless certain types of power saws are available to them. However, there are many details of the actual construction of halved joints that are essential for the builders but with which the designer need not be concerned: the selection and combination of saw blades for making wide cuts, the technique for checking the setting of the blades to ensure the proper depth of cut, etc.

Obviously, familiarity with such details will help a designer, at least in achieving greater confidence in preparing instructions for the builders, but they are peripheral to design, however important they may be in construction.

To discuss construction fully would almost double the size of this book. Therefore, I have included only those items of information that are absolutely necessary for designers, omitting any considerations that can reasonably be left to the skill and judgment of the construction supervisor. In particular, I have included items that designers are normally expected to specify in their instructions.

Designers should remember, however, that any discussion of established techniques and materials is a guide, not a restriction. The work of good designers is characterized by constant innovation: the use of new materials, and of old materials in a new way. In every instance, the good designer uses resources so as to best serve the needs of a particular play, using traditional methods when they apply, but altering freely when new techniques will serve the play more effectively.

The discussion of scenic resources will be separated into four main divisions. Flats and three-dimensional scenery (with accompanying sections on methods of painting and shaping) are covered in this chapter. Lighting and scene shifting are covered in Chapter 4.

FLATS

Flats are the most frequently used elements of scenery, and the traditional methods of flat construction are often used in building three-dimensional scenery. A flat is a frame made of wood, very much like a picture frame, which is covered on one side with cloth. The cloth is then painted with scene paint.

Flats are most often used to represent walls; when they are joined side by side, with the cracks between them covered and the surface painted properly, they are indistinguishable from plaster, wood, or stone.

All texts (including the first edition of this one) once recommended white pine as the best lumber for stage use. It has now become so scarce and so expensive that it can no longer be considered practical for scenery. Instead, lumber must be chosen from the types locally available at reasonable prices. Hardwood is to be avoided as expensive, heavy, and difficult to work. Ponderosa, cedar, fir, southern pine, and redwood are possibilities, although none of them is quite so convenient or usable as white pine.

Lumber

Lumber is sold in lengths of even-numbered feet (10'-0'', 12'-0'', 14'-0'', etc.). Consequently, it is most economical to design the scenery to match one of those lengths. Lumber described by a dealer as 12'-0'' long will be at least that length; it may be slightly longer, perhaps as much as an inch. Consequently, a designer can confidently assume that if a piece of scenery requires a board 12'-0'' long, it can be readily cut from a board so identified by the dealer. The thickness and width of lumber, however, are *less* than specified; thus, a board described as 2'' thick and 4'' wide is likely to be only 1¾'' thick and 3½'' wide. Furthermore, the deviation from the nominal measurements will not be uniform and may vary from board to board even in the same lot. Such deviation is not normally the concern of designers. They specify and draw the full dimensions, and the set-construction workers make the necessary adjustments so that the scenery matches the designers' specifications. Occasionally, however, the difference may be significant to a designer. If, for example, a designer wants a plain molding 4″ wide around a door opening, the designer cannot specify the use of a 4″ board, since the board will actually be somewhat narrower.

Two sizes of lumber are normally used in constructing flats: 1″×3″ (called "one by three") for the outside framing and horizontal braces and 1″×2″ for diagonal braces.

Flat Construction

Two pieces of wood may be joined in a variety of ways, each method having its own special advantages and disadvantages. Professionally made flats are often built with mortise-and-tenon joints, which have the advantage of great strength. But such joints are nearly impossible to separate if it should be desirable to alter the flat, and they are extremely difficult to make well without special equipment. Consequently, the great majority of flats used in American theaters are fastened together with butt joints, which are fast and easy to make, which may be readily separated, and which have adequate strength for most scenic requirements.

A butt joint for a flat is constructed by placing the two pieces of wood on the same surface, with the end of one piece in contact with the side of the other, so as to form the shape of an L. A triangle of three-layer plywood, called a *corner block,* is then placed on top of the two pieces of wood and nailed to them, the points of the nails being bent over as they come through the wood.

Sound flat construction requires that several precautions be used in making joints, but only one of them is the concern of the designer: the placement of the corner blocks and *keystones* (defined on page 43). Often, two flats must be joined at right angles. If the corner blocks have been nailed over the joints with their edges clear out to the edges of the framing lumber, an unacceptable gap will appear between the two flats when they are placed together. To avoid that, the corner blocks must be set back from the edges of the frame a distance at least equal to the thickness of the framing lumber. Since the flats are seldom placed together end to end, it is not necessary to hold the corner blocks back an inch from the top and bottom edges of the flats; however, even there it is better to set them back by about a quarter of an inch, to prevent the plywood from catching on irregularities in the stage floor and splintering when the flat is slid along. Those gaps should be indicated in the working drawings that are prepared as guides for the construction crew.

In most theaters, flats are returned to storage after the last performance of a play and are used again in constructing sets for the next play. Some flats may thus be used in a long series of settings. Since it is not possible to predict how the flats will be fitted together for future sets, it is preferable to specify routinely that corner blocks and keystones be held back a standard distance from the side edges of all flats, even though holding the corner blocks away from the edges slightly weakens the joints and makes them somewhat more difficult to construct.

The single exception to that practice is a flat that for some reason (perhaps its unusual shape) will never be used again. In such a case it is better to indicate on the drawings that the plywood is to be attached almost even with the edge of the framing. The towers in the *Simon Big-Ears* set are an example of such a design (see *Figures 9-6* and *16-24*).

The Reuse of Flats

The vertical pieces of lumber forming the side edges of a flat are called *stiles;* the horizontal pieces forming the top and bottom of the flat are called *rails.* The *rails* should extend the whole width of the flat, with the stiles cut to fit between them so that the end grain of the stiles will not touch the floor and splinter when the flat is slid across the stage.

Flats require internal bracing to hold the sides straight and the joints square. For very narrow flats, one or two horizontal pieces of 1 × 3 lumber, fastened between the stiles, are sufficient; they are called *toggles.* Flats wider than 2'-0'' also need two diagonal corner braces, set at 45° angles inside the frame and fastened to the rails and stiles. To provide adequate strength, both corner braces must be fastened to the same edge of the flat, so that they are not parallel to each other. For an ordinary flat without an opening, one end of each diagonal brace is fastened to the same stile, the other end of one is attached to the top rail, and the end of the other is attached to the bottom rail. However, if the flat has an opening for a door, there may not be enough space for a diagonal brace at the bottom of the flat; in that case, both braces are placed at the top, with one end of each fastened to the top rail and the other ends fastened to the stiles.

The construction of a standard flat of traditional design is indicated at the left of *Figure 3-1.* The back of the flat is shown in order to display the various elements more clearly. The toggle bar is fastened by trapezoids of ¼'' plywood, called *keystones,* held back 1'' from the edges of the flat and nailed like the corner blocks. The ends of the corner braces are cut at 45° angles, and the braces are then fitted across the corners and fastened at each end with half a keystone, which is also held back 1'' from the edge of the flat.

The Standard Design

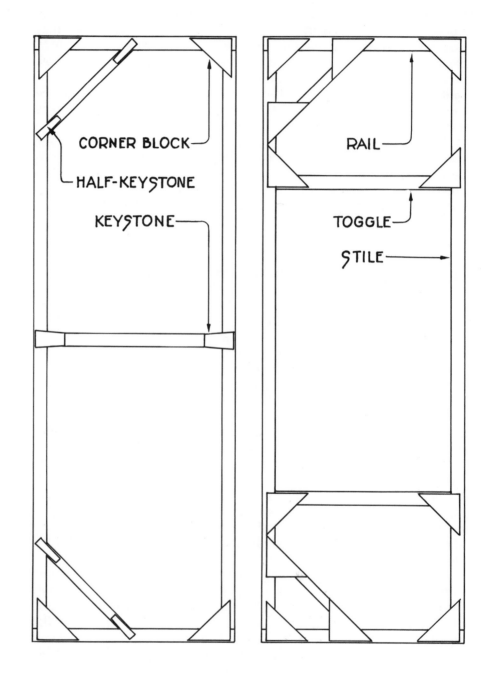

CORNER BLOCK

HALF-KEYSTONE

KEYSTONE

RAIL

TOGGLE

STILE

Figure 3-1. The standard *(left)* and preferred designs for the construction of flats.

It is possible to make flats more readily usable by introducing some variations in the standard design. The architecture of a theater is a major factor in determining the most effective heights for flats; it also affects the placement and dimensions of such elements as doors, windows, molding and paneling, and pictures hung on the walls. An artist who designs a series of sets for the same theater is likely to place such elements at the same height in many of the sets and, for example, to use windows of similar dimensions, particularly with regard to their height and their distance from the floor. Such elements, as well as pictures and applied molding, often require special bracing at the back of the flat. If designers can determine the height at which they will most often need such braces, a good deal of work can be saved by routinely designing flats so that the toggle bars are uniformly fitted into the flats at the most useful position. For 12'-0" flats, this level might well be 3'-0" from the end of the flat; if so, all flats should be regularly designed with the toggle bars in that position. If a particular design requires that pictures be hung, or molding attached, the supports will already be present, and no construction time will have to be spent on moving them or adding temporary nonce supports.

It is also preferable to use plywood triangles for attaching the bracing lumber, as well as at the corners of the flats. Because triangles provide more nailing surface than keystones or half-keystones, it is possible to hold them back from the edge of the flat a full inch, like the corner blocks, and also to attach them so they extend beyond the bracing on only one side of the lumber. The toggle edges closest to the center of the flat can consequently be kept free, so that a clean rectangular opening can be cut in the flat to receive a window without having to trim or replace the plywood fastener. And finally, it is good practice to fasten the toggle-bar triangles to the stiles with screws instead of nails, so that they may be more easily moved if a particular design requires some position other than the standard. The drawing on the right in *Figure 3-1* illustrates the preferred method of designing and constructing flats. The proposed design specifies two toggle bars for each flat, to provide support at the most convenient positions. If only strength were considered, a single toggle in the center of a 10'-0" flat would be sufficient, and it might be satisfactory even for a 12'-0" flat, but longer flats will require additional toggles; the distance between toggle bars or toggle and rail should never exceed five or six feet.

The rails, stiles, and toggles of ordinary flats are made of 1×3 lumber; corner braces are cut from 1×2. For very long flats, it may be preferable to make all or part of the rails and stiles out of 1×4 lumber, and where reduction of weight is more important than strength, it may occasionally

A Preferred
Design

Lumber
Dimensions

be desirable to use 1 × 2 lumber for the rails and stiles as well as for the bracing. For example, the *Simon Big-Ears* set was made of 1 × 2 lumber, since the set was to be transported by truck to several theaters, and since the flats were small enough not to require great strength.

Corner Blocks

The plywood triangles used to fasten lumber together may be of a wide range of sizes. The most commonly used size is made by cutting a 10″ × 10″ square of plywood diagonally across. Increasing the size of a corner block makes it possible to spread the nails farther apart, with a resulting increase in strength. Where little strain is put on the joint, it may be possible to use 8″ corner blocks, and in special circumstances even to reduce them to 6″. When the end of a diagonal brace fits into the corner of a flat, even a 10″ corner block may not provide enough surface to fasten it securely, so that it may be desirable to increase the size to 12″ or more.

In most theaters, corner blocks are cut from scrap plywood. It is desirable to adopt a standard size and specify it automatically, unless the design requires larger or smaller dimensions. The construction crew can then routinely cut all plywood into standard corner blocks as scraps accumulate, thus maintaining a constant supply. By arrangement with the construction supervisor, it may be possible for designers to omit dimensions of standard-sized corner blocks in their drawings, indicating the sizes of only those that are larger or smaller.

Standardization of Flats

Since flats will normally be used over and over again, it is good design practice to standardize their height and width and, whenever possible, to design to the standard sizes. The most effective height for flats varies from theater to theater, depending largely on the architecture of the theaters; however, 12′-0″ is perhaps the most common height. In the nineteenth century, when many stage sets were shipped by train from town to town, 5′-9″ was adopted as the maximum width for flats, since larger flats could not be easily loaded through the doors of freight cars. Most scenery canvas is 6′-0″ wide, and since the edges must be trimmed off in covering flats, the 5′-9″ limitation is still a practical one. Furthermore, a wider flat is unwieldy to handle and difficult to store.

However, it seems more practical to standardize flat widths at intervals of 1′-0″, and the designer may find it more convenient to set 5′-0″ as the extreme width for ordinary use. To provide greater flexibility, it may be desirable to build a few flats 1′-6″ and 2′-6″ wide, which can be combined with other widths to produce total dimensions at 6″ intervals.

Occasionally the requirements of a set will make it desirable to use flats of odd dimensions. So far as possible, the flats should be designed so that the unusual flats can be constructed by adding temporary pieces to existing standard-sized flats. If a completely new flat must be built, it should be designed so that the edges may be removed after the show so as to leave flats of standard size. For example, if the design requires a flat 4'-3" wide, the best practice would be to construct it by adding a 1×3 board to the edge of a standard 4'-0" flat. Since the added board will not be quite 3" wide, it will be necessary to leave a small gap between it and the stile of the flat; this gap can be covered by gluing a strip of cloth over it on the front surface of the flat. The edging should be attached to the stile of the flat by plywood triangles, placed so as to miss the corner blocks of the flat and fastened with screws to permit their easy removal after the final curtain.

Occasionally flats are designed with an irregular edge (for example, when they are intended to simulate pilasters or columns). Often, such an irregularity can be cut out of a piece of corrugated cardboard and tacked to the edge of the flat, and the joint can be covered with a patch of scenery canvas *(Figure 3-2)*. For large projections, or edgings that may have to resist strain during the play, it is possible to screw a properly shaped strip of plywood to the front of the flat, cover the joint with a strip of scenery canvas, and then remove the additions when the flat is ready for storage at the end of the show. If the joint is objectionably apparent, the plywood strip may be attached so that its surface is in the same plane as the front of the flat by adding a 1×2 strip behind it and running plywood triangles across the joint, fastening them to both the 1×2 and the corner blocks on the flat *(see Figure 3-3)*.

The irregularly edged flat most frequently used is called a *groundrow.* One of the problems of outdoor scenery is hiding the line where the stage floor meets the back wall; the groundrow is designed to solve that problem. It consists in effect of a flat standing on its side, with an irregular edge applied to the upper stile, cut so as to simulate distant hills, the skyline of a city, a fence, or some other scenic element. For an extremely irregular groundrow it may be necessary to constuct it as a separate unit, rather than basing it on a stock flat. Since the groundrow is most often placed out of the way at the back of the stage, it does not usually need much support. It is customary to support it by a couple of *jacks,* wooden triangles hinged to the back of the groundrow. They are designed so that the flat slants slightly backward for greater stability. For a very long groundrow, it may be necessary to use three or more such jacks, and if there is

Unusual
Dimensions

Irregular Edges

Groundrows

Figure 3-2. The use of cardboard in constructing irregular edges on flats. This wing is from a set for Sheridan's *The Critic*. It is shown from the back at the left; from the front at the right. Shaped extensions were added to the edge of the flat at three corners. The three-dimensional shaping on the front was simulated by painting and spattering. (See also *Figure 14-1*.)

any danger of the unit's being tipped over during the action of the play, a hinged foot iron (or even a large ordinary hinge) may be fastened to the back corner of the jack and screwed firmly to the stage floor.

For convenience in handling, it may be desirable to build a groundrow in two sections, hinged vertically, so that they can be folded together to make a unit only half as long as when extended. If the groundrow must be stored at the side of the stage during part of the play, the reduction in size may be worth the additional construction time required.

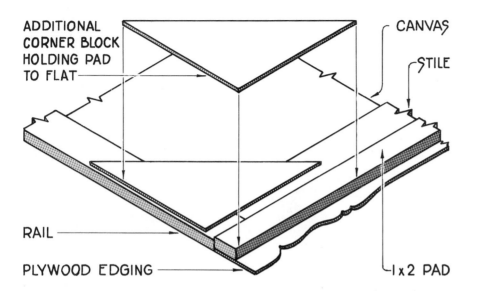

ADDITIONAL
CORNER BLOCK
HOLDING PAD
TO FLAT

CANVAS

STILE

RAIL

PLYWOOD EDGING

1 x 2 PAD

Figure 3-3. Adding plywood edges to flats. The edging is cut from ¼'' plywood. A 1 × 2 pad is nailed to the straight edge of the plywood, the flat is laid face down, the edging is placed in contact with it, and the two are fastened together by additional corner blocks. The drawing shows the lower right corner of the flat, from the back.

The scenery represented by a groundrow can sometimes be made more convincingly three-dimensional if it is divided into sections and placed on separate groundrows that are positioned one behind the other, separated by gaps of two or three feet. *Figure 3-4* illustrates a set of three such groundrows, the near one showing low hills and a curving road in the middle distance, the second one showing somewhat more distant hills and a building, and the third representing mountains far in the background. To be visible, each groundrow must be higher than the one in front of it. If there is any haze or dust in the air, the colors of scenic elements such as buildings and foliage become steadily lightened as their distance from the viewer increases. This effect, which easel painters call *aerial perspective,* can be simulated more easily with multiple groundrows than with single groundrows, by successive whitening and greying of the paint mixes for groundrows representing more distant parts of the scenery and by lighting the groundrows differently.

Aerial
Perspective

Another device that is sometimes effective is called a *shadow box (Figure 3-5);* it is most frequently used to represent buildings with lighted windows. For the shadow box, the shape of the groundrow (showing, for

Shadow Boxes

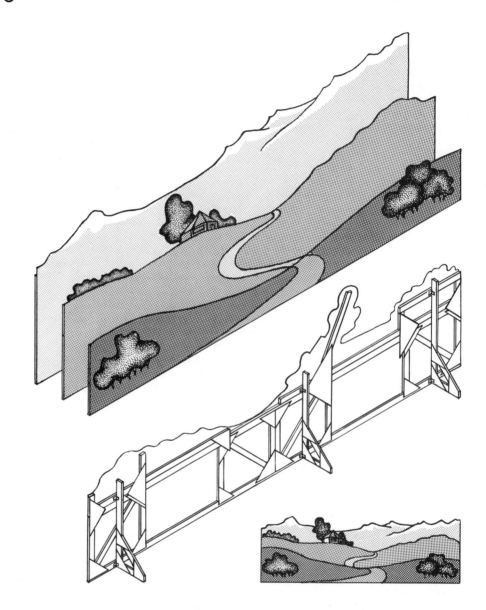

Figure 3-4. Groundrows. The center drawing shows the second groundrow from the back. It is made of two stock flats, hinged end to end, with a plywood edge added at the top, the entire unit being supported by three jacks. The top and center drawings show the groundrows from a position that does not match that of any member of the audience. The bottom drawing shows the three groundrows from the audience's viewpoint, drawn to a smaller scale.

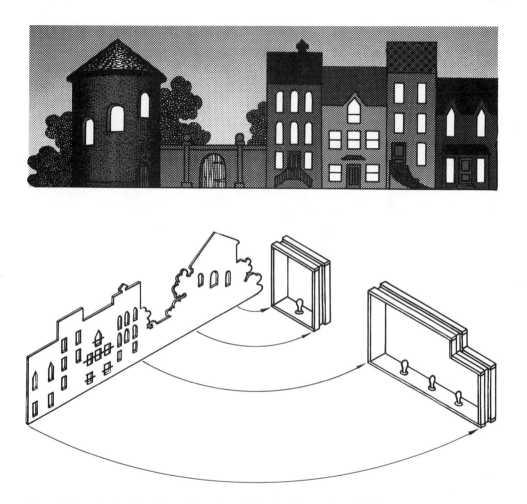

Figure 3-5. A shadow box. The top picture shows the shadow box from the viewpoint of the audience; the reflected light shines through openings in the front, suggesting lighted windows. The bottom drawing shows the front moved aside to reveal the boxes that contain the lights and that form the reflecting surfaces.

instance, the skyline of a city) is cut in duplicate. Holes representing windows are cut in one of the shapes, and the front surface of the second shape is painted some highly reflective color, perhaps white or light yellow. The two shapes are then fastened together at some distance, 6″ to 12″ or 18″, to form a kind of irregular box, and the edges and joints are carefully covered to make them lightproof. When the unit is placed on stage, a few ordinary electric lights are set inside it so that the light

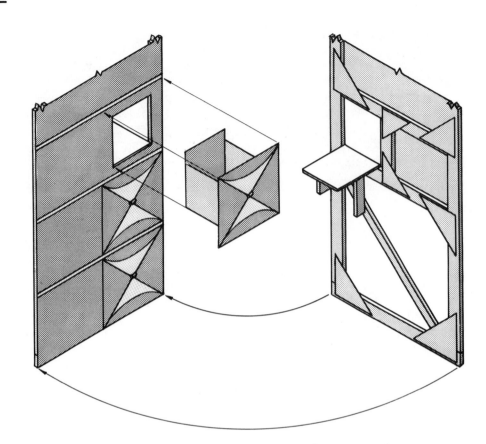

Figure 3-6. Fitting a filing cabinet into a wall. The crew cut a special hole in the canvas for the top drawer, framed the opening on the back, and added a shelf on which the drawer could slide. The drawer was essentially a cardboard box, with the back shaped so as to extend above the toggle at the top of the opening, to prevent an actor from accidentally pulling it out too far. (The zigzag lines at the top of the drawing, called *break lines,* are conventional symbols indicating that only part of the flat is shown.)

reflects from the back surface and shines through the holes in the front, simulating lighted windows. If such a shadow box is made wide enough, it will be freestanding and will not need jacks or other bracing. If only a small part of a groundrow represents buildings, a small shadow box may be added to it to provide lighted windows only in the area where they are needed.

Openings   Most sets require that some flats have openings, usually so that doors and windows may be fitted in, but often to represent balustrades and for other purposes. Usually, additional framing pieces must be added to the back of the flat to define the edges of such openings and to support the weight of pieces that are added. For example, the office set for the second act of *Harvey (Figure 3-6)* was designed with a three-drawer filing cabinet built into the wall. Since only one drawer was actually used in the play, the two bottom drawers were simulated by gluing cardboard shapes to the front of the flat. For the top drawer, a rectangular opening was cut in the canvas and framed by two special toggle bars connected by short vertical pieces, which had been added to the back of the flat. The file drawer slid in and out on a shelf attached to the framing.

Construction workers automatically canvas the entire area of a flat; consequently, if a section is to be left open, the designer must specify that by printing "Do not canvas."

Irregular Openings

When an opening is irregular in shape, it may not be practical to outline it with wood bracing. The standard procedure is to cut the canvas to the desired shape and then glue coarse netting across the back to hold the edges in place; with proper lighting, the netting will be nearly or completely invisible from the audience. An alternative method is to glue sections of corrugated cardboard on the back of the flat around the edge of the canvas after it has been cut, and then trim the cardboard to match the canvas after the glue has hardened. This method was used to stiffen the edges of the painted drapes in the set for *The Critic (Figures 14-1 and 16-20)* and the shaped edges of the fireplace opening in the *Harvey* set *(Figure 3-8)*.

Doors and Windows

Doors and windows may be built as integral parts of the flats, but more often they are constructed as separate units, shoved into the openings in the flats, and fastened by a hinge arrangement *(Figure 3-7)*. Such a unit is essentially a shallow box, with the door forming the bottom of the box. Wooden trim is fastened to the front of the door frame. The unit is then pushed through the opening in the flat from the front, until the trim strikes the surface of the flat; the hinges that have been attached to the side of the frame are swung down so that the vertical pieces of the flat frame are pinched between them and the facing trim, and the unit is ready to be used. Doors in sets are regularly designed to swing offstage, and doors in the side walls are fastened with the hinges on the upstage side (away from the audience). Those placements make actors' entrances slightly easier and more effective; in addition, doors so arranged help hide offstage areas from the audience.

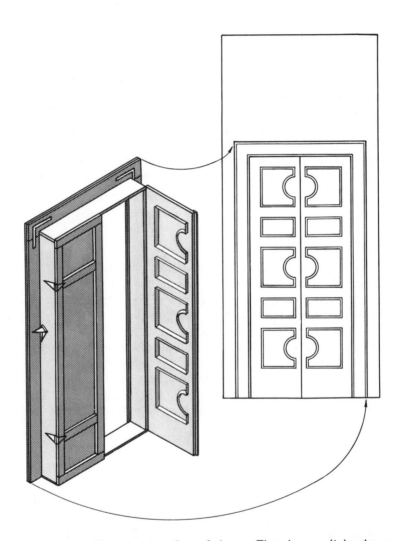

Figure 3-7. The construction of doors. The door unit is shown by itself at the left. At the right it is in place in the flat. Doors are often designed to fit inside the casing; in this drawing, they are shown fitted against the back of the casing, which is preferable because it does not require such precise construction, and the cracks around the edges are automatically masked by the door itself. For a double door, the center crack can be masked as shown, by a strip of thin wood or plywood attached to the back of one leaf; however, the actors must then be trained to open that door first. Various hinge arrangements are possible; these doors have a flap of each hinge bent around the edge of the lumber.

Cutting through the bottom rail of a flat to make space for a door weakens the flat greatly; usually additional strength must be supplied to hold the flat steady during performance. One method is to fasten each leg of the flat with its own stage brace. The legs may also be fastened firmly to the floor with foot irons or with jacks like those used for groundrows, except that the jacks must be made in the form of right-angled triangles, to permit the door flat to stand vertical. The strength of the flat may also be restored by screwing a *sill iron* under the bottom edge. A sill iron is a strap of metal that is ¾'' wide and as long as the width of flat. It has holes in it through which screws may be inserted to hold it to the flat frame. The holes have a conical shape, so that the heads of the screws can be countersunk.

Strengthening Openings

Often, it is possible to design scenery so that an opening can be cut in the canvas without removing part of the rail. The fireplace for *Harvey* (*Figure 3-8*), for instance, was designed with a shell-shaped opening, held up off the floor by more than the width of the rail, so that special strengthening for the flat was not necessary. It is even possible to leave the original rail in place at the bottom of a door opening. The danger of actors' tripping over it can be somewhat reduced by cutting out the top half or two-thirds of the rail so that it projects not more than 1'' above the floor of the stage. If the set is available in time for actors to get accustomed to using the entrance, it is probable that it will cause little difficulty. An alternative method is to make the bottom rail out of a 1 × 2 laid flat; if desired, the top edges may be beveled to still further reduce the chance of tripping. A strip of ½'' plywood may also be used in the same way.

Anything added to the bottom of an existing flat, even a sill iron, will increase the height of the flat. Occasionally the difference in size may not be noticeable, but usually it will be necessary to cut back the bottom of the flat enough to make the height standard after the sill iron or wooden strip has been fastened on.

Of the methods discussed, the sill iron is the most desirable. If flat widths are standardized, a supply of sill irons should be accumulated to match the sizes of flats in which doors are most frequently used.

Occasionally the designer may want to use a door or other opening larger than any of the standard flat sizes. Rather than build a special flat into which such an opening can be cut, it may be preferable to build a small flat the size of the wall area above the opening; this can then be attached to two standard flats, leaving the desired opening between them. The two flats may be joined by any of the methods described above, although in this case the preferred method for supporting them rigidly is to use a jack or stage brace at each side of the opening.

Headers

A small flat placed above an opening is called a *header.* It may be rectangular or shaped (for example, to suggest an arch). *Figure 3-9* illustrates the design of headers of both types.

Figure 3-8. Unframed openings in flats. This fireplace, from a set for Mary Chase's *Harvey,* was designed so that the opening could be cut out of the canvas without destroying the framing. To stiffen the edges, corrugated cardboard was glued to the back around the opening and trimmed to match the canvas. A front view of the wall unit is shown at the right. The three-dimensional mantel was built as a separate unit. The picture frame was also constructed separately, of corrugated cardboard decorated with rope. The design around the frame was painted to simulate three-dimensional carving. Backing for the fire-place opening was supplied by tacking black canvas to the back of the flat.

Window Glass   Glass is avoided in windows on the stage, since it may reflect a glare of light to certain members of the audience and can easily be broken. Often the windows can be left open, and that is nearly always the case when they are hung with curtains. However, if it seems desirable, ordinary galvanized screenwire may be tacked over the back of the opening, giving some of the sheen of glass without its mirror effect.

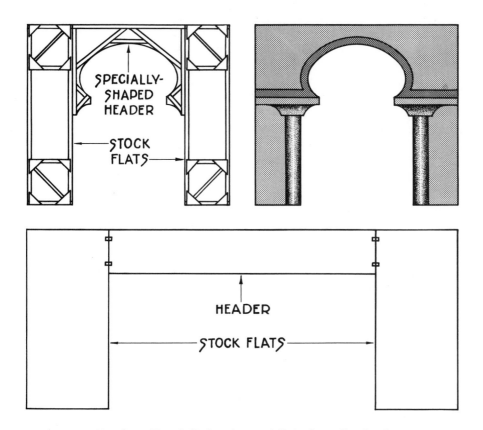

Figure 3-9. Headers. *Top left:* header and flats from the back; *top right,* the same unit from the front. The shaped header can be cut from plywood, so that the surfacing itself holds the frame together, and corner blocks need not be used. As in *Figure 3-2,* it is interesting to notice how much more extensive the shaping appears when it is extended by painting across the surface of the flats. The drawing at the bottom shows a rectangular header. The dutchmen have been omitted to reveal the hinges.

Nearly always, the audience must be prevented from looking through openings in flats to the backstage area. Scenic elements used to hide stage areas are called *masking.* A general discussion of masking problems is given in Chapter 6, but two special instances will be described here.

    Sometimes stage fireplaces require realistic space behind the opening, where fuel, paper or other objects must be placed or where a realistic fire must be simulated. The simplest method of masking the opening for such a fireplace is to build two or three small flats, hinge them together, paint them black, and stand them on the floor behind the opening.

Fireplace and Bookcase Masking

Often, however, a fireplace is used only decoratively, or the mantel is used but not the space behind the opening. A simple method of masking the opening is to cover it by gluing canvas on the back of the flat, painting the canvas black where it is visible to the audience. The same method may be used for constructing bookshelves if it is not necessary to put books or other objects on them. After an opening in the flat has been framed and cut, 1 × 1 strips of wood are fastened horizontally across it to represent the shelves, and a rectangle of black canvas is glued to the back of the flat, masking the opening. Spines may then be cut from real books, or imitations made, and fastened to the shelves. Such bookshelves are not completely convincing, but they are satisfactory, except in an extremely realistic setting.

Thickness Pieces

A wall made of flats fastened edge to edge simulates an ordinary wall convincingly except for one detail: it is not as thick as most walls. An audience is never able to see the edges of all of the walls of a set, but it is desirable to add *thickness pieces* at points where the edges are visible.

Narrow flats are frequently used as thickness pieces. When they are fastened to the walls, the thickness of the flats from which the walls are made is added to the width of the thickness-piece flats; they should consequently be designed so that the total dimension will equal the desired thickness. For walls less than 1'-0'' thick, it may be possible to use solid pieces of lumber for the thickness pieces. Either 1'' lumber or some thickness of plywood may be used; and ½'' plywood is more effective than ¼'' because of its greater rigidity.

Usually, 1'' lumber must be nailed with the edge butted against the back surface of the flat, to prevent reducing an opening or extending the width of the flat. Often, it may be possible to nail ½'' plywood to the edge of the flat, and the addition of ¼'' plywood would hardly ever alter the dimensions of flats or openings so as to make any detectable difference in the design. If plywood must be attached at the back of the flat rather than the edge, a blocked butt joint may be used, with additional stiffening if necessary.

For irregular openings, such as arches, the thickness pieces may be made of corrugated cardboard or some other flexible material, which is fastened to the edges of the openings at enough points to produce the desired shape. If necessary, special supports may be added to the back of the flat to help define the edge.

Joining Flats

Fastening a series of flats together to form a set involves two problems that are the concern of the designer: they must be assembled in such a way that they can be readily moved from the scene shop to the stage, and the joints must be concealed so as not to be noticeable to the audience. If more than one set is used in a play, the flats must also be joined so that the first set can be taken apart and stored and the other set assembled during the time available, usually an intermission.

Flats that meet at an angle of about 90° can be fastened at the back by lashing. Special hardware is attached to the adjacent stiles, and a rope is laced to the hardware and tied. This method of fastening is especially valuable because the flats can be set up and taken apart very quickly during shifts. If the flat that is most nearly vertical to the front edge of the stage is butted against the front or back face of the other flat, the crack is automatically closed, and no other treatment is necessary.

Lashing

For flats that must be combined to form a continuous surface, as for a wall, the most effective method of joining is to hinge them together, placing the hinges on the front (canvassed) side. A strip of cloth is then glued on the front of the flats to cover the crack and the hinges. Such a strip is called a *dutchman*.

Dutchmanning

    Joining by means of hinges and dutchmen is also effective for flats that meet at angles. When flats stand at approximately 90° to each other, the joint between them is inconspicuous enough that dutchmen are not necessary, and such joints are usually made by lashing. However, when it is possible to fold them without producing an unmanageable unit, a slightly neater joint can be produced by using hinges and a dutchman.

Any number of flats may be hinged together and dutchmanned, and often an entire wall of a set may thus be joined into a single unit, without making it too heavy to handle. Any two flats so joined will fold together, with the canvassed surfaces inside. However, if more than two flats are assembled, there may be difficulty in folding them compactly without straining the hinges. If three flats are arranged so that one of the outside flats is not more than half the width of the center flat, it may be possible to handle them folded, although the unit will be somewhat awkward.

Multifolds

    By hinging a vertical wooden strip between two flats, it is possible to assemble any three flats so that they may be folded compactly. The folding stile, called a *spacer*, must be at least as wide as one flap of the hinge. Since the use of spacers increases the width of the unit, the additional width must be taken into account in preparing the design. Similar treatment may be used for a four- or five-fold, or in fact for any number of flats. (See *Figure 3-10*.)

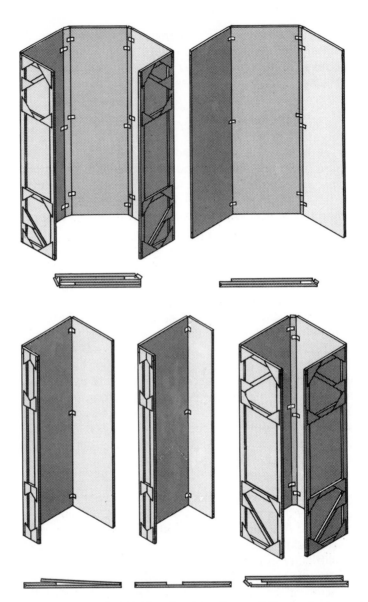

Figure 3-10. Multifolds. Combinations of three, four, and five flats are shown. When the center of three flats is wider than the combined width of the end flats *(bottom, center)*, the unit will fold without added spacers. Sometimes a three-fold can be handled without great difficulty, even though it does not fold compactly *(bottom, left)*. Each unit is shown in two views: completely folded and standing partly opened. Dutchmen have been omitted to reveal the hinging. The small circles in the folded views indicate hinges.

The methods for joining flats that have been discussed so far have been aimed at hiding the joint. The same effect can be produced paradoxically by making it more conspicuous.

It is even possible to reduce the visibility of a joint by painting the adjacent flats in contrasting colors. For example, if a wall is designed with one section papered and the other covered with wood paneling, a moderately tight joint between flats that coincides with the edges of the paneled and papered areas will be almost invisible, without further covering. A somewhat similar device is to break the line of the wall at the joint, setting a section of the wall back slightly, in a kind of bay. Such a break may be very slight and still effectively conceal the fact that the wall is built in separable units.

The crack between flats may be covered by a pilaster. The pilaster may be constructed as a separate unit and fastened on the face of the flats after they are in place, or it may be permanently fastened to the front of one of the flats before they are in place. In the latter case, half of the pilaster will extend to cover the edge of the adjoining flat when it has been put in place.

Often, some decorative elements such as cornices, fireplaces, and pictures are constructed separately and are hung on the flats after they have been assembled on stage. Such elements are usually built as single units, without construction cracks. Where they cross joints between flats, they conceal the portions of the cracks behind them. Furthermore, they are likely to attract attention more than the flats. Consequently, if as much as half of an undutchmanned joint is hidden by such elements, the audience may be distracted from noticing the crack, although the rest of it may actually be visible.

Carefully applied dutchmanning can make a joint invisible, but it makes it impossible to disassemble the flats if they must be shifted. The designer therefore needs to be familiar with the alternative methods. *Figure 3-11* illustrates several of the methods that have been discussed.

When flats are assembled on stage, they are usually held in place by *stage braces,* devices that may be easily adjusted and quickly set up and removed. A stage brace has hooks at one end, which catch on a brace cleat fastened on the back of a flat. At the other end of the brace is a metal strap with holes through which a large fastener, called a *stage screw,* can be driven into the stage floor. The braces are made so that their length can be easily adjusted, and the bottom end is placed well behind the flat to form a firm triangle.

Flats joined side by side in the same plane, however, require additional stiffening in order to remain straight. Such stiffening is provided by lengths of 1 × 3, called *battens,* run horizontally along the back of the

Figure 3-11. Hiding joints where dutchmen cannot be used. Five methods of making joints less conspicuous are illustrated (indicated by the arrows). (1) Adjoining flats have been painted different colors, one with a wallpaper design, the other to simulate paneling. (2) Brightly colored objects (cornice, painting, etc.) have been placed in front of the joint. (3) The wallpaper has been designed so that the joint coincides with a line in the pattern. (4) A small jog has been inserted into the wall, so the flats meet at right angles. (5) The joint has been completely hidden by a separate pilaster.

wall and fastened firmly to the flats. Usually a wall requires two battens, one close to the top and one about a third of the way up from the floor, if doors or other openings do not prevent such a placement.

Battens may be slanted to avoid openings in the flats, and if it is impossible to run a batten in a straight line entirely across them, two or more battens may be used. However, both diagonal and horizontal battens function only if each batten is fastened at two separate points on each side of the joint to be stiffened; the farther apart such fastening points are, the more rigidly the flats will be held in line.

Battens may be fastened to the flats in several ways. The simplest is to lay the wall face down on the stage floor and nail the battens to the back. Another method is to slip S-hooks on the toggle bars of the flats and then set the battens into the open halves of the hooks.

A defect of both of those methods is that the face of the batten is parallel with the wall. Much greater stiffening strength is obtained by fastening the batten on edge. This is done by hinging it to the stiles, placing the hinges on alternate sides of the batten so that it cannot fold flat in either direction. If loose-pin hinges are used, the batten may be removed during shifting, and the wall may be folded for temporary storage at the side of the stage. Battens set in S-hooks may be removed and replaced even more easily, but battens nailed to the flats cannot be readily removed during a performance.

Plywood

One of the most useful technical developments of the past century is the invention of plywood. In its manufacture, very large thin sheets of wood are cut from logs. These sheets are extremely weak in one direction and somewhat stronger in the other. A number of such sheets are placed in a pile, with the grain of successive sheets running at right angles, and they are glued together under pressure. The result is a laminated board of large size, with much greater strength than a piece of ordinary lumber of the same thickness.

The most common type of plywood contains three layers and is ¼'' thick, 4'-0'' wide, and 8'-0'' long. Since the two outside layers run in the same direction, and only the center layer is placed with the grain running crosswise, ¼'' plywood is considerably stronger in one direction than in the other. Plywood is also readily available in thicknesses of ½'' and ¾''; usually, the thicker plywood is made up of more than three layers, so that it has more uniform strength in the two directions.

The greater strength of plywood makes it extremely useful in the theater. Its most common use is as corner blocks for flats, although it is also used for edging groundrows, for surfacing furniture, and for a large number of miscellaneous purposes. It is heavier than cardboard, but much lighter than other lumber providing equal strength. Sheets ¾'' thick or more are ideal for platform flooring.

Plywood is available in a variety of finishes and costs. Sometimes the outside layers are made of especially expensive woods, and they may be already sanded and varnished or painted, so that they are ready for use in furniture or as paneling without further processing. Quarter-inch plywood is usually sanded smooth, but it is unfinished otherwise. Plywood is often used so that one side is hidden, and it can be bought with only one surface carefully finished. Such wood, described as "good-one-side," is acceptable for almost all theatrical uses, and it is cheaper than sheets that have been finished on both sides. The thicker plywoods are available with still less finishing, both surfaces being left fairly rough. This type is cheapest of all, and it is usually entirely acceptable in the theater. It is most likely to be used for platform flooring, and since the surface will be covered with padding and canvas, the roughness is of no significance. Plywood is such a convenient and adaptable material that it is important for the designer to be familiar with it. However, the selection of the type and grade of plywood is usually made by the construction supervisor rather than the designer, and consequently a number of the factors that must be considered in making that selection have been omitted from this discussion.

Quarter-inch plywood is slightly flexible in one direction and can be bent around a fairly sharp curve in the other direction; consequently, a strip of plywood can be used for such purposes as edging a circular platform, around which it can easily be bent by hand and nailed into place.

Plywood differs from ordinary lumber in one further characteristic: the actual size is very close to the nominal dimensions, so that the designer can safely assume that adding a layer of ½'' plywood to a structure does in fact increase it by ½'', and that a 4'-0'' × 8'-0'' sheet of plywood will fit precisely on a platform base of the same dimensions.

Molding In addition to plywood sheets and ordinary boards, lumber is available in special shapes called moldings. These come in a wide variety of shapes and sizes. They are formed by cutting off parts of boards so as to produce special cross-sectional patterns. Perhaps the most familiar molding is ordinary quarter round, which is produced by rounding off one corner of a strip of lumber, forming a cross section shaped like a quarter of a circle. Extremely elaborate molding shapes are available, but most of them are not scaled so as to project effectively at theatrical distances, and in addition they are very expensive; consequently, large moldings for sets are usually produced by combining the simpler and cheaper forms, along with straight stripping and ordinary boards, often 1 × 2s. The combination of simple molding patterns to form a cornice is illustrated in *Figure 3-12.*

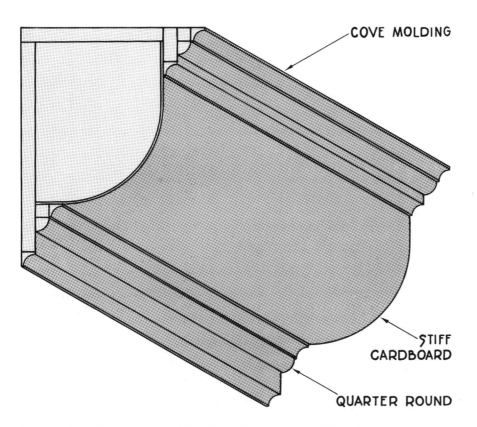

COVE MOLDING

STIFF
CARDBOARD

QUARTER ROUND

Figure 3-12.   The use of molding for a large cornice. The cheapest moldings (¾'' cove molding and quarter round) are combined with 1×1 stripping, stock 1×2 and 1×3 lumber, and a cardboard sheet to form an apparently massive structure.

Figures 3-13 and *3-14* show cove molding used to simulate carvings on a pillar.

Related to moldings are dowels and simple 1×1 strips. Dowels are made from square strips with all four corners rounded to produce a circular cross section. They are available in many sizes, from ⅛'' in diameter up to 2'' or more. Most lumber yards stock them only in lengths of about 3'-0'', although the heavier dowels can often be bought in lengths up to 20'-0''. They have many miscellaneous uses in set design—as legs for tables, in making room-dividers, in simulating iron railings, and in many other ways.

The 1×1 strips are also adapted to a variety of uses. They can be combined with moldings, they can be used to stiffen cardboard units (as in the ornamental screen for *The Solid Gold Cadillac,* illustrated in *Figure*

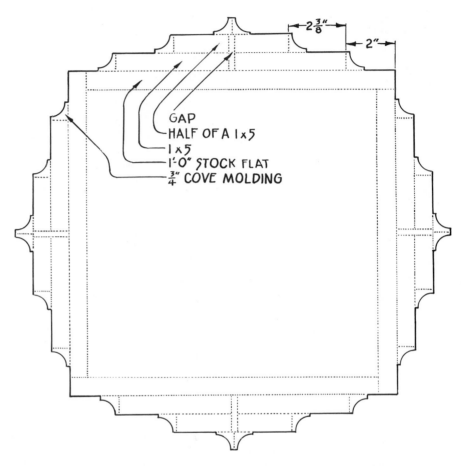

Figure 3-13. Cove molding used to simulate carving on a pillar. The basic form is square, made of four 1'-0'' flats nailed together (shown in cross-section). Vertical boards are nailed outside the flats and edged with cove molding to produce a roughly circular outline.

3-33), and they can be used for constructing decorative units where strength is not important. The *fleur-de-lis* grillwork in the set for *The Madwoman of Chaillot,* shown in *Figure 8-1,* was built on a framework of 1 × 1s painted gold to simulate metal. These strips can readily be prepared in the scene shop by ripping wider boards. Sometimes lumber yards do not stock 1 × 2s in sufficient quantity for theatrical use; in that case, they fill orders by ripping 1'' strips from 1 × 3s. Normally, such strips would be discarded, but if they are included in the order, they may be added to the stock in the scene shop, and a permanent supply may be maintained.

Figure 3-14. Pillars for *The Lark* built to the design shown in *Figure 3-13*.

THREE-DIMENSIONAL SCENERY

The current century has seen a greatly increased use of three-dimensional scenery, as distinguished from flats. The most common three-dimensional units are platforms and stairs.

Platforms   Most platforms are in the shape of a rectangular box, with a solid top and open-frame sides. The pattern for the supporting frames is somewhat similar to that for flats: butt joints, fastened by corner blocks, are used, and each side is made rigid by two diagonal braces. The major difference between platform and flat construction is that in platforms the crosspiece at the bottom (equivalent to the bottom flat rail) is fitted between the stiles (the legs of the platform) and raised approximately an inch off the floor, so that the platform is supported at isolated points, rather than continuously along its entire lower rim, making it less likely to rock on irregularities in the stage floor.

By far the best flooring is heavy plywood, generally ¾'' five-ply. The construction and design of a platform is largely determined by the uses it must serve, the number of people who must stand on it at once, the weight of other units it must support, etc. Generally, a sound rule is to design the platform so that no point on the top is more than 1'-6'' from a support; thus, a platform larger than 3'-0'' × 3'-0'' should have extra supports.

Safety is especially important in platform design, and it becomes increasingly significant as platform height is increased. Here, as elsewhere in the theater, it is sound practice to design with a 50% margin of safety; for example, if four actors must stand on a platform at the same time, it should be designed so as to be strong enough to support six. For all but the lowest platforms, lumber at least 1'' × 4'' should be used for the supporting frames, rather than 1 × 3; and for larger platforms, lumber sizes should be increased so as to keep well within safety margins. Good grade 2 × 4 lumber provides much greater strength, and in special cases it may be wise to use 2 × 6 or 4 × 4. *Scenery for the Theatre,* by Burris-Meyer and Cole, may be consulted for information about the strength of lumber of various types and sizes. Aside from safety, a platform should be strong enough not to sag or sway visibly when it is being used.

The top of a platform should be padded with cloth or newspaper (tacked so it will not shift when the platform is used). Scenery canvas is spread over the padding, brought around the edges, and tacked firmly to the underside of the plywood top. In designing platforms it is important to remember that the total height is made up of the height of the supports plus the thickness of the top. Where platforms must fit closely, it may even be necessary to include the thickness of the padding in figuring the height of the leg units.

Folding Platforms

Rigid platforms are easiest to build. However, they require so much storage space that they are impractical for most theaters. Folding platforms (also called *parallels*) require much less storage space. The tops are built as separate units, and the supports are hinged so that they can be folded compactly.

Almost every stagecraft book describes an individual design for folding platforms. Designers who constantly use platforms in their sets might find it desirable to study the designs given by different writers, so as to determine the types that most closely fit their own theater, scene shop, materials, and personal taste. A few relatively standard types will be described here.

The simplest pattern is essentially the same as that for a rigid platform, except that the supporting frames are hinged together rather than being nailed. Two corners diagonally opposite each other have the hinges placed on the inside of the unit; for the other two corners, half of each hinge is placed on the inside and half on the outside (see *Figure 3-15*). Lengths of 1 × 2 should be nailed or screwed to the underside of the top, held back from the edge by a distance equal to the thickness of the side units, to prevent the top from shifting during use. The battens need not extend for the full distance.

If such a platform has permanent internal supports, the space between the supports, and between each support and the ends of the platform, must be at least equal to the width of the platform, or it will not fold compactly. However, the supports may be constructed separately, so that they can be lifted out before the platform is stored. To hold them in place when the platform is in use, metal straps should be screwed to the top of the supports. Such straps must be countersunk, so that the top will rest firmly on the support. To hold the supports vertical, 1 × 2 battens should be fastened to the inside of the side frames, forming grooves into which the supports can be slipped *(Figure 3-16)*. An alternative method is to fasten the supports with loose-pin hinges, which can be readily disassembled for storing. When stored, platforms designed to fold as shown in *Figure 3-15* have a total thickness of 2″ to 3″, and their length is equal to the length of the platform plus its width.

Platforms that will not increase in length when folded may be constructed by placing all hinges on the inside and using tight-pin hinges for two opposite corners and loose-pin hinges for the others. When the platforms are folded for storing, the pins are removed from the loose-pin hinges, and the two side-and-end units are folded individually and nested (see *Figure 3-17*). One additional pattern uses tight-pin hinges throughout. Each end of the platform is supported by two frames, each one half the width of the platform. They are hinged together on the outside of the unit *(Figure 3-16)*.

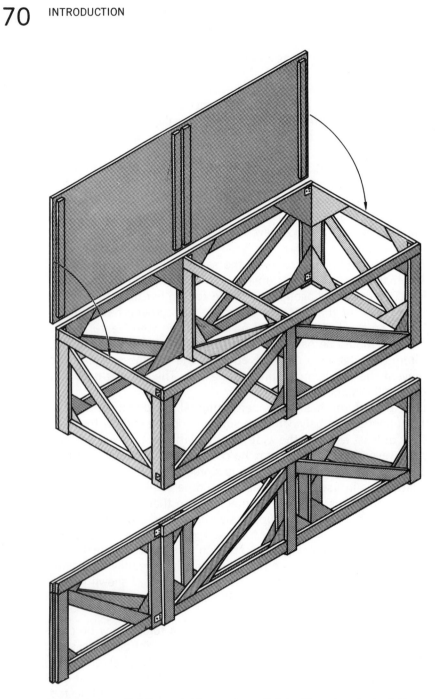

Figure 3-15. Folding platforms (parallels). The simplest of the folding platform designs. *Top:* the platform set up for use, with the top raised to reveal the frame. *Bottom:* the supporting frame folded for storage.

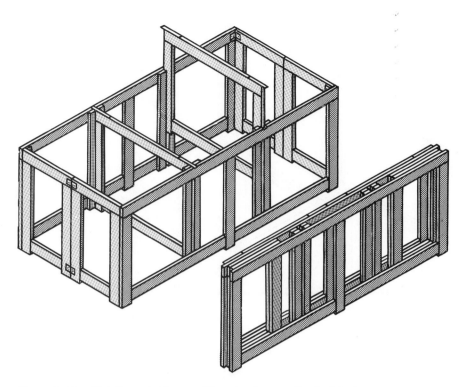

Figure 3-16. Folding platforms. The most complicated but convenient of the three designs is shown. Each end is made in two sections, hinged to fold inward. Internal supports are lifted out for storage: one is shown slightly raised. Countersunk metal straps catch on the side frames to prevent the center supports from falling through when the platform is lifted. (The top, diagonal braces, and corner-blocks are omitted.)

Circular Platforms

Platforms other than rectangular ones may be built similarly. The most commonly used of such shapes are circular platforms. They may be supported by triangular units similar to the rectangular supports. For a very large platform, it is possible to make a top that can be transported easily by using double layers of plywood, so arranged that the joints of one layer cross solid areas of the other. Matching holes for bolts are bored through both layers, with space for countersinking the heads of the bolts in the top layer. The platform top may then be moved in sections, assembled by bolting the sections together, and then disassembled for storing. This method was used for the circus ring in a production of *J.B.* (see *Figure 3-18*).

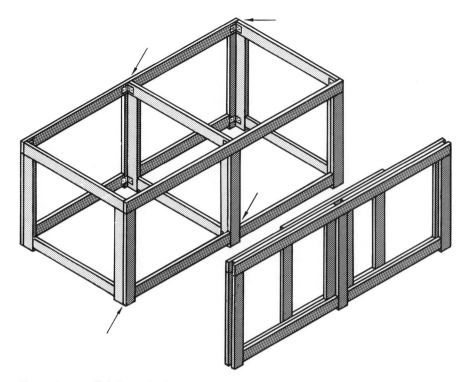

Figure 3-17. Folding platforms. In this design, four joints (indicated by arrows) are fastened by loose-pin hinges, the other hinges being tight-pin. For storage, the loose pins are pulled and the supporting frames folded and nested. (To make the drawings clearer, the platform top and the diagonal braces and corner-blocks have been omitted.)

Platform Facing

Ordinarily, platforms are built with the sides left open, revealing the supports. If it is desirable to hide some of the sides of the platforms used for a particular production, temporary facing may be fastened on, made of ¼'' plywood, heavy cardboard, or any other material sufficiently rigid not to shake when the platform is used.

Standardizing Platforms

Building platforms is difficult and time-consuming. Their design, therefore, should be carefully standardized to make them readily reusable; they should be built in sizes and shapes allowing for effective recombination and easy storage. Heights should be designed in multiples of 6'', so that

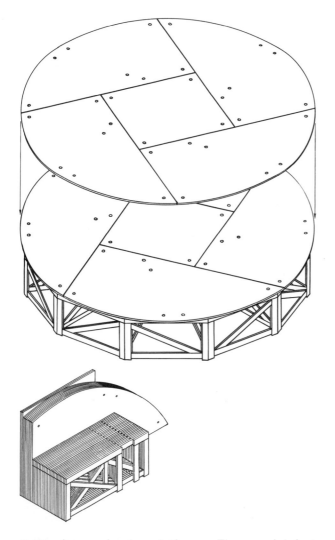

Figure 3-18. Large circular platforms. The special feature of this design is the construction of the platform top. It is composed of two layers of ½'' plywood, identical except that they are turned so that the joints in one layer cross solid sections of the other. The center section is 4'-0'' × 4'-0''; each of the curved units is cut from a single 4' × 8' sheet of plywood; the diameter of the top is 12'-0''. Holes for bolts are drilled through both layers, the holes for the top layer being countersunk so that the heads of the bolts will fit into the wood. The top can then be disassembled by removing the bolts, and when the supporting frames are folded, the entire platform can be stored in a relatively small space, as shown in the bottom drawing. (Both pictures are drawn to the same scale.)

they will match step units, and lengths and widths should be adapted to the size of the stage. Most often, varying levels for a stage set are produced by combining platforms of various standard sizes, rather than building a new single unit. All the platforms are taken from stock when possible, and new standard-size platforms are added to stock as necessary. Special variations in platforms may be achieved by building temporary additions. The additions often need not be fastened to the standard units, but may simply be set beside or on top of them.

Ramps

Ramps are platforms with slanted tops (see *Figure 3-19*). Visually, they are extremely effective in sets, but they are included less frequently than standard platforms because they are more difficult for actors to use. Their construction is identical with that of ordinary platforms, except that the supports must be designed to match the slant desired.

Stairs Stairs may be designed to stand alone (independent) or to use an attached platform for partial support (dependent), and they may be straight or curved.

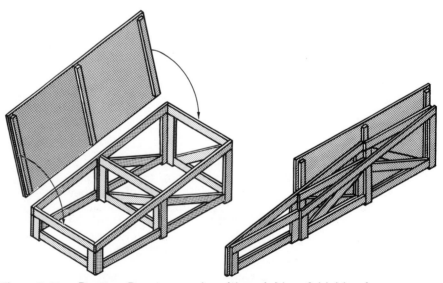

Figure 3-19. Ramps. Ramps may be either rigid or foldable. A folding ramp is shown. Any of the methods for constructing folding platforms may also be used for ramps. (The hinges and corner-blocks have been omitted from the drawing.)

Independent Stairs

The construction of independent stairs is similar to that of a ramp, except that the slanted top edges of the sides are notched so that small rectangles, forming the steps, may be fastened to them. The steps themselves are called *treads;* the vertical spaces between the top surfaces of adjacent steps are called *risers,* and the notched supports are called *carriages.* Because the notching greatly weakens the supporting lumber, the lumber must be much wider than for a ramp: 1 × 10 lumber is commonly used. The treads may be made of ¾'' plywood. The carriages should not be farther than 2'-0'' apart, but the treads may extend as far as 2'' or 3'' to the sides, beyond the carriages, so that a step unit 2'-6'' wide may be built with two carriages. Wider units require an additional carriage in the center. As in the case of platforms, other methods of construction are possible; a few are shown in *Figure 3-20.*

The student should be warned against an error in stair design that almost every beginning designer makes at least once: miscalculating the height of the risers. To design them correctly, the designer must subtract the thickness of the tread from the total height of the bottom step only. All other risers are built to match the full step height. Thus, if the treads are made of ½'' plywood and the completed steps are intended to rise at 6'' intervals, the support for the bottom step must be 5½'' high, that for the next step 11½'', the third, 17½'', etc. This formula seems illogical at first thought, but careful analysis, or the measurement of an actual step unit, will demonstrate that it is correct.

Stairs usually lead to a platform. Therefore, it is customary to build a flight that is one step fewer than the design calls for, using the platform itself as the final step. Occasionally, the designer may prefer to run the stairs all the way up to the platform level.

Stairs should be firmly fastened to the floor (with foot irons), to the platform (with clamps, hinges, or bolts), or to both.

Dependent Stairs

For dependent stairs, the lower end rests on the floor, and the upper step is fastened to the platform. A batten is bolted across the end of the platform at the correct height, and a matching batten at the back of the top step rests on it. The two battens are prevented from slipping apart by cleats screwed or bolted to the stair batten, with ends placed down so that they can be hooked over the platform batten. An alternative method is to fasten the cleats to the batten on the platform (see *Figure 3-21*).

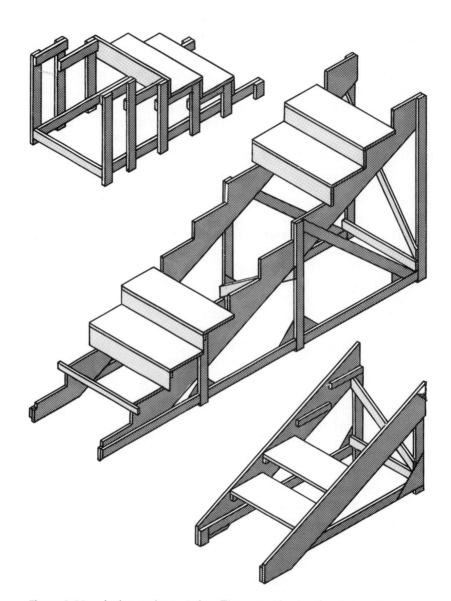

Figure 3-20. Independent stairs. Three methods of construction are shown. The top unit is especially recommended, as it is simple and sturdy. For longer flights, diagonal bracing should be added. The center drawing illustrates the standard design, in which the steps are supported in notches cut into the edges of wide lumber. The bottom drawing shows the fastest method. This design is also the weakest of the three. It should not be used for long flights or anywhere else where safety is a significant factor.

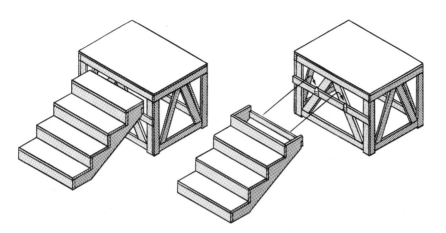

Figure 3-21. Dependent stairs. The stairs are shown at the left fastened to a platform; at the right, they have been separated, and the top tread has been removed to reveal the method of fastening. The batten at the back of the top step is lifted over the metal cleats screwed to the batten on the platform, and rests on that batten. The cleats may be fastened to the batten on the platform, as shown, or they may be fastened to the back of the batten on the steps, pointing down, as described in the text.

Curved Stairs

Curved stairs are highly decorative, but difficult to store, and they require a great deal of space on stage. They may be constructed like straight stairs, with the steps especially cut to conform to the desired curve. It will be necessary to make each carriage in two or more sections, angled so as to roughly follow the curve of the steps. Since each step strikes each carriage at a slightly different angle, cutting the carriages for this type of construction requires very close measurement.

Curved stairs may also be built by making a separate rectangular support for each step; these are then set at the desired angles and held in place by diagonal braces. (See *Figures 3-22* and *3-23.*) The front of each step rests on the support, which will place it at the intended height; the back of each step rests on a batten fastened to the front of the frame supporting the next highest step. Curved stairs are nearly always designed as independent units.

Appearance

Stair units are used both on stage and off stage, in the latter case to enable actors to reach platforms by which they must enter. For offstage

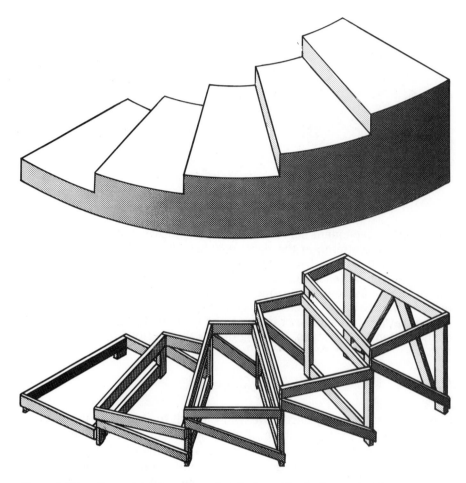

Figure 3-22. Curved stairs. The simplest method of constructing curved stairs is shown. The design is somewhat similar to
that shown in the top drawing in *Figure 3-20*, except that one
side of each step is longer than the other, to provide for the
curvature. The bottom drawing shows the internal supports,
with treads, risers, and surfacing removed.

access stairs, the primary limiting factor is safety: appearance need not be
considered. For step units that are to be seen by the audience, appearance
is important—not only the appearance of the units themselves but also the
appearance of actors as they use them. The graceful use of stairs requires
that the risers be lower than is usual in ordinary buildings: a 6″ riser is
usually best.

Offstage access stairs need not have closed risers, but most onstage
stairs will require them. They should be made of ¼″ plywood, so that they

Figure 3-23. A set for Shakespeare's *The Taming of the Shrew,* incorporating three flights of curved stairs, two low and one high. All were built by the method shown in *Figure 3-22,* using 1 × 3s for the framework, with siding of ¼'' plywood.

will resist accidental kicking. The risers should be fastened to the carriages first, then the treads should be butted up against the risers. If the risers are nailed to the treads from the back, they will give additional support against sagging. If risers are not filled in, the steps can be made firmer by cutting lengths of 1 × 2 equal to the width, of the stairs and nailing one across the carriages, just under each tread. If necessary, additional lengths of 1 × 2 or 1 × 3 can be cut to fit between the carriages and nailed so as to support the back of the treads.

The framing of onstage steps is usually concealed by means of a flat specially built to fit. It should be covered with ¼'' plywood or heavy cardboard rather than canvas, which is likely to shake when the stairs are used. If the unit is to have a railing, the support balustrade and railing may be attached to the flat, which is then fastened to the step unit with loose-pin hinges or picture hooks or, if the set need not be shifted, may be nailed, screwed, or bolted in place. (See *Figure 3-24.*)

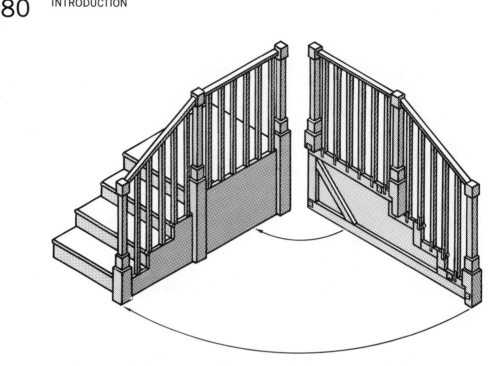

Figure 3-24. Balustrades. *Left:* a stair unit, joined to a landing platform, with attached balustrade and facing; *right:* the balustrade unit swung around to reveal its construction. Since the surfacing is ¼'' plywood, corner blocks are not necessary. The entire unit is fastened to the steps and platform by loose-pin hinges, one leaf of each hinge being screwed to the balustrade, and the other to a matching position on the steps or platform. If the balustrade must withstand significant strain (for example, if an actor is to grasp the handrail and vault over it to the floor), the loose-pin hinges would not provide sufficient strength, and the balustrade should be bolted to the steps and platform.

More Complex Structures

So far, the discussion of three-dimensional scenery has been concerned with relatively simple units. Although freer forms are more difficult to design and construct, they are an important theatrical resource and should not be neglected.

Most similar to platforms, ramps, and step units are freestanding architectural structures, more or less closely related to ordinary architecture. Combinations of platforms, ramps, arches, columns, and step units may be used effectively by actors. Such units may be essentially abstract designs, suggestive of contemporary sculpture, which may have esthetic interest in their own right.

Since regular forms seldom occur in nature, the imitation or suggestion of natural objects may require the building of highly irregular structures. Rocks and trees are the most common of these forms.

Practical Elements

Any element in a set that must be used by the actor is referred to as *practical.* Thus, a practical window is one that may be opened; a practical rock is one that an actor may climb or stand on. Nonpractical elements are those that are intended only to be seen by the audience. Although the construction of practical and nonpractical units is similar, the practical obviously have the added problem of having to be designed to resist whatever strain they will be subjected to while being used in the play. As with platforms, it is good practice to design any scenic unit strong enough to resist 50% more strain that will actually be applied.

Substructure

A practical rock must be built essentially like a rigid platform, with surfaces near enough to level that actors can stand or climb on them, and with sufficient support to bear the actors' weight. The first step in designing such a unit is to sketch its general shape. The sketch is then analyzed to determine how it may be used and to identify the surfaces that must resist strain. Supporting frames are then designed, with whatever bracing is necessary to keep them firm. To these weight-bearing supports are added wooden frames designed to match key points in the major surface lines of the total structure. (See *Figure 3-25.*)

Surfacing

After this entire framework has been constructed, the surface shaping is done. First, ordinary chicken wire is stapled firmly to the structure and pressed and pulled until it matches the desired shape. Then a coating of papier-mâché is applied. Papier-mâché consists of strips of paper, usually newspaper, dipped in a glue mixture and fastened across the surface of the chicken wire. The strips are crisscrossed until the unit is entirely covered. Three or four such layers are used, and then a final layer made up of strips of cloth is added in the same way. The result is a firm, gelatinous structure, which can be given texture by molding; the cloth may even be wrinkled to suggest rock crevices or the bark of a tree. Such a structure requires two or three days to dry, but when it is dry it is tough and hard and will resist great strain without cracking. Most of the strength comes from the final layer of cloth; paper alone makes a very weak structure,

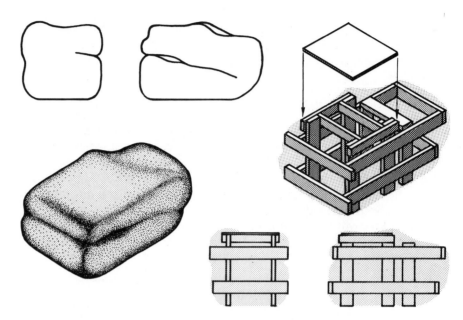

Figure 3-25. Practical rocks. This rock was included in Michael David's design for *Oedipus at Colonus* (see *Figure 6-4*). It served as a seat for Oedipus. The outline drawings at the top show one end and one side of the rock in orthographic projection. At the right, the supporting frame is shown in isometric and orthographic projection. The completed rock is shown at the lower left.

which may be acceptable for nonpractical units but will crack if the unit is used in any way. It is better to add the cloth layer even to nonpractical units, since directors sometimes decide to have actors use units that were originally intended to be only decorative, and since the tougher structure need not be protected so carefully during erection and shifting of the set. When dry, the unit is painted with ordinary scene paint.

Trees and Columns

A similar procedure may be used for constructing columns, tree trunks, and other three-dimensional elements. For columns, arcs of the proper size are cut from 1 × 4 or wider lumber and nailed together to form complete circles, with a hole in the center (see *Figure 3-26*). Thin strips of wood or plywood are then nailed vertically to the outside of the circles. Pliable cardboard is tacked around the outside of the column to conceal the edges of the stripping, and scenery canvas is glued and tacked on for a

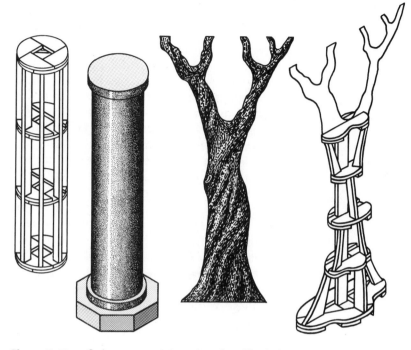

Figure 3-26. Columns and tree trunks. Their internal structure is similar, except that columns are usually circular in cross section, and trunks irregular. In each case, a series of cross sections are constructed and then fastened together by vertical supports. The vertical supports shown in the drawing at the right are staggered, to make it easier to drive nails into both ends of each support. Small tree branches are cut from ¼'' plywood, which are rounded by applying papier-mâché. The trunk is finished by stapling it to a layer of chickenwire, which is then coated with papier-mâché, over which canvas is pulled and molded to form ridges suggesting bark. The column is finished by bending a fairly strong but pliable surfacing around it, nailing the surfacing in place, and adding base and capital.

final coat. Trees may be constructed in the same way, although the horizontal supports will be irregular rather than circular, conforming to the shape of the trunk.

The method described can be used only for large trunks and branches; it is possible to construct fully three-dimensional trees by fastening dead branches cut from real trees to the large branches of the structure, concealing the joints by cloth or papier-mâché molded so as to make a smooth transition. Foliage is more difficult to simulate, and to produce a realistically leaved large tree takes more time than is usually available. Unless the set is extremely realistic and brightly lit, foliage can often be simplified and suggested rather than constructed in detail. A standard procedure is to hang one or more strips of netting horizontally at the top of the stage, so that the branches of the tree extend up behind the netting. Canvas is cut with an irregular edge to suggest leaf shapes, glued to the netting, and painted in varying shades of green, in areas of a size and shape similar to leaves. Where the netting is not needed to support the canvas, it can be trimmed away. Such a structure may be effective, especially if the light is concentrated toward the base of the tree.

A still simpler method is to design a frankly conventionalized pattern that abstracts some of the characteristics of foliage without attempting to conceal the tree's artificiality. Michael David's design for *Oedipus at Colonus (Figure 6-4)* is an example of this method: the foliage shapes are freeform and nongeometric, like real foliage; they include various shades of green (although David chose blue-green mixes rather than the yellow-green that is commoner in real foliage); and the colors are placed so that the lightest are at the edges of the masses, where, in real foliage, the sunlight would show through most strongly. The result is a conventionalized symbol that expresses foliage without attempting to deceive the eye.

SCENE PAINT

Nearly all scenic elements that are visible to the audience are finished by being coated with scene paint. The esthetic use of color is discussed in Chapter 9; the present discussion will be limited to describing the characteristics of scene paint and the methods of applying it.

In recent years, theater technicians have been experimenting with many of the new types of paint. Each of the paints has special advantages and disadvantages, as compared with traditional scene paint. One characteristic that may occasionally be of great importance is that many of the new paints are waterproof after they have thoroughly dried. Since traditional scene paint is highly soluble in water, the new paints are much to be preferred for performances in outdoor theaters, in partially enclosed summer theaters where there is some danger of scenery getting wet, or even where scenery must be transported from the scene shop in one building to the stage in another. Deplorable as such an arrangement is, it is still found occasionally, even in the campuses of large universities, and if water-soluble paint is used, a spell of bad weather can delay the transportation of the scenery by days, sometimes with disastrous effect on the production work. The traditional paint, however, has advantages of its own: it its cheaper than the newer paints, it is available in especially brilliant colors, and some construction supervisors find it more controllable than the synthetic paints. Some supervisors prefer it simply because of its familiarity. Certainly, it is still widely used.

Traditional paint is sold in the form of a fine powder. It has to be mixed with water to the desired consistency, and a quantity of liquified animal glue must be added to it. When ready for application, the scene paint is a moderately thick liquid that dries quickly. It may be used on almost any surface, although scenery canvas is especially adapted to it. It dries to a mat finish, which prevents it from reflecting spotlights like a mirror back into the eyes of the audience.

Scene paint may be applied in many different ways and is available in a wide range of colors, including metallic powders. All of the colors can be freely intermixed to match any color specified by the designer.

In most instances, scenic units are first painted with a uniform base coat of scene paint, in a single color. The glue-water-pigment formula by which the paint is mixed (assuming that traditional scene paint is used), the method by which it is applied (spraying or brushing), the type of brushes used, and the techniques for handling the brushes are all subject to the control of the construction supervisor and consequently need not be specified by the designer. The designer's responsibility consists only of providing a sample of the color to be used.

Spattering

Usually, however, the texture of the base coat is varied in some way, and since the appearance of the finished set depends on the technique used, designers are expected to supply instructions for texturing; therefore, they must be familiar with the available techniques. Stagecraft texts regularly describe numerous methods for altering the visual texture of the base coat. One technique, however, is used so frequently as to be the standard method of application; it is called *spattering.*

The first step in spattering is to paint the flat or other scenic unit a solid color (the base coat). The painter then dips the tips of the bristles of a large brush in slightly thinned scene paint of a different color and applies it to the first coat by swinging the brush toward the surface with a snap of the wrist and stopping it suddenly, sometimes by striking it against a board held in the other hand. The momentum of the brush forces the bristles to continue swinging forward, and as they stop, drops of paint fly from them and fall on the painted surface.

Control

The size and distribution of the resulting spots of paint can be controlled somewhat by varying the wetness of the brush, the force with which it is swung, the direction of the swing, and the distance from the painted surface at which the swing is stopped. Skilled scene painters can produce a uniform coating of dots of paint across the entire area of a flat, or they can shade the coating from heavy to light; the spots may be applied so large as to be separately visible to the whole audience or so small as to be completely invisible from the first row of seats. (See *Figure 3-27*.)

Furthermore, spattering is readily correctable, since if, for example, too much red is spattered in one part of a flat, the area can be respattered, this time with base coat, to conceal part of the red.

Functions

Spattering serves several purposes in scenery. The least important is that of correcting an error in the basic color (for instance, if not enough blue has been used in mixing a blue-green). Even after the flat has been painted, the color can be altered by spattering it with the missing pigment, without repainting the set.

The most important effect of spattering is esthetic: a spattered flat has an appearance of greater vibrancy, vividness, and aliveness, as compared with a flat painted in what, from the audience, seems to be the identical color, but for which the various pigments have been mixed together before painting and applied as a uniform coat. The greater vividness of the spattered flat is so striking that designers should specify that all scenic units be spattered as a regular procedure, omitting spattering only when they especially want the effect of flat painting.

Unspattered flats create an impression of purity of color, simplicity, and clarity, as contrasted with the vibrancy and richness provided by spattering. The *Simon Big-Ears* set (*Figure 9-6*) provides an illustration of the use of both flat painting and spattering. The walls and towers were heavily spattered to produce richness, vibrancy, shading, and a suggestion of the texture of stone; then the foliage was added in flat paint and left unspattered so as to contrast more sharply with the stone surface and to provide an impression of simplicity and smoothness that seemed better suited to the texture of natural leaves. A second example, and an extreme one, is the set for *A Thurber Carnival* (*Figures 2-2, 2-3,* and *2-4*), which was left completely unspattered. The set was intended to suggest a Thurber drawing, so the flats were painted solid white to imitate paper, and the decorative elements were added with black lines.

Concealing Defects

A final effect of spattering is less important esthetically, but of great practical value. Because spattering breaks up and obscures lines, it is of great

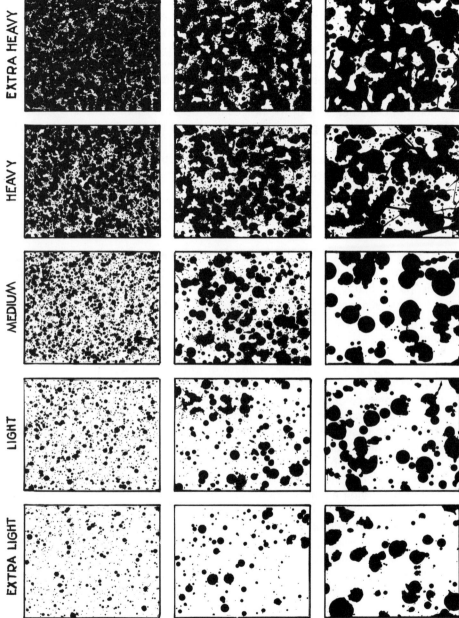

Figure 3-27. The range of spatter. Most often, medium-sized spatter dots are used, fading from heavy to extra light. The spatter samples are shown here somewhat reduced; the original swatches were 2½″ × 3″.

value in hiding minor defects and deviations in scenery. Not only will it correct and conceal many errors, but the designer can frequently rely on it to simplify construction methods. When two flats are fastened together by hinging them on the face, and then a dutchman is glued over them, the bulge produced by the pivot of the hinge will be clearly visible. The edges of the hinge-leaves will also be visible, and even the edges of the dutchman may be detectable. If the flat is then painted uniformly, all of those irregularities are still likely to show. It is possible to avoid them by cutting holes in the stiles so that the hinges can be sunk even with the surfaces of the flats and by using especially thin material for the dutchman, but such a solution is often prohibitively expensive of time. If the flats are well spattered, the bulges and edges will be effectively concealed, unless the flats are to be brightly lit at an angle almost parallel with the surface—an unusual situation.

Spatter Colors

Spattering can be used simply to add texture and richness to a base coat of paint, without altering the color, or it can be used as a more vivid means of mixing colors than stirring them together into the base coat.

If designers want to spatter without changing the color of the base coat, they should specify one of two patterns of spatter mixture. The simplest is to spatter the base coat with two colors of paint, one produced by mixing a small amount of black with some of the base coat, the other produced by mixing a similar amount of white. The black and white largely cancel each other, producing a visible texture with only a slight alteration in the basic color of the flat.

The second method produces somewhat greater vividness. The position of the base coat on the color wheel (*Figure 9-4*) is first determined: let us assume that a primary blue has been used for it. The pigments on each side of the base coat (in this case, blue-purple and blue-green) are then selected from the color wheel. The two spatter mixes are then prepared by adding each of the new colors to a quantity of the base coat.

More frequently, the base coat will not fall at one of the primary positions on the color wheel, but will be itself a mixture of two pigments; thus, if it is orange, it already contains yellow and red mixed together, usually also including some black and white. Of the two primaries already present in the mixture, one is lighter and one darker. The spatter colors should be produced by adding white and the lighter of the two primaries to a quantity of the base coat, and black and the darker of the two primaries to another quantity of the base. For an orange (or brown) base, these formulas would require the addition of yellow-and-white and red-and-black; for purple, the additives would be red-and-white and blue-and-black; for green, they would be yellow-and-white and blue-and-black.

Reinforcing Light

The final function of spattering is to reinforce lighting. In the *Simon Big-Ears* set, for special reasons, all of the effects of differential lighting were produced by alterations in the base coats and by variations in spattering. But even under normal conditions, it is usually good practice to reinforce the lighting pattern by spattering the areas of the flats that are to be less brightly lit more heavily with the darker of the two spatter mixtures and spattering the lit areas of the flats more heavily with the lighter. In practice, that means that nearly always the coat of dark spatter is applied most heavily at the top of the flats, fading evenly toward the bottom, and the coat of lighter spatter is applied heavily at the bottom, fading evenly toward the top.

Designers should feel free to use or not use spattering according to the effect they want to produce, but it is so frequently desirable that it would not be unusual to design an entire season of plays in which every element of every set was spattered.

Texturing

If spatter is applied in small spots, the flats seem smooth; if the dots of color are large, the flats appear rough; consequently, the designer should specify the size and quantity of spatter to be applied, although usually such descriptions as "heavy, coarse spatter," "light, coarse spatter," and "medium, fine spatter" are sufficient. A designer who wants more precise control of the spatter coat should supervise the construction crew while they spatter the flats.

Even at its coarsest, spatter produces a relatively uniform texture. Still greater variation can be achieved by using other techniques of applying spots of color to the base coat. Such methods are rarely used and are more likely to be invented by the designer to produce a special effect, rather than being standard techniques. A designer who is interested will find various unusual methods of applying paint in texts on stagecraft; only a few examples will be mentioned here.

Dry-brush techniques involve the use of a brush that has so little paint in it that it makes isolated streaks, rather than a solid strip of color. The dry-brush effect can sometimes be used to suggest thatch, striations like those of "combed" plywood, or grooves in brickwork. A feather duster can be used as a large, very coarse brush. If the tips of the feathers are dipped in paint, the duster can be used to apply color in large, irregular blobs or streaks: the brush can be drawn across the surface to produce striations, it can be twirled to produce whirls of paint, or it can be dotted over the

Dry Brush

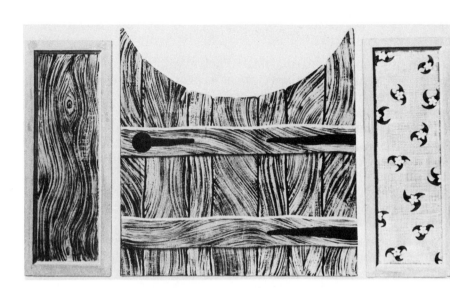

Figure 3-28. Dry-brush techniques. *Left:* Dry brush is used to simulate wood graining. *Center:* A coarse graining is applied to a rustic door. (The hardware and the edges of the boards are painted solid, not with dry brush.) *Right:* Dry-brushed lines are applied horizontally and vertically to suggest a clothlike texture, as a background for a floral motif.

surface to simulate the effect of an extremely coarse spatter. (See *Figure 3-28.*)

Twisted Cloth

A piece of canvas or burlap can be twisted or wadded to produce an irregular surface; when dipped in scene paint it can then be rolled or pressed against a flat, producing various irregular patterns of paint. (See *Figure 3-29.*) Such an application might be useful in simulating the texture of a rock surface.

Puddling

A technique that is of occasional value is called *puddling;* unlike the methods just described, it produces a base coat that is itself varied, rather than adding variegations to a previously painted and dried base. In puddling, the flat is laid horizontal, and the surface is covered with irregular areas of paint of different colors. While they are still wet, the edges are blended, so that when the coat has dried it consists of irregular splotches that fade into each other. Usually, the various colors are closely related, so that a flat might be puddled with half a dozen mixes of light brown, all produced by mixing additional pigments with quantities of the same basic brown paint. When such a flat has dried, mortar lines painted across the

Figure 3-29. The use of cloth in applying scene paint. Each panel was painted with a base coat, and then a texture was applied by dipping canvas in paint and pressing it against the surface. For the center panel, a strip of canvas was folded in accordion pleats, and only the edges were used for printing. For the top and bottom panels, the canvas was wadded to produce an irregular pattern. Lines were added to suggest mortar and (*bottom panel*) a wallpaper pattern. The final step has been omitted from half of each panel to reveal the cloth printing more clearly.

surface will create the effect of a varicolored stone wall. The same techniques might be used for painting foliage: a puddled base of various shades of leaf green could be laid down first, and, when it was dry, individual leaf shapes could be painted over it, so that the base would be visually interpreted as indistinct foliage between the nearer, defined leaf shapes.

Stenciling   Often the repetition of identical elements in sets involves no particular problems (for example, when an identical design is used for all the doors, or the walls are covered with a series of identical panels). Repeated motifs arranged to form an all-over textured pattern, however, do require the use of special techniques. The commonest of such designs are those simulating wallpaper.

Regularly spaced designs may be analyzed so as to reveal an underlying simple geometrical grid. It is most practical for the designer to start with the grid and build the design over it. Nearly all such grids are variations of a checkerboard or diamond pattern; the checkerboard may be varied by substituting rectangles for squares, the diamond by slanting the lines at different angles. One important variation of the diamond pattern is produced by drawing the short diagonals of diamonds with angles of 60° and 120°; the result is a grid made up of equilateral triangles.

In designing such a pattern, the artist should first lay out a grid, then draw in a motif that corresponds to one of the units of the grid. The entire design can be completed by copying the motif in each of the other units.

Such designs are usually applied to scenery by stencils. The entire design may be painted through holes in the stencil, or the stencil may simply be used to mark the design on the surface. The design may then be painted by hand. Often, the workers will lay key points of the grid on the surface of the flat with a tape measure and straight edge, as a guide in placing the stencil. However the pattern is applied, it is extremely helpful if guidepoints can be incorporated into it, so spaced that when one copy of the pattern has been marked, the stencil can be shifted so that the guidepoint at its bottom (for example) matches the top guidepoint that has already been marked, with the result that the stencil is in the proper position for making the next copy. Often, such points can be incorporated unobtrusively into the design. An example of this method is the wallpaper design used for *Harvey (Figure 3-30),* in which the four small circles served as guidepoints for automatic spacing. If the points do not fit esthetically into the design, they can be placed to coincide with areas that will be painted, and the dividing bridges can be painted out after the design has been marked.

Cutting stencils is time-consuming, and they are easily damaged, so it is good practice to create a design that will be as rugged as possible, especially if the paint is applied with the stencil in place. Following are a few hints that will help in producing designs that will be practical for stencil application.

No stencil can be cut with a protected (solid) area inside an open area. The simplest example of such a shape is that of a doughnut: the circle marking the hole in the doughnut would fall out when the stencil was cut. Solid pointed areas, extending into open sections, are weak; open

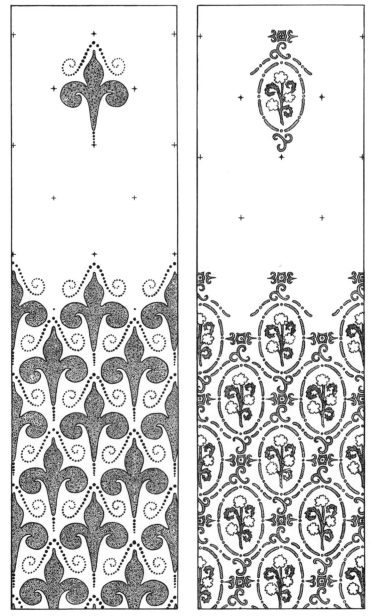

Figure 3-30. Stencil design. *Left,* wallpaper for a production of Molière's *The Imaginary Invalid; right,* wallpaper for Mary Chase's *Harvey.* At the top of each panel, the grid of guide points for laying out the pattern is shown, with a single motif drawn in place. At the bottom of the panels, the patterns are shown complete.

Figure 3-31. A wallpaper design for Act I of *The Importance of Being Earnest,* illustrating the use of bridges for strengthening stencils. At the top a stencil is shown as it was actually cut; twenty-four bridges were placed where they would not interfere with key points in the pattern. The motif was pounced on the flat in chalk, and the pattern was then painted by hand, carrying the lines across the spaces left by the bridges.

areas, however, may have pointed shapes. Thin solid strips are weak, and should be avoided. (See *Figure 3-31.*)

Obviously, no important esthetic effect should be dispensed with simply to promote ease of stenciling. If a pattern cannot be designed effectively without violating some of the suggestions above, it is possible to correct the objectionable features by adding bridges across open areas to strengthen points of weakness. Thus, three or four bridges could be used to join the center of a doughnut shape with the surrounding solid area. After the design has been painted, the stencil can be removed, and the areas that have been left blank under the bridges can be filled in freehand. In adding temporary bridges, which have no esthetic function in the design, it is important not to obscure the lines of the design. Thus, bridges should often be held back from the end of an open space, so that the lines of the design itself will be clear to the painters.

Stamping

A new method of applying wallpaper designs to flats has been developed. It is especially suited to bold designs without small details. (See *Figure 7-3.*) The motif is cut from the elastic sheet plastic manufactured to be used for rug pads. A slightly larger rectangle of Upson board is flexed and tied so that it retains a slightly rounded shape, and the plastic is fastened to it with white glue.

Using a small (two-inch) paint brush, the artist coats the plastic with scene paint, turns the unit upside down, and prints the motif by pressing the plastic against the flat with a rocking motion. This method saves an enormous amount of time, as compared with painting the same motifs by hand or with a stencil.

Randomizing

The repetition of identical motifs, evenly spaced across a surface, is not the only way to produce an effect of texture. Motifs may be used that share certain qualities in common, but differ in other ways; for example, color may be kept constant while shape and arrangement are varied. The method of designing such a pattern is called *randomizing.*

The principle of unified variety requires that the different elements be related to each other, even though there is no precise repetition. The designer's first step, then, is to determine the limits within which the elements may vary. For a stone wall, the designer may decide that all stones must be rectangular (excluding squares and other shapes); that no rectangle may have one set of sides more than twice the length of the other sides; and that no rectangle may be longer than 18″ or shorter than 6″.

To prepare instructions for the scene shop, the designer draws the required shapes on a scaled representation of the wall. Let us say that the overall dimensions of the wall are 4'-0″ × 12'-0″. The designer first draws a rectangle representing one of the stones (let us say with a length of 18″) somewhere close to the center of the wall. Then, in the areas between this initial stone and the edges of the wall, the designer draws additional stones, being careful not to space them precisely in the centers of the areas, not to place them vertically or horizontally even with each other, and not to make any two of exactly the same dimensions. Then moving to somewhat smaller dimensions, the designer draws other stones slightly off center in each of the areas between the stones already drawn. As more and more stones are drawn, the spaces between them will become steadily smaller, until they are within the range of dimensions adopted for the stones. The designer then draws the stones so as to completely fill in the remaining areas. (See *Figure 3-32.*) While operating within the established limits, the designer is careful not to produce unintended patterns by concentrating related sizes and shapes in one part of the wall, by lining up edges, or by producing unintentional symmetrical arrangements. Working constantly over the entire area, rather than starting at one corner and filling each area, will help greatly in achieving the effect of random arrangement. Exactly the same methods of arrangement may be used for randomizing color and texture. The random effect is very useful for reducing the degree of rigidity in a design. Since it adds variety, it may greatly increase the interest of a design, so long as it does not destroy the unity.

Randomizing a Screen

It may be helpful to describe a more complex application of randomizing—for instance, that used in the curved shapes of the ornamental screen for *The Solid Gold Cadillac (Figure 3-33.)*

The screen as a whole was composed of vertical rectangles of the same height but of two slightly different widths, joined alternately side by side. Each of the narrower units contained three large, relatively rigid ornaments based on the square and circle. For greater variety, the wider units were filled with vertical bronze bars, alternating with metallic strips having irregular curved edges and insets of colored enamel in the center. Corrugated cardboard was used to simulate metal for the irregular strips. For rigidity, a vertical strip of 1×1 lumber was fastened behind each metallic unit. Since the metal strips had to hide the wood support, they had to be designed with a solid 1″ vertical strip in the center; consequently, a thin rectangle representing this strip was drawn first. The edges of the metal strips were intended to be made up of long sine-curves or S-curves, varying irregularly, with the two edges asymmetrical. On the basis of several trial sketches, it was decided that the extreme limit of each edge should be 1½″ from the edge of the central 1″ strip. To prevent the accidental development of symmetry, the specifications directed

Figure 3-32. Randomizing: a stone wall. The numbers indicate the order in which the rectangles representing stones were placed in the drawing. The first stone was drawn close to the center of the wall; then a number of stones were scattered irregularly across the open spaces, followed by a third group. The center drawing shows the placement of the fourth, fifth, and sixth groups of stones. The bottom drawing shows the completed wall, with mortar added, the corners of the stones rounded, and the edges highlighted and shadowed.

that about four complete S-curves be drawn on one side of each strip, and about five on the other. Since the unit was intended to give an impression of free variation, these curves were drawn freehand. In actual construction, four vertical lines were first drawn on the cardboard, the center pair 1'' apart, and the outside lines 1½'' from the center lines, thus producing

Figure 3-33.   Randomizing: a screen. The method of randomizing the curved sections is shown to a larger scale (*bottom*). A grid of four lines was drawn: the center lines were 1″ apart, and the outside lines were 1½″ from the center lines. One edge was divided into four sections and the other into five, and undulating curves were drawn matching the marks. (*The Solid Gold Cadillac*.)

two wide stripes with a narrower stripe between them. Measuring by eye, the designer marked one of the wide stripes into five approximately equal lengths, the other into four. An undulating curve was then drawn in each of the outside stripes, designed so that similar points on the curve roughly matched the divisions that had been marked. The curves were inspected for smoothness, corrected if necessary, and then cut. When fastened to the frame, the entire unit was painted gold. Lines were then drawn inside the irregular strips, ¾″ from each edge. Where the strips were 1½″ wide or less (that is, where the inside lines touched or crossed), they were left gold; where there was a space between the inside lines, the area was painted in colors designed to simulate enamel. Six colors were used, distributed so that no two successive areas were painted the same color, and so that each individual color appeared in an even randomized arrangement throughout the entire screen.

The description of the process, which might be called controlled variation, may seem unduly complicated. It is entirely practical in actual design and construction. The method consists essentially of two types of decisions: selecting the elements that are to be varied and defining the limits within which variation is permissible. The result of those two decisions is that the design necessarily displays both unity and variety.

A set made of flats representing an ordinary room can be made much more convincing and interesting if the basic design is supplemented with added three-dimensional details, such as a cornice at the ceiling, pictures hanging in three-dimensional frames, columns, pilasters, fireplace mantels, and paneling. Such elements are usually constructed separately, and hung on the flats with picture hooks. Often, however, a designer can greatly reduce the amount of time needed to build a set by simulating the three-dimensional effect with painting. The walls in *Figure 3-34* are an example of *trompe l'oeil* painting. The towers in the *Simon Big-Ears* set *(Figures 9-6 and 16-25)* are another example. Because the entire set had to be transported by a single truck, it was necessary to build the towers flat in order to save shipping space. They were painted to suggest roundness so as to be completely convincing to the audience.

Trompe L'oeil
Painting

A complete discussion of the methods of simulating three dimensions in paint would be beyond the scope of this book; the student is advised to study the effects of light in expressing roundness and thickness in ordinary life, as well as the methods used by easel painters. However, a few suggestions will be given here.

The Patterns of Reflection

Examination of a moderately smooth column, preferably not in direct sunlight, will demonstrate some of the phenomena of lighting. Looking at it with their backs to the source of light, students will notice that the part of the surface closest to them is most brightly lit, in the form of a more or less sharply defined vertical streak. As the surface moves away from this strip, it becomes steadily darker, with the least light reflected from the areas at, or close to, the edges of the visible half of the column.

Examination of a paneled door is also helpful; in this case, it may be easier to analyze if it is in direct sunlight. If the door has sunken panels, the top edge of each panel will be in shadow, and the bottom edge will reflect a highlight clearly brighter than the rest of the wood. Unless the

Figure 3-34. *Trompe l'oeil* painting. Inexperienced students painted the rough stone blocks of the wall, using drybrushing and spatter to represent the shadows and highlights that would result if the blocks were lit from the upper left corner of the picture. *(The Lion in Winter.)*

sun is directly overhead, one side edge will also be shadowed, and the other side edge will be highlighted, the arrangement depending on the direction of the light.

Figure 3-35. The flats making up the wings have shaped edges, but details and thickness pieces are represented by paint. (Sheridan's *The Rivals*.)

Painting in Three Dimensions

Imitating the appearance of three dimensions on a flat surface involves painting the areas with colors that will duplicate the pattern of reflection of the three-dimensional object. For example, paneling can be simulated on flats by drawing strips to represent molding and then painting them in two colors, one distinctly darker and the other much lighter than the surrounding surfaces. (See *Figure 3-35.*) The imitation can be made more acceptable if some actually three-dimensional details are added. For instance, if an elaborate molding 6″ wide is to be painted along a wall, it can be made more convincing by fastening a simple molding at the top and bottom edges and simulating only the center section with paint.

The *Simon Big-Ears* towers are shaped like a column, with the base broadened. The painters were instructed to paint each tower in nine vertical strips, broader at the bottom than at the top to match its shape. Because the designer intended to suggest that the light was coming from the center of the stage, the mixes were not arranged symmetrically: the lightest tint was placed in the fourth strip (counting from the edge of each tower that was closest to the center of the stage), and the strips on each side of it were made progressively darker. The edges between each pair of strips were then blended, and the entire flat was finally spattered differentially, with a light spatter concentrated at strip 4 and fading to the edges, and a dark spatter starting at the edges and fading toward the lightest strip. (See *Figures 9-6* and *16-25*.)

Texture in Paint

The shadows, middle colors, and highlights of rounded objects with rough surfaces blend together at the edges; the smoother the surface, the more distinct the edges between the various degrees of brightness are, and on highly polished surfaces, such as metal, each separate area may be uniformly dark or bright, with a hard, sharp edge. It was intended to suggest that the *Simon Big-Ears* towers were made of rough stone, so they were carefully blended; for a polished marble column, the shadows and broad highlight would have been painted with considerably greater definition, and a thin, sharp, almost white streak would have been run up the center of the highlight area.

The Direction of Light

The positions of bright and dark areas on a three-dimensional object are determined by the direction from which light strikes it. Most often, the light comes from overhead, in the daytime from the sun and at night from ceiling lights. Under those conditions, a raised molding attached to the wall, for example, would be brightly lit along its top surface. The bottom surface would be in shadow, and the middle area would be lighter than the shadow and darker than the highlight. Occasionally, the major light comes from below; for example, a glowing fire might make the underside of a raised molding on the wall near it brighter than the top.

In imitating the effect of light falling on scenery, a designer may use one of three fundamental patterns. The most realistic is to adjust the shadows and highlights to match the direction of the spotlights and other lights that will actually be used for the set; such painting is especially convincing if it is reinforced with some actual three-dimensional details.

Since stage lighting is often complex, however, and since it may be necessary for the designer to complete the painting designs before the lighting has been planned, it may often be preferable to use a generalized version of the pattern of stage lighting. Usually, the center of the stage area is more brightly lit than other areas, since it is the strongest position on stage and the one most heavily used by actors. Consequently, three-dimensional shapes can be simulated by painting them as if the light came from a point in the center of the stage, about head height (that is, six feet above the floor).

Let us suppose that the designer has decided to face all of the walls with panels sunk below the surface, extending from the floor up three feet, the paneling to be simulated by painting. First, the edges of the panels are indicated as narrow strips, perhaps half an inch wide. Assuming that the light comes from a point six feet above the center of the stage floor, the horizontal strip at the top of each panel, and the vertical strip closest to the center of the stage, are painted dark; then the other strips are painted light. Of course, if it was intended that the panels be raised from the surface, instead of sunk into it, the pattern of highlight and shadow would be reversed. This pattern of shading, in which the source of light is assumed to be the center of the stage, is the most useful of the three possible treatments and is convincing for all but the most realistic sets.

The third possibility is the least convincing, but also the simplest. For some unidentified reason, when there is no clear indication of the direction from which light is falling on an object, one assumes that it is being lit at an angle of 45°, from the upper left corner. Because of this psychological phenomenon, *trompe l'oeil* painting can be done with reasonable effectiveness by applying highlights and shadows as if all the light on the stage came from that direction. Since this pattern does not match the actual direction of light used for most stage sets, this is the least realistic of the three treatments, but especially for a frankly artificial set (for example, a wing-and-drop set for an old-fashioned melodrama), its great simplicity may make it the preferred solution. In particular, if the flats are painted in the scene shop before they are assembled, this pattern eliminates the necessity for constant checking to determine the position of each flat in the completed set.

THREE-DIMENSIONAL SHAPING

Aside from the imitation of lighting, the effect of three dimensions requires an adjustment in the shapes of the scenic units. In the *Antony and Cleopatra* set *(Figure 6-19)* the pillars and horizontal beams were fully three-dimensional, with thickness pieces constructed full size. If they were to be simulated in two dimensions, it would be necessary to design the front flats with extensions to represent the thicknesses, which could then be painted a different shade or tint, to suggest that they were in a different plane than the fronts of the arches.

More complex shapes are illustrated in *Figures 2-18, 6-14,* and *9-1* (see also *Figure 16-25*). In the *Simon Big-Ears* set, the towers were placed well apart on the stage, so that the audience turned left and right to see them. They were designed with the intention of suggesting that circular windows were cut in them; if the towers had been built three-dimensionally, the thickness of the wall at the edge of the window closest to the center of the stage would have been invisible to the audience, but the thickness at the offstage edge would have been clearly visible through the opening. Furthermore, since the audience looked up at the windows, the thickness piece would have seemed widest at the upper offstage edge of each window. In simulating this effect on the two-dimensional flats, the window opening was first drawn symmetrically, and then the thickness added by drawing a similar curve matching the pattern of visibility. The holes actually cut in the canvas were consequently asymmetrically shaped. Painting the area representing the thickness piece produced a convincing simulation of three dimensions.

The false proscenium and sets for *The Importance of Being Earnest* (see *Figures 2-18, 6-14, 16-22,* and *16-23*) illustrate the extreme use of three-dimensional painting. One further example is the columns designed for a set for *The Marriage of Figaro (Figure 7-4)*. These were built as entirely two-dimensional units, in order to speed up the construction work and to leave as much as possible of the stage floor open for use by the actors. However, the design was intended to suggest extreme three-dimensional shaping, particularly in the scrolls at the bottom of each column, which were designed to appear as if extending forward at an angle of 90° to each other. The primary result of that position would have been to reveal the edges of the curved shapes; consequently, they were included in the design and construction and painted to differentiate them clearly from the other surface. In addition, the segments of the twisted pattern that made up the vertical section of the columns were shadowed and highlighted to suggest roundness.

Chapters 13 and 14 describe in detail the method of preparing perspective paintings of stage sets. A two-dimensional unit shaped to indicate roundness and thickness is, in effect, simply a section cut from such a painting, drawn full scale and set up on the stage. Students will find the process clearer after they have completed their study of perspective.

Papier-Mâché   Papier-mâché is an extremely useful material for constructing three-dimensional elements. For repeated units, such as the capitals of columns, it is possible to make them quickly by first modeling the unit in clay, then making a negative mold of plaster of paris. When the plaster of paris has dried, the clay is removed, the inner surface of the mold is coated lightly with vaseline or aluminum foil, and copies of the unit are made by pressing in papier-mâché, beginning with strips of cloth and then adding two or three layers of paper.

Some decades ago, a synthetic product called Celastic was marketed. It is, in effect, a substitute for papier-mâché. It is made soft when dipped into a special liquid; then it is shaped and allowed to harden. Since the walls of the units are thinner than those made of papier-mâché, it is preferable for such uses as constructing masks and simulating armor; it is widely used in the construction of jewelry. Its major disadvantage is its greater cost: in contrast, the expenditure for even large papier-mâché structures is so low as to be negligible. Individual preferences vary: some workers find papier-mâché unpleasantly messy, others prefer it to the synthetic products. Normally, designers can leave the choice of the type of material to be used to the construction supervisors, who will make their decisions on the basis of their own preferences and the available time and materials. From the viewpoint of actors and audience, the two types of material are interchangeable.

Papier-mâché and Celastic are both examples of *plastics,* in the basic sense of the word, which designates moldable materials. Within recent decades, chemical experiments have resulted in the development of a large number of synthetic plastics, most of them made from petroleum. Their use in the theater is still experimental, although some designers have handled them very effectively. They are available in many different forms, including clear sheets resembling glass, rigid foam, elastic foam, rods and tubes, liquids that can be poured into molds to harden and that can be either colored or left clear, and sprays, one of which has the peculiar property of expanding as it sets.

Plastics   Plastics constitute a genuinely valuable addition to theatrical resources, but there are certain objections to their use. The most important is that they involve significant fire and health hazards, which require that they be handled with extreme care; the other is that their present cost is high, and certain to rise as the supply of petroleum shrinks. Perhaps the plastics most useful in scenery construction are the foam that is sold in the form of white blocks, which can be carved with tools or heated wires, and the elastic foam sheets that are intended for rug pads but are ideal for padding platform tops and the treads of stairs.[1]

1   For a more complete discussion of the use of plastics in the theater, see Burris-Meyer and Cole, third edition, or Welker, *Stagecraft,* pages 203–217.

Figure 3-36. Rope decoration. The picture frame was made of corrugated cardboard, with thin rope glued along the lines of the pattern. Water-based putty was then added to make the design look more three-dimensional.

Rope Decoration

Rope is an extremely useful decorative material. It may be glued on wood or cardboard frames in complex designs to simulate wood carving, fastened to wire or wood strips to represent metal grillwork, tacked to flats to simulate wooden molding, and so on. (See *Figures 3-36* and *3-37.*)

Wire

Ordinary coat-hanger wire can be used effectively in many ways. The chandeliers for *Blithe Spirit* (*Figure 2-13*), as well as those for Sheridan's play *The Critic* (*Figures 3-38* and *14-1*), were made from coathanger wire, which was then painted gold and hung with crystals. Since the wire will hold its shape when bent, it can be used to simulate vines or metal grillwork, with rope tied or glued to it for greater visibility.

Moderately fine wire of the type known as stovepipe wire is especially valuable because it is nearly invisible on stage and can be used to suspend

Figure 3-37. Rope decoration. The grillwork is simulated by a frame of 1 × 2s, with dowels as banisters, each wrapped with a spiral of rope. The corner motif and the S shapes were bent from coat-hanger wire, and rope was glued to the front of each. The shield was cut from two sheets of quarter-inch plywood; roofing nails were then driven part way into the wood, leaving the heads about a half inch above the surface of the wood. Nylon rope was run from one of the nails at the outside edge of the shield to the matching nail in the center and back to the next nail at the edge, continuing until the pattern was complete. Finally, the shield was painted, and the rope and nails were dry-brushed with gold. The picture frames were made of corrugated cardboard. Rope of various types was glued to the surface to simulate wood carving, the frames were painted and antiqued, and the rope was dry-brushed with gold.

Figure 3-38. The use of wire. The candlestick, including sockets, was made of coathanger wire fastened to a plywood base. The foliage shapes were cut from double thicknesses of paper, glued to the wire, and gilded. (See also *Figure 2-13* for a chandelier formed of wire and hung with plastic beads, with amber Christmas-tree lights fastened inside the fringe of beads.)

decorative elements in midair. Dull-finished nylon fishing line can be used in the same way, although its extreme flexibility requires that units fastened by fishing line be anchored more securely than units fastened with stovepipe wire.

One extremely valuable material is ordinary corrugated cardboard. It may be bought in large sheets—although unlimited supplies in various sizes are available free. Some products, such as furniture, are shipped in boxes made of large sheets of the cardboard. Usually, business houses discard the boxes and may have to pay to have them hauled away. A little exploration will reveal local merchants who will be willing to donate the boxes to the theater.

Corrugated cardboard is moderately strong in one direction and extremely weak in the other. It can often be effectively used for table tops and for reinforcing irregular openings in flats or covering columns and pilasters. Its strength can be increased greatly by laminating two or more sheets, with the grain running in opposite directions; the inside surfaces are coated with a glue mixture and dried under moderate pressure. At best, corrugated cardboard lacks the strength of other building materials, but if units are carefully designed, they will be surprisingly sturdy. Cardboard tables, chairs, columns, and picture frames will be more than adequate for stage use. (See *Figures 3-39, 3-40,* and *3-41.*) One set of end tables made from corrugated cardboard was returned to the scene shop after being used as designed; without attempting to protect the tables, the crew used them in the scene shop as tables, as step stools, and to hold lumber for sawing. Even with such treatment, they retained their strength and shape for more than three years.

Tables, balustrades, and other scenic units made from corrugated cardboard have the advantage of cheapness, but their most striking quality is their lightness. A table that would require two people to move it if it were made with even a light wood frame may be light enough for one person to carry in one hand if made from cardboard.

The successful use of corrugated cardboard requires careful application of the principles of construction strength; wherever possible, advantage should be taken of the strength afforded by triangles.

Folds are made in the cardboard by scoring the sheet with a nail or a blunt knife and then carefully folding along the scored line. Joints are fastened by gluing heavy paper across the crack, much like dutchmen on flats. The paper used for surfacing the cardboard itself is ideal for this purpose; if the cardboard is soaked in warm water for a few minutes, the layers will separate, and the surface paper can be pulled off for use in joining. With a little care, it is possible to cut part way through the cardboard and strip off one surface and the corrugation below, exposing the bottom layer of paper; if that layer is coated with glue, it can then be pressed against the surface to be joined to it, forming an automatic dutchman.

Because of the lightness of the cardboard, it is practical to construct elements solid that would have had to be made hollow if they were built from wood. For example, a 3"-thick railing for a stone balustrade can be

Corrugated
Cardboard

Figure 3-39. Cardboard construction. The love seat has a plywood base, with the curved surfaces filled in with cardboard. The table and stool are entirely of cardboard, except for rope decoration and a fitted pillow. The stool is made of two layers, to provide the arched leg effect. The top of the table is made of four layers; the legs vary from two to ten.

built up from laminated cardboard without increasing the weight significantly. The flexibility of the cardboard can also be used in shaping elements: a base 3″ high and 2″ thick can be built around the bottom of a column by cutting a 3″-strip of cardboard with the corrugations running across the strip, coating it with glue, and winding it around the bottom of the column to the thickness of 2″.

The corrugations will show if raw edges of the cardboard are left visible. They may not be noticeable from the audience, but they can be completely concealed by attaching a strip of paper (which can be heavy or light: even newspaper or discarded mimeograph paper can be used) around the edge, gluing it to the top and bottom surfaces of the cardboard sheet. With a little care, it will be possible to design the units so that most edges are hidden by the paper dutchmen used in construction, so that only a few concealing strips need be used.

When construction has been completed, the units are painted with ordinary scene paint.

Figure 3-40. Corrugated cardboard stools are placed together to form a bier for a mock funeral (*A Funny Thing Happened on the Way to the Forum*).

JOINERY

Many different methods of joining lumber have been developed, but only those that are especially useful in the theater will be described here. Some

Figure 3-41. A small console table made of corrugated cardboard and ¼″ cotton rope, gilded (designed for Coward's *Blithe Spirit*).

joints that were formerly widely used in the theater have been made obsolete by the development or increased availability of new materials, particularly plywood, and they have also been omitted from this discussion, although they are still occasionally used. The accurate cutting of joints, their precise fitting, and their solid fastening require a number of skills and are facilitated by special techniques; these, however, are not the concern of designers and consequently will not be discussed. What designers should know is the types of joints most theatrically useful, the types of structures to which they are adapted, and their advantages and disadvantages. Since building must sometimes be done to meet pressing deadlines, it is also important that designers have some knowledge of the length of time required for the various types of joints, so that in an emergency they can choose the faster ones and omit those that would stretch the work unacceptably. And finally, designers should not specify the construction of joints requiring special tools unless they are sure that those tools are actually available to the construction crew. All of those items of information are included in the following discussion. For easier comparison, the analysis is given in semitabular form.

1. **The butt joint**
   Description: The end, side, or edge of one piece of lumber is placed flat against one surface of another piece of lumber and fastened either by nailing through both pieces or by attaching a piece of plywood or other fastener across the joint. (See *Figure 3-42.*)
   Use: This is an all-purpose joint, used to join the stiles, rails, and toggles of flats, as well as to construct furniture, platforms, etc.
   Disadvantages: It is only moderately strong, although normally adequate for theater purposes. If a plywood piece is used, the thickness of the lumber is increased by ¼''.
   Advantages: It can be made quickly, with hand tools and without special skill.

2. **The mitered joint**
   Description: This is identical to the butt joint, except that the end of at least one of the pieces of lumber is cut at an angle other than 90°, 45° being the commonest.
   Use: It is most frequently used in the theater for the diagonal braces of flats; it is also occasionally used for picture frames and molding applied to walls to simulate paneling. (See *Figure 3-43.*)
   Advantages: Its most important advantage is that it provides the triangles that are essential to a rigid structure in flats. In picture frames, molding, etc., the mitered joint changes the angle of the strip without destroying the decorative pattern or shape; for example, it is the only joint by which lengths of quarter round can be joined at an angle without throwing the surface into different planes.
   Disadvantages: It has the same disadvantages as the butt joint, in addition to being somewhat more difficult to cut.

3. **The lap joint**
   Description: One piece of lumber is nailed on top of another. (See *Figure 3-44.*)

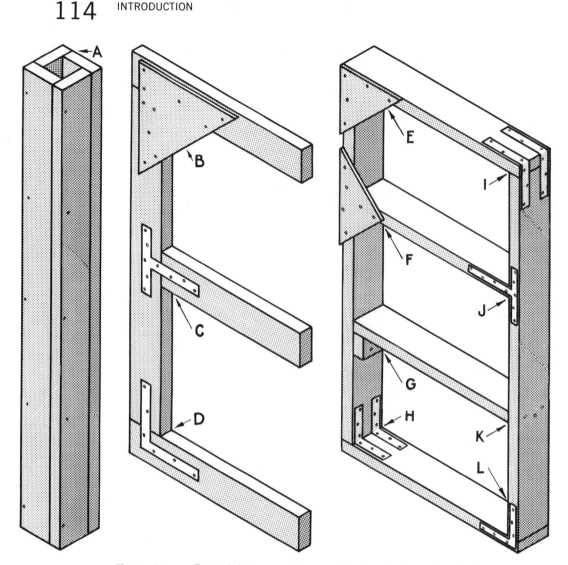

Figure 3-42. Butt joints. Twelve methods of fastening butt joints are shown. In the drawing at the left, the joints are fastened by nailing directly through the two pieces of lumber. This style of butt joint can often be used in constructing parts of furniture, small pillars, newel posts, etc. The butt joints shown in the middle drawing are most often used in constructing flats, in which case they are fastened with corner blocks (joint *B*). Joints *C* and *D* are fastened with strap-metal braces. The joints shown at the right are often used in making shelf units. Joints *E* and *F* are fastened with corner blocks, *G* is fastened by an added block of wood (see also *Figure 3-49*), and *K* is held together by nails driven through the vertical board. The other joints are fastened with strap metal of various shapes.

Figure 3-43. Mitered joints. The top left figure illustrates the mitered joint's unique property of altering the direction of a patterned molding without destroying the pattern.

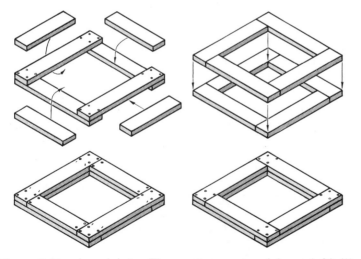

Figure 3-44. Lap joints. The center square (*above left*) illustrates the commonest form of the lap joint. If short pieces are used to fill in the gaps, the surfaces become level (*below left*). The arrangement shown at the right produces a similar figure without added pieces. (In the bottom left figure the short lines on the top surface represent the points of clinched nails.)

Use: Most frequently used where the joint is to be hidden, as in the frames for rocks.

Advantages: A strong joint, especially if glued. The fastest and easiest joint to construct; requires only hand tools.

Disadvantages: The joint is twice as thick as the lumber used, and the two pieces of lumber are in different planes. (But adding a second strip of lumber to each of the two composing the joint makes the surfaces even, although the weight will be nearly doubled.)

4. The running lap joint

Description: A series of lengths of lumber are laid in a line end to end, and then a second series is laid on top of them, placed so that the joints of one layer lie close to the centers of the boards making up the other layer. The two layers are then nailed, screwed, or bolted together.

Use: This is a means of joining sections of lumber to form a unit longer than the length of individual boards in stock. It is most frequently used for stiffening the top and bottom of a large drop, in which case the edge of the canvas is placed over the first layer of lumber and the second layer is laid on top of it. When completed, the two layers of lumber hold the canvas firmly between them. (See *Figure 3-45.*)

Advantages: May be made very quickly and easily, requiring very little cutting and only hand tools.

Disadvantages: The weight and thickness of the unit are twice that of a single layer of the lumber used.

5. The scarf joint

Description: Two pieces of lumber are laid on edge and cut in a long, slanting line. The cut surfaces are then placed on top of each other and fastened by gluing and nailing. (See *Figure 3-46.*)

Use: Infrequently used in the theater, but valuable when stock lumber is too short and the added weight and dimensions of a running lap joint are unacceptable.

Advantages: May be used to produce lumber of any length, without increasing the thickness.

Disadvantages: It is difficult to cut, even with a power saw.

6. The halved joint

Description: The halved joint is essentially a lap joint in which the area of contact in each piece of lumber has

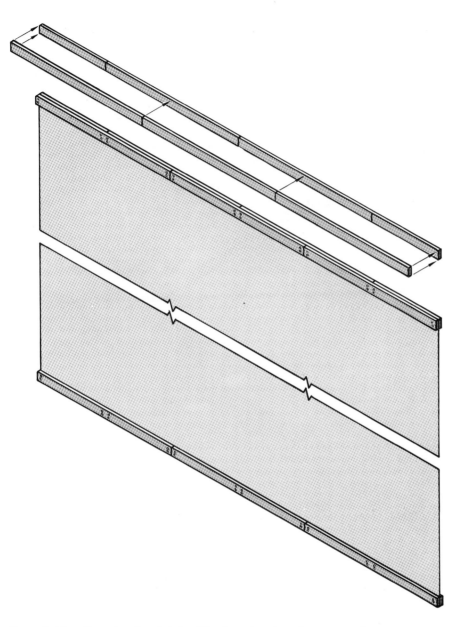

Figure 3-45. Running lap joints. The top drawing shows a series of boards to be joined into a single structure by running lap joints. The bottom drawing shows the running lap joint used to construct stiffeners for the top and bottom of a canvas drop. The canvas is placed between the layers of lumber before they are nailed together and is held in place by the same nails that fasten the boards.

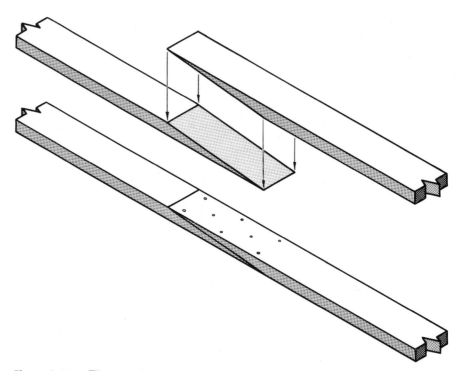

Figure 3-46. The scarf joint. This can only be cut satisfactorily with a power saw.

been cut to half its original thickness. It is fastened by gluing and nailing. (See *Figure 3-47.*)

Use: The joint is useful in building screens or furniture where corner blocks would show, and where it would be undesirable to have the two pieces of lumber in different planes.

Advantages: The joint has the same thickness as the pieces of lumber of which it is composed, and it does not require a corner block.

Disadvantages: Even when glued, the joint will be weaker than the solid lumber. The joint requires a radial-arm or table saw, although with such a saw it is easy and fast to cut.

7. The notched joint

Description: A rectangular cut is made in one of the pieces of lumber, matching the thickness and width of the second piece, which is fitted into the notch and nailed in place. (See *Figure 3-48.*)

Use: The notched joint is primarily useful for such structures as bookcases, where the shelves must bear considerable weight.

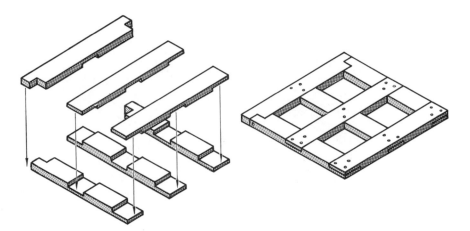

Figure 3-47. Halved joints. Two types of halved joints are shown, in various positions. The pieces are shown separated at the left; assembled at the right.

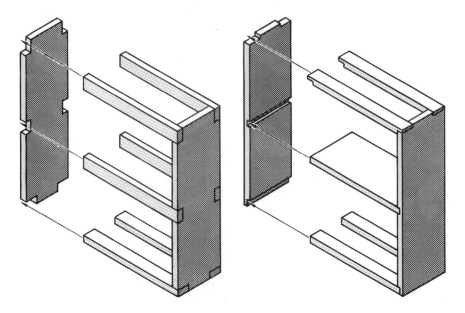

Figure 3-48. Notched joints. Various types and positions of notched joints are shown. The joints at the top of the right figure are combinations of halved joints and notched joints. If the structures shown were to be used as shelves, only the center shelf in the right drawing could be used as drawn; the others would have to be completed by the addition of rectangles of plywood or other material laid across them and nailed in place.

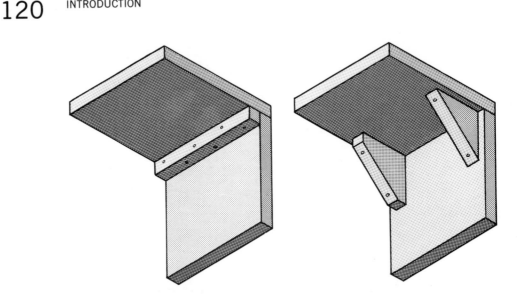

Figure 3-49. Blocked joints. Blocked butt joints are shown, although any type of joint may be blocked. Three types of blocks are illustrated. The two at the right provide more strength than the third. Since little holding power is added by the points of the triangle at the right, they are often cut off (as shown in the center block), especially where space is limited, as in bracing certain types of door frames.

Advantages: Offers great resistance to force at right angles to the surface of the unnotched lumber.

Disadvantages: Requires a power saw, although it is fast and easy to cut. Does not offer much resistance to force at right angles to the surface of the notched lumber.

8. The blocked joint

Description: This joint is essentially a double butt joint, in which a third piece of lumber is butted against both of the two pieces of lumber being joined. (See *Figure 3-49.*)

Use: It is a substitute for a notched joint when the added piece is acceptable.

Advantages: It is fast and easy to construct, and it is stronger than a butt joint.

Disadvantages: The third piece of lumber may be unsightly. It is somewhat weaker than a notched joint.

Fastening Joints   Two pieces of lumber may be fastened by gluing, nailing, screwing, or bolting (listed in the order of increasing strength).

Ground carpenter's glue, used also as a binder for scene paint, is normally used in the scene shop for gluing lumber, because it is readily available, cheap, and strong. Joints are not usually glued in building scenery; gluing is seldom used alone, and is used in conjunction with other fastening materials only when additional strength is necessary, or when joints are likely to loosen in use, as for chairs and stools.

Nails are available in many sizes and styles, including roofing nails, common nails, clout nails, box nails, twisted nails, and double-headed nails, as well as others less useful in the theater.

Nails

Nails offer considerable resistance to force applied perpendicular to the length of the nail; they offer little resistance to force applied lengthwise. Where possible, units that must resist strain should be designed so that the force is transmitted by compression from one piece of lumber to another, and nails are used simply to prevent the pieces from shifting. The seat of a stool, for example, should be designed so that it rests on the legs, rather than being nailed between them. Since nails will not effectively resist a long-continued steady force applied lengthwise, they should not be used to fasten any structure that is to be hung overhead, if the structure is heavy enough to injure someone if it fell (in practice, that means nails are never used for anything that is to be hung over the actors' heads). Of course, that rule does not apply to flats or other units that are hung so that no strain is placed on nailed joints, for instance, if they are supported by hanger irons caught under the bottom edge.

Clinching

The holding power of nails can be increased enormously by using nails that will extend entirely through the joint, with an exposed point of at least ¼''. The point is then driven sidewise and forced firmly into the surface of the wood. Nails bent in that way are said to be *clinched*. Clout nails are soft nails especially designed for theatrical use; they are the preferred nails for fastening corner blocks in constructing flats. They must be clinched; unclinched clout nails have almost no holding power. Threaded or twisted nails have much greater holding power than common nails of the same size, and nails coated with rosin also have additional strength. When common nails tend to split the lumber, as in constructing furniture, much thinner rosin-coated box nails may be substituted, with little loss in strength.

Head Designs

Roofing nails are actually very large and sturdy tacks. They are used in the theater to fasten cardboard and other weak materials to lumber, since the large surface of the head offers more protection against the cardboard's tearing loose.

Double-headed nails sound at first hearing like legendary objects of the left-handed monkey-wrench variety, but they actually exist, and they are of extreme, although only occasional, value in the theater. The two heads are placed at the same end of the nail, separated by about ¼''; it looks as if the head and a short section of an ordinary nail have been cut off and welded to the center of the head of another nail. This type is used for firm but temporary joining of lumber. For example, if a wall is to be stiffened by a batten nailed to the back of the flats, doubleheaded nails are preferred. The nails are driven in so that the first head is tight against the surface of the batten; the nails then hold as firmly as ordinary nails driven in all the way. When the set is taken apart, one can slip the claws of a hammer between the two heads and grip the second head to pull out the nail, without having to dig into the wood or pry the boards apart to start the nail.

Screws   Screws, which are also obtainable in a wide variety of shapes and sizes, have significantly greater holding power than nails. They take more time to insert but have the advantage of being readily removable, so they are to be preferred for attaching toggles to stiles. Screws cannot be reset in the same holes without considerable loss of holding power.

Bolts   Bolts, in various sizes and styles, are by far the strongest fastening device available. They should always be used when joining units that are to be flown in such a way as to put any strain on the joints. They should also be used for assembling high platforms or any other structure in which safety is a major factor.

Bolts hold by pinching the joined lumber between the head of the bolt and the nut. Wrenches supply so much force that it is possible to turn the nut so that it digs into the wood. With soft wood, especially for large platforms where safety is an important consideration, there may be some danger that the strain on the bolt will pull the head and nut into the wood, loosening the joint. This can be prevented by slipping a metal washer between the head and the lumber and between the nut and the lumber; the washer provides a greater surface of contact, increasing the resistance to unwanted enlargement of the bolt hole.

Holes must be drilled through the lumber to be bolted together, matching the diameter of the shaft of the bolts. They may be removed and reset in the same holes without loss of holding power, so they are especially useful for large platforms or other structures that must be disassembled for storage.

Other metallic units have been developed for joining scenery. The most useful of them is the loose-pin hinge, which matches the butt joint in versatility and frequency of use in the theater. The loose-pin hinge differs from the tight-pin hinge in that the flaps of the hinge are joined by a heavy wire, with a hook at one end to prevent its falling through. (See *Figure 3-50.*) Two units or pieces of lumber joined by loose-pin hinges may be left permanently fastened together, or they may be separated by slipping

Hinges

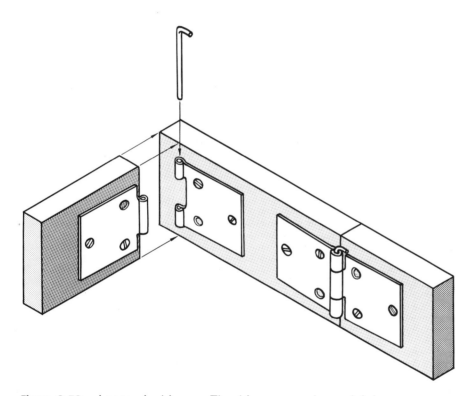

Figure 3-50.   Loose-pin hinges. The hinges are shown joining three sections of lumber, two at right angles and two in the same plane. The pin has been pulled from the left hinge, and the flaps separated. It is customary to use only two screws in each flap of a hinge, to avoid splitting lumber. Loose-pin hinges do not lie flat against the surface of the wood, so their edges appear here at a slight angle to the edges of the lumber.

out the pins and lifting them apart. For reassembling, the units are fitted together so that the two halves of the hinge meet, and the pins are slipped into place. Fitting requires a little care, but it can be done fast enough to be practical for scene shifts. Loose-pin hinges are used in such a variety of ways that only suggestive examples can be given: to fasten stiffening battens to the back of a wall; to fasten flats together at the corners of walls; to hang cornices at the top of flats; to fasten light platforms together; to join the leaves of screens; to hang mantels on fireplaces; to attach doors to their frames; to join flats into a single plane.

Few scene shops have a sufficient supply of loose-pin hinges; therefore, when units need not be separated during the run of a show (as in the case of flats hinged on the face, with the joint and hinges covered by dutchmen), it is generally preferable to specify tight-pin hinges, so that the loose-pins may be saved for units that must be separated and rejoined.

Strap-Metal Fasteners and Picture Hooks

Strap metal, cut in various shapes and drilled to provide holes for screws, may be used to join lumber; in effect, it functions as a substitute for ¼" plywood, having the advantages of being thinner and of supplying so much greater strength that much smaller dimensions are acceptable. The three most useful shapes are simple straps, L-shaped braces (which may be flat or bent), and T-shaped braces. (See *Figure 3-51*.) The L-shaped braces are especially useful for reinforcing the joints of furniture, where corner blocks or other wooden reinforcement would be unsightly.

S-hooks are devices for attaching 1" lumber (See *Figure 3-52*.) They have the advantage of being self-contained units that do not have to be fastened in place with screws.

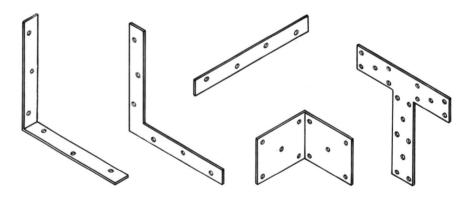

Figure 3-51. Strap-metal fasteners. These fasteners are available in several sizes, with screw holes drilled in varying patterns. The commonest patterns are shown.

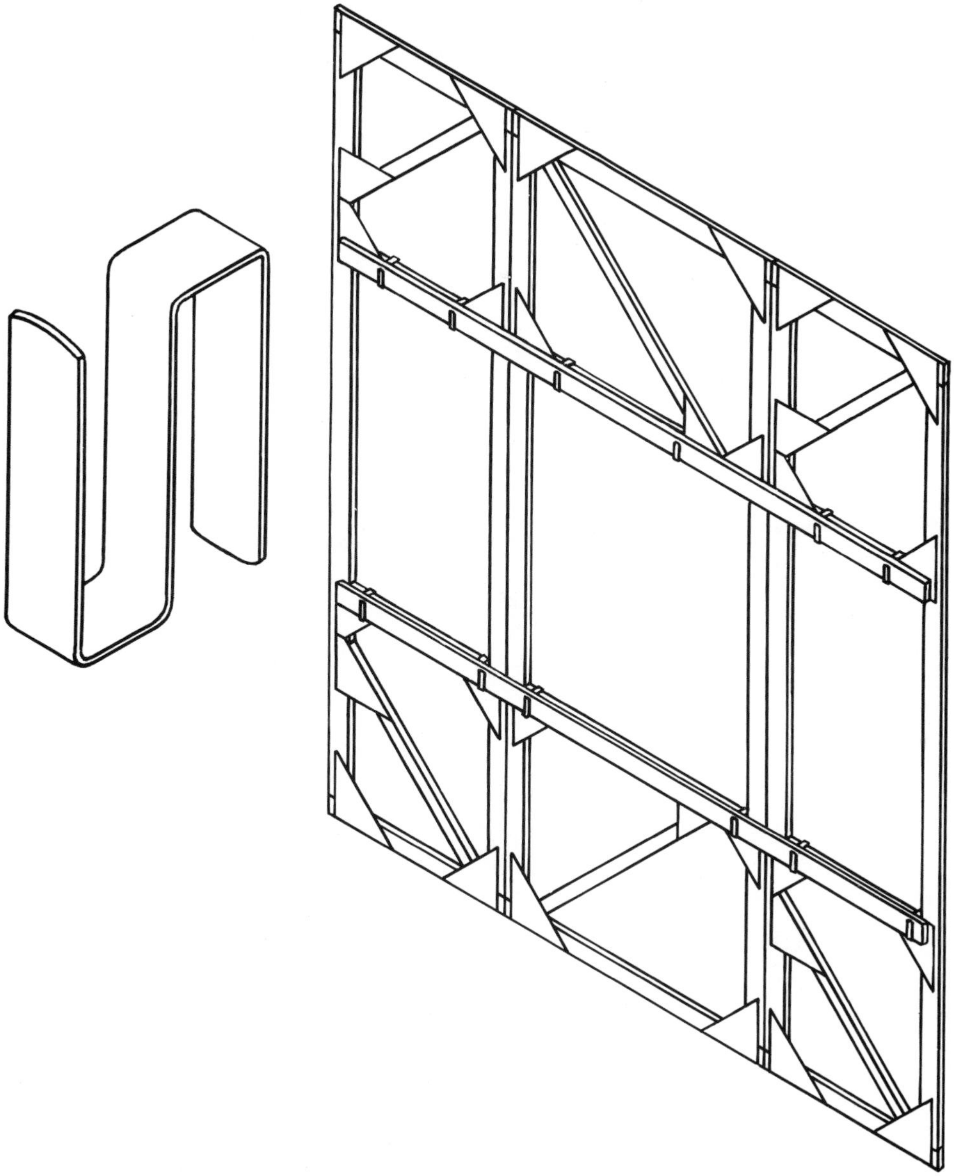

Figure 3-52. S-hooks. A single S-hook is shown at the left. At the right, three flats are shown stiffened by two battens at toggle level, held in place by S-hooks. Two S-hooks are used on each toggle of each flat, spaced as close to the stiles as the corner blocks will allow. One end of each fastener is hooked over the toggle, and the batten is set down inside the other end.

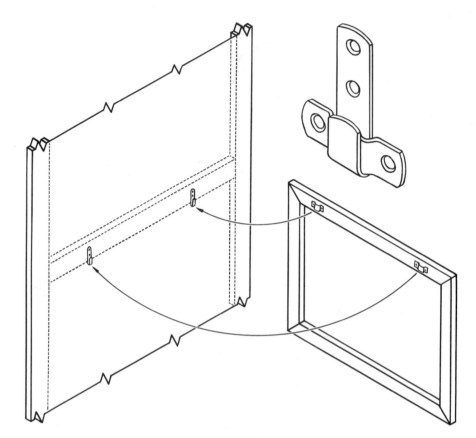

Figure 3-53. Picture hooks and eyes. *Lower right,* a picture frame shown from the rear, with picture eyes attached to it. *Left,* the center section of a flat, from the front; the hidden framing is indicated by dashed lines. The hooks are screwed to the toggle, through the canvas, and the picture is hung by catching the hooks in the eyes.

Picture hooks and eyes are devices that can be used for hanging units of moderate weight on walls, platforms, etc. Pictures, pilasters, cornices, and stair facings may be fastened by picture hooks. They may be used for many of the same purposes as loose-pin hinges and are faster to disassemble and set in place. (See *Figure 3-53*.)

Rigidity in
Design

When two pieces of rigid material, such as lumber, are placed with surfaces in contact, as in the lap joint, and then fastened at two points, they form a solid rigid structure. Three pieces fastened together in an open triangle (one end of each is fastened at a single point to one end of another) also form a rigid structure. No other arrangement of lumber is rigid: if four pieces are joined in the same way, the result is a square, rectangle, or trapezoid, and its shape can readily be changed by applying force against the sides in various directions. Pentagons, hexagons, and assemblies with still greater numbers of pieces are still more flexible.

In practical design, those facts can be reduced to the simple principle that the only rigid figure that can be constructed by joining separate pieces of lumber is the triangle. Consequently, whenever a unit (such as a flat, a platform, or a piece of furniture) must be built from a series of pieces of lumber, the design must provide for enough triangles to maintain its shape.

Not only is the triangle rigid, but it imparts its rigidity to other parts of structures in which it appears. A square made up of four strips of lumber joined at the corners can be shifted into various positions, but if a fifth strip is fastened diagonally across it, two triangles are produced, the entire figure immediately becomes rigid, and its shape cannot be changed without breaking the lumber or separating the joints. It is not even necessary to span the distance from corner to corner; a small diagonal brace fitted into one corner of a square will produce a triangle, the rigidity of which is then extended to the entire figure.

The principles just presented, although theoretically sound, require some practical qualification. They assume that the fastenings are tight and firm; in actual practice, all joints have some play in them. If a 12'-0'' stile is attached to a 5'-0'' rail by a single corner block, the plywood triangle provides the necessary triangular form; but if two people take hold of the free ends of the boards and force them together, the enormous leverage will break the joint loose. Even if only light force is applied, the minute play allowed because the nails are not gripped with absolute tightness by the lumber will be magnified at the ends of the boards, so that it may be possible to swing the free end of the longer board as much as an inch or two from its true position, even without breaking the joint.

This, then, suggests an additional practical principle: although theoretically any size of triangle provides rigidity, in practice the larger the triangle the more resistance it presents to deformation.

Furthermore, the triangle formed by a diagonal brace set into the corner of a flat resists strain much more strongly in one diirection than in another. If a flat were constructed with a single diagonal brace in one corner, and then pressure were exerted on the corner of the flat diagonally opposite, pushing toward the brace, only a little force would be required to break open the joint, pulling the nails through the wood. Force exerted against one of the other corners, however, would tend to press the braced stile and rail together, toward the brace; no significant force would be applied to the nails themselves. Instead, it would be transmitted to the diagonal brace, and the joints would fail only if the force were so great as to tear the corner block apart or crush the lumber used for the diagonal brace. It is for this reason, then, that diagonal braces are fastened to the same side of the flat, rather than in opposite corners. Inspection of sketches showing the two arrangements, or the construction and experimental forcing of actual frames, will demonstrate that placing the diagonal braces in opposite corners produces great resistance to force applied in one direction, but very little resistance to force applied in the other direction, whereas the standard design provides adequate resistance to force applied in any direction.

At the beginning of their work in the theater, the designers may occasionally run across rigid structures in which there seem to be no triangular elements. Inspection will demonstrate that triangles are present, although they may be hidden by surfacing, or by being filled in and extended, even perhaps with curved outlines. The critical factor, of course, is the pattern formed by the points of fastening, not the outline of the materials used.

Hiding Braces

Unfortunately, diagonal bracing is often inharmonious with the esthetic patterns of a design. If artists want an effect of squareness, verticality, and horizontality, they may have difficulty supplying triangles of sufficient size and number to provide adequate rigidity. This is especially true in furniture, where diagonal bracing of legs may spoil the visual design desired. Solutions for this problem depend on a designer's ingenuity. A few suggestions may be of assistance.

It may be possible to add surfacing (of cardboard, plywood, or even canvas) that will hide the intrusive structural supports. Increasing the dimensions of some of the elements, such as the legs of a chair, may make it possible to spread the fastening nails, screws, or bolts so as to achieve sufficient triangular support, although the lumber itself retains its rectangular shape. Attention may be distracted from bracing by adding painted or three-dimensional decoration to the esthetically significant lines of the design; ordinarily the braces can be painted black, making them nearly unnoticeable. This method was used in concealing the functioning legs of the chairs for *Antony and Cleopatra,* since the apparent legs were too weak to support the chair seats. Although in this case the hidden members were vertical rather than diagonal, the same method will help hide slanted supports (see *Figure 7-5*).

For platforms, it may be possible to extend the structure off stage, with the ends hidden by other scenic elements; triangles added to the design in the offstage sections will then transfer their own rigidity to the parts of the platform visible to the audience. An extreme example of this appears in the *Antony and Cleopatra* set, where a very large platform extended entirely across the back of the stage. The flooring was 9'-4'' above the stage, and the design required that no supports be visible for a space 11'-4'' wide in the center of the platform. In addition, the platform had to bear the weight of five actors without detectable sagging. The design solution was to extend the platform well out beyond the area visible to the audience and to include large triangles of 2 × 4 lumber in the offstage area, with hypotenuses and sides 10'-0'' to 15'-0'' in length. Incidentally, access stairs were supplied by adding steps to the hypotenuses of the triangular supports at one side of the stage.

Metal

More and more designers are experimenting with metal, especially steel, as a replacement for wood in scenic structures. The main advantage of steel derives from its greater strength, which makes it possible, for example, to build stairs and platforms with much smaller legs and framing. In addition, metal bars can be welded firmly together, making it possible to omit some diagonal bracing without significant loss of rigidity. As a result, platform, ramp, and stair supports can be made much less visible than if lumber were used. A delicate or lacy effect can sometimes be produced more easily with metal than with wood. For example, the frame of the roof shown in *Figure 4-9* was made of welded steel (the outlines of the shingles and the upstairs window were cut from quarter-inch plywood). The steel frame provided rigidity for the structure that could have been achieved with wood only at the expense of accepting a clumsy and heavy effect.

Some sheet metal is used in scenic construction, but more often metal is in the form of round or square tubing. Various ingenious clamps have been designed to hold the pieces together, making it easier to salvage material for reuse.

The major disadvantage of metal is its great expense as compared with lumber; not only does the material itself cost several times as much as the lumber needed for the same structure, but welding equipment must be provided in the scene shop. As lumber prices continue to rise, metal may become more competitive; at present, its use must be considered experimental, or suitable only for those special situations when extra strength, small size, or delicacy of effect make it preferable.

STAGE PROPERTIES

When designing stage props, designers are likely to have the most difficulty planning the construction of furniture. Only occasionally will they be able to use furniture that was actually designed and built for use in the home; they will therefore constantly need to prepare instructions for the construction of furniture of all types. The adaptation of various styles of decoration is discussed in Chapter 8; the expansion and emphasis necessary for producing what is called projection are discussed in Chapter 6; here we are concerned with methods of construction.

The artist will find it easiest to think of each piece of furniture as separated into the basic structure and the decoration. The primary purpose of the structural design is to supply whatever strength and rigidity the action of the play requires; the applied decoration determines the style and emotional impression of the piece of furniture.

The Pattern of Furniture

The easiest construction pattern for most furniture, including chairs, davenports, and tables, is an open boxlike framework, with all parts joined at right angles. Since diagonal bracing is inharmonious with many styles of design, such devices as strap fasteners and bracing with invisible wire may be used.

A piece of furniture, then, is first planned as a simple boxlike shape. Often, it is possible to incorporate sizable bracing units in furniture, provided they will be concealed during the performance of the play. For example, if a kitchen table is to be covered with a cloth, ordinary corner blocks can be used to fasten joints that will be hidden by the cloth. Similarly, decorative plywood surfacing may be used to hide bracing and joints.

The characteristics of plywood make it extremely useful in adding decorative shaping to the basic structure. It can be readily cut in the most complex curves, and it can be bent when desired. Furthermore, because of its great strength, a decorative surfacing of plywood can be used as a fastener, so that it becomes in effect a shaped corner block. Where it is not necessary to bend the surfacing, ½'' plywood may be used in place of ¼'', with a resulting increase in strength; it is especially useful for chair and davenport seats.

Variations in form can be further emphasized by applied decorations, with papier-mâché and rope fastened on to simulate wood carving, and the entire unit painted to emphasize the decoration, perhaps with gilding on the raised surfaces. Often, structural supports that are still visible can be made unnoticeable by painting them black.

Strength Requirements

Furniture especially designed for one production can often be used again in later productions, if it is redecorated; consequently, it is desirable to build it strong enough to withstand any ordinary handling. Occasionally, providing full strength will require more time than is available, or it will increase the weight of the furniture so as to make it unsuited for a particular production. In that case, the designer may want to ask the director to describe exactly how the furniture is to be used, so that the designer can plan within narrow limits of strength. For example, if actors are to sit or stand on a table, it must be built to support their weight; but if it is used only to hold a small vase of flowers, it can be much weaker, with resulting saving in materials, construction work, and shifting time. Thus, ordinary corrugated cardboard might be substituted for beaver board or plywood for the top of the table. Even in this case, however, it is wise to follow the standard procedure of designing each scenic structure with a 50% margin of safety, so that a table top that must bear a weight of 10 pounds should be constructed so as to support 15.

Some examples of furniture designs are shown in *Figures 2-6, 2-7, 2-16, 3-39, 3-40, 3-41, 6-17, 6-20, 6-21, 7-2,* and *7-5;* they illustrate the methods described above.

4

Scenic Resources: Lighting and Shifting

The early chapters of the text emphasized the integrity of theater production in which the various subordinate arts of the theater are joined harmoniously to produce a unified effect. The relationships among these contributing arts vary: some are much more closely related than others. Planning the arrangement and movements of the actors is a major responsibility of the director, but it is only slightly less a concern of the designer. Even the costumes and hand properties constitute a significant part of the stage picture and are relevant to the designer's work, although they are usually handled by different members of the production staff. In this chapter we will discuss lighting and shifting, two other aspects that are relevant to the designer.

LIGHTING

Of all the aspects of production that can be distinguished from set design, the most closely related is lighting. In European theaters, the lighting design for a set is usually planned by someone other than the set designer;

in America, it is more common for both designs to be prepared by the same person, and even when lighting is assigned to a specialist, he or she is likely to work in close cooperation with the set designer, and most often under the set designer's direction.

The esthetic principles applicable to lighting design are in great degree identical with those of sound scenic design; the materials and specific techniques differ considerably. Designers should extend their knowledge of lighting as fully as possible, preferably by enrolling in a course devoted entirely to lighting and by working on the lighting crew for a series of productions. In a book focused on set design, it is not possible to include more than a brief indication of the methods of lighting, with special emphasis on its esthetic potentialities.

Light in the theater may be divided into three categories:

1. Reflected light, the most frequently used of these categories, in which the functional elements are the flats, furniture, or actors on which the light falls

2. Direct light, in which the light travels in a straight line from the source to the viewer's eyes, either simply through the air, as in the case of a candle, or through a translucent medium such as a lampshade

3. Projection, in which the functional element is a shadow falling on a drop or flat

Reflected Light   Reflected light may be divided into two types, general and specific.

General

General lighting, which is produced by foot lights, border lights (footlights hung overhead above the stage), and floodlights, is characterized by lesser focus and definition. Its color and brightness may be controlled, but the area of the stage on which it falls is subject to only minimal control. Before the invention of the electric light, when the major problem in the theater was simply to provide visibility, candles or other sources of light were placed at every possible point, with little attempt at controlling distribution. In the modern theater, general lighting is used primarily to light walls, drops, or cycloramas intended to represent the sky. It is sometimes also used, at a low level, to fill in and slightly lighten areas between the pools of light cast by spotlights.

Specific

Major illumination comes from spotlights, which are generally directed in an overlapping pattern so as to almost or entirely cover the total acting area. It is common to divide the stage floor into six areas: the center, left,

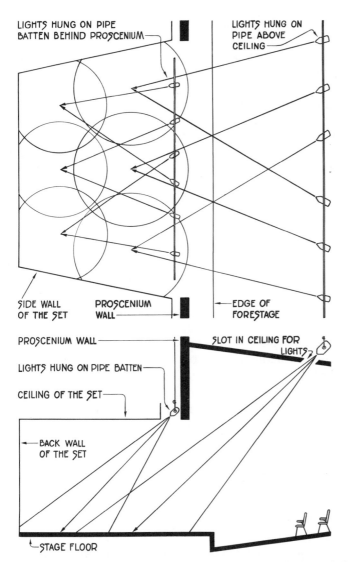

Figure 4-1. The basic spotlight pattern. The ground plan of the stage is shown at the top, and a cross-section of the stage and the front part of the auditorium is shown below it. Both are drawn to the same scale so that the diagrams can be easily compared. The back half of the stage is lit by spotlights hung on a pipe batten immediately behind the proscenium arch; the front half by spotlights aimed through a slot in the ceiling of the auditorium. The set shown is the simplest type of box set. The pattern shown is a basic one, and the lighting of other types of box sets, however complicated, can best be analyzed in terms of their relationship with this arrangement.

and right at the front of the stage and the matching areas at the back of the stage. Two spotlights, at angles of 45°, are pointed at each area. (See *Figure 4-1.*) Ordinarily, each of such a pair of spotlights is given a separate color, one "cool" and the other "warm" (see Chapter 7 for a discussion of these terms). The spotlights are not spaced on the stage floor, but are placed to fully light the actors' heads. Since the pools of light are very wide when they reach the stage, there is considerable spill, which makes the rest of the actors' bodies visible, as well as the furniture and the set itself. Such an arrangement usually produces parabolic pools of light along the walls. In an extremely realistic setting and play, such pools of light may seem inharmonious and objectionable. In that case, the edges may be softened by throwing the lights partly out of focus, or by placing special masks in front of them. In addition, footlights and other general illumination may be used, partially dimmed, to increase the overall lighting so as to further conceal the placement of the spots.

The contemporary trend, however, is toward a franker theatricality, which accepts spotlights, even when obviously visible, as part of the medium. Differential lighting is a powerful factor in controlling the attention of the audience; lighting a set so that the intensity is greatest at the level where the actors perform, diminishing gradually toward the top of the flats, is of great assistance in focusing the attention on the actors, where it should be focused. In addition, the spotlights may well produce an interesting pattern, which contributes to the esthetic effect of the set.

All theaters have some method of lighting the stage when technical work is being done. Such lights, called *work lights,* generally throw a uniform flood over the entire stage area. The value of differential lighting can be persuasively demonstrated by lighting a set as it would be lit for a performance and then switching to work lights; the best-designed set looks astonishingly crude and inexpressive under work lights.

Direct Light   The second type of lights mentioned, in which the audience is allowed to see the light source directly, is generally to be avoided in the theater. Even a single candle flame can become blindingly distracting when an audience must watch it for a long time. Even as accents, unshaded direct lights tend to be too sharp, competing with the actors for the audience's attention. Like most rules, this may be ignored occasionally with excellent effect, but designers should plan to use direct lights only after careful thought. If a designer wants to include a chandelier with unshaded lights, bulbs of very small wattage may be used, perhaps dimmed, to provide the desired glitter without painful distraction. If a shade for a candle or floor lamp is acceptable, the amount of light can be controlled by inserting additional layers of paper or other translucent material until the light is no longer distracting.

The remaining type of lighting, projection, is a valuable part of the set designer's resources, although it involves many difficulties and restrictions. All projection consists of a light source that is directed at a reflecting surface, with a means of interrupting part of the light so as to cast a shadow. The shadow may be produced by interrupting all of the light in one area of the beam or by subtracting only light of a certain color, producing a partial shadow in the complementary color. The interrupter may be an opaque sheet, cut to a specified shape; a large pane of glass on which opaque or transparent designs have been painted; or a slide, produced photographically.

The disadvantages of scenic projection are many. Projection can be used only on a nearly dark stage; lighting for acting areas must be concentrated as far as possible from the reflecting surface, for if unwanted light spills or reflects from the floor or furniture, the projected image will be washed out or destroyed. Actors must play in front of projected scenery; consequently, they cannot use it as they may use three-dimensional scenery or scenery that is made up of flats. Projectors are difficult to hide on stage, and available machines may not be powerful enough to project effectively from the back of the auditorium. Some of these problems are likely to be solved in the near future. Projectors are now available that are far more powerful than those of the past. Although the cost of the new equipment makes it prohibitive at present, prices are likely to go down as manufacture is expanded.

Those restrictions usually make projection impractical. However, there are certain advantages. Elaborate designs may be painted, and reproduced photographically for projection, at a small fraction of the cost in time and material that would be required to duplicate them by ordinary construction. Projected scenery may be changed instantly, especially if two projectors are used for each reflecting surface. The scenery may be faded from one slide to another, with a dreamlike effect.

Like other aspects of set design, innovations in the use of projection were first made in Europe, where extensive experimentation took place. An early and especially notable example of projection in the United States was used in the production of Strindberg's *Dream Play* at the University of Minnesota. The scenery was designed by Dr. Frank M. Whiting. Five of the settings are reproduced in Dr. Whiting's book *An Introduction to the Theatre,* and they will repay study, although they suggest only a small part of the effectiveness of the actual production. (See also *Figure 4-2.*)

The Effects Machine

Two special types of projection should be mentioned. One is the effects machine, which can be used to project clouds, falling rain, and similar

Figure 4-2.   Projected scenery: Strindberg's *The Dream Play.* In this production, designed by Dr. Frank Whiting, all scenery was projected. Three screens were provided: a sky drop at the back of the stage and an irregular wing on each side at the front of the stage. Two projectors were aimed at each screen, so that scenery could be changed by crossfading from one set of projectors to the other, with a dreamlike effect. [By permission of Dr. Frank Whiting.]

moving patterns on a sky, particularly if the surface representing the sky is at the back of a deep stage. The machines, and slides providing various effects, can be purchased or rented from theatrical supply houses.

The interest of a few years ago in psychedelia resulted in the increased use of effects machines, often to project nonrepresentational patterns or spots of color, moving across a backdrop on stage or across the entire acting area. Especially in less realistic plays, and when combined with music, painted patterns, sound effects, and other sensory stimuli, the resulting experience can be exciting and interesting. A somewhat similar effect can be produced by placing opaque patterns, constructed or natural, in front of the light sources, so that the stage, for example, is covered with the moving shadows of leaves, as in Jo Mielziner's set for *The Death of a Salesman.*

Linnebach Projectors

The other special device for projection is the *Linnebach projector.* It is essentially only a shadow box. One side of the lightproof box is made of a large sheet of glass or transparent plastic (which may be curved, if desired) on which a design is fastened or painted; designs can be cut from opaque or colored material, or painted with opaque or transparent pigments. Inside the box, as far as possible from the transparent sheet, is a light bulb. The transparent slide is turned toward the reflecting surface, and the light switched on. Since there is no lens, the projected image will be fuzzy and indistinct. Sharpness can be improved slightly by selecting a light bulb that throws the maximum light with the smallest filament.

Sharpness depends on the size of the slide, its distance from the light bulb, the size of the filament that is the actual source of light, and the distance between the slide and the surface on which the image is projected. These factors operate as follows: the sharpness of the image is increased by increasing the size of the slide and its distance from the light bulb and by reducing the size of the filament and the distance between the slide and the reflecting surface.

The Linnebach projector can be used only for effects that do not require a sharp image, and its use is consequently very limited. However, it may be effective for projecting stationary cloud shapes, swirling yellow lines suggesting a dust storm, shadowy tree shapes seen at twilight, and abstract patterns. While its use is limited, it can be made quickly and cheaply, and it will produce effects that cannot be achieved by ordinary methods of set construction and painting.

SHIFTING

If more than one set must be used for the performance of a play, space must be available for storing the additional set or sets while they are not being used, and there must be practical means for removing one set at the end of a scene and replacing it with the set for the next scene. This substitution of one set for another is called *shifting*.

Planning the shifts is normally the responsibility of the technical director or construction supervisor, not the designer; however, the sets must be designed so as to make efficient shifting possible. A full discussion of shifting is beyond the scope of this book; the student will find adequate discussions in Burris-Meyer and Cole and in many other stagecraft texts. The major methods will be mentioned only briefly here.

Time is of great importance in shifting. Usually a full intermission of ten or fifteen minutes is available for a shift, but occasionally successive scenes will be played without intermission, and the shift must be made in the minimum time possible, preferably less than sixty seconds. One of the fastest methods of shifting scenery, especially if it is made up of flats, is to fly it. This method requires special architectural construction for the stage area: a unit of steel beams (called a *grid*) must be supported horizontally above the stage floor at a height that permits raising the scenery up until it is hidden from the audience. To the beams are fastened pulleys, around which ropes are run. One end of each rope hangs down so that it can be attached to the scenery; the other end runs across under the grid and down a frame at the side of the stage. Weights are fastened to the offstage ends of the ropes to counterbalance the weight of the scenic units, and the scenery can then be raised out of the way high overhead by pulling on the ropes. With an adequate system, the major elements of three or more sets can be flown in this way, and set changes can be made quickly by raising one set at the end of a scene and lowering another set for the next scene.

Hardly ever are all of the elements of a set flown; in particular, furniture, platforms, and stairs are likely to be removed by hand after the flats have been raised. However, with an adequate shifting crew, one set can be removed and a second put in place very quickly if major elements are flown.

Flying

During the early part of this century, a number of theaters were built with a *revolving stage*; many of them are still in use, and the revolve is occasionally included in theaters being built today.

Like all theatrical techniques and resources, the revolving stage has both advantages and disadvantages. It was built in varying forms, more or less mechanized, and to a greater or lesser degree an integral part of the architecture of the theater. The revolving stage consists of a circular platform supported on casters and pivoted at the center so that it may be turned. In its simplest form, such a platform rests on the stage floor and is turned by hand; at its most elaborate, a matching hole is cut into the stage, the circular section is sunk into the hole so that its top is level with the surrounding areas, and it is turned by electrical machinery.

The early advocates of the revolving stage saw it as a major solution of the problem of shifting. Two sets could be fastened on the revolve, back to back, so that one faced the audience. At the conclusion of the first scene, the platform was turned so that the second set faced the audience, and while it was in use, stagehands replaced the first set with the scenery for the third scene. Using this method, each set occupied half of the circular platform. By designing sets so that each required less space, it was

The Revolving Stage

possible to squeeze three on the revolve at the same time and change scenery simply by turning the platform.

Experience in working with the revolving stage, however, quickly demonstrated that it has serious limitations. If the platform is used for two sets, only half of it is available for each, so that the depth of the stage is automatically reduced by 50%. In a new theater, the reduction can be compensated for by doubling the depth of the stage, but the addition to the cost of the building is very great. If the revolving stage is used to hold three sets, the space available for each is still further reduced, and each tends to be forced into the shape of a piece of pie, a fact that can be disguised by the designer only at the expense of great time and ingenuity. Furthermore, if all three sets are intended to remain on the revolve throughout the performance, actors generally have to enter and exit through the two sets not being used at the moment; consequently, the doors, arches, and other openings for one set must match those of the sets behind it, which imposes severe restrictions on the design.

Since the ordinary stage is essentially rectangular, the largest revolve that can be fitted between the curtain and the back wall leaves open areas at the sides and large open areas at the corners. Scenery that is to be revolved must therefore be placed only in the center of the stage, so masking problems become extreme. The ordinary box set, in particular, is almost entirely unrelated to the placement of scenery that is enforced by the shape of the revolve.

Several revolve patterns were developed in an attempt to solve these problems. (See *Figure 4-3.*) Multiple revolves were designed, in various arrangements, so that scenery could be placed in the areas beyond the edge of a single circle. One pattern consisted of two revolves, side by side, with their edges touching in the center of the stage. Another pattern added two small circles at the front corners of the stage. Although such arrangements matched the typical floor plan of scenery more closely than a single revolve, significant areas of the stage still remained outside the circles. Furthermore, if a set was designed so that different parts of it were placed on three revolving platforms, it was necessary to keep the three sections of the scenery separate. Disguising the resulting joints placed a further burden on the ingenuity of the designer, whose use of familiar technical resources was restricted. No colonnade, wall, stairs, or other continuous structure could be extended beyond the edge of any of the three platforms, and use of dutchmen, pilasters, and other devices for concealing joints was impossible.

In spite of its limitations, however, the revolving stage is genuinely useful, and designers can consider themselves fortunate if their theater includes one, even though they are likely to use it for only a few productions each season. Masking problems can be solved by designing sets with side flats that can be swung into position beyond the revolve after the revolve has been turned. (See *Figures 4-4* and *4-5.*)

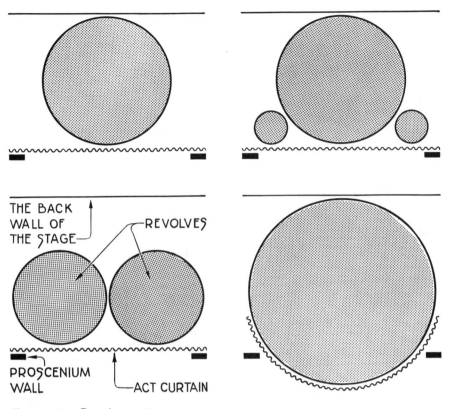

THE BACK WALL OF THE STAGE

REVOLVES

PROSCENIUM WALL

ACT CURTAIN

Figure 4-3. Revolve patterns.

The revolve is least useful as a simple shifting device and most valuable as a special esthetic resource—an integral part of the performance, carried on in the sight of the audience. It would be difficult to find a play in which the revolve could be used realistically, but few plays demand a fully realistic treatment.

While in graduate school, Dr. Osborne Allen Brines, III, designed a set for *The Madwoman of Chaillot*. The stage had a doughnut-shaped revolve in which a ring turned around a stationary central circle. For the first act, which takes place at an outdoor cafe in Paris, Dr. Brines set the dining tables and chairs in the center section, placing park benches, street signs, and other elements on the revolving ring. (See *Figures 4-6* and *4-7*.) It was thus possible to alter emphasis by swinging the revolve around, moving a particular bench into center downstage position and then, when desired, moving it past the focus of attention. The movement, made during the action of the play, was well suited to this fantasy.

At first reading, it might seem that Ketti Frings's *Look Homeward, Angel* is not suited to a revolving stage, because the initial impression is

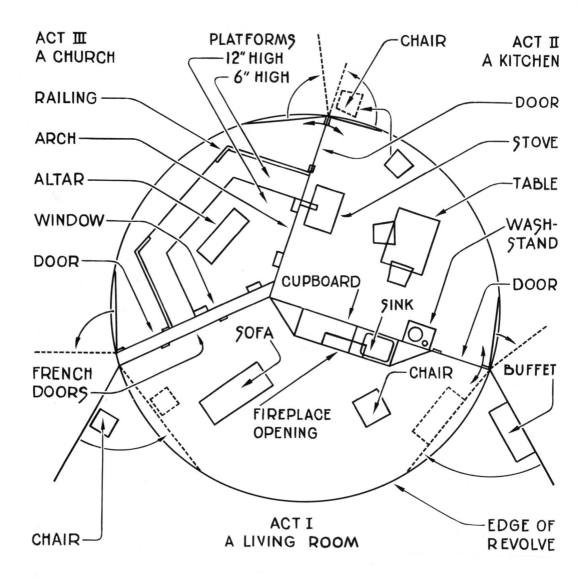

ACT III
A CHURCH

ACT II
A KITCHEN

PLATFORMS
12" HIGH
6" HIGH

CHAIR

RAILING

DOOR

ARCH

STOVE

ALTAR

TABLE

WINDOW

WASH-
STAND

DOOR

DOOR

CUPBOARD

SINK

FRENCH
DOORS

SOFA

CHAIR

BUFFET

FIREPLACE
OPENING

CHAIR

ACT I
A LIVING ROOM

EDGE OF
REVOLVE

Figure 4-4. The use of the revolving stage. Three sets are shown on the simplest form of revolve. The set for the first act is in playing position. At the end of the act, the furniture and flats extending beyond the edge of the revolve will be swung in to positions indicated by dashed lines on the revolve, the revolve will be turned to bring the Act II set into playing position, and the end flats for Act II will be swung out to the positions shown by dashed lines. (Perspectives of these three sets are shown in *Figure 4-5.*)

Figure 4-5. The use of the revolving stage. Because the sets are of different widths, the act curtains are opened at varying distances, to provide masking for the wings.

Figure 4-6. Set for Act I of *The Madwoman of Chaillot.*
(Designed by Dr. Osborne Allen Brines, III.)

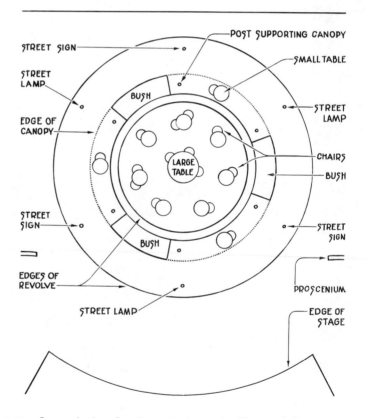

Figure 4-7. Ground plan for the set shown in *Figure 4-6*.

one of realism. However, there are many nonrealistic elements in the play.

Based on Thomas Wolfe's mammoth novel of the same name, the play consists of a series of episodes separated in time and taking place in several different locales. Characters do not grow significantly during any single episode, so that the episodes are like a series of slides flashed on a screen, with abrupt breaks between them, rather than a smoothly flowing motion picture. In some of the scenes, the locale changes during the action, flowing, for instance, from a bedroom, to the front hall of the house, out to the porch, and into the yard.

The design for one production making use of a revolve provided a house realistic in detail but with sections removed to make the interior visible. (See *Figures 4-8, 4-9, 4-10, and 4-11.*) The area outside the revolve was painted green and treated as the yard. The major set was turned not only within sight of the audience, but while it was actually in use. One scene, for example, began in a bedroom, with the set turned so that the room was pointed directly toward the audience. After a discussion between Eugene and Laura, Eugene went into the hall to telephone, and as he moved from one area to the other, the set swung smoothly around to turn the front of the house toward the audience, who could follow the action through the glass door and the large windows that filled the front wall. Eugene's mother could be seen dimly, entering the dark hall at the back, and a dialog followed, at the end of which Eugene emerged from the house and walked down the steps, across the yard, and off stage. Although the movement of the set was entirely visible, it was so thoroughly integrated with the action of the play that it seemed inevitably right. Furthermore, the set matched the style of the play in that each locale was treated realistically, but they were somewhat arbitrarily juxtaposed.

A set for the light musical comedy *Once Upon a Mattress* was designed for the same stage used by Dr. Brines. Multiple locales are specified by the script, and the set for this totally unrealistic play was handled quite arbitrarily. Low platforms were put in the area in the center of the stage, and thrones for the king and queen were set on two of them. On the revolve was placed a double flight of curved stairs, seven feet wide, used in part for the action specified in the script but more significantly as an abstract structure to display the dancers, who are an important part of the cast. (See *Figures 4-12* and *4-13.*) Revolving the set 180° revealed the outside of the castle (*Figure 4-14*), with an arched entrance and crenellated walls. Two towers were placed at the front corners of the stage, partly for masking, but also to accommodate some of the action of the play. At one point an actress swings into view suspended in a giant birdcage; this was fastened out of sight behind the stage right tower, and a concealed ladder was provided so that the actress could climb up to the cage just before she was to appear, rather than having to sit in midair

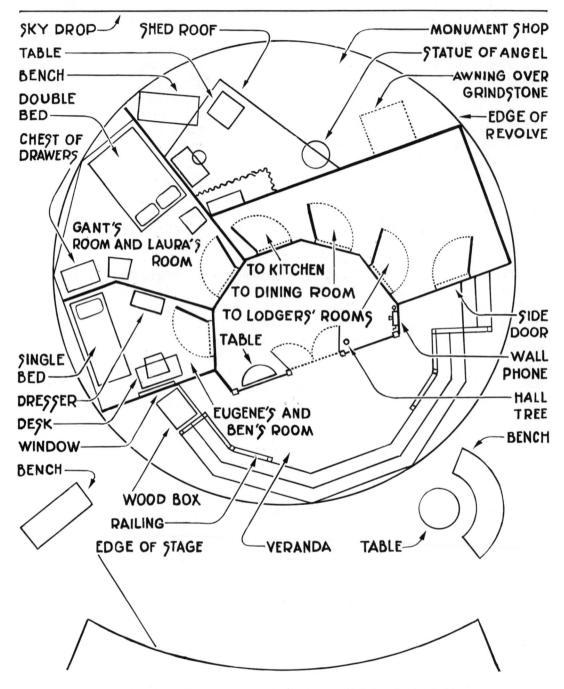

Figure 4-8. Ground plan of set for Ketti Frings's *Look Homeward, Angel.*

Figure 4-9. The Gant boarding house, *Look Homeward, Angel*.

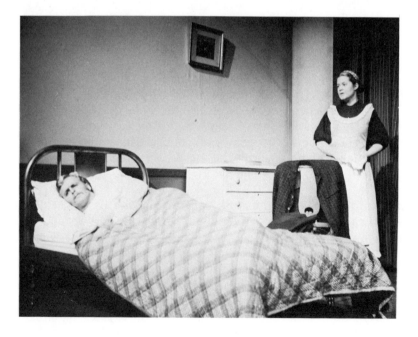

Figure 4-10. Ben's room, *Look Homeward, Angel*.

Figure 4-11. The monument shop, *Look Homeward, Angel.*

through half the show. The matching tower at the left had a curtained entrance that, when opened, revealed the laboratory of the magician, with blazing fire and steaming cauldron. Again, the revolve was turned in sight of the audience and while being used by actors and dancers, a treatment that was completely in harmony with the make-believe spirit of the play.

Wagon Shifting   A third method of shifting is to use large platforms with casters, called *wagons,* which can be quickly rolled on and off stage. Such a wagon may be large enough to hold an entire set, or it may be designed to carry only the major units. Obviously, if two or three sets are to be mounted on full wagon stages, a great deal of backstage space must be available.

    One pattern of wagon shifting involves three wagons, each as large as the entire acting area. One is placed just off stage on the left, the other on the right, and the third at the back of the stage. For the first scene, one of the three wagons is pushed into position; at the end of the scene it is rolled back into its storage position, and a second wagon is moved into

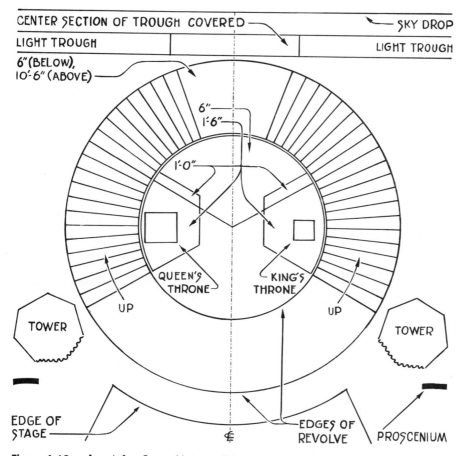

Figure 4-12.   A set for *Once Upon a Mattress,* using a revolving ring (shown in the interior position).

place. To facilitate setting the wagons properly, tracks may be laid on the floor by nailing strips of 1 × 2 or 1 × 3 to guide the wheels.

Another wagon pattern controls the movement of the wagons by means of pivots. When one of the wagons is in position on stage, its down-left corner is fastened to the stage floor by means of a pivot. At the end of the scene, stagehands push it so that it swings around, with the pivot as the center of the path of movement, until its left edge is parallel with the proscenium wall, and what had been the front edge of the platform (when it was in performing position) is vertical to the back wall of the stage. A second wagon, pivoted similarly but at the down-right corner, is then swung into place. These movements require that the casters be set with their sides at right angles to the line joining them with the pivot, rather than being lined up with the edges of the platform. If space is available, a

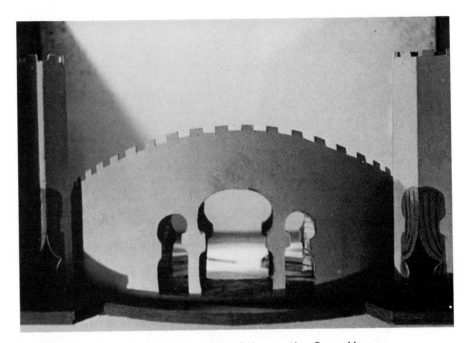

Figure 4-13.   A model of the outside of the castle, *Once Upon a Mattress.* Since it was made primarily for the director's use, this model was painted broadly, but not in detail. For instance, the walls, shown as a solid color in the model, were painted to simulate stone blocks in the finished set (see *Figure 2-6* for a similar effect).

third wagon can be placed at the back of the stage, as in the pattern described above, and pushed into place after both of the pivoted wagons have been swung to the offstage position. (See *Figure 4-15.*)

Wagon stages are entirely practical, and the offstage space they require is no more than should be provided in any well-designed theater; in actual fact, however, architects seldom do include adequate wing space for stages. Provision for flying is more common, although sometimes it is designed so as to be unusable. Members of the audience can see farther up at the back of the stage than at the front, so that while a flat at the front of the stage might be hidden by raising it just slightly above the top of the proscenium opening, a flat raised to the same height at the back of the stage would still be largely visible.

Shifting by Hand   Older theaters may have no usable space for flying or for shifting by wagon. In that case, it may be necessary to shift all scenery by hand,

Figure 4-14. A model of the throne room, *Once Upon a Mattress.*

storing it in the wings when it is not being used during the performance. The designer's preliminary study of the theater plant will include a record of the available offstage space. For a multiset show, fast and efficient shifting by hand requires the use of whatever inventiveness and ingenuity the designer may have. The scenery must be designed so that it can be separated into units, each of which can be shifted by the number of crew members available, in the time provided. Paths of movement must be practical; for example stagehands removing a large wall of the first set should keep out of the path of those moving on stage a large wall of the second. Where flats must be separated in shifting, the joints must be concealed by devices other than dutchmen. Shifting and storage of wall units can often be facilitated by using easily removable stiffeners, such as battens placed in S-hooks rather than nailed permanently to the flats; the units may then be folded and moved more quickly. Heavy scenic units such as platforms and stairs can be supplied with casters to make them easier to shift, and even walls can be raised and shifted by rolling tip jacks, described in standard stagecraft texts.

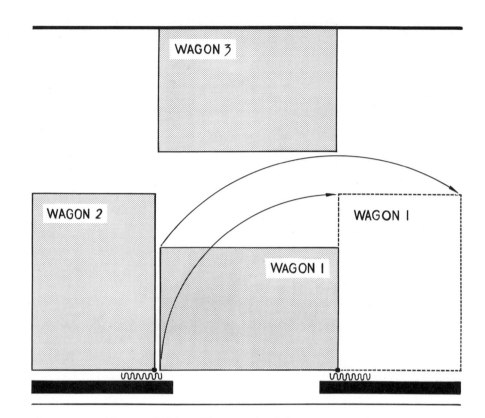

Figure 4-15. Wagon shifting. The standard three-wagon pattern is shown, with wagon 1 in position for performance. At the end of Act I, the wagon is swung to its offstage position (indicated by dashed lines), and wagon 2 is moved into playing position. The dots at the downstage corners of the wagons indicate their pivots. The line behind wagon 3 represents the back wall of the stage, the heavy black bars indicate the proscenium wall, and the curved lines between the proscenium wall and the wagons are conventional symbols representing the act curtain. The bottom line indicates the edge of the stage. The audience (not shown) extends below the picture.

Special Solutions   Careful study will suggest solutions for particular problems. Some of the sets illustrated in this book involved devices developed under the stress of varying degrees of desperation. Storage space for the five sets required for *Our American Cousin* was inadequate; that problem was solved by using both sides of the flats; for example, the set for the heroine's cottage was painted on the back of the flats used for the drawing room in the opening scene. It would have been possible to build the flats with halved joints, so that the back surface would not have been varied by corner blocks and could have been separately canvassed; however, an analysis of the available construction time indicated that the sets could not be built unless stock flats were used. The solution to the masking problem consisted of nailing rectangles of cardboard across the tops and bottoms of the flats to conceal the corner blocks and diagonal braces. The cardboard was then painted to simulate a thatched roof and a stone foundation. A few of the toggles were moved so as to place all of them at the same height. Finally, the canvas was painted to suggest stucco, and the framing of the flats was finished in a contrasting color, simulating a half-timbered construction. A few details were added, including windows, flower boxes, and a vine curling around the door.

The sets for the Oedipus plays (*Figures 6-3* and *6-4*) illustrate an extreme solution of storage and shifting problems. In designing the sets, Michael David assumed that they would not be used in a single performance, but the director decided to present both plays, which are long one-acters, in the same evening. Since each set covered most of the stage floor with platforms of quite different shapes, and since the theater did not provide offstage space for storing more than a few platforms, the problem of handling both sets was a difficult one.

The solution adopted resulted from the discovery that the *Oedipus at Colonus* platforms in most instances were higher than those for *King Oedipus.* The platforms for the *King Oedipus* set were consequently built as designed; the working drawings for the *Colonus* platforms were replanned so that they could be set down over the first set. The visible and practical surfaces of the platforms were consequently identical with the original designs, but the legs varied greatly in height, to enable them to fit on the irregular supporting surface. In a few cases, it was necessary to finish the *King Oedipus* platforms on two or more sides, and then turn them during the shift, so that the visible surfaces would bear the correct color.

Storage space was used as economically as possible; some of the *Colonus* platforms were actually stored on stage during the performance of the first play; for example, the two large pillars, each formed by a pair of flats set at right angles, were used to hide some of the smaller *Colonus* platforms for which there was no space off stage.

STAGECRAFT AND THE DESIGNER

Obviously, the more fully designers are familiar with the materials and methods that are available for set construction, the more practically they can design. Their primary need, however, is not to acquire skill in construction themselves, but to learn what they can reasonably ask their construction crews to do. Many details that are of great importance in constructing scenery have been omitted from this discussion, with attention focused on the items that are most important from the standpoint of design. The materials and techniques described constitute designers' physical resources, from which they must select and combine those that will help them achieve the desired esthetic effects, which are, of course, the only purpose and justification for set construction.

PART II

STEPS IN DESIGNING

5

THE
PRELIMINARY
ANAlysis

DESIGN RESTRICTIONS

All designers in the practical theater work within a series of restrictions. There are, of course, the restrictions of the script itself, although designers may not feel them as limitations, since their whole function is to prepare designs that will express the intention of the playwright as fully as possible.

However, other restrictions are often irritating: budget limitations, for instance, and the architecture of the theater, including the size of the stage, the available lighting facilities, and even the dimensions of the door of the scene shop. Less identifiable, but equally important, may be the restrictions imposed by the skill—or lack of it—of the construction crew.

An impatient and arrogant refusal to accept such limitations is a characteristic of amateur or dilettante artists. It is absurd to design scenic units that must be built in the scene shop but are too large to get through its door; to design a charming set providing seats for six actors when in fact seven must sit down at once; to design a set costing $2000 when only $500 is available. Throughout the centuries, great artists have adjusted realistically to the resources available to them, rather than refusing to function at all under conditions short of ideal; the ideal is never found in the theater. Great designers have frequently compensated for restrictions

159

by combining materials and specified techniques to produce effects un-imagined by previous artists.

The first step in designing a set, then, is determining the limitations to which the designer must conform.

Budget

The director or business manager should be consulted with regard to the funds available for scenery. If neither can give solid information about budget, referring to records for previous years will indicate how much is regularly spent on scenery. Often, appropriations for scenery are made for an entire season, rather than for each play. In that case, the designer should examine all of the plays scheduled for the season in an attempt to decide what their relative cost is likely to be. If one play will require many elaborate sets and another a single simple set, the designer should plan to spend considerably different sums of money for the two productions.

Economy

Economy in design consists primarily of making the fullest possible use of standard units—standard-size flats, platforms, etc., that are already in stock or that have been purchased for the current production and can be added to the theater's stock of scenery after the play is over. If scenic units such as platforms can be used in several productions, their cost can be divided and spread over an extended period of time, making it possible to justify the construction of units too expensive to include in the budget for any single play. The next most important factor in economical design is to specify low-cost materials where possible. Normally, in the nonprofessional theater the cost of construction is not a factor, since workers are not usually paid.

Inventory

Designers should also ask for the scenic inventory, which will identify the flats and other scenic units in stock, so that they may incorporate them into their designs where possible.

Construction Skill

To know the level of skill of the people who will build a set, the designer has to have worked with them for several productions. If the designer is new to the theater, the director or an experienced member of the technical staff may be able to provide information on the quality and type of work that can practically be expected from the crew; additional information can be obtained by examining photographs of sets built in recent years. As important as basic skill is the speed at which the crew is able to work, although that is still more difficult to determine before watching them in operation. Since most theatrical work is done to rigid deadlines, it is important that the designer not demand work of the construction crew that they cannot reasonably complete in the time available.

Inventory should be taken of the equipment in the scene shop. The type and quantity of power equipment should be given special attention. In one theater, the first production after the purchase of a new power saw was *The Solid Gold Cadillac.* For the set, the designer specified the construction of fifty halved joints, which were made very easily on the new saw; the previous year, such a design would have been totally impractical.

Equipment

When visiting the scene shop, designers should check on the space available for construction, the size of the largest opening by which the scenery may be moved out of the shop, and the methods and route by which it is transported to the stage. Ordinarily, they will design scenic units that can be handled comfortably in the space available; occasionally, for special effects, they may want to utilize construction and transportation space down to the last half-inch.

Dimensional Limitations

And finally, designers must get information about the architecture of the theater. Again, it is absurd to design a set 24'-0" deep if the stage is only 23'-0"; or to design a set so that important entrances or other elements are invisible to a large section of the audience. As an essential part of the designer's tools, every theater should have a supply of drawings giving the necessary architectural information. If such drawings are not already available, the designer must prepare them before beginning work on the set for a particular play.

Theater Architecture

The Floor Plan

The most important of these drawings is an accurate floor plan showing the stage and auditorium of the theater. (See *Figure 5-1.*) In the auditorium area, the first and last rows of seats should be drawn; for a particular theater it may be necessary to include other seats, for reasons that will be described in the next chapter. If the theater has a balcony, it should be included in the plan.

The part of the drawing showing the stage should include the proscenium wall, with its opening indicated, as well as the side and back walls of the stage area. Any permanent structures in the stage and offstage areas should be indicated, including such things as lighting dimmers, catwalk ladders, and even radiators. In addition, stairs should be drawn, whether they are backstage or in front of the curtain, leading from the

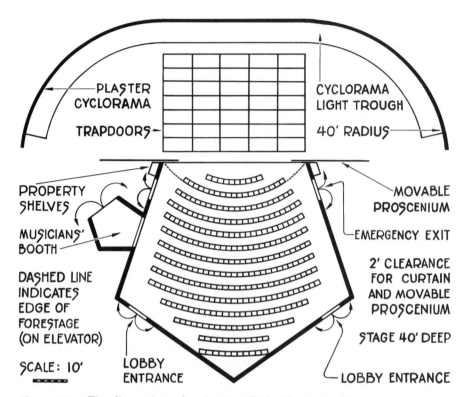

PLASTER
CYCLORAMA

CYCLORAMA
LIGHT TROUGH

TRAPDOORS

40' RADIUS

PROPERTY
SHELVES

MOVABLE
PROSCENIUM

MUSICIANS'
BOOTH

EMERGENCY EXIT

DASHED LINE
INDICATES
EDGE OF
FORESTAGE
(ON ELEVATOR)

2' CLEARANCE
FOR CURTAIN
AND MOVABLE
PROSCENIUM

SCALE: 10'

LOBBY
ENTRANCE

STAGE 40' DEEP

LOBBY ENTRANCE

Figure 5-1. The floor plan of a theater. This illustrates the type
of drawing designers need as a basis for their work. For their
own theaters, they will prefer to omit the labels. In addition, it
is not necessary to include every seat; only the seats needed for
checking sight lines need be included. [From a building
designed by the author to house the speech and theater programs of a midwestern college.]

stage to the auditorium floor. If the walls of the stage have pillars or indentations, those irregularities should also be carefully marked.

In a floor plan the areas should be measured to (at least) the closest
½″. It is helpful to include the space needed for a free operation of the
front curtain.

The selection of the scale for this floor plan, as for any theatrical
drawing, is based on convenience. One of the common sizes of artists'
cardboard is 22″ × 28″; larger sheets are difficult to handle easily. At the
scale of ⅜″ = 1'-0″, cardboard of that size provides space for drawing an
area a little larger than 58'-0″ × 74'-0″, which should be adequate for
most theaters.

A rough sketch should be made of the auditorium and stage areas, and the precise measurements should be recorded on it as they are determined.

Only one copy of the drawing need be made to this scale. However, the designer needs multiple copies of the same drawing on a much smaller scale. They may be produced by having a line cut made from the large drawing, and a supply run off by a printer. Almost equally effective, however, are copies duplicated by mimeograph or the spirit process, using a specially drawn stencil or master. Either letter-sized (8½" × 11") or legal-sized (8½" × 14") paper may be used. The following table shows the areas that can be represented at three scales.

Scales	Letter-Sized Paper	Legal-Sized Paper
¼" = 1'-0"	34' × 44'	34' × 56'
³/₁₆" = 1'-0"	45' × 58'	45' × 74'
⅛" = 1'-0"	68' × 88'	68' × 112'

The scales indicated are smaller than those most commonly used for theatrical drawings, but they have special convenience in making rough sketches.

The Cross Section

Measurement for the cross-sectional drawing is much more difficult, although the elements to be included are likely to be fewer. The drawing represents the appearance of the theater if it were sliced lengthwise by a giant knife, cutting through the walls, floor, and ceiling on the center line of the auditorium. (See *Figure 5-2.*) The center seats of the first and last rows should be included. If some seats are closer to the stage than the center seat of the first row (for instance, if the row curves toward the stage), the position of the seat closest to the stage should also be included in the drawing, even though it does not actually fall on the center line. Special care should be taken to reproduce the slope of the auditorium floor accurately, and the ceiling of the auditorium should be shown, with the slots provided for lights, as well as the grid over the stage. The balcony is also important in a cross section.

This drawing should be prepared to two scales, and duplicated copies of the smaller version should be provided. It is convenient to use the scales used for the floor plan; the length of the two drawings will be identical, and the height of the cross section view may well be less than the width of the floor plan, so there should be no difficulty in reproducing it at the same scale on the same sizes of paper and cardboard.

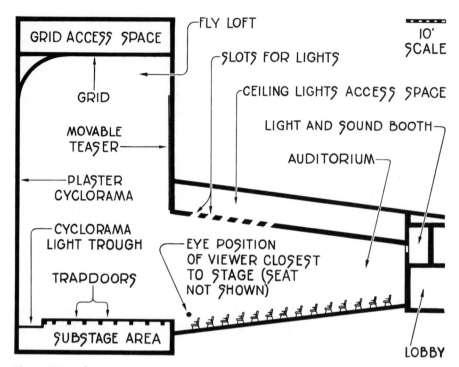

Figure 5-2. A cross section of the theater shown in *Figure 5-1*. This illustrates the second drawing needed by the designer.

The drawings described are used primarily to check the visibility of scenic elements from positions in the audience; their use is discussed in detail in the next chapter.

THE FIRST READING AND ANALYSIS

Having collected the necessary information with regard to budget, crews, available scenery, equipment, and architecture, the designer is ready at last to turn to the script.

His first step should be to read the play, as he would if he were simply reading it for pleasure: to learn the story, and to get a general impression of the effect of the play as a whole.

Having finished his reading, he is ready to begin a detailed analysis of design problems. He will already have identified the general mood of the play. He will also have noticed the locale of the play: that it takes place (if it is Pinter's *The Dumb Waiter*) in the basement of a building in London, etc. He may want to turn again to the description of the setting supplied by the author and study it carefully.

At this point, the designer should be given a warning that may seem to contradict a basic principle discussed in Chapter 1. Although he should study the scenic description given in the script, he should feel free to develop his own design independently: the author's suggestions may be helpful, but they are suggestions, not restrictions, and may, if it seems wise, be completely rejected.

How can we justify such a practice, if it is the designer's function to express and support the intention of the playwright? The answer to that question is that as a specialist in set design, the designer can make sounder decisions in that area than the playwright.

The designer should ignore floor plans or photographs of sets used in previous productions of the play. There are several reasons for this policy. The simplest and most obvious is that a design must be created in terms of the theater in which it is to be used, and a design that may have been superb for a particular Broadway theater is almost certain to be less than ideally suited to a different situation. Novices in the theater often assume that Broadway conditions are ideal; as a matter of fact, the best theaters in America are found on college and university campuses, and the design used in the Broadway production of a play may incorporate numerous compromises and defects. In any case, a design created for one theater, whether good or bad, would not be suited to any other theater except one that was an exact architectural duplicate.

It is possible to produce an effective drama program by renting a theater and hiring companies to bring performances for local presentation. Directing, acting, costuming, set design, and all other aspects of production are then handled by artists who are part of the company. Such a program may be of great value, but those who arrange it are managers, not artists. Even if only part of a production is drawn from external sources (costumes rented, set designs copied from previous productions), to that extent those responsible for the program become managers, not artists. Certainly, allowing oneself to be identified as a scenic designer on a play program when actually one has copied all or part of the work of an actual designer is to function unethically, and probably illegally.

Finally, a sound design is the result of an orderly step-by-step procedure, involving careful analysis and the making of a long series of decisions in logical order. For a designer even to glance at someone else's finished design is to reverse the process. If the design is a very bad one, it may have little effect; but if the design is good, it is likely to set up a vivid picture in the designer's mind, making it impossible to focus on the analysis and decisions that must, in sound design, be preliminary to the final result.

In this connection, it may be helpful also to discuss a fundamental error in design that characterizes the work of most beginners. Novices typically attempt to produce a design as a single act. In planning scenery, they are most likely to begin by making a perspective sketch, showing how the scenery is to look when finished; they then assume that all that is necessary to complete the design is to redraw it more carefully to scale. But a perspective sketch implies and enforces a large number of decisions that the artist in such a case has not made: it implies a particular floor plan; specific dimensions for furniture, walls, and other scenic elements; a pattern of movement, imposed on the actors by the placement of doors, windows, furniture, etc.—an overall esthetic effect. All of those aspects of design are vitally important, and sound decisions concerning them require the full focus of the designer's attention; they should not be decided by accident, while the designer is concentrating on other problems. For example, the set's effect on the arrangement and movements of actors should be planned during a separate step of the design process, when the designer is able to concentrate on it totally, to the exclusion of other design problems.

A warning should perhaps be included against a possible misinterpretation if students should have the chance of observing their instructors or some other skilled designer at work. With growing experience, designers are often able to master their techniques so fully that they are able to make automatically and at great speed decisions that in the beginning required considerable time and full attention. For example, they may be able to substitute imaginative analysis for actual drawing, to explore design problems and make decisions on the basis of visualizations. Consequently, to the observer, it may seem that they have skipped steps in the design process when actually they have handled them with speed and efficiency; in particular, this skill is likely to operate during the exploratory parts of their work. As students gain experience, they can expect their own work to become steadily more efficient and faster, with a reduction in the more laborious note-taking and voluminous sketching. During their initial study, however, it is far safer for them to make haste slowly and to plod where later, perhaps, they may run.

The sound, skilled, and (in the best sense) professional artists, therefore, break the total process of design into a series of separate problems and deal with one at a time, purposely pushing the other aspects of design as far as possible toward the bottom of consciousness. In that way, they are able to devote their whole attention to each decision individually.

This procedure is so foreign to most people untrained in art that it may at first seem somewhat awkward. Students may find, when they are concentrating on one aspect of design, that ideas and questions connected with other problems constantly flash into their minds, and they may be tempted at least to stop and jot thoughts down. They should resist that temptation strongly, concentrating exclusively on the problem at hand.

At first, that may prove irritating, but soon it will become habitual and will seem the natural and easy way to work. The primary justification for the method is that it results in better finished designs: it guarantees the best design a designer is capable of, since each decision is the result of conscious analysis of the particular aspect of the design, arrived at under ideal conditions, when the designer is able to bring full attention to it, undistracted by other problems.

The method has a second advantage, which while of less artistic importance may be equally gratifying to the designer: it produces a feeling of comfort and confidence. Most beginning students of set design feel a paralyzing fear of the art, a confusion and feeling of inadequacy that are often summarized by the comment "I don't know where to begin." The sound professional approach solves that problem by indicating precisely where to begin and what step to take next, third, fourth, etc. To produce a completed design at a single step is almost impossible; but to attack one small problem and then, having solved it, to move on to another, makes the whole procedure logical, effective, and assuring. Students who resist this basic principle of art will never become sound designers; students who accept it wholeheartedly may be confident of steady growth in their mastery of the art.

6

DESIGNING
THE
MACHINE

The designer's first reading of the script has given him a general acquaintance with the outline of the story, the mood and style of the play, the times and places in which the action occurs, and the author's suggestions regarding setting. His next major concern is to develop a setting that the director can use effectively in arranging the positions of the actors on stage and in planning their movements during the action of the play.

ACTION REQUIREMENTS

The first step in this procedure is to determine precisely the script's minimum requirements regarding action. To do that, the designer turns again to the first page of the script and begins a careful analysis of what the actors actually do. In his first reading, he was primarily interested in the story of the play, so he concentrated on the dialog, perhaps skimming the stage directions. Now he will probably concentrate on the stage directions, skimming the dialog, although he must study it closely enough to make sure that he does not miss actions that are implied by the speeches but not mentioned in the stage directions.

Stage Directions

In working with classic plays, it is well to remember that full stage directions are a very recent development in playwriting; since most classic authors worked closely with the companies that produced their plays, often they did not include any directions in the script, but gave them to the actors orally. Stage directions, and even act and scene divisions, in ancient Greek and Roman drama and in much Elizabethan drama, including Shakespeare's, were often not written by the playwright, but added by later editors. In such cases, designers are not bound by them in the slightest; they need not give them even the degree of attention that they would give to stage directions written by the playwright.

Thus, if an edition of a Shakespearean play identifies a scene as taking place in a garden, the designer may quite properly ignore the note unless the setting is clearly indicated by the dialog. While only rash designers would casually overrule a great master of the theater, they may safely assume that their judgment with regard to set design is superior to that of the persons who have annotated the scripts.

Minimal
Requirements

At this point in his study, the designer should concentrate on *minimal action requirements*. If he cares to jot down information about scenic elements that are desirable but not absolutely necessary, he should mark them in such a way as to clearly distinguish them from the essentials, perhaps by putting such notes in brackets.

As he analyzes the script, he notices each time an actor enters or exits and checks the dialog to identify where the actor has come from or is going to. Each time an actor sits, the designer notices what he does while sitting. His actions may require, for instance, that his chair have a coffee table in front of it so that he can spread out papers to work with, or that a davenport be provided large enough for him to stretch out on. If the stage directions instruct him to walk to the fireplace and examine a photograph on the mantel, the designer will check to make sure that the fireplace is actually essential and that the photograph cannot be hung on the wall or set on a piano. If an actress must stumble over a step and catch herself against the wall, the designer notes not only that there must be a step, but also that the wall must be reinforced so that it will not shake or punch through when the actress throws her hand against it. If the action of the play requires that a burglar stalk an actor until he is caught in a cul-de-sac among the furniture, the designer notes that such an arrangement must be included in the design. If the maid must eavesdrop on a quarrel between a married couple, the designer adds a note reminding himself that a good eavesdropping nook must be provided.

In particular, the designer should keep track of how many people are sitting at each moment of the play. In Mary Chase's farce *Harvey*, Elwood Dowd has as his constant companion a white rabbit six feet tall, named

Harvey, who is invisible to everyone (including the audience) except Elwood. At the end of Act I, Elwood pulls up a chair for Harvey to sit in while Elwood reads him a chapter from a novel by Jane Austen. At an early rehearsal of the play at one college, students who had taken the course in set design were greatly amused to discover that, in counting the number of chairs needed by the actors, the designer had forgotten to include one for Harvey, with the result that the design had to be revised. That is a most unusual case, of course, but it demonstrates vividly the necessity for analyzing the seating requirements accurately throughout a play. This step is an irksome one, but it is vitally important for preparing a sound design, and if it were neglected it might well mean that a design, when completed, would be discovered to be impractical and would have to be discarded.

BLOCKING

The next step is somewhat more interesting. It consists of moving beyond the minimal physical requirements of the set to its part in the esthetic effects created by the arrangement and movement of the actors.

The design of the arrangement and movement of actors on stage is called *blocking*. This is a kind of omnibus term, that is used in several ways: to indicate the design itself, the act of creating it, and the process of teaching it to actors. We have identified the major function of most sets in somewhat figurative language by saying that a set must serve as a machine for organizing the arrangement and movement of actors on stage; using the technical term, we could restate that more directly by saying that a good set will offer the director maximum assistance in producing an effective blocking design.

The actual blocking of a play is planned by the director, not by the set designer. This aspect of the set is so important, however, that in the conference during which the director evaluates a proposed set design, he or she is likely to turn first to its blockability and to weigh this one factor more heavily than any other. The designer, then, need not plan the blocking, but he or she must be able to judge the efficiency of the set design in assisting the director's work. A thorough understanding of blocking is consequently vital to mastery of set design.

Blocking serves several purposes in the total esthetic pattern of a play. Perhaps its primary function is to help control the spectators' focus of attention. Ordinarily, at any specific moment in the play, the story is being

Controlling Attention

carried forward by a particular actor; if the spectators are to follow the play, their attention must be focused on that actor.

Experience has clearly demonstrated that the pattern in which actors are arranged on stage is a powerful factor in controlling the focus of attention of the audience. In fact, if actors are properly arranged on stage, even a passerby who stops at the door of the theater and glances in at the stage casually should instinctively look first at the actor who is at that moment carrying the story of the play forward. It is easy to produce any number of static arrangements that will so control the spectator's focus of attention, and if that focus was supposed to be maintained for long periods on a single actor, blocking would be easy. However, in a typical play, the focus remains on one actor for only a brief moment, then it flashes to a second and a third and back to the first. Designing blocking so that the audience, without any feeling of strain or forcing, will follow such a swiftly moving pattern of attention is a major esthetic problem, and directors devote perhaps as much time to solving it as to any other single part of their work.

Unfortunately, no clear-cut rules have yet been developed to objectively identify the factors affecting the audience's pattern of attention. In the absence of such rules, designers and directors must use their own taste and imagination to predict how the audience will react to the actual performance. But even though blocking necessarily involves great uncertainty, it will be helpful for the designer to consider a few principles that experience suggests may be valid.

Contrast

Perhaps the most important factor in controlling attention is contrast, of any type; this seems to take precedence over all other factors. Thus, if a stage is filled with a howling, swirling mob, except for a single man sitting quiet and unmoving in a chair in the center, the audience's attention will be focused on him. If all the members of a cast are sitting at a table, except for one woman who is standing, the audience will focus on her.

Speech

Speech is a powerful factor in attracting attention: the audience tends always to look at the actor who is speaking. Since at almost every moment in a play the story is carried forward by the actor who is speaking, this factor is of the greatest assistance to the director in focusing the spectators' attention properly.

Movement

Movement attracts attention. Normally, a director plans at least a small movement to accompany almost every speech, to reinforce the influence on the audience's attention exerted by the speech itself. In the past, when actors have attempted to "steal scenes," they most frequently used the principle of the attractiveness of movement. Thus, an actress lying on a sofa might distract the attention of the audience from an actor's speech by using a series of movements—patting her lips with her handkerchief, fanning herself, or yawning.

Height

Height attracts attention. When Regina, in *The Little Foxes,* stops on the stair landing and turns to her family, seated in the living room below her, to say to them brutally, "Why don't you all go home!," the audience's attention is focused on her not only because they have been following her movement, not only because she is speaking, not only because she is standing while the others are sitting, but also because she is on a higher level than the other actors. It is for this reason that directors and actors so enjoy sets that enable them to use a variety of levels.

Stage Areas

Certain areas of the stage are more likely to attract the audience's attention than others; such areas are called *strong.* The center of the stage is apparently the strongest area, with the downstage left and right corners next strongest and the upstage corners weakest.

Since the position of an actor or a scenic unit on the stage is of such importance, a special system of terms has been developed to identify the parts of a stage. Although they are primarily used by actors and directors, the designer will find it convenient to be familiar with them. Actually, various similar sets of terms and stage divisions are used by different workers in the theater; the simplest and most generally useful will be discussed.

The first step in describing the geography of the stage is to mark off the edges of the acting area, that is, the space normally defined by scenery and used by the performers. The acting area is usually thought of as extending toward the audience as far as the proscenium wall; its front edge is therefore defined by a line connecting the back corners of the wall, at the edges of the proscenium opening. For a deep stage, the acting area may extend only part of the way back, perhaps 15'-0"; if the stage is shallow, it may be necessary to include all of the space between the front edge and the back wall. In any case, the back edge of the acting area consists of a line parallel with the front edge.

For reasons that will be discussed later in the chapter, the side edges of the acting area are slanted, rather than being drawn at right angles to the front and back. The back edge is shorter than the front edge, so that the four edges of the acting area form a trapezoid.

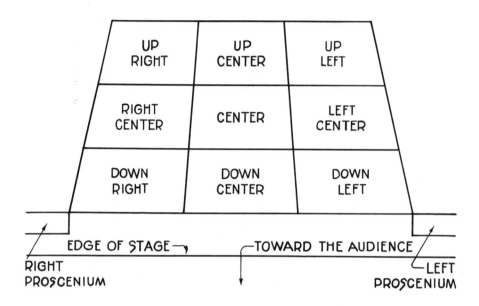

Figure 6-1. Stage geography.

The subdivisions of this basic shape are marked by dividing each edge into three equal parts and connecting matching points on opposite edges with straight lines, forming nine quadrilateral shapes (*Figure 6-1*). The center one is called *center*; the others are identified by combinations of the terms *center, left, right, up,* and *down.* Areas toward the back of the stage are referred to as *upstage,* and those toward the front are said to be *downstage.*

The application of the terms *right* and *left* would of course vary according to the position from which the stage was viewed; in order to keep the description uniform, the areas are named from the viewpoint of an actor standing in the center of the stage and facing directly toward the audience. The division directly in front of him is said to be *down center;* the area behind him is *up center;* the space immediately to his right is *right center,* just in front of it is the *down-right* area, and just above it the *up-right* area. The areas at the left are given corresponding names. It should be pointed out that these terms are the reverse of those that would be used by members of the audience.

Since the designer works from various viewpoints, the standard terms will sometimes match his momentary position and sometimes contradict it. However, it is more effective to use the terms uniformly. For example, in discussing the designer's perspective painting of the set, which is made from the viewpoint of the audience, it is more useful to use the traditional terms, even though the down-left area will actually appear at the right of the picture.

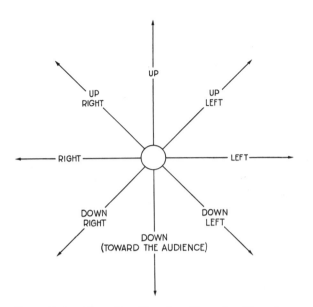

Figure 6-2. The directional pattern for the stage.

Besides naming areas, some of the same terms are also used directionally; thus a stagehand might be instructed to move a table down stage two inches. When used directionally, the point at which the actor or piece of furniture is standing is considered to be center, so that only the terms *up, down, right,* and *left* (or their combinations) are used. (See *Figure 6-2.*) In addition, the terms *on* and *off stage* are common. They are less precisely definable, but they generally refer to direction with regard to the center area; thus, to move a platform farther on stage is to move it toward the center.

Angle

The angle at which actors are placed helps them control the audience's attention: the more directly they face the audience, the more likely the audience is to focus on them. Unfortunately, however, the strongest position (facing the audience directly) is not usually available in the theater. In some plays and theatrical styles the actors acknowledge the presence of the audience and speak directly to them. Thornton Wilder uses that technique in *Our Town:* one of the actors, called the Stage Manager, begins the performance with a speech to the audience. Occasionally, a director may introduce this device into a play where it was not intended to be used. For example, in one production of *The Solid Gold Cadillac,* the stockholders' meeting was staged by bringing up the lights in the auditorium, and the members of the audience were addressed as if they were stockholders attending the meeting. Two of the actors were seated in the audience at the beginning of the play. Far more often, however, actors are instructed to create the impression that they are unaware of the presence of the audience and are speaking only to each other; even in *Our Town,* the great majority of the scenes are played as if the actors were unconscious of the presence of onlookers.

In order to maintain that illusion, actors are instructed never to look directly at the audience, an instruction that is obviously difficult to follow if they are placed in chairs, davenports, or other furniture that automatically force them to face the front edge of the stage. Consequently, the designer should carefully avoid such positions for furniture, preferably slanting davenports and other furniture to facilitate their use by the actors. Such slanting is easy along the side walls, but if the back wall of the set is parallel with the front of the stage, it may tend to pull the furniture placed near it into the same parallel position. Chairs or other furniture standing against the back wall and used only briefly in the play may be placed directly facing the audience, but any units that are to be used for long periods of time should be angled.

Some scenes almost always present difficulties to the designer. One particularly troublesome problem is the arrangement of actors around a dining table. If the table is placed parallel with the edge of the stage, and four actors are seated at it in the normal position, one of them will not only have his back turned directly toward the audience, but he will hide the view of the actor opposite him. If the table is angled so that one corner points toward the front of the stage, the arrangement is improved, but only slightly. Even if only two actors use the table, seating them at opposite ends when it is in parallel position limits the audience to a profile view, and slanting the table throws one of them into the extremely weak position in which the audience sees him at the three-quarter angle from the back.

There is no really acceptable solution to this problem, so the designer must resort to uncomfortable dodges and tricks. One solution is to angle the table slightly, lengthen it so that two actors can be seated along the upstage edge, and then explain the avoidance of the downstage side by some such device as pushing a teacart in front of it. If only two actors must use the table, it is probably best to point one corner directly toward the audience and seat them on adjacent sides, with the downstage edges left open. In any case, the designer should place the table and shift the chairs around in an attempt to provide sight lines that are as effective as possible.

Almost the only time the arrangement for a group eating at a table on stage is fully acceptable is when they are seated at the speakers' table at a banquet. In ordinary life, such tables are regularly left open on one side to provide visibility for the audience; therefore, on the stage all of the actors can be similarly placed on the upstage side and the ends of a long speakers' table without producing a distractingly unnatural pattern. *Figure 16-17* illustrates one solution for the problem of arranging actors at a table, although like nearly all such arrangements it is a somewhat uncomfortable compromise between the pattern of ordinary life and the theatrical requirements of visibility.

Within the limits imposed by the restrictions that have been discussed, however, the arrangement of furniture, stairs, and other scenic units is of great value in controlling the angle at which actors face the audience, producing varying degrees of emphasis on the different characters that help control the viewers' focus of attention.

Scenic Pointing

The focus of attention of the actors influences the attention of the audience. When actors turn and look, or even point, in a particular direction, the audience is likely to follow them. A set may be designed to serve something of the same function: in effect, to point to an actor. The set for *Antony and Cleopatra (Figure 6-19)* was designed as a series of arches through which the audience looked. Running under this arcade was a flight of stairs, four of which (if we include the stage floor) were enlarged to form landings. The result was that the opening under the last arch became a kind of picture, massively framed; if the audience had looked at the set without actors, the scenic design would undoubtedly have pulled their attention to that area. Consequently, when Cleopatra and Antony entered at the back of the stage and paused momentarily under the last arch, the fact that other characters had turned to watch their entrance was reinforced by the design of the entire set, so that the queen and the general irresistibly dominated the stage picture. (Of course there were many other operative factors that have not been analyzed in this discussion, including the pattern of lighting and the design of the costumes.)

Lighting

Lighting, a powerful resource in controlling attention, can be used to reinforce blocking patterns. An audience instinctively turns toward the most brilliantly lighted area on stage. Chapter 4 described the method of lighting in which the stage is divided into a series of acting areas, each one lighted by a pair of spotlights. For each particular moment in the play, the acting area where the audience's attention should be focused is normally more brightly lighted than any of the other areas. As the focus shifts about the stage, the light crew makes constant adjustments in the pattern of illumination, playing the light board somewhat like a musical instrument. Usually, of course, it is hoped that such changes will not be consciously noticed by the audience; the changes themselves are minimal, only suffi-cient to shift the balance of illumination so that the momentarily critical area dominates, and the changes are made smoothly. Such unobtrusive increase or decrease in illumination is referred to as *sneaking up* or *down.* But even though changes in lighting most often operate subliminally, their influence on attention is of great importance. It is for that reason (as was indicated in Chapter 4) that sets are nearly always differentially lighted vertically, with the top half of a set much darker than the lower half, to focus attention on the actors.

Other Functions
of Blocking

Besides controlling the attention of the audience, blocking serves other functions. In fact, it fulfills all of the functions of the set itself.

Locale

One function is to give information to the audience about the locale of the play. In the main, that is done by including in the set functional and decorative elements that would be found in a similar setting in ordinary life: doors and windows, furniture, fireplaces, garden benches, trees, paths, etc. The arrangement of such elements, when they are actually used by actors, strongly influences the actors' movements, as well as their momentarily static patterns. If the set requires a bay window, a staircase, an outside and an inside door, a fireplace, three chairs, and a davenport, those elements could obviously be arranged in many different ways. But actors would probably find no two such arrangements exactly equal in usa-bility. It is the designer's responsibility to work out the arrangement that will facilitate the most effective pattern of movement for the actors.

Mood

Like the set, blocking must harmonize with, and be expressive of, the mood of the play. No generally-agreed-on principles have been developed with regard to the expression of mood by the arrangement and movement of actors, so only tentative suggestions can be made to supplement the designer's intuitive imagination.

Short, fast, broken, staccato movement seems best suited to farce, and long, slow, legato movement seems best suited to tragedy. On the other hand, anger suggests fast, broken movement, while smooth move-ment seems most harmonious with pleasant emotions. The expression of mood by movement is illustrated in the blocking diagram for *Antony and Cleopatra (Figure 6-3).*

A careful study of Michael David's designs for Sophocles' *King Oedipus* and *Oedipus at Colonus (Figures 6-4, 6-5, 6-6, 6-7,* and *6-8)* will also be of value in this connection, as well as in other aspects of set

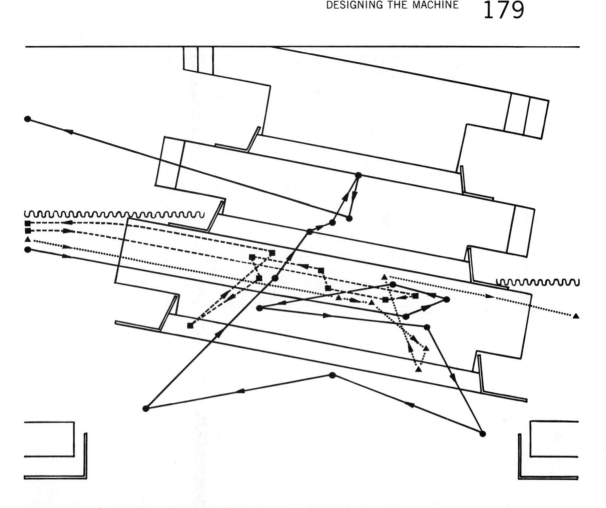

Figure 6-3. A blocking diagram. This is one of hundreds of blocking diagrams prepared by the director for a production of Shakespeare's *Antony and Cleopatra,* using the set shown in *Figure 6-19.* The part of the play diagrammed is Scene 4, Act I, which lasted 3½ minutes. Three characters appear: Caesar is represented by circles and a solid line, Lepidus by squares and a dashed line, and a messenger by triangles and a dotted line. Each line segment indicates a movement; each symbol indicates where a character pauses. Even without the script, certain conclusions can be drawn from the diagram itself. Caesar clearly dominates the scene, although the other characters play significant parts in it. Caesar's movements are broader; he acts on three major levels, yet does not move away from the center area. The mood, too, can be guessed from the movement patterns. Caesar, for example, strides across the stage in undeviating lines. The zigzag pattern of his movements suggests agitation, but their directness implies firmness. His dominant emotion is extreme anger.

Figure 6-4. Set for Sophocles' *King Oedipus*, designed by Michael David.

Figure 6-5. Set for Sophocles' *Oedipus at Colonus*, designed by Michael David.

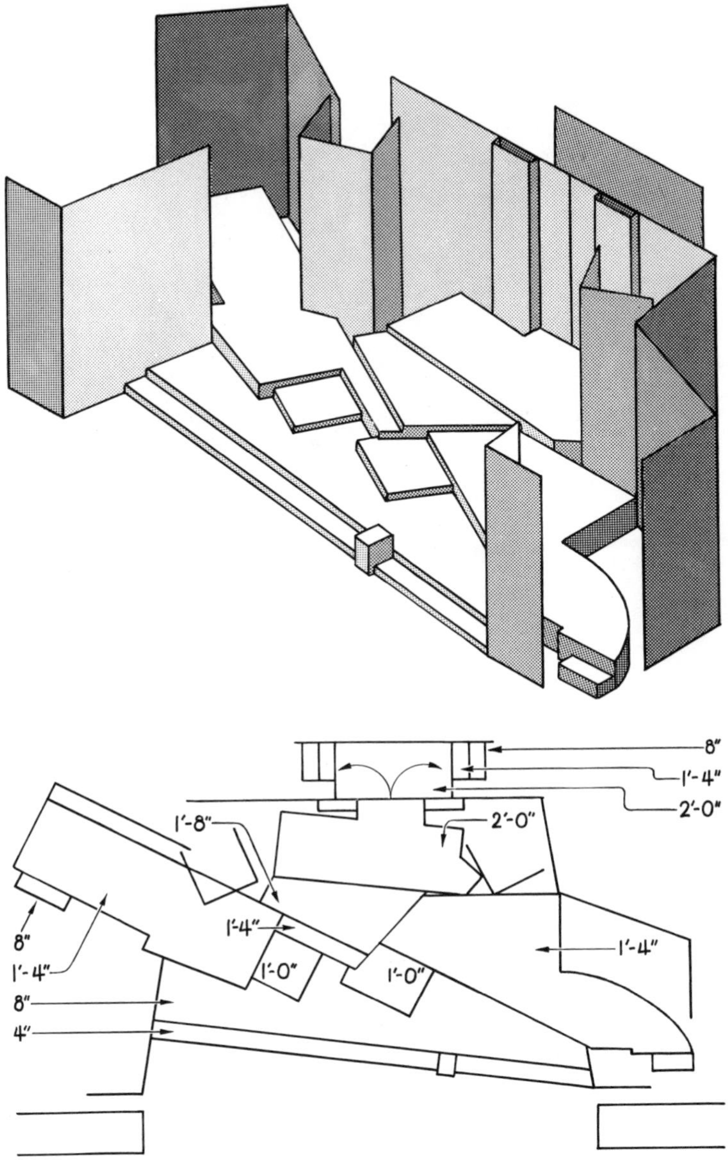

Figure 6-6. A set for Sophocles' *King Oedipus,* shown in isometric projection and ground plan. The figures on the ground
plan indicate the height of levels above the stage floor. The two
rectangles at the bottom of the drawing represent the proscenium wall. For the appearance of the set from the audience, see
Figure 6-4. [Designed by Michael David.]

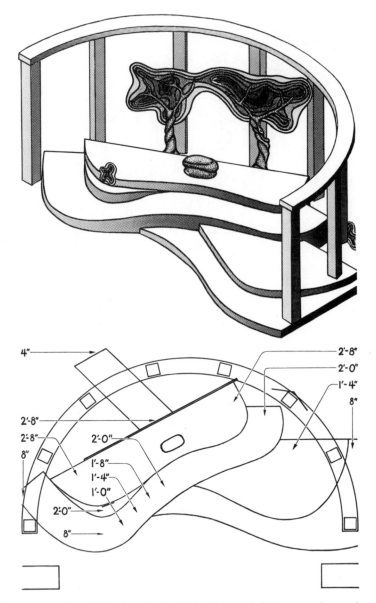

Figure 6-7. A set for Sophocles' *Oedipus at Colonus,* shown in isometric projection and ground plan. The figures on the ground plan indicate the heights of levels above the stage floor. Two ramps are included; the one at the top is invisible to the audience. The use of levels in this set is difficult to sense without examining the actual set in the theater; it is shown in *Figure 6-5* as it appeared from the viewpoint of the audience. [Designed by Michael David.]

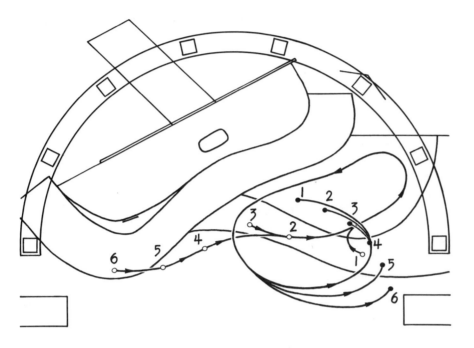

Figure 6-8. Blocking approaches dance. This is one of the blocking diagrams prepared for the production of *Oedipus at Colonus* using Michael David's set (*Figure 6-5.*) The section of the play diagrammed is a poetic passage that was recited by the chorus while they moved from one position to another. Six members of the chorus appeared in this brief section of the play. Their starting positions are indicated by open circles; their final positions by solid circles. The actor indicated by number 1 moved first, followed by the others in numerical order. They moved along the paths shown. Each pair of circles marked by the same number represents a single actor. A comparison with *Figure 6-3* will demonstrate vividly how clearly even the minimal information given in a blocking diagram can suggest mood.

design. *King Oedipus* is a violent and bitter tragedy, with anger as its dominant emotion and hysterical grief perhaps second in importance. Anger appears in *Oedipus at Colonus,* but clearly subordinated; the major emotion is one for which there is no name in the language, combining sweetness, resignation, sadness, and exaltation. If students will study Michael David's ground plans and then turn to the perspective paintings, imagining actors moving around the stage, they will see that the design for each play enforces and facilitates a type and pattern of movement suited to the mood of the play: the *King Oedipus* set is designed in a series of irregular straight steps, while the *Colonus* set is made up of gentle curves, with major shifts in level produced by ramps rather than steps.

Closely related to the general mood of a play are the emotional relationships between the various characters; such relationships must be expressed by the actors, and a well-designed set will make that expression easier for them. *King Oedipus,* for example, is made up largely of a series of short scenes, most often involving only two major characters, although occasionally three are included. In effect, the personality of Oedipus is displayed by setting him in contrast in one scene with Creon, in another with Tiresias, in another with an old herdsman, and in other scenes with his queen, Jocasta. The tones of the various scenes are very different, but each involves high tension, and the relationship of the characters involved shifts constantly through the episode. Thus, in his scenes with Tiresias, Oedipus is at one moment dominant as he violently attacks the old blind seer, at the next moment Tiresias achieves dominance as he angrily defends himself; even in the scene in which Oedipus has his old slave tortured, the king begins in full command and then is reduced to terror by the news he forces from the slave.

For each scene to be effective, each member of the audience must sense the swift changes in the relationships of the characters; perhaps highly skilled actors could make the changes clear even on a bare stage, but a well-designed set should make such communication easier for them.

A study of Michael David's floor plan *(Figure 6-6)* will demonstrate how much assistance he has given the director and actors in solving this problem. The highest platform stands directly in front of the entrance to the palace, so that whenever Oedipus enters he is immediately on a level at which he physically dominates all of the other characters, expressing his emotional position at the beginning of each episode. As the scene continues, he moves naturally down to a middle level, from which he can step up or down easily, so that by a single movement in the right direction he can either strengthen or weaken his position in relation to the other major character in the scene. In effect, then, the irregular platforms constitute a kind of keyboard on which the actor can play a flexibly changing melody of emotion; of course, the other characters have similar resources, although less extensive than those provided for Oedipus. Incidentally, although the arrangement of platforms at first glance seems highly irregular and accidental, the designer has included three separate paths by which an actor may move from the stage floor to the highest platform by low steps of uniform height (4''); at the same time he has supplied irregular paths in which the actor may step at larger intervals, up to more than a foot. Thus, Jocasta is able to make graceful, easy crosses, and Oedipus, in moments of emotional stress, can match his mood by more broken paths revealing greater physical effort.

The assistance Michael David has given to the actors in expressing the variations in their relationships is so important that to any actor, director, or set designer the pattern of platforms is by far the most significant aspect of his design. Yet, the steps form only a minor part of the total stage picture, so that most members of the audience are likely to be unaware of their importance; in fact, a major reason for their effectiveness is that they function unobtrusively but unmistakably, throwing the viewers' attention where it should be focused, on the actors themselves. It is not surprising that Michael David spent the major share of his time while working on the set in the design of the platform series, and that in using the set the director and actors came to feel that the apparently haphazard arrangement had the inevitability and rightness that characterize all sound and careful design.

Blocking as Choreography

The focus of attention, adjustment to functional scenic elements, and expression of mood all have esthetic implications, but the total esthetic effect of movement includes something additional. In this aspect, drama approaches dance. If dance is defined as movement organized into a communicative, meaningful, and affective pattern, then good blocking is to some extent dance. (See *Figures 6-3* and *6-8.*)

The organization of three-dimensional space into a work of art, as in architecture, sculpture, and set design, involves two kinds of space, which may be called negative and positive. The walls, floors, ceilings, and stairs of a building occupy space and are strikingly visible. But they also define and enclose open space, in which the activities involved in the use of the building go on. The area occupied by the architectural elements themselves can be called *positive space;* the area they define and enclose, *negative space.*

In the nineteenth century, the attention of architects, critics, and the general public was focused on the positive element of buildings, and the negative space was often squeezed, distorted, and mishandled in order to preserve the pattern of the outside walls of a building. The most revolutionary development in architectural design in modern times has been the reversal of this emphasis, so that attention is now focused primarily on the (negative) space enclosed by the walls of a building rather than on the positive space occupied by the walls themselves. This is expressed by the architectural cliché that in the nineteenth century buildings were designed from the outside in, whereas they are now designed from the inside out.

In set design, Adolphe Appia pointed in the same direction. His revolutionary early designs were especially effective in shaping negative space for use by the actors and at the same time handling the visual elements expressively. Throughout his career, his focus on negative space steadily increased, with a growing deemphasis on positive space, so that his later designs seem somewhat less effective. In the finest designs both types of space would be handled with equal skill, but short of that ideal, the design of negative space—that is, the shaping of the three-dimensional area to be used by the actors—should be given priority over the purely visual or pictorial positive space. Unfortunately, judges of design contests tend to focus in the old-fashioned way on the set as picture, with scant attention to the design of the space it encloses. The same defect regularly appears in many otherwise beautiful and impressive books containing collections of set designs; they may use modern motifs and materials and superficially modern decorative styles, but in their basic esthetic they are often fundamentally Victorian.

The shape of space (negative as well as positive) has esthetic implications. As Solness climbs higher and higher toward his doom in Ibsen's *Master Builder,* his ascent itself helps create emphasis. The confined areas in which Ibsen's *Hedda Gabler* and *An Enemy of the People* are set help express the pressures of life on Hedda and the attack of the townspeople on Dr. Stockman. The confinement of the action of Albee's *Who's Afraid of Virginia Woolf?* to a somewhat seedy, dark, restricted living room contributes significantly to the effect of the play; the outdoor scenes inserted into the movie made from the play are an esthetic intrusion, weakening the effect rather than strengthening it. On the other hand, the feeling of infinite space that is produced by some sets for *Oklahoma* is of great importance in expressing the mood of the play and in providing ample negative space for the free use of the actors and dancers.

The effective handling of negative space is the most important function of the set designer, and the most significant test of his ability. Of course, other elements should be handled as well as possible, but a design stands or falls primarily on the basis of this element. The designer must be able to recognize the special esthetic effect of the script and create a shape enclosed by the walls and other elements of a set that will harmonize with, and express, that esthetic, especially when the space is used by the actors. Since negative space is so important a part of scenery, any set design can be usefully studied with regard to that factor. In this book, it may be especially useful to examine the sets for the Oedipus plays (*Figures 6-4* and *6-5), The Tempest (Figures 2-14, 9-7,* and *9-8), The Lark (Figures 2-7, 6-20,* and *6-21), Of Thee I Sing (Figures 9-9* and *9-10), The Rimers of Eldritch (Figures 6-23* and *6-24),* and *Rosencrantz and Guildenstern Are Dead (Figures 1-6* and *7-1).* Obviously, the design of negative space is related not only to esthetics, but also to mood, action requirements, and the communication of information about locale.

It is excessive to say that the pattern of movement designed for every play should have sufficient interest and meaning to hold an audience's attention if it was presented alone, without the dialog, but it is surely sound to say that ideally blocking should approach that pitch. Every set should be so designed as to facilitate as fully as possible the creation of such a pattern of movement by the director, a pattern combining as great a variety as possible while producing an effect of esthetic unity.

PERSPECTIVE ALTERATION

Before moving on to the production of the first exploratory sketches, it may be helpful to discuss *perspective alteration,* an aspect of design that derives from geometrical and emotional aspects of visual perception.

A stage set representing an ordinary room almost always has the side walls opened at a larger angle than 90°; in fact, the majority of sets have no walls meeting at right angles. Slanted walls are said to be *raked.* Because this is such a constant factor in set design, it is important for the designer to understand the reasons for what at first glance may seem like an arbitrary and unnatural practice.

      The angling of side walls may be justified on simple practical grounds. If the student will draw the floor plan of an actual room on the stage area in the diagram of his theater and check sight lines from various seats, he will discover that each side wall is nearly invisible to about a third of the audience; slanting the walls in the customary fashion not only improves visibility, but also makes the views from the different seats more uniform, so that two people sitting far apart in the theater have much more nearly the same picture of the set than they would if the walls actually met at right angles.

      However, this practice can be justified on another basis, which is more significant because it is esthetic rather than mechanical. The relationships that playwrights hope to establish between their audiences and the characters in their plays vary. At one extreme, a playwright such as Bertolt Brecht wants his audiences not to share the experiences of the characters in the play. Brecht goes so far as to say that the action of the play must be "distanced," that the audiences must be "alienated." Something of the same relationship existed in the classical performances in the Chinese theater. Other examples could be cited, but at present they must still be regarded as exceptional. In the great majority of plays, the playwrights' intention is to focus the attention of the members of the audience—to so catch them up in the action, problems, and setting of the drama that they forget the rest of the audience sitting around them and share the experiences the actors are recreating on stage. This quality of

Raking

sharing other people's emotions and experiences is called *empathy.* The essence of empathy is taking someone else's point of view, looking at things with his eyes, analyzing them with his mind, and reacting to them with his emotions. That is, of course, strictly impossible, but if we cannot actually sit in someone else's chair and see things with his eyes, we can do it imaginatively.

The purpose of the designer, then, is to help spectators place themselves in imagination on stage, as observant even if silent members of the cast; the set should make them feel, not that they are distant observers, sitting 40 feet away and watching a series of actions in which they have no part, but that they are centrally involved in the setting.

That aim affects set design in two critical ways. Suppose a spectator is sitting in an actual living room, perhaps 15'-0'' long by 12'-0'' wide; suppose she is sitting in a chair placed in the center of one of the long walls, close to the wall. The top drawing in *Figure 6-9* shows the appearance of such a room, seen from the spectator's position, including the space within the cone of focused vision. Now suppose that the room is transported bodily to the stage, Belasco-fashion, without alteration except for the omission of the fourth wall, which is invisible to our imaginary spectator, since she has her back to it. Suppose that the spectator is then given a seat in the auditorium. Obviously, she would get a slightly different view of the room from each seat in the auditorium, but let us select for her the most typical seat, exactly in the center of the auditorium, let us say 40 feet from the front edge of the stage. The center drawing in *Figure 6-9* shows what the room would look like from that viewpoint. A comparison with the top drawing will demonstrate that the real room, unaltered, looks different from the two points of view; on stage, the ceiling seems lower and the side walls have narrowed, with the result that the back wall dominates the picture.

Figure 6-9. Reality and theatricality. The top and center pictures have the same floor plan, but different viewing distances; the center and bottom pictures have the same viewing distance, but different floor plans. To make comparisons easier, the position of the picture plane has been varied to produce pictures of the same width. *Top:* a living room, viewed by someone sitting in a chair with her back to one wall. *Center:* the same section of the room, placed on stage without alteration and viewed from the auditorium's center. The most important alteration is in the apparent loss of depth. *Bottom:* a stage set, in which all of the objects have been redesigned. (See *Figure 6-10* for the matching floor plans.)

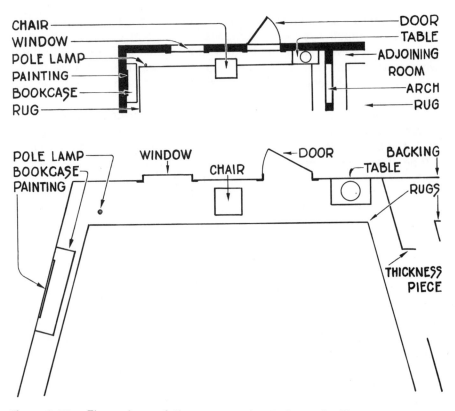

Figure 6-10. Floor plans of the room and set shown in *Figure 6-9*. The floor plan of the actual room is shown at the top, that of the stage set at the bottom. Only that part of the room that would lie within the cone of focused vision of the person sitting as described in *Figure 6-9* is included in the floor plans and the perspectives.

Architectural facts require that the spectator actually sit in a position in the theater similar to that described above; esthetic considerations, however, require that her visual experience in the theater match as closely as possible that illustrated in the top drawing. To achieve such an effect, then, the room presented on stage cannot be a simple reproduction of a real room, but must be altered in design. The perspective drawing at the bottom of *Figure 6-9* indicates the appearance of the adjusted set from the spectator's seat in the center of the auditorium. (*Figure 6-10* shows the floor plan of the set.) A comparison of the three perspectives will demonstrate the value of slanting the side walls to achieve a more convincing duplication of the visual experience of ordinary life.

Many scenes in ordinary life, particularly outdoor scenes, are not dominated by straight lines or right angles. Nevertheless, when they are simulated on stage, the same kind of spreading must be done if the visual experience of the spectator is to match that of ordinary experience. Even a setting showing a forest or an irregular garden will in fact involve visual spreading, however disguised.

Projection, the second perspective alteration, is made necessary by the fact that as we move farther from any object, it becomes visually smaller. A door that looks large from a distance of six feet may seem quite small and unimpressive if we move out to normal viewing distance in the theater (say 40 feet). A wallpaper pattern made up of sprays of white flowers on a blue background may be charmingly effective across a normal room but become simply a textured blur from 40 feet away. To counteract this perspective diminution, the door would have to be greatly enlarged for use in the theater, and the wallpaper pattern would have to be redesigned on a larger scale, with perhaps simpler motifs and greater contrast between the pattern and the background. This process of compensating for perspective diminution in the theater is called *projection,* and it is essential to all aspects of the art; acting, sound effects, makeup, costumes, set design, etc., must all be projected to seem natural to the audience. It is for that reason that real furniture, real plants and flowers, ordinary decorative paintings, and normal clothing not only are ineffective on stage, but seem unreal.

Projection

Scenic Enlargement

The problem of projection was extreme in the enormous Theater of Dionysus, in ancient Athens. The average spectator was so far from the stage that it was found necessary not only to enlarge such scenic elements as doors and walls but also to expand the actors themselves. Low stilts were fastened to their shoes to make them taller, and enormous masks were built, which amplified and thus projected their features; the combined result was to increase the actors' heights by a foot or a foot and a half. Their costumes were then padded to match, so that they would not appear unnaturally thin. From up close, they appeared of superhuman size; from the audience, they seemed to be of normal size.

Expansion of actors is almost unknown in the modern theater. The designer must ordinarily assume the size of the actors as a given and unalterable fact that operates as a limit to the projective expansion of scenic elements. It is simple enough to design a chair that will look, from a distance of 40 feet, exactly like an ordinary chair from eight feet away; but when an actor sat in the enlarged chair, the difference in scale would make him look ridiculous. Consequently, perspective adjustment must be compromised. The designer should carry it as far as possible toward the goal of compensating for perspective diminution, stopping short of the point where the expansion would call attention to itself and to the difference in scale of the actors. Many architectural features and objects found in ordinary life are standardized in size; this is particularly true of such things as typewriters, telephones, and the height of chair seats and desk tops. Many other things, however, occur in many different sizes. Doors may vary from 1'-6'' in width up to 4'-0'' or more; a window may be tiny or occupy a whole wall; books, drapery designs, pictures hung on the wall, trays, coffee tables, wastebaskets, etc., may be daintily minute or huge. Where a range of sizes is available, the artist may effectively design in the upper half or third of the normal range, without enlarging the elements incredibly or distractingly.

Forced Perspective

The reverse of perspective projection constitutes a valuable technique known as *forced perspective;* it is used to make stages and sets look deeper than they actually are. This technique has been used ever since the theory of perspective was first applied to set design, centuries ago.

As has been indicated, the appearance of a scenic element depends to a great extent on its distance from the viewer. The closer an object is to the viewer, the larger it appears, so that if a colonnade were built running from front to back of the stage, the columns in front would be seen as distinctly taller and broader than those at the back. In addition, the spatial relationships of parts of an object change as it is moved away from the viewer. Thus, if two large boxes of the same size were placed on stage with their open sides toward the audience, one of them at the edge of the stage and the other against the back wall, the spectators would see proportionately more of the sides of the front box.

The Method of Forcing

The technique of forced perspective involves simply an exaggeration of the spatial alteration and shrinking effects of actual perspective. Suppose, for example, that the designer includes in a set a series of large arches, each one parallel with the front of the stage and placed one behind the other so that the audience looks through each to the next one. If the stage is 30'-0'' deep, and ten arches are provided, the farthest arch will appear clearly smaller than the front one. Suppose, however, that the stage can be made still deeper, and the arches respaced so that the last one is 60'-0'' behind the front one; it will appear still smaller. Essentially the same effect can be produced by designing and building the arch to a smaller size, so that when it is placed 30'-0'' from the first arch, its visual dimensions will match those of the full-sized arch at the greater distance.

The method of determining the correct dimensions for perspective forcing can be worked out from the discussion of perspective projection in

Chapter 13. Rather than duplicating that discussion, I will state it here in an abbreviated form, which will be clear only after the student has mastered the material in the later chapter.

1. Extend the perspective grid (described in Chapter 13) to the distance to be simulated.
2. Draw the scenic unit, in perspective, as it would appear at that distance.
3. Identify the actual distance at which the unit will appear in the set.
4. Using the scale provided by the perspective grid for that actual dimension, measure the drawing of the unit.
5. Prepare working drawings specifying the shape of the unit as shown in the perspective drawing, with the dimensions as determined in step 4.

This method will not only provide the correct dimensions for building the unit in forced perspective, but will also define its shape accurately.

The Limits of Forcing

There is a limit to the acceptable use of forced perspective. In effect, the method squeezes a deep set into a shallower space; but the actors' bodies will not be altered, so that while a front arch in the colonnade described may be suitably related to their heights, the arches toward the back may be noticeably, and even ridiculously, out of proportion. Units placed well behind the acting area, so as to be separated from the actors throughout the play, may be designed quite freely in forced perspective. Even in the case of the colonnade described, the forcing of the perspective scale may be unnoticeable if it is possible to restrict the action to the front half of the stage. Forced perspective is most frequently used in ground-rows, which are usually placed close to the back wall, and that use is so common as to be standard. It is a somewhat troublesome design technique, but if used carefully, it is a valuable scenic resource. It is not at all impossible to produce a practical set design that doubles the apparent depth of a stage, and with great care, the effect might be still further extended. To watch a performance in such a set and then examine the set from on stage after the last curtain is a startling experience.

In this book, forced perspective is illustrated most clearly in sets for two plays. In the *Antony and Cleopatra* set *(Figures 6-3* and *6-19),* it was intended that the individual arches composing the set appear identical in size to the audience; actually, their heights varied from 15'-0'' to 8'-3'', with the result that the stage appeared to be about twice as deep as it actually was.

In the wing-and-drop sets designed for *The Importance of Being Earnest (Figures 2-18, 6-14, and 6-15),* the stage picture is broken into four planes, composed of three sets of wings and the back wall. Similar pillars, wallpaper patterns, and other details appear throughout the set, but beyond the first pair of wings they are diminished in false perspective; thus, the wallpaper pattern for the Act I set was drawn to four different scales. Forced perspective is also illustrated in the groundrow in *Figures 7-6, 7-7,* and *7-8.*

THE PATTERNS OF SCENERY

Each set design constitutes a pattern that is in some ways unique. However, it is helpful, especially for the beginning designer, to think of sets as belonging to three broad types, although of course no such classification can be more than a convenience when applied to works of art.

The Box Set

Perhaps the most familiar of the three types is called the *box set.* In its simplest form, it closely resembles a five-sided box, with the back and side walls of the set (usually made up of flats) forming three sides of the box, the stage floor the fourth side, and the ceiling resting on the walls the fifth side; sometimes such sets are used without a ceiling, although they would still be included in the same category. The sixth side is missing, and the structure is turned so that this open side is pointed toward the audience, parallel with the front edge of the stage. (See *Figure 6-11.*)

The box set differs in shape from an ordinary wooden or cardboard box in two ways: openings must be cut in the walls to allow actors to enter and exit; and the side walls are farther apart at the front than at the back, in conformity with the principle of perspective spreading.

The box set is seldom used in this simplest form. Many variations are possible (see *Figure 6-12*): stairs may be introduced; walls may be made irregular with bays and extensions; one side wall may be built longer than the other, forcing the back wall to slant so that it is no longer parallel with the front of the stage; and the side walls may stand at different angles to the front of the stage. Perhaps the most extreme variation is to omit the back wall altogether, lengthening the side walls and swinging them together at the back so that only one corner of a box is shown, with the proscenium opening cutting diagonally across it.

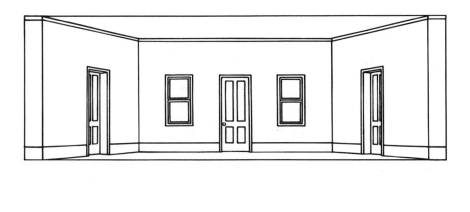

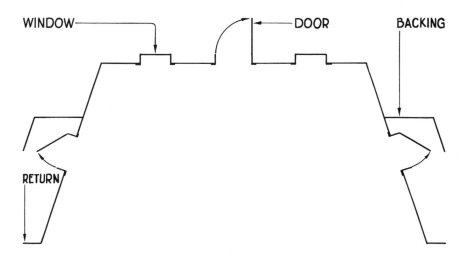

Figure 6-11. The basic box set pattern. The simplest pattern is shown. Sets are seldom designed in this basic form, but more complex patterns can best be analyzed as variations of this one. Some of the possible variations are illustrated in *Figure 6-12.*

The box set is only a little over a hundred years old, and there is currently a slight tendency to reduce its use; however, in varied and disguised form it is still probably designed more frequently than either of the other two types, since it is the most effective means of representing the interior of a room. In addition, it is the easiest type of set to build, since it is made largely from flats that in most theaters can be taken from stock; and it makes it easy to hide backstage areas from the sight of the audience, a problem that is more difficult to solve for other types of setting.

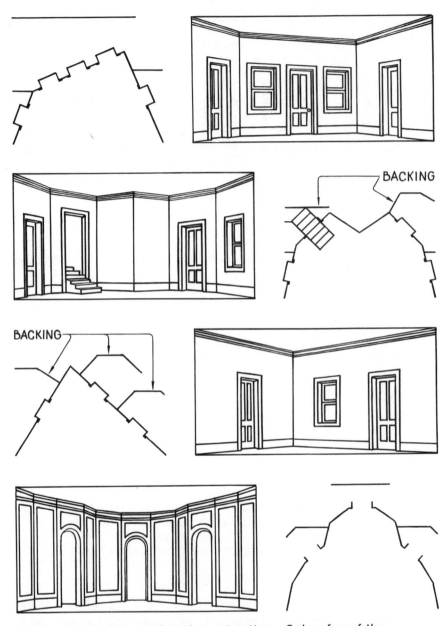

Figure 6-12. Variations of the box set pattern. Only a few of the enormous number of possible variations are shown, each one in ground plan and perspective. In the top set, the back wall is angled; in the second set, it is replaced by four short wall segments, arranged in the shape of an *M*. The third set shows the side walls swung together. In the bottom set, the three walls of the basic box set are replaced by eleven narrow walls.

Returns

Unless the side walls are sharply angled so that the front edges extend far off stage (an awkward arrangement), some members of the audience will be able to see past them, into the offstage wing spaces. It is customary to mask this area by attaching a special flat, called a *return,* to the edge of each side wall, extending off stage parallel with the front edge of the stage. Such flats are not an integral part of the set, and they may be painted a neutral color, preferably black. More commonly, the decorative pattern of the side wall is carried around the corner and applied to the return. Besides masking, returns also help guide the act curtain past the edges of the side walls.

Ceilings

The space above the set must also be masked, to hide the ropes by which the scenery is hung. Even if the scenery is not flown, the simulation of an ordinary room requires that a ceiling be provided. Ceilings are somewhat troublesome; they interfere with lighting the stage, they are difficult to set in place, they tend to foul the lines leading to the grid, and they are somewhat difficult to stiffen so that they will not sag. However, they have two great advantages: (1) they make an interior set much more convincing, and (2) they add solidity to the set, since the weight of the ceiling resting on the tops of the flats makes the entire structure more rigid.

Various types of ceilings have been devised, including the single-flat ceiling, the book ceiling, and the rolled ceiling. Any good book on stagecraft will give detailed instructions for constructing all three types. The generally most convenient one is the book ceiling. It is made in the form of two large flats, long enough to extend from one side of the stage to the other and wide enough so that their combined width is at least equal to the depth of the ordinary set; the precise dimensions are dependent on the size of a particular stage (especially the proscenium opening) and the depth of set a particular designer normally specifies. The flats are hinged together on the face to form a two-fold, with hinges not more than 3'-0'' apart and with the joint dutchmanned. The flats are hung from the back by the hinged joint. When the rest of the scenery has been put in place, the leaves of the ceiling are spread apart, and it is lowered until it rests on the tops of the flats that make up the walls of the set; usually, it will extend slightly beyond them at the sides and back.

Since the length of the individual flats is greater than the length of available lumber, pieces must be fastened together with scarf joints for the ceiling stiles. Normally, only one ceiling is built for a particular theater; it can be repainted for each show to match the set, but it should not usually require rebuilding. Because it is permanent equipment, and because its size and use involve considerable stress, it should be built with special care, and the corner blocks should be 12″ on a side. The ceiling is suspended by special ceiling plates, which are bolted to it, and which have rings to which the ropes can be tied.

The ceiling has a tendency to sag; consequently it may be necessary to stiffen it in the center by permanently fastening a 1 × 3 or 1 × 4 board on edge perpendicular to the surface of the ceiling, close to the hinged joint, on the back of the unit. It is preferable that the ceiling not extend all the way to the front of the set; holding it back a foot or more provides more space for the beams of spotlights, especially those used to light the back of the acting area. To provide masking, a narrow flat should be added, perhaps 12″ or 18″ wide, running the full width of the ceiling and fastened permanently just above the front edge. This masking unit also functions, like the center stiffener, to prevent the front edge of the ceiling from sagging.

It is possible to mask the overhead area in other ways, especially by using horizontal beams running parallel with the front edge of the stage. If they are designed correctly, they will provide adequate masking while still leaving open spaces between them, which can be used as passages for light. The method of checking the adequacy of the masking is described later in the chapter.

False Prosceniums

Usually, the proscenium opening is thought of as a scenically neutral frame that serves primarily to define the acting area and separate it from the auditorium space. However, it may be temporarily rebuilt in harmony with the set for a particular play; the temporary structure, called *a false proscenium,* becomes an integral part of the set design. Since the new proscenium may, in effect, extend the set forward in front of the curtain, the director may take advantage of the added space to enlarge the area used by the actors; consequently, a false proscenium is a useful device for stages that do not have adequate depth.

The ordinary methods of building flats are used in constructing false prosceniums. They may be two-dimensional, and they may be placed either in front of the proscenium wall or behind it, extending out into the edges of the proscenium opening. Thickness can be simulated by *trompe l'oeil* painting, or the false proscenium may be built completely three-dimensional; in that case, it is most likely to be designed to fit both in front of, and inside of, the real proscenium.

False prosceniums differ from other scenic units only in minor ways. Because they are closer to the audience, they must be built and finished somewhat more carefully. Since they outline the entire proscenium opening, they are likely to be larger than any other scenic units and consequently require design and construction that provide sufficient bracing and rigidity. Their size alone makes them somewhat more difficult to build than normal flats, but not prohibitively so. Their effects of enlarging the scenic space and of fitting the scenic frame to a particular set design make them extremely useful devices that designers should regularly consider in planning their sets.

The same techniques that provide economy of material and construction time in building ordinary flats also apply to false prosceniums. Most often, analysis of a design will demonstrate that much of the structure can be made up of flats already in stock. Even a false proscenium with a highly irregular outline can usually be built by fastening standard flats together to form a basic rectangular structure, producing the special shapes by adding edging units, either cut from thin plywood or built in the form of irregular flats by normal framing and canvassing methods.

Extremely effective false prosceniums have been used by many set designers, and the student should be able to find interesting examples in the many published collections of set designs. In this book, the device is illustrated by the false prosceniums included in the sets for *Antony and Cleopatra (Figure 6-19)* and *The Importance of Being Earnest (Figures 2-18, 6-14,* and *6-15).*

False prosceniums are most frequently used for box sets, although they are equally adapted to the wing-and-drop pattern and, if properly designed, may also be used for three-dimensional sets.

Before the introduction of the box set, the *wing-and-drop* set had been standard. The back walls of the two types of sets are essentially the same, although the back for the wing-and-drop was sometimes made of a piece of unframed cloth (hence the term *drop*), rather than in the form of flats. The essential difference was in the treatment of the side walls, and a resulting difference in overhead masking.

The side walls of a box set are usually made up of a series of flats, placed side by side to form a solid wall at a simulated angle of 90° to the front edge of the stage. If these individual flats were separated, and each one turned so that it was parallel with the front edge of the stage, the result would be a series of what are called *wings,* which, together with the back wall, would constitute a wing-and-drop set. The box-set ceiling will not fit on such a set, and its removal opens the overhead space to the sight of the audience. Masking was accomplished by hanging a short drop or a flat overhead, with its long edges parallel to the floor, connecting the two wings of a pair. Such masking devices were called *borders.* Any number of wings-and-borders could be used in a set, although four or five pairs of wings were most common. (See *Figure 6-13.*)

The details of the scenery were then painted on the wings, drops, and borders, the edges of which could be straight or shaped to match the

The
Wing-and-Drop
Set

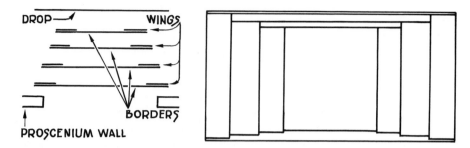

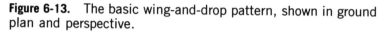

Figure 6-13. The basic wing-and-drop pattern, shown in ground plan and perspective.

structures which they were supposed to represent. (See *Figures 6-14* and *6-15.*)

During the last part of the nineteenth century and the early part of the twentieth, the wing-and-drop pattern was strongly attacked by designers who were interested in popularizing three-dimensional scenery. The major defect of the wing-and-drop is that it does not effectively simulate the appearance of most rooms, since it does not permit the ceiling and side walls to be built as continuous structures. However, colonnades and arcades, and rooms from the more heavily decorated periods, with heavy beams and bays, are readily adaptable to the wing-and-drop style. The pattern provides easy masking and is especially suitable to exterior sets. Elements such as buildings, trees, and bushes are separated in real life, so that constructing them as isolated wings does not distort them, as it does solid side walls.

The wing-and-drop style has some additional advantages. It permits very fast shifting, requires little storage space, and makes possible the use of a large number of sets. For a play requiring five different sets, for example, the wings for each set could be stood in place in groups, those for the first set hiding the others during the first scene. At the end of the scene, the setting could be changed by simply sliding the first wing in each group off stage to reveal the second, which would already be in place. A similar number of drops could be hung one behind another, and the first raised to reveal the second, thus completing the scene shift.

Perhaps the greatest advantage of the style was its cheapness and simplicity of construction, which enabled designers to achieve a degree of elaborateness and spectacle that would otherwise have been impossible for them. The student may find it interesting to examine some of the widely reproduced designs of Piranesi and the Galli-Bibiena family, which have a magnificence and splendor that constitute a major defense for the wing-and-drop as a legitimate scenic method.

The wing-and-drop style went out of fashion more than half a century ago, but it is still frequently used for period plays, especially nineteenth-

Figure 6-14. A modern imitation of the nineteenth-century wing-and-drop style: a set for *The Importance of Being Earnest,* Act III. All details except the furniture are painted on flats with specially shaped edges. [Photograph by Austin Studio.]

Figure 6-15. A modern version of the nineteenth-century woodwing style. Borders and wings are edged with S curves to suggest leaf shapes. (*The Importance of Being Earnest,* Act II.)

century melodramas, and it is occasionally used in modified and disguised form even for contemporary plays. The sets in this book for Sheridan's *The Rivals (Figure 3-35)* and *The Critic (Figure 14-1)* and Wilde's *The Importance of Being Earnest (Figures 2-18, 6-14,* and *6-15)* are intended to match closely the early wing-and-drop style. Those for *Story Theater (Figure 1-3), Antony and Cleopatra (Figure 6-19),* Beckett's *Waiting for Godot (Figure 2-5),* and Lorca's *Blood Wedding (Figure 6-18)* display some wing-and-drop influence.

Three-Dimensional Scenery

It is much more difficult to describe three-dimensional scenery than that of the other patterns, since each set typically has a highly individual ground plan. It may be helpful to divide this category into two subgroups: scenery in which the main function of the additional thickness is visual and scenery in which the main function is practical (that is, scenery the actors actually use during the performance).

The first type is more closely related to scenery made up of flats, which in the nineteenth century regularly simulated a third dimension by means of painted shadows and thickness pieces (and frequently did so more effectively than most modern commentators are willing to admit). Solid elements were often combined with the basic assembly of flats, so that many ordinary box sets, when dressed with thickness pieces, pilasters, inset doors and windows, bays, window seats, full-sized fireplaces, bookcases, and picture frames, created a very convincing appearance of solidity. When such elements are moved out from the walls to which they are attached, so that columns become free-standing colonnades, fountains appear as detached structures, and staircases curve up from the center of the stage rather than being sunk into the wall, the set becomes categorizable as three-dimensional without having changed in any very radical way from a freely handled and fully decorated box set made up primarily of flats. (See *Figure 6-16.*)

Only one further change is necessary to move such a set into the final category, the fully practical three-dimensional. The change is essentially one of emphasis: the three-dimensional elements are enlarged, joined together to form impressive free-standing structures, and flats are either dispensed with or relegated to the level of unobtrusive masking devices. (See *Figure 6-17.*) The major elements of three-dimensional sets of this type are platforms, stairs, columns, and arches, although abstract shapes may be designed that are not adaptations or reflections of architectural elements. Functionally, three-dimensional sets of this type are distinguished by the fact that actors make free use of them, standing on the platforms, climbing the stairs, and swinging from one part of the structure to another somewhat like children on playground equipment.

Scenery of this type may have major esthetic interest in its own right, and it makes more effective use of height as a device for expressing vary-

Figure 6-16. A three-dimensional set that differs only moderately from the familiar box set pattern.

Figure 6-17. A three-dimensional set almost entirely free of the box set. Although it provides ledges for actors to sit and walk on, it functions visually as a free-standing structure, silhouetted against an abstract pattern of light projected against a sky cyclorama.

ing degrees of dominance among the characters in the play, and for controlling the attention of the audience, than any set that relies only on the single level of the stage floor. Designing sets of this type involves two major difficulties: because the artists are less controlled by architectural traditions, they must make bolder and more imaginative decisions; and to the extent that solid walls are discarded, masking the offstage areas from the view of the audience becomes more difficult. The advantages of practical three-dimensional sets are so great that beginning designers should make a conscious effort to push their own style in this direction, especially because they are likely unconsciously to favor the more familiar box set.

SPECIAL SCENIC PATTERNS

Several styles of scenery have been developed that make possible a significant saving in materials and construction time. Each style also carries with it esthetic implications, so designers may choose to use them even when economy is not a problem. These patterns can be adapted to all of the types of scenery that have been discussed above.

Unit Sets

The term *unit set* is used to describe what are actually two separate scenic devices. One of them involves the construction of a basic frame with a series of openings (which may be rectangular or otherwise shaped). This unit functions as a kind of neutral skeleton: the focus of attention is on plugs (usually flat but sometimes three-dimensional) that are placed behind the openings to complete the stage picture. The set can be shifted by removing the plugs and replacing them with others of different design. The set for Lorca's *Blood Wedding* shown in *Figure 6-18* is of this type.

Figure 6-18. Type 1 unit sets: Lorca's *Blood Wedding.* The basic set consists of five asymmetrical arches (shown at the top, with back lighting to suggest moonlight). *Center:* The two side arches are backed by flats painted bright yellow yellow-orange. The furniture is painted the same color and decorated with peasant designs. *Bottom:* White flats are fitted into the side arches, and the double-arch unit is filled in with a half door and a white window flat. Altogether, five sets were provided for the play, each one making use of the same basic arrangement of arches, but varying in lighting, furniture, backing walls, and color scheme.

The second type of unit set consists of a group of different elements that can be rearranged to form varying patterns.

Unit sets of both types, of course, are useful only for multiset shows. Practically, they have the advantages of reducing cost, requiring less storage space off stage during the run of the show, and increasing the speed of set changes. Their esthetic effect, however, is much more important. The immobile frame of the first type of unit set constitutes a very strong unifying element in the various sets, not only because it remains as a constant part of each stage picture, but also because it defines a ground plan that remains essentially uniform throughout the show.

The second type of unit set contributes almost equal unity, but more subtly; the arrangement of the scenic elements may be planned so as to greatly alter the stage picture, but the presence of the same forms in each picture provides a solid unifying element, however extremely the separate arrangements vary. The sets for *Twelfth Night* shown in *Figures 7-6, 7-7, and 7-8* illustrate a rather simple unit set of the second type.

The practical and esthetic advantages of the unit set make it an important part of the designer's resources. Its inherent artificiality tends to push the design in the direction of theatricality, so that it is less suited to naturalistic drama, but it is an effective method for the majority of plays that are written in theatrical rather than naturalistic styles. The designer is likely to find the second of the two types more usable, since it provides a degree of unity comparable to the first type without its visual and blocking rigidity of ground plan.

Multipurpose Abstraction

Although both types of unit set are simpler to construct than fully realistic settings, they still require some rearrangement of scenic units for each successive locale, which usually involves closing the curtain and interrupting the flow of the play. With plays such as those by Shakespeare, this can greatly alter the feeling of the performance by breaking up the continuity of the script into a series of staccato scenes that are sharply marked off from each other, rather than being fluidly joined.

This type of play can be illustrated by a single example, *Antony and Cleopatra*. The play is broken into forty-two scenes, in twenty-six different locales. Of these locales, nineteen are used only once, four are used twice, two are used three times, and one is used nine times. There are nine interior locales—rooms of buildings located in Egypt, Rome, and Athens. A tenth, at Cleopatra's tomb, and an eleventh, on the deck of Pompey's ship, may be regarded as either interior or exterior. The fifteen remaining locales are outdoors, including the hills near Alexandria, nearly a dozen different places on battlefields, a street in Rome, and a street in Alexandria, Egypt. Some of the scenes are very long, but two successive scenes last for only seven seconds each, another is eight seconds long, one is nine, one is ten, and many others are only a little longer. The quick succession of short scenes is intended to produce an impression of speed and excitement. To provide a full realistic setting for each (as has been done) is to destroy the intended effect. In one notorious production of *Hamlet,* the set changes required as long a total time as the action of the entire play! Even to snap the curtain shut, rearrange a few units, and open it as quickly as possible would unacceptably impede the action.

Figure 6-19 shows one designer's solution to the *Antony and Cleopatra* problem. The stage was covered with a flight of stairs, with alternate steps made deep enough to serve as individual acting areas. Pairs of slanted pillars were joined by headers, defining four entrances at stage right and three at the left. Because more of the play takes place in Egypt than anywhere else, the set was decorated in Egyptian motifs. The stage, however, was treated as essentially unlocalized. Properties, including tables and chairs and a sedan cot were brought in by servants to give some occasional suggestion of place, but primarily, the dialog itself was relied on to indicate locale, as in the original Elizabethan production. The only major change of set took place during an intermission, when the second and third headers were removed to reveal Cleopatra and her women standing just behind the last header on a concealed platform, the dialog identifying the scene as taking place in her "monument." The stage floor and low steps thus served multiple purposes, as a battlefield, a street, and even a room in the palace, with the action flowing uninterruptedly as Shakespeare intended it.

Figure 6-19.   A multipurpose set for Shakespeare's *Antony and Cleopatra.*

This kind of play appears not only in the Elizabethan period but also in earlier and later periods. Contemporary plays of this type include *Of Thee I Sing, The Rimers of Eldritch, Story Theater, The Death of a Salesman,* and several of Eugene O'Neill's plays.

Such multiset, short-scene plays may be set by a method at least distantly related to the Elizabethan and ancient Greek theaters, and faintly suggested by the *Antony and Cleopatra* example.

We tend to think of the Elizabethan stage as fundamentally a single squarish platform, and the Greek theater as a long shallow shelf, but they were much more flexible than that, as a glance at the plays (especially the Greek comedies) will clearly demonstrate. Both theaters were essentially unlocalized acting machines, providing a variety of acting areas, trap doors, stairs, mechanisms for flying actors, and entrances.

The modern designer can develop a structure that has those characteristics, even though superficially it may resemble neither theater in appearance any more than they resembled each other. The classic structures had to satisfy the requirements of a wide range of plays, including those to be written after they were built; the modern designer has the simpler task of meeting only the requirements of a single play. As one consequence, he can afford to decorate his set more precisely in harmony with the mood of the particular production.

Such a structure may be related to abstract sculpture; it is more likely to be suggestive of architecture, making use of platforms, arches, colonnades, entrance openings, and flights of stairs. Directors can use the setting by exploiting whatever hints it may provide of locale (using openings as entrances, using a nook to suggest a prison cell, following a broken path around the stage and over platforms and steps for a chase scene, etc.). These suggestions can be reinforced by providing a few items of furniture or properties, which may be carried on by servants or the principal actors themselves. At first thought it might seem that such a setting would appear bare and inadequate. In fact, given only a few hints, the imagination of the audience will clothe the stage with all the details that full design and industrious construction could furnish, and more. When Lorenzo says

> How sweet the moonlight sleeps upon this bank!
> Here will we sit and let the sounds of music
> Creep in our ears. . . .
> Sit, Jessica. Look how the floor of heaven
> Is thick inlaid with patines of bright gold.

the imagination of the audience, assisted by a faint wisp of music in the background, will provide a more beautiful moonlit bank and star-spangled sky than any set designer, construction crew, or lighting instruments could create.

It should be emphasized that this type of scenery, called *multipurpose abstraction,* is not an easy shortcut to design. Indeed, the easiest setting for the designer is probably the fully realistic. The abstract set must be multipurpose—that is, it must genuinely serve all the purposes of the play. When Othello is brought to trial before the Duke and Senators of Venice, the set must create an impression of the pomp and richness of the Venetian court; it must provide the officials with an elevated and impressive position that will enable them to dominate the accused, although they are sitting while he is standing; there must be areas where the arresting officials can stand guard, out of the way, unobtrusive yet ominous. And the setting must be so designed that when Othello begins his great speech—

> Most potent, grave, and reverend signiors,
> My very noble and approved good masters,
> That I have ta'en away this old man's daughter,
> It is most true; true, I have married her;
> The very head and front of my offending
> Hath this extent, no more.

—he can confront the officials without turning his back toward the audience. He must have room to move while still maintaining the fact of his confinement, and as his defense grows steadily stronger, he must be able to rise (esthetically, if not physically) to a position of triumphant dominance, where it seems unnecessary even to make a formal statement of acquittal. Solving the problems inherent in just this scene would tax the ingenuity of many designers, yet all the other requirements of the play must also be considered. Multipurpose abstract sets are in fact the most difficult to design effectively, even though they may often be by far the best solution to the problems of a particular production.

The performance possibilities of abstract sets are likely to be less evident at first glance than those of any other type of scenery, and directors are likely to use them with more individuality. Such a set creates its own esthetic, defining negative space and decorating positive space. Abstract scenery typically exploits negative space more fully than any other type of setting. The following designs make use of multipurpose abstraction in varying degrees: *Rosencrantz and Guildenstern Are Dead (Figures 1-6 and 7-1), The Taming of the Shrew (Figure 3-23), The Tempest (Figures 2-14, 9-7, and 9-8),* and *The Lark (Figures 2-7, 6-20, and 6-21).*

The set for *The Rimers of Eldritch,* shown in *Figures 6-23, 6-24,* and *15-9,* can also be considered an example of multipurpose abstract scenery, although some of the stage areas are so sharply localized that the set

Figure 6-20. A multipurpose set for *The Lark:* the throne room.

Figure 6-21. The trial scene in *The Lark*.

Figure 6-22. Simultaneous staging. More than half a dozen small sets are combined in this production of a medieval liturgical play, ranging from heaven at the left of the picture, through the Sea of Galilee *(right center),* to hell *(right),* represented as the mouth of a monster, from which devils emerge.

is cited in the next section to illustrate simultaneous staging. This ambiguity is a reminder that however useful categories of scenery may be, they are to some extent artificial. Every well-designed set precisely fits the play it is prepared for, and it creates its own category; good designers start with the script and the experience that the director hopes to create for the audience, not with some external, preconceived set category that the script is then altered to fit.

The liturgical dramas of the middle ages were written as a series of short scenes. They were first performed in the churches, and each scene was localized for the congregation by a conspicuous property or a visual symbol related to the action. For instance, when the friends of Jesus stopped to buy ointments to anoint his body, a table symbolized the shop. Especially popular were scenes taking place in hell, which was identified by the head of an enormous monster with gaping jaws, out of which ran actors dressed as devils. (See *Figure 6-22.*)

    These minisets were arranged in various patterns; in one church in France they were placed in a row facing the congregation. The actors would stop at the first scenic symbol and perform one scene, then they would move to the second, representing a change of setting. Although only one section of the acting area was used for each scene, all of the scenic

Simultaneous
Staging

elements were visible throughout the performance; this type of arrangement is known as *simultaneous staging.*

Some modern plays specify sets in which different locales are represented simultaneously. Examples are Eugene O'Neill's *Desire Under the Elms,* Tennessee Williams's *Summer and Smoke,* Dylan Thomas's *Under Milk Wood,* and Arthur Miller's *The Death of a Salesman* and simultaneous staging may be applied to other multiset shows, even when not suggested by the script. Plays that are best suited to this treatment are those made up of short scenes, with frequent shifts of locale. Since simultaneous staging requires restricting each scene to a special area of the stage, using it for plays where the action is limited to a single set for a long period of time can restrict the actors undesirably and produce a noticeable imbalance in the use of the stage area. Occasionally a minor setting can be incorporated into the major set so as to be unobtrusive throughout most of the play. For example, an exterior balcony, used for a prolog or for a brief appearance of one or two characters at the end of the play, may be built above the ceiling of a set showing the interior of a room.

A set for Lanford Wilson's *The Rimers of Eldritch (Figure 6-23*; see also *Figures 6-24* and *15-9)* illustrates a close approach to the medieval pattern, developed for a contemporary play. The script is an unusual one, involving about a dozen identifiable locales, as well as some action that takes place without clear localization. Furthermore, the actors shift from one setting to another without interruption of the action, particularly in the courthouse-church scenes, where, without changing their positions on stage, the jury suddenly becomes the choir in a church, and the judge becomes a preacher. One or two of the settings are used only briefly, for example, the grocery store.

The set shown in *Figure 6-24* at first glance suggests multipurpose abstraction: it is made of a series of apparently randomly placed platforms, the offstage outline of which roughly follows a semicircle. But closer analysis, or attendance at the production, would demonstrate that between half a dozen and a dozen identifiably localized areas are included, all but two arranged around the offstage edge of the structure. Moving from stage right to stage left (the spectator's left to right), they are the cafe, the Johnson home, the church-courtroom, the Jackson house, the Atkins house, and the Truit front porch. An unobtrusive counter is set on the lowest platform, at center, to localize the area as belonging to the store during the brief scene there.

The central area of the set is essentially unlocalized. It is used for parts of the play that are choreographic and that do not have precise locale. It is also an adjunct to whatever localized area may be in use at the moment; for example, when the Atkins house is in use, the adjoining unlocalized platforms may represent the yard or other areas near the house, providing approach and entrance space. Even localized areas may be used in this way; for instance, actors entering the cafe can approach it

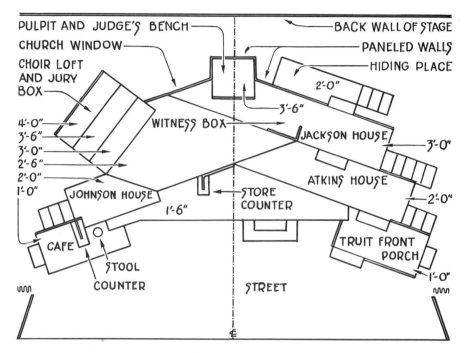

Figure 6-23. Simultaneous staging for a modern play: *The Rimers of Eldritch.* (See also *Figure 15-9* for a model of the set.)

Figure 6-24. Set for *The Rimers of Eldritch.*

across the stage floor or down through the Johnson home. The strip of stage running along the front of the entire structure was used by the actors as a clearly localized street, giving access to the cafe, the Truit porch, and the central platforms. The ambiguous area used for both the climactic church scene and the courtroom scenes is given emphasis by placing it at upstage center and raising it higher than the rest of the set. The backing for this area is also ambiguous, incorporating paneled walls suggestive of a courtroom, but with a stained-glass church window inserted. In production, the transitions between the courtroom and church were indicated by bringing up spotlights placed behind and above the stained-glass window for the church scenes and fading the lights down for the courtroom scenes. There was a clear alteration in the appearance of the area, providing an unobtrusive but unmistakable clue to the audience.

At the end of the play, two of the actors must disappear from the stage during a blackout, but their voices must still be clearly audible for the final speech or two. The set provides for this by means of the upper left platform. It is a foot below the Jackson house level, so it is invisible to the audience. The wall backing the courtroom area, left of the judge's position, extends four feet along the hidden platform. Thus it was easy for the two actors to step down to the concealed platform during the blackout, move to a position behind the backing wall, face the audience, and deliver their final lines clearly while remaining out of sight.

It will be seen that this set, with localized areas arranged in a curved line and joined by an unlocalized area, matches the medieval pattern of mansions and *platea* very closely. It should be pointed out that this arrangement sprang from the designer's analysis of the script and was not imposed upon it by starting with the simultaneous staging pattern and then adapting the play to fit the pattern. The similarity to the medieval setting is thus fundamentally coincidental; nevertheless, the set demonstrates that even an unusual style may occasionally be well suited to a contemporary play.

The Thrust Stage   One further development remains to be mentioned. It is called the *thrust,* or *open, stage,* a characteristic mark of which is the absence of a proscenium wall. The majority of existing theaters are still of the proscenium type, but the majority of new theaters are provided with thrust stages, so designers are likely to work in theaters of both types.

The proscenium functions to frame the stage picture. Esthetically, the proscenium defines the acting area, separating it clearly from the section of the auditorium where the viewers sit. When reinforced by differential lighting, with the stage space behind the proscenium brightly lit and the auditorium darkened, the proscenium serves to focus the attention of each member of the audience on the actors and their scenic environment and away from the other viewers. Mechanically, the proscenium wall serves as a major masking device, hiding waiting actors, scenic supports, lighting instruments, and machinery for shifting.

The most significant effect of the thrust stage is that it sets up a relationship between audience and actors that is different from that produced by the proscenium; exactly what that relationship is has not yet been defined, and the range of its potentialities remains to be fully explored. The typical thrust stage is lower than the proscenium stage, it has steps leading to the auditorium floor, and it is moved forward closer to the audience. In its most extreme form the thrust stage may have no front curtain.

The removal of the proscenium makes it possible to produce visual effects that are not practical when using the traditional closed sets; at the same time, it presents the designer with new mechanical and esthetic problems. Exploring the resources of the open stage and solving its special problems will be major concerns of designers during the next few years.

The proscenium, like a picture frame, tends to somewhat reduce the sense of three-dimensionality, whereas the open stage emphasizes it. The greater sense of space that is an inherent characteristic of the open stage enables designers to make more effective use of architectural and sculptural patterns, which they may find both more challenging and more interesting. The proscenium stage tends to push designers slightly toward naturalism; the open stage influences all elements of production strongly in the direction of greater theatricality. The new stage arrangement is least suited to the conventional box set, and it tends to increase the visual emphasis on such properties as waving flags and such effects as billowing smoke. Mechanically, opening the stage to the audience makes shifting more difficult and obtrusive, so that such techniques as simultaneous staging and unit sets become especially useful.

THE FIRST SKETCHES

The designer is now at last ready to make his first exploratory sketches. At this point, he has become thoroughly familiar with the scenic requirements of his script: he has an impression of its mood, he has traced its story and identified its locale, and he has prepared a list indicating the scenic elements that are absolutely necessary for the production. Taking one of the small-scale floor plans of his theater, he sketches on it an arrangement of those elements, roughly marking the positions of walls, doors, and furniture, as well as any other items on his list.

Sketching Methods

Some designers prefer to make their first sketches on blank paper, transferring them to scaled diagrams of the theater only when they have got through the first tentative trials. Another technique is to draw a series of sketches on the same sheet, on top of one another. In that case, the designer should make his first sketch very light, just dark enough to be visible; then each successive sketch may be made slightly darker. Anywhere from three to five sketches may be drawn on top of each other without confusing them, if the designer is careful. That method has no value if a particular sketch is to be totally abandoned, but it may be helpful if the major lines of one sketch are carried over into the next; for example, if a fireplace is to be shifted from one wall to another without changing the shape of the room, it may be easier to draw both positions on the same diagram. That is especially true if the designer is uncertain as to which of the two positions is preferable.

Finally, the designer may find it convenient to cut floor plans of scenic elements out of colored paper, measuring them to the same scale as was used in preparing the diagram of the theater; for example, small squares, cut 18″ (to scale), may be used to represent chairs, a long rectangle a davenport, and a strip a fireplace. These cutouts can then be moved around the diagram of the stage, and various arrangements can be tried out without drawing them permanently on the sheet.

The Rough Check

Having made his first sketch, the designer then runs through the play in imagination, picturing the paths of actors' movements as they enact the major scenes of the play. At this point, he need not check with the playscript itself; what is wanted is simply a rough, approximate estimate of the workability of the sketch, particularly the identification of any aspects of it that will make it difficult or impossible for the actors to perform.

Typically, serious defects in the arrangement will become immediately apparent. Perhaps the designer will discover that a table placed in a strong position to emphasize a breakfast episode hides the easy chair in which one of the characters must later enact an important death scene; or that when the villain drops a box (supposedly containing the severed hand of his latest victim) beside the davenport, the box, instead of being forcefully placed at the focus of attention, is hidden by actors who can stand nowhere except in front of it.

If such defects appear, the designer takes a second copy of the floor plan and sketches a revised arrangement, intended to correct the defects of his first sketch. This is then subjected to the same analysis.

Exploring Alternatives

The emphasis on defects, however, is not an entirely accurate one. Even if the set shown in the first sketch seems to function well, the designer should continue to construct alternative arrangements, testing each for its relative effectiveness. Ideally, he should draw as many different designs as possible, until either his time or his imagination is exhausted, so that he may make his final selection with confidence that it is not simply adequate, but the most effective he is able to devise. This suspension of decision until all practically possible alternatives have been explored is another distinction between the skilled professional and the amateur, who is more likely to leap desperately at the first usable design he develops, defending it to himself and to others with frightened intensity. Characteristically, the amateur is likely to be satisfied with his first sketch, whereas the skilled professional is more likely to be dissatisfied even with his final design, since he is aware of how many additional possibilities he was unable to explore, either because of lack of time or because of the limits to his own mental and imaginative flexibility.

As the designer becomes more experienced, he will find that he steadily grows in his awareness of more and more diversified solutions to problems of design. The new designer is likely to reach the limit of his imagination very quickly, finding that successive sketches constitute only minutely varied repetitions of his first few ideas. Since he cannot wait for further experience to open up new areas to explore, it may be helpful to suggest some rather artificial tricks that may start him thinking in a different direction. The difficulty may be that his mind is so filled with the one or two basic patterns he has developed that he is unable to look at the design problem from any other point of view. He must therefore try to destroy the pattern in his mind and shift to a new angle.

One method is actually to shift the orientation of the original sketch: the designer should redraw the back wall, placing it in the position of one of the side walls, and shift all the rest of the set, including the furniture, into the new position. Such an arrangement will undoubtedly be unacceptable in many ways. The artist should then attack those new problems, moving the furniture, altering the positions of the windows and doors, to produce the best arrangement possible, with the back wall in its new place on the floor plan.

Next, the designer might try reversing his treatment of one or more major elements in the design. Suppose he has drawn a large bay at the center of the back wall, extending back behind the main line of the wall perhaps 8'-0''. He should make a second sketch in which the same curved wall section appears, but pushed forward into the room. Again, the new pattern will require major alteration of other elements in the design.

Suppose the designer's first sketch contains a stage area raised 8'' above the stage floor by means of platforms. He might reverse the areas, sinking his platform area to the level of the stage floor and raising the rest of the stage above it.

It is not to be expected that sketches based on such devices will always, or even as much as half the time, result immediately in designs that are improvements over the original plans, although that may happen occasionally. These tricks, however, will help the artist break through the restrictions of his first designs and may well start him on new sketches that attack the problem from an entirely different point of view.

Particularly at this point in the process of designing, the artist should avoid discarding any idea without testing it in an actual sketch. In fact, he should think of this step as a process of systematic exploration of design solutions. He will ultimately select only one for actual use, but the broader and more complete his exploration, the better the final solution is likely to be. Even if he should at last return to his first sketch as the best one he has made, he will do so with confidence that he has demonstrated its superiority and has not missed a better solution for lack of analysis of the problem.

How many sketches he will develop depends on factors that cannot be assessed here. Some designers make a very large number of trial sketches; others do much of their analysis in imagination, making fewer actual sketches on paper. The first of those two procedures is safest for the beginning designer. The complexity of the playscript itself is undoubtedly a factor, and in general it would seem that the better the script the longer it takes to design for it: certainly, Mary Chase's *Harvey* presents fewer design problems than Shakespeare's *Antony and Cleopatra*. Probably, increasing experience will slowly reduce the number of preliminary sketches that a designer must make. One experienced designer typically makes from 20 to 30 such sketches for each set design; if the student designer's fortieth sketch satisfies his test for adequacy, he can probably feel that he is functioning well.

When he has carried his exploratory sketching as far as his time and ability will permit, the designer selects from all of his drawings the one that his rough checking indicates is most effective as a machine for organizing the arrangement and movements of the actors.

The First Script Check

Once the designer has selected the most effective sketch, he turns to the script and subjects the sketch to a closer check, following all major movements through the play, imagining the actors using the set as he has indicated it, and checking at each moment for the effectiveness of their positions and movements in relation to the total blocking pattern. This more detailed check is likely to result in still further adjustments in the design, although it is to be hoped that they will be matters of detail, and that it will not be necessary to discard the design altogether and start over again. If that should happen, it would probably be an indication that the designer had not done his preliminary steps adequately.

THE SCALED DRAWING

When the sketch has passed the script check, whether or not additional adjustment has been necessary, the designer is ready for the next step. This consists of preparing an accurate scaled drawing of the ground plan that he has already drawn in sketch form.

For this drawing, it is wise to use a larger scale than that of the diagram showing the entire theater. The designer should have available a drawing giving the floor plan of the stage itself, including the proscenium opening and, if possible, the offstage areas. If such a drawing is not already at hand, he should prepare one.

This drawing constitutes a permanent part of the designer's equipment, and since it is useful only if properly drawn, it should be made with care.

The Ground-Plan Grid

The sheet of cardboard on which the drawing is made should be as large as can be handled conveniently; the standard 22″ × 28″ size is satisfactory. The most convenient scale is ¾″ = 1′-0″, which allows an area representing 29′-0″ × 37′-0″ to be drawn on the standard sheet; if the stage is larger, it is preferable to use a larger sheet of cardboard rather than reduce the scale.

The essential diagram consists of a rectangle with dimensions equal to the depth of the stage and the width of the proscenium opening. This should be laid out in light pencil, centered horizontally on the cardboard, with the bottom margin considerably larger than the top. It is convenient if the front edge of the stage and the side walls of the offstage areas can also be included, but it is better to leave them out than to reduce the scale of the entire drawing. The proscenium wall should be outlined; it will probably extend off the edge of the cardboard on each side.

Most proscenium openings are built to full feet (32′-0″ rather than 32′-3″). As an example, let us assume a proscenium opening of that dimension, a stage depth of 24′-0″, a proscenium wall 2′-0″ thick, and a forestage 4′-0″ deep (measuring from the back edge of the proscenium wall). The drawing, then, will show a centered rectangle 24′-0″ × 32′-0″. Directly below it, running from each corner to the edge of the cardboard, will be two long rectangles 2′-0″ wide, representing the proscenium wall. And 2′-0″ below the bottom edge of the proscenium wall will be a horizontal line, either running to the edges of the cardboard or stopping at the proper points, representing the edge of the forestage. The large rectangle thus represents the full acting area and hence the major area in which scenery can be placed, with its top edge marking the position of the back wall of the stage.

The next step is to mark off all of the edges of that rectangle at intervals of ¾'', representing a foot on the actual stage. If the width of the stage consists of an odd number of feet, the midpoints of the top and bottom edges of the rectangle should also be marked. When this has been done, the drawing is ready for inking.

Color Coding

For reasons that will be discussed later, it is important that the lines of the diagram be relatively faint and that they be drawn in two colors. Red and green are suggested. To make sure that the lines are not too obtrusive, the designer should dilute the ink with water. Ordinary fountain-pen ink is better for this purpose than the more expensive drawing ink, and it will stand a surprising amount of dilution. Clean bottles should first be filled about two-thirds of the way with water, then ink should be added a drop at a time until the right concentration is reached. The diagram is to be used as a guide under tracing paper; the inked lines should be clear enough to be easily legible through the tracing paper, but no brighter. The designer can check the color of the ink solution by drawing lines with a clean pen dipped into it and checking the lines as soon as they are dry by laying a scrap of tracing paper over them to see whether they are easily visible.

When the ink solutions have been prepared, the vertical center line of the stage rectangle should be drawn in red by connecting the center points of the top and bottom edges. (All of the lines of the drawing should be made with the finest penpoint available.) Alternate lines parallel with the center line should also be drawn with red. If the stage width is an odd number of feet, the three red lines in the center will be 1'-6'' apart; all other red lines will be 2'-0'' apart. If the stage is an even number of feet in width, all red lines will be 2'-0'' apart. The bottom line of the rectangle should then be drawn in red, and alternate horizontal lines should be filled in with the same color.

As soon as the red lines are dry, the remaining lines of the rectangle should be drawn in green. Finally, the lines lying outside the acting area (representing the proscenium wall and the edge of the stage) should be traced with undiluted black ink, and the space that must be allowed for the movement of the front curtain should be indicated by drawing a short black line across the side edges of the grid at the proper distance behind the proscenium wall (probably somewhere between 1'-0'' and 1'-6'').

Using the Grid

In effect, the diagram described constitutes a floor plan of the stage divided into 1'-0'' squares, forming a large number of easily distinguishable reference points. The grid operates as a two-dimensional ruler, making it much easier to lay out the lines of a set than if the drawing were done on a blank sheet. Since it is intended for permanent use, no marks representing a particular set should be made on it directly. Instead, the set should be drawn on a sheet of tracing paper fastened to the grid by small strips of masking tape. The tracing paper should be larger than the stage area but somewhat smaller than the entire sheet of cardboard.

When the drawing has been completed, the tracing paper must be removed and repositioned on a new sheet of cardboard; consequently it is important that reference points be marked, and it is sound practice for the designer to train himself to habitually trace them before starting to draw the set itself. The most effective points to mark are the corners of the stage rectangle, as well as the points at which the center line crosses the top and bottom edges; these marks should be in the form of tiny + signs, which are more accurate and more legible than dots.

The designer's preliminary sketch is made freehand and consequently will deviate considerably from precise accuracy. The purpose of the gridded drawing is to transfer the sketch to a larger scale and at the same time to adjust its accidental deviations, producing an accurate scaled drawing.

The construction crew must utimately build the scenery in conformity to the angles, dimensions, and arrangements set down in this drawing, and when the set is assembled on stage, it must match the ground plan. Wherever possible, it is sound practice to arrange the lines of the set so as to make the construction and erection of the set as simple and efficient as possible. For example, where it can be done, walls should be placed so that their corners coincide with easily identifiable points on the grid; it is preferable to slant a side wall so that its back corner is 8'-0" from the center line, rather than 8'-1¾". If the wall at the back of a hall behind an archway can be placed precisely on the grid line 20'-0" from the front edge of the stage, that is better than placing it 19'-10½" from the edge. Even furniture that does not stand parallel either to the lines of the grid or to one of the side walls may be placed so that one leg, for example, stands exactly in the center of one of the grid squares, and another leg rests on one of the grid lines.

No esthetic effect should be abandoned simply to make the drawing or the placement of the actual set on the stage easier, but where the measurement can be simplified without damaging the effectiveness of the design, the more practical arrangement should always be preferred. Often, the measurements that must be made in erecting the set can be made easier by shifting a scenic element as little as half an inch, and such a shift may be completely undetectable from the audience. If the designer must choose between increasing the difficulty of construction or assembly and preserving the esthetic effectiveness of his design, then of course he should preserve the design, but it is a mark of amateurism to demand complexity of technical work without any resulting increase in esthetic effect.

Adjustments   The more accurate drawing may reveal unsuspected problems in the design, especially for the beginning artist. In particular, he is likely to discover that furniture, when drawn to measure, occupies more space than he had expected: that the hero, for example, cannot maneuver his wheelchair between the desk and the davenport. As the designer becomes more experienced, he can expect that such problems will occur less frequently. When they do occur, however, he must in effect return to the sketching step and attempt to make whatever adjustments are necessary. At this point it may be especially helpful for him to cut paper shapes accurately scaled to the sizes of the various pieces of furniture and move them on the paper until he has developed a satisfactory arrangement; he can then mark the key points, remove the paper silhouettes, and complete the outlines.

SIGHT-LINE CHECKING

An experienced designer is aware of the problems of visibility and masking at every point in his designing, including his first exploratory sketches. However, precise checking of those factors can be done only after an accurate scaled ground plan has been completed.

Since it is the function of the designer to provide an effective visual background for the actors, he is necessarily concerned with the visibility of the various elements in his design from the different seats in the auditorium. If, for example, the hero's climactic speech must be delivered from a stair landing, then the designer must determine that the landing he has provided will be clearly visible to every member of the audience.

In an ideally designed theater, all backstage machinery, doors, and such miscellaneous paraphernalia as radiators and heat ducts are invisible to the audience, even when there is no scenery on stage. Such design is entirely within the range of possibility, but, unfortunately, most theater architects do not achieve it, so that even with a box set some members of the audience may be able to see backstage areas that obviously do not belong to the set: they may be able to look through french doors and see a radiator fastened to the back wall of the stage, where they should actually see the bushes and flowers of a garden, or they may be able to look overhead and see the ropes by which scenery is suspended from the grid, the lighting equipment, and even the grid itself. In addition, the movements of actors and technicians backstage during the performance may be visible. In such cases, the designer must provide scenery especially planned to conceal the areas, objects, and people that the audience should not see; such scenic elements are called *masking.*

The adequacy of the artist's designs, with regard to both visibility and masking, is checked by means of sight lines, drawn across the floor plan and the cross-section view of the theater. Since the position of the seats in the auditorium is a necessary factor in such checking, the large floor plan showing the entire stage and auditorium must be used.

Sight lines may be drawn freehand across the preliminary sketches. More precise checking must be done on an accurate scaled drawing of the set. Since the two drawings showing both the stage and the auditorium are part of the designer's permanent equipment, he should not mark on them directly, but should first cover them with tracing paper, and then carefully draw the set, as well as the sight lines, on the tracing paper. These drawings will not be reproduced in permanent form, so it is not necessary to mark guide points on them.

Horizontal Sight Lines

All members of the audience see the set from their own distance and angle. Let us select a single viewer for demonstrating the use of the floor plan: for example, the person sitting in the center seat of the last row. With a ruler, draw a line from this seat to the edge of the left proscenium, and extend it till it touches the back wall of the stage. Then swing the end of the ruler over to the opposite side of the stage and draw a second line from the seat to the right proscenium and on back to the back wall. The two lines, with the back wall and the front edge of the acting area, will form a trapezoid defining the area visible to the person sitting in this particular seat: he will be able to see an actor or a piece of scenery placed inside that area, but anything outside the edges of the trapezoid will be invisible to him. This method can be used to determine whether a scenic element is visible when it is intended that the audience see it, or whether areas that are not supposed to be seen are effectively hidden.

In this process, which is known as checking sight lines, it is not necessary to consider every seat in the house. (See *Figure 6-25,* where the critical seats are in the fourth row.) Usually, only two seats need to be checked: the extreme left and right seats in the front row. In most theaters, elements that are visible to members of the audience sitting in both those seats will be visible to all the rest of the audience, and elements that are hidden from them will be hidden from everyone. Checking with a few additional seats will determine, for any particular theater, whether the two extreme front-row seats do give adequate information about visibility for the entire audience; if they do not, the designer should analyze the plan to determine the fewest sets of sight lines that must be checked and which seats are critical.

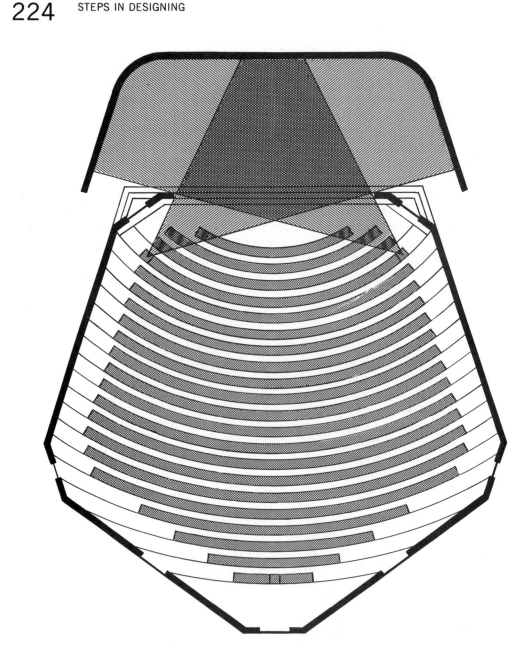

Figure 6-25. Checking horizontal visibility. In the theater shown, the end seats in the fourth row are the key seats for checking horizontal visibility. The area visible from each seat is shaded; the five-sided double-shaded area represents the portion of the stage that is visible to all of the members of the audience. (Auditorium of a convention and assembly building designed by the author for a midwestern boys' school.)

For the ordinary theater, the two sets of sight lines drawn from the end seats of the front row define the maximum area with which the designer has to work; all scenery that is essential to the play must be placed within the resulting trapezoid. Few plays, however, are performed on a completely bare stage. Each scenic element placed on stage produces additional sight lines. These should be checked during the process of design, whenever doubt arises with regard to visibility, and the entire set must be given a final sight-line check before the work proceeds beyond the ground-plan stage.

Masking

The designer focuses first on placing important scenic elements where they are clearly visible to all the members of the audience. Then he turns his attention to the problem of hiding areas of the stage that he does not want the audience to see. For interior settings, this mainly consists of preventing the audience from looking through doors, windows, and other openings to the backstage area.

When a stage door leads to another room, masking ordinarily consists of setting a wall of the offstage room behind the door, at a distance great enough not to get in the way of the actors who must enter or exit. Such a wall need not be complete; only the area the audience can see need be built. The minimum width for such a wall is determined by drawing sight lines from the critical seats (normally, the end seats of the first row) through the edges of the door opening. (See *Figure 6-26.*) A line is then drawn on the plan so that it crosses the outside sight lines. Measuring that line will indicate, to scale, the minimum width required for complete masking.

Obviously, the farther the masking is placed from the door, the wider it must be, so it is convenient to place it as close to the opening as is consistent with easy use of the entrance by the actors. The dimension indicated by this method is a minimum; masking is nearly always built considerably wider than this minimum, so that even if the masking piece is not set in place with hairline precision, the opening will be entirely covered. If stage space is limited, a masking piece 4″ to 6″ wider than the distance between the sight lines may be adequate, thus allowing a 2″ to 3″ margin for error on each edge; designing the masking a foot or more wider than the area to be masked allows a more comfortable margin for error and should be done, if practical. The maximum width of the masking is determined only by convenience, particularly the amount of space back stage. When the masking is largely hidden (as by the leaf of a door), and when it is not likely to attract great attention, two or three stock flats may be hinged together, dutchmanned, and painted to serve as masking; such a unit will stand by itself, with the flats set at an angle, and may require

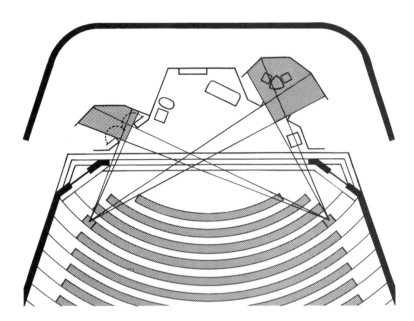

Figure 6-26. Checking horizontal masking. The drawing shows the front part of the same theater shown in *Figure 6-25,* with a stage set in place. Sight lines are drawn through the door openings from each of the critical seats; the fact that each sight line strikes a backing flat indicates that the backing is adequate. The shading indicates the extent of the areas beyond the doors that are visible to the audience, although no single member of the audience would be able to see all the areas marked.

no bracing. If the set must be shifted, it can readily be folded and moved to the side of the stage for production storage by one or two stagehands.

Vertical Sight Lines

Vertical sight lines usually present fewer problems than horizontal, but they must be checked with equal care. In this case, the critical seats are those closest to and farthest from the stage, usually the end seats in the front row and the center seat in the back row. If the theater has a balcony, sight lines must also be drawn from the highest seat, usually the center seat of the last row. Again, the sight lines are used to determine whether the audience can see actors and scenic elements that should be visible, and whether areas that should be invisible are hidden, either by the major scenic units or by masking.

In checking vertical sight lines, it is usually not necessary to include every scenic element in the cross-section drawing. In the main, two questions must be answered: whether actors who are placed above the stage floor (on stairs, on platforms, or flown) will be visible from the farthest seats, and whether the overhead area is effectively masked for the members of the audience who sit closest to the stage. Consequently, the designer usually needs to draw only the outlines of platforms or stairs and of ceiling structures. The height of the proscenium opening is significant, although the critical height is the level beyond which the audience cannot see; thus, if the height of the architectural opening is reduced by a short curtain hung across it, the functioning top of the opening is the bottom of the teaser curtain.

Two examples of the use of vertical sight lines will be given: one illustrating the problem of masking, the other the problem of visibility.

Masking with Beams

Often, ceilings in stage sets are simulated by running false beams parallel to the front of the stage. Such beams are made by joining two flats at right angles, one hanging on edge facing the audience and the second serving as a thickness piece, attached horizontally at the lower edge of the vertical flat. If such beams are to be convincing, no member of the audience must be able to see between them: in design terms, each beam must mask the opening between itself and the beam in front of it. Whether beams as designed will mask adequately can be determined by drawing them to scale (in cross section) on a cross-section drawing of the theater and extending sight lines from the seat closest to the stage. (See *Figure 6-27.*)

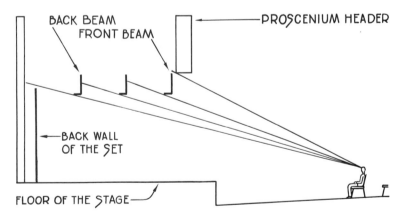

Figure 6-27. Checking vertical masking. The back wall and three overhead beams are shown, in cross section. The adequacy of the masking is checked by drawing sight lines for the seat closest to the stage. As shown, the front and back beams fail to mask properly. The center beam masks adequately, since the sight lines strike scenic units (the center and back beams). The errors in masking can be corrected by enlarging the scenic units or adjusting their positions.

If the beams mask adequately, each sight line connecting the seat with the far edge of the thickness piece of one of the beams will run into the vertical flat of the beam behind it (except for the last beam, where the sight line should strike the back wall of the set). If the sight line runs above the next beam, then the beams must be placed closer together, or their dimensions must be changed by making the vertical flats wider or the thickness pieces wider, or both.

Visibility

For the set for the Albion production of *Antony and Cleopatra,* the risers of the steps that fill most of the stage were originally specified as 8'' high, making the back step 4'-0'' above the stage floor. Actors standing at that height would be clearly visible to the entire audience. However, the climactic scene of the play requires that Cleopatra be on a platform high enough to place her well above actors standing below. In order to give maximum visibility to the actress in that scene, the designer decided to place the platform at the back of the stage, over the 4'-0'' level of the stairs. Safety requirements necessitated a platform floor that, with its support, would be 4'' thick. This platform was drawn to scale on a cross-sectional diagram of the theater. Since the actress was about 5'-6'' tall, a point was marked on the drawing at that distance, to scale, above the floor of the high platform. Checking the sight lines for the first row indicated that the actress would be clearly visible, but sight lines drawn from the back row demonstrated that the upper half of her body would be hidden from that position. (See *Figure 6-28.*) As a result, the dimensions of the flight of steps were cut in half, making it possible to reduce the height of her platform by 2'-0''. Checking the back-row sight lines indicated that in the new position the actress would be effectively visible.

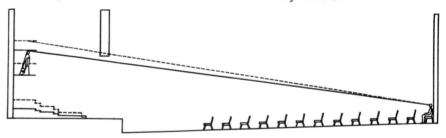

Figure 6-28. Checking vertical visibility. Here, the critical viewpoint is that of the spectator farthest from the stage. The dashed lines indicate the original sight line and the stairs and high platform as originally designed. The actress's head would have reached as high as the dashed sight line, and she would not have been fully visible to spectators in the last row. The dimensions were therefore reduced as indicated by the solid lines.

With a little experience, a designer will discover that it is not always necessary to check all four sight lines (two from each critical seat). Often, the only sight lines needed for checking the masking behind a door in the side wall of a set are the upstage line drawn from the extreme front row seat on the same side of the auditorium, and the downstage line drawn from the matching seat on the other side. For vertical checking of visibility, often only the upper sight line from the last row need be drawn, and for vertical masking, only the upper sight line from the front row may be necessary. Simple inspection of the drawings may indicate that visibility or masking is adequate from one seat, and that sight lines need actually be drawn only from the other seat; sometimes even a single sight line is sufficient. But all sight lines should be drawn wherever there is any doubt about the adequacy of visibility or masking of the design.

THE FINAL SCRIPT CHECK

After the ground plan has been drawn carefully and to scale, the design must be submitted to a final rigorous test. The artist should go through the script once more, this time checking every movement, however slight, and the arrangement of all of the actors at every moment of the play. Obviously, many different blocking patterns could be developed for a particular play with any set that had been designed for it, and the designer need not select from among alternative possibilities; but he must make certain that his design makes it possible for the director to arrange the actors effectively at every moment in the play, and that the pattern of movement can be designed so as to conform to the practical and esthetic requirements of the play.

GETTING THE DIRECTOR'S APPROVAL

Some excellent directors are unable to read a ground plan; that is, they must see a model or perspective drawing of a set before they are able to visualize how it can be used. If the designer is working with such a director, he must carry his design through to that stage before conferring with the director. Most directors, however, are able to test at least the functional adequacy of a set from the ground plan alone. In that case, the designer may prefer to submit his drawing to the director to be sure that the director has no objections to the design. It is likely that the director will want to give only tentative approval to the design at this stage, but the designer will know that he is not continuing with a design that the director finds unacceptable.

It will be a great help to the director in evaluating the drawing if the heights of all levels above the stage floor are indicated on the drawing. For example, the designer should print 2'-6'' in the center of the rectangle representing a platform of that height. It is more effective to indicate such heights as measured from the stage floor, rather than from adjacent levels. It is customary to identify height figures by enclosing each dimension in a circle. Often, for steps or small platforms, there is not enough space for such a marker; in that case, the word *high* can be added to the dimension, an explanatory note can be given in the margin, or circled dimensions can be placed in the margin, with arrows pointing to the matching levels. Here, as always, any mechanical rule can properly be altered if there is a resulting increase in legibility or convenience.

7

DESIGNING
for
Mood

In Chapter 2, the second function of scenery was identified as the expression or reinforcement of the mood of a play. Here, the word *mood* is used broadly to indicate all of the emotions the playwright hopes to stimulate the audience to feel during the performance of the play. An essential responsibility of the set designer is to assist the actors and other theater artists in producing that emotional response.

Each playwright typically handles emotion in an individual way, and plays vary not only in the intensity of emotions they arouse, but also in the kinds of emotions. Many different elements contribute to the emotional effect of a play: the events that make up the story, the personalities of the characters, even the experiences of the audience outside the theater. In addition, the playwright's own attitude toward the story is important, as is the verbal style of the dialog. All of these emotional elements, and any others that may appear in the play, are what, for lack of a better term, we will call *mood*.

The importance of designing scenery to express the mood of a play has only recently been fully recognized. For the first 2000 years of the history of the theater, any correspondence between the style or tone of a play and the scenic background was accidental; as we have seen, in

231

ancient Greece and Elizabethan England tragedies and farces were presented against essentially the same background. That a set should be emotionally expressive was first definitively stated and demonstrated in the designs and theoretical works of Adolphe Appia. But during the more than half a century since Appia, the emotional function of scenery has become generally accepted as second in importance only to its function as a machine for organizing the action of the play.

Designing for mood involves two problems, one minor and the other major. The minor problem is the difficulty of describing the mood of a play; the major one is how to express that mood visually.

Language is extremely deficient in emotional terms, and those that exist have never been defined with ideal precision. Even the familiar standard terms that we easily use in discussing drama are impossible to define acceptably: for example, *tragedy, comedy, farce, musical comedy, melodrama.* Euripides' *Ion* is listed among the Greek tragedies; yet it has a happy ending, it has strong elements that suggest musical comedy, and its general tone is one of bittersweet lightness.

Each play, then, must be examined on its own terms; the designer will find it helpful to describe its mood and tone as clearly as possible, but finally he must arrive at a vividly realized feeling of the mood of the play that will be essentially indescribable. In this situation, it is important that he bring his realization of mood to as sharp a conscious focus as possible.

FOCUSING ON TONE AND STYLE

The designer has already sensed something of the mood of the play in reading it for the first time, and incidentally during his further study of the script while designing his machine. Now he should turn to the script again and study it carefully, focusing on the tone and style. Certainly, the emotions expressed by the actors are of major significance, but he should notice also the attitudes of the playwright toward the characters, and he should try to imagine the reactions of the audience as they watch the performance. The verbal style of the script is also significant. In particular, the degree to which the verbal style matches that of ordinary conversation is of great importance in producing an effect of naturalism or artificiality; it constitutes an invaluable clue for the designer with regard to the degree of realism he should incorporate in his set.

When analyzing the mood of any play, the designer first has to study each scene in detail. He should make brief notes on every emotion and mood he finds expressed or hinted at. He must also note the varying tempos and rhythms. Even a one-act play may evoke a wide range of contrasting emotions. For example, Euripides' "tragedy" *Alcestis* includes mythic and realistic elements, moments of solemnity and moments of low comedy, passages of anguish and passages of sweetness. In addition, it has a very wide variety of tempo and rhythm, extending from the slow gentleness of Alcestis' scenes to the excited tumbling mood of Hercules'.

It should be obvious that not even an extended analysis could do more than indirectly suggest the actual tone of a play. There are no words, for instance, that will precisely categorize the emotions Euripides has combined; they can be felt very clearly by anyone focusing on them while studying the script, but they are essentially unnamable.

UNITY IN VARIETY

When the designer has finished his attempt to identify individually all of the moods and emotions in the script, he should lay the script aside and lean back and try to get as clear as possible an impression of the general effect of the play; that is, he must begin his study by concentrating on the sources of emotional variety in the play, but he must end it by concentrating on the element of emotional unity.

Euripides, for instance, has achieved in *Alcestis* an effect of unity at least matching the variety of his material; but its total effect is even more indescribable than the individual elements, so that anyone who wants to experience it must go to the play itself.

AFFECTIVE SYMBOLS

The visible elements of a set must have esthetic and emotional effects even if they are wholly realistic. The sleazy nightclub used in *Cabaret,* the depressing institutional lounge where *One Flew Over the Cuckoo's Nest* is set, the open-air seaside setting of Plautus's *Rope,* all help express the basic emotions of the plays, even if they are handled with simple realism, without concern for their overtones.

A less realistic treatment gives the designer more opportunity to use scenery expressively. Often, if the designer searches for it, he may be able to find a scenic element that will have strong emotional suggestion. So long as the emotions expressed match those intended by the script, his scenic element will probably fit harmoniously into the production, even if it is not required by a literal reproduction of the setting of the action.

Most often, such elements function as symbols, with emotional overtones. Any collection of set designs is likely to provide a number of examples. The distinguished designer Jo Mielziner frequently illustrated this device in his work. His design for Maxwell Anderson's *Winterset* used a moderately abstracted painting of the Brooklyn Bridge shrouded in fog as a backdrop, evocatively suggesting the spirit of the play. Other examples are the leaf shadows in *Death of a Salesman,* the drop for *The King and I* showing Siamese buildings, and the tangled barbed wire used in *After the Fall* to suggest the atmosphere of a concentration camp.[1]

Affective symbols also appear in several of the sets illustrated in this book. The set for *The Lark (Figure 6-20)* includes elaborately shaped pillars and Gothic arches suggestive of the middle ages, not only literally but in spirit. In addition, a visual focus for the set was provided by a stained-glass window, six feet wide and twelve feet high, which was used symbolically in the production: when Joan heard supernatural voices, spots behind the window were brought up, casting a vividly colored glowing pattern across Joan and out beyond on the stage floor; when the voices disappeared, the spots were brought down; when the voices did not speak, the window remained unlit. A similar symbol was used in *The Rimers of Eldritch (Figure 6-24)* to indicate the transition from courtroom to church, as has already been described. For a production of the antiwar play *We Bombed in New Haven,* one designer painted the entire set, walls and floor, in the unpleasant pattern and drab greens used for military camouflage.

A particularly successful affective symbol was used for a production of *Rosencrantz and Guildenstern Are Dead.* The title characters are minor and rather passive members of the cast of *Hamlet,* acted upon rather than acting, pawns in the hands of others more powerful than themselves. Although the modern play focuses on them, they retain the same characteristics. It seemed to the designer that they were presented as helplessly caught in a trap, as animals lost in a maze, running along the paths looking for a way out but finding nothing but cul-de-sacs. When he came to prepare his design, the maze simile seemed most expressive, so the set became a literal maze, with twisted paths leading nowhere. (See *Figure 7-1.*) One reviewer commented: "the set clearly contributes through its indefinable number of directions, false turns, and many levels to the depiction of the two characters who can eventually find no other possibility for themselves except death."

1.   These as well as other examples are illustrated in Jo Mielziner, *Designing for the Theatre: A Memoir and a Portfolio* (New York: Bramhall House, 1965.)

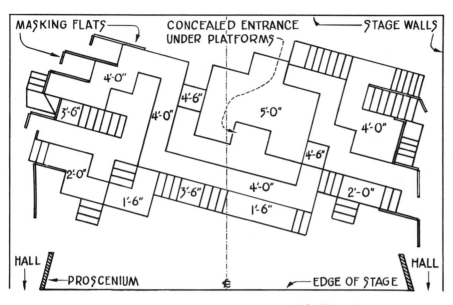

MASKING FLATS——— CONCEALED ENTRANCE ——STAGE WALLS
UNDER PLATFORMS

4'-0"

4'-6"

3'-6"   4'-0"   5'-0"

4'-0"

4'-6"

2'-0"

1'-6"   3'-6"   4'-0"   2'-0"

1'-6"

HALL   ⌐——PROSCENIUM   ₵   ⌐——EDGE OF STAGE   HALL

Figure 7-1. The set as a maze: *Rosencrantz and Guildenstern Are Dead.* (See also *Figure 1-6.*)

Symbols are not always so successful, and what seems like an excellent idea may evaporate on the drawing board or—even worse—may be discovered to be ineffective only after the scenery has been built. An example illustrated here *(Figures 7-2 and 7-3)* consists of two sets for *Hedda Gabler,* both developed by the same designer. Ibsen's plays are especially suited to the use of affective symbols, because he so often uses them himself (see *Ghosts, The Wild Duck, Peer Gynt,* and *A Doll's House,* as well as many other less obvious examples).

Hedda Gabler is the tragic story of a woman who feels she has been caught in a trap, the walls of which steadily close in on her until her only escape is suicide. The pressures of society are symbolized by the house in which the play is set. Once, during a walk with her fiance, trying desperately to find something to keep the conversation going, Hedda had expressed admiration for a particular large Victorian house, one that she actually disliked. As his wedding present to her, her fiance bought the house, to which they moved after their honeymoon. It thus becomes, symbolically, a kind of trap, visually suggesting the forces around her that will finally lead to her death. Throughout the play, the walls seem to be closing in more and more, like those of the dungeon in "The Pit and the Pendulum."

For his first production of the play, the designer attempted to express this ominous confinement by reducing the size of the living room in which the play is set; in his words, "It didn't work; all I got was a small room"

Figure 7-2. A set for *Hedda Gabler*, designed as a confining room.

Figure 7-3. Falling walls as a symbol: *Hedda Gabler.*

(Figure 7-2). The second time he was assigned to design a set for the play, he decided to look for a different symbol. He broke the walls of the room into sections, showing each one as falling forward, as if about to crush the people in the room *(Figure 7-3)*. The wall sections were of various widths, but on the average about six feet. Gaps were left between them, through which only darkness was visible. Each panel was set so that the top was a foot farther toward the center of the stage than the bottom—in other words, each leaned forward by a foot (they were supported by invisible wires). To increase the impression, the designer had them constructed in forced perspective, being wider at the top than at the bottom. In addition, a large and apparently very heavy cornice was added at the top of each flat.

As described, the set may seem so far from realism as to be dysfunctional; in fact, as the curtain rose, one's first impression was of an ordinary living room, and although the distortions were clearly visible throughout the play, the primary effect was not to destroy the identification of locale but to express the emotions intended. Although there are many ways to set this play, the director and designer were satisfied with the set described, feeling that it expressed the mood of the play as a realistic treatment could not have done.

These sets illustrate both the dangers and the possibilities of symbolic design. When design strays from the literal, the designer's task becomes more difficult, but the resultant set may be more interesting. Symbolic ideas must be viewed with suspicion and tested with great care, but when they work they are extremely effective.

MOOD IN VISUAL TERMS

Even the most realistic elements, of course, have emotional implications. The designer now has his list of notes reminding him—inadequately—of the various elements of emotion, mood, and tone that appear in his play. More important, he has so absorbed these elements that he has a clear image in his mind not only of them individually but also of the general overall mood.

His next step, then, is to turn to the ground plan he has designed and so clothe it that it will, as far as possible, evoke that mood and support the actors in their expression of it.

This brings us to the second, and most serious, problem in this aspect of design. It is one with which we are already familiar: there are no universally-agreed-on principles or rules with regard to the visual expression of mood. It is common experience that there is a vivid relation between setting and emotion. The apparent mood of a particular scene may vary greatly even when the only visual change is that the sun comes out from under a cloud and pours a golden light over the landscape. Some rooms seem cheerful, others depressing; some warm and intimate, others cold and impersonal. One writer, describing the emotions suggested by natural scenery, says "Some dank gardens seem to cry aloud for murder."

It is the designer's responsibility, then, to create the equivalent of a garden that cries aloud for murder, if his play is a mystery; to design a setting suited to brilliant and romantic deeds, if he is designing for *Cyrano de Bergerac;* or to design a set for raucous low comedy, if he is designing for *The Merry Wives of Windsor.* In the absence of objective principles, he must again apply the criterion of his own taste, imagining, as accurately as possible, what the reaction of an audience would be as it watched a particular play performed in a scenic environment of a particular design. And he can apply whatever principles experience suggests, even though they are, at this point in our knowledge, still an imperfect guide.

Scale

One basic factor in the emotional reaction to visual environment is scale. That is the primary source of the effect that the pyramids of Egypt have on every visitor. A tiny pyramid of stone, perhaps three inches high, intended to be used as a paperweight, produces a totally different effect from a pyramid stretching high into the sky, so large that a person standing close beside it cannot see it as a whole. A massive arch, rising eighty feet in the air with pillars three feet square, creates an entirely different impression from an arch of the same pattern reduced to a height of two feet and set in the wall to serve as a window.

In assessing the scale of a scenic element, the unit of measure is the human body. That is immediately obvious with regard to objects that are intimately used by actors. A telephone 18″ long would seem enormous; one 5″ long would seem like a toy; both, on stage, would look ridiculous— a perfectly legitimate effect, of course, for certain types of plays. An ordinary chair has a seat about 18″ square; a chair with a seat 3′-0″ square, especially if its other dimensions were enlarged proportionately, would look massive. The distinction, in scale, between a huge, impressive throne and a delicate seat for the dressing table may well be only a matter of a few inches. A door that exactly frames an actor—that is just wide enough and just high enough to enable him to walk through it without stooping or turning sidewise—will seem small; a door 10′-0″ wide and 15′-0″ high will seem overwhelming.

But scale in the theater does not operate on quite the same basis as in ordinary life. In Chapter 6, we discovered that objects must be expanded on stage in order to seem to be of ordinary size. The *normal* theatrical dimension, then—the dimension that makes objects seem ordi-

Figure 7-4. Variations in scale: columns for Shakespeare's *Antony and Cleopatra* and Mozart's comic opera *The Marriage of Figaro.*

nary, neither large nor small—is this expanded dimension, which should be taken as the basis of measurement. Objects larger than this dimension will seem large; objects smaller will seem small. It is for that reason that an ordinary chair, for example, looks small and delicate on stage.

Two examples of the expressive use of scale are the columns designed for *Antony and Cleopatra* and *The Marriage of Figaro (Figure 7-4).* Everything about the Shakespearean play is massive in scale; consequently, the columns designed for it were about 3'-0'' square. They rose to support a heavy crosspiece of similar dimensions, the underside of which was 13'-0'' above the stage floor. Mozart's opera, on the other hand, is a frothy and delicate farce. Columns used in a set for it were only 6'' wide and 10'-0'' high.

Thickness is an important factor in suggesting scale. The *Antony and Cleopatra* columns derive their impression of mass as much from the thickness pieces as from the dimensions of the front of the columns. Thickness pieces constitute a small part of a set, as built, since they are added only to the few edges of walls that are visible to the audience, but they contribute enormously to establishing the scale of mass—to identifying the set as heavy or as delicate and light.

Generally, differences in scale operate in two ways. A large scale seems most harmonious with tragedy; a small scale with comedy. In addition, a large scale suggests crudity; a small scale, refinement and delicacy. The first act of Thornton Wilder's *The Skin of Our Teeth* is set in a living room of a prehistoric home, immediately before one of the ice ages. To suggest crudity of construction, the furniture was designed with square legs almost 4″ wide. In *Antony and Cleopatra,* on the other hand, the design of the furniture attempted to suggest the sophistication and refinement of the Egyptian court by specifying furniture with legs about 1½″ wide, with decoration designed to make them look still slimmer. (See *Figure 7-5.*)

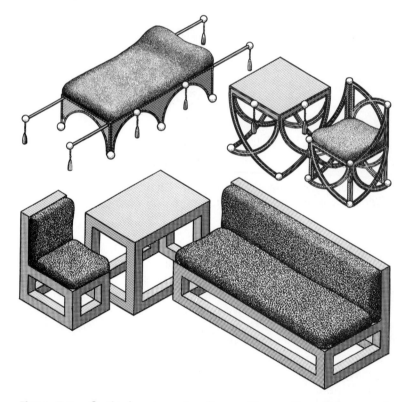

Figure 7-5. Scale in stage furniture. *Above:* The *Antony and Cleopatra* furniture was designed to suggest the refinement of the Egyptian court. *Below:* Furniture for *The Skin of Our Teeth* has legs 4″ square to suggest the crudeness of prehistoric construction.

Related to the scale used in design is the degree of visual texture employed. A set may be composed of broad, unbroken surfaces or built up from many small elements. Two sets representing rooms may have almost identical floor plans, yet vary greatly in the amount of detail: one may have three straight walls, while the other has walls that, while following essentially the same paths on the floor, are broken into a large number of nooks and crannies. Decoratively, one room may be painted a solid color, the other covered with a highly detailed wallpaper design, complicated wood paneling, cornices, an elaborate fireplace, pictures hung in heavily decorated frames, and complexly shaped drapes. The degree of busyness of a design operates much like scale, in suggesting mood. A relatively open design seems to suggest seriousness or tragedy; a busy design suggests farce, comedy, delicacy, and artificiality.

Busyness

     The sets illustrated in this book display a wide range of busyness, from the extremely open sets for *Blood Wedding (Figure 6-18.)* to the extremely busy design for the first act of *The Importance of Being Earnest (Figure 2-18)*. It may be interesting to evaluate the decisions of the designers with regard to the relationship of the moods of the various plays and the degrees of busyness appearing in the sets.

Related to both scale and busyness is the type of line employed in design. Long, straight lines suggest seriousness and tragedy; short lines, joined to form broken paths, changing direction frequently, suggest farce or comedy. Similar effects are produced by curves: long, simple curves seem better suited to tragedy; complex curves that frequently change direction suggest comedy. Curved lines have grace and sweetness; straight lines seem more severe.

Line

Symmetry suggests stability, balance, rigidity, artificiality, and rest; asymmetry suggests movement, imbalance, flexibility, naturalness, and tension. The qualities of asymmetry are more characteristic of drama than those suggested by symmetry: most plays are intended to produce a feeling of movement, excitement, and tension, rather than relaxation and immobility. Consequently, asymmetrical designs are much more frequently suited to stage scenery than symmetrical designs. Since there is a strong tendency for a beginning designer to plan symmetrically, students should consciously remind themselves to consider asymmetrical arrangements for each play they design. It is not intended to suggest that designers forbid themselves the use of symmetry, but simply that they resist their natural tendency to prefer symmetrical designs sufficiently to enable them to analyze each script in its own terms and then design the type of set that will be best suited to it.

The Symmetry-Asymmetry Continuum

The asymmetry of set designs may vary over a wide range, from sets so asymmetrical that no element in the left half matches any element in the right to sets where the two halves are identical except for a single minor detail. In fact, the designer can most effectively think of symmetry as occupying a broad scale, with total asymmetry at one end and total symmetry at the other. In the main, a set should occupy a point on the scale matching the degree of tension inherent in the script (although other factors, such as the degree of artificiality in the playscript, are also operative).

Among the sets illustrated here, several are entirely, or almost entirely, symmetrical: *Once Upon a Mattress (Figures 4-12, 4-13,* and *4-14), The Importance of Being Earnest (Figures 6-14* and *6-15), Simon Big-Ears (Figure 9-6),* and *Of Thee I Sing (Figure 9-10).* Others are extremely asymmetrical (see especially *The Tempest, Figures 9-7* and *9-8).* It will be profitable to examine all of the illustrations to evaluate the degree of success with which this aspect of design has been adjusted to the moods of the various plays.

An example of the use of varying degrees of symmetry is a set design for Shakespeare's *Twelfth Night (Figures 7-6, 7-7,* and *7-8).* The play, like all the other plays of Shakespeare, is extremely varied, defying categorizing, except perhaps for the hybrid term *tragicomedy.* In the production for which this design was created, two intermissions were inserted into the play, resulting in a first act of moderate length, a very long second act, and a very short third act. The first act dealt largely with what is called *exposition*—that is, with the introduction of the characters, an indication of what had happened before the play opened, and a statement of the problem of the play. The major section of the plot occupied the second act, an extremely varied one full of tension and uncertainty. In the short last act, the knots of the plot were cut through, the conflicts among all the characters were resolved, and the play ended happily with not one marriage, but three, the curtain coming down on the jester singing as he danced away to attend the wedding celebrations.

The play is a light, bright, fantastic one, and the designer attempted to match it with a set having similar qualities. The same scenic elements were used for each act, but arranged in three different patterns. For the first act, the units were arranged symmetrically, but the blocking was designed so that no scene used the entire stage; thus one scene might be played in the front left third of the stage, and the next well back at the center of the stage. Only the area used for a particular scene was lighted. The set thus combined elements of symmetry and asymmetry; although the floor plan was symmetrical, for the audience the actual stage picture was asymmetrical through almost all of the act.

For the second act—full of movement, tension, and uncertainty—the units were arranged in an extremely asymmetrical pattern.

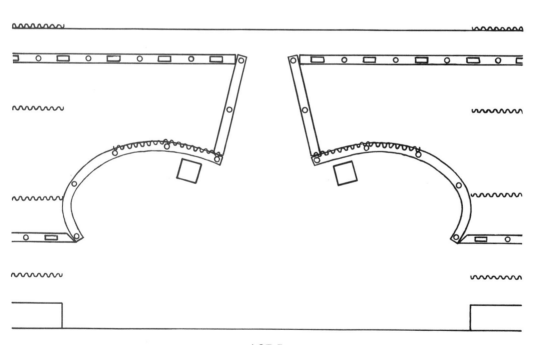

ACT I

Figure 7-6. The ground plan and perspective of a set for Act I of Shakespeare's *Twelfth Night.* The director inserted two inter-missions in the performance, thus breaking the play into three acts. The same scenic elements were rearranged for the dif-ferent acts, making this a type 2 unit set. The rows of pillars define acting areas.

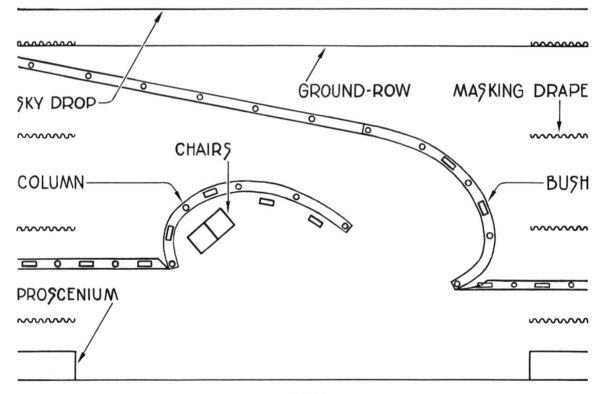

SKY DROP

GROUND-ROW

MASKING DRAPE

CHAIRS

COLUMN

BUSH

PROSCENIUM

ACT II

Figure 7-7. Act II, *Twelfth Night.* Note the asymmetry of the design.

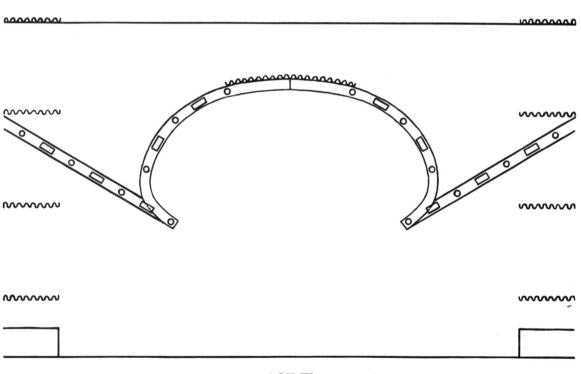

ACT III

Figure 7-8. Act III, *Twelfth Night.* The set for the short final act
is strongly symmetrical.

For the third act, the arrangement was completely symmetrical, taking the shape of an oval arcade with one open side facing the audience, suggesting a picture frame or perhaps an outdoor setting especially designed for a garden wedding. At the opening of the act, the actors were arranged irregularly about the stage. As the action of the play proceeded, each actor gradually moved into a position that created a formal symmetrical arrangement (the type that used to be called a *tableau*) just before the fall of the curtain.

For the audience, then, the arrangement of scenery and actors was basically asymmetrical throughout most of the play, moving from moderate asymmetry, through a long period of extreme asymmetry, to a final symmetrical picture expressive of the artificiality and sweetness of the last scene.

Avoiding Symmetry

Since beginning designers are likely to find themselves steadily pulled in the direction of symmetry, it may be helpful to suggest a simple trick by means of which a symmetrical design can be made asymmetrical. It should be emphasized that this is only a mechanical device and consequently should be used only to rescue a set in an emergency, not as a habitual principle of set design. The trick is to take the ground plan and turn it slightly so that the center line of the design crosses the center line of the stage at an angle; the result is an appreciable increase in visual tension, often with an improvement in its dramatic quality (see *Figures 1-6, 4-8, 6-3,* and *7-1).*

The Major Lines

One other aspect of the orientation of design elements is the direction of the major lines. In analyzing the lines of a set, we may divide them into three groups: vertical, horizontal, and diagonal or slanted. Of the three, horizontal lines suggest the greatest stability, and diagonals the greatest tension. The *Antony and Cleopatra* set *(Figure 6-19)* is the most obvious example of the use of both types of line: the horizontals of the steps and the tops of the arches suggest rigidity and solidity; the slanted lines of the columns create a clear feeling of tension. Vertical lines create an esthetic impression of soaring and lift. Throughout most of *Antony and Cleopatra,* the set combined horizontals and diagonals in a state of balanced tension; when the horizontals of the middle arches were removed for the last act, the set was dominated by the soaring, slightly slanted verticals of the third-arch columns, which helped support the rising tension and exaltation of Cleopatra's death scene. Michael David's sets for the Oedipus plays also illustrate the skillful use of orientation: the violence of *King Oedipus (Figure 6-4)* is expressed to some degree by the vertical thrust of the massive blood-red rectangle that dominates the set; the quieter and more relaxed mood of *Oedipus at Colonus (Figure 6-5)* is suggested by the basic horizontality of the rolling earth shapes.

The influence of color on mood is a powerful one, but in this aspect of design there are even fewer generally accepted principles than in the other areas. Many authors confidently identify the emotional effects of various colors, but their analyses not only contradict each other but contradict ordinary experience. The following comments are consequently offered very tentatively, and designers must rely heavily on their own taste.

Color

Perhaps the most important point to make about color is a denial of a common view. Many colors have conventional associations with emotions: that is, custom has identified them as expressive of certain feelings. Thus, white is conventionally suggestive of purity, purple of royalty, red of passion, and black of mourning. Such associations are part of the language and folklore of our culture, although other cultures have different associations (for instance, in some cultures white rather than black is associated with mourning, and bright orange is the symbol of purity). The important thing for designers to remember is that if such associations function in the theater at all, it is so weakly as to be almost negligible. A designer who relies on black decorations to make a set look tragic may discover that the effect is just the opposite.

One emotional reaction to color is generally agreed on, and that is the ability of colors to suggest various degrees of heat. Even here, however, there is disagreement about the effect of specific colors. It is generally agreed that red is a warm color, and pure blue a cold one. When these two are mixed, the warmth dominates, so that the resulting purple seems warm, although less so than red. Yellow is a slightly warm color; when mixed with red it produces orange, which is clearly warm. Because yellow is not strongly warm, however, when it is mixed with the cool color blue, the resulting green is cool rather than warm. Black seems slightly warm and white slightly cool; thus, the pastel colors produced by mixing large amounts of white with other pigments seem airy and moderately cool, although the predominant tone will still be that of the basic color. Thus, red mixed freely with white produces pink, which seems warm, but much less so than pure red. In the same way, black mixed with green produces an effect still cool but less so than pure green. When black and white are mixed together the effect of the black clearly dominates, so that greys are slightly warm rather than cool; however, the warmth of the black is so weak that it may be counteracted by mixing a little of one of the cool colors with grey; thus, grey with a small addition of blue will appear cool. Of course, the addition of one of the warm colors makes grey even warmer, so that a grey with a little yellow in it will appear clearly warm.

White and Black Admixtures

Aside from the degree of warmth, the admixture of black or white with a pure color produces other psychological effects. White seems to lighten a color emotionally as well as visually; as more and more white is added to green, for example, the resulting mixture becomes light, airy, and delicate. The addition of black to a color produces an effect of richness; green with a considerable amount of black mixed in seems rich, solid, and sophisticated.

The pure colors vary in their apparent similarity to white and black; the primary and secondary colors are listed below, beginning with the color that is most like white and ending with the one most like black.

(White)
Yellow
Orange
Green
Red
Purple
Blue
(Black)

The significance of that listing for designers is that the degree to which a color is changed by mixing white (or black) with it depends on how far apart the two pigments are on the list. Thus, even a little white mixed with blue produces a sharp and obvious change in the blue, whereas a great deal of white must be mixed with yellow to produce much detectable change. Even a little black mixed with yellow so muddies the color as to make it seem not yellow; and black mixed with orange produces such a different effect that, in English, a separate name has been created for the resulting color: brown.

The emotional effects of various mixtures can be combined. For example, green mixed with a large amount of white will appear light, fresh, and delicate; adding black to green makes it appear rich and sophisticated. Mixing both white and black with green will produce a color that combines lightness and sophistication, although with some loss in freshness and delicacy.

The Moods of Dark and Light

It is frequently said that dark colors harmonize best with tragedy and bright colors with comedy, and that seems true to some degree. However, so many other factors affect the relationship of colors to mood that designers should remember this principle as only one of many. Michael David's designs for the Sophoclean tragedies are largely in light and bright colors; the *Antony and Cleopatra* set is basically a light yellow, though it has been somewhat sophisticated by the addition of black. On the other hand, the *Simon Big-Ears* set was painted in light, fresh colors (surprisingly similar to the color scheme for *Antony and Cleopatra,* although the proportions of the colors used are quite different). Of all the folk clichés, the one that seems falsest to ordinary experience is the automatic association of black with sadness. Pure black, in fact, is far more likely to produce an effect of sparkling gaiety. The absurdity of the traditional view can readily be demonstrated by imagining a blonde actress wearing a shiny black dress and a string of pearls: the effect would be anything but depressing. Probably black is most likely to express somber emotions when it is mixed with other colors rather than used by itself: certainly, if a particular series of colors had been selected for a set, mixing black with each would lower the tone of the entire color scheme and produce an effect of richness and sobriety that would clearly shift it toward harmony with more serious emotions.

Contrast

An additional element in the effect of color is the degree of contrast incorporated in the design. Sharp contrast seems best suited to comedy, low contrast to tragedy, although, like the previous principle, this is only one of many factors involved in designing a color scheme.

The Ambiguity of Association

And, finally, the emotional effects of colors are powerfully influenced by their associations with objects having the same color. The apparent freshness of yellow-green and the warmth of orange are undoubtedly partly due to their association with budding trees and the glow of a fire. Such associations would be easy to use in the theater except that they are highly ambiguous. In ordinary experience, objects of the same color often produce contradictory emotional reactions. A moderately dark red may produce a strong negative reaction when it is associated with blood, but the same red may be the color of a beautiful flower or a ripe tomato. The blue of the sky may seem cool, but the same blue in a flame may suggest more heat than an orange flame would: "white hot" is hotter than "red hot." Although the ambiguity of familiar emotional associations with colors prevents designers from using them in any simple way, it enables them to control the effect of color on an audience. The same color may be used to produce quite different effects in scenery by including in the design an explanation of its association. Thus, leaf green may seem sweet and fresh and cool when painted on a groundrow representing distant hills; it may seem horrible when used for the inside of a space ship filled with men from Mars whose skin has been made up with the same color. A yellow mixed with grey may seem warm and pleasant when used for the wall of a stone building seen through a window; it will seem sickly and nauseating when it is used to paint the walls of a hospital room.

It is to be hoped that we will sometime have objective principles that can be followed in using color to express and support emotion in the theater; it is too powerful a factor to be controlled only by hunch and intuition. In the absence of such principles, designers should develop the habit of studying the effects of color in ordinary life; they should examine colored reproductions of the work of other set designers; and for each of their own designs they should use their own taste to evaluate as wide a range of color schemes as time will allow.

8

DESIGNING
for
LOCALE

People who are not theater specialists, if asked to name the primary function of scenery, would be likely to answer, "to indicate where a play is supposed to take place." Probably, beginning designers most often start with the assumption that their major job is to design scenery that will perform that function. It is, then, not negligible, although in the practical art of the theater it is distinctly less important than the two aspects of scenery that have already been discussed. A set that serves almost exclusively to facilitate the action of the play may be a very fine set; a set the only function of which is to indicate where the play takes place would probably be highly inadequate.

Nineteenth-century stage sets were essentially large flat paintings, in front of which the actors performed; all details of the locale, including any furniture that was not actually used by the actors, were painted on flat surfaces. (See *Figures 2-18, 9-1,* and *14-1* for modern re-creations of such sets.) Appia rebelled against that practice by developing essentially three-dimensional scenery, which the actors played in, on, and around. Throughout his career, he moved steadily toward a greater concentration on the set as a machine, so that some of his later sets included little or no information about locale. At first, however, his designs suggested locale very effectively. His method combined selection and abstraction, and it was so influential that it is now the standard procedure for set design.

SELECTIVE REALISM

Belasco's transporting of an actual slum bedroom to the stage of his theater to serve as the setting for a play might be described as an attempt to
achieve *total realism;* the most common current method of design is *selective realism.* Let us imagine the setting a play would have if the action
occurred in real life, rather than on the stage. Which play we consider is of
little importance, but let us choose *The Solid Gold Cadillac,* by Howard
Teichmann and George S. Kaufman. The play calls for five sets: an auditorium where the stockholders of a large corporation hold a meeting; a government office in Washington; and three of the corporation offices—a very
large one, a medium-sized one, and one little bigger than a cubbyhole.

In a real building, the corporation offices would include an enormous
amount of detail. If Belasco were to try to move one of them to the stage,
he would have to move three large walls, one of them perhaps made of
glass; many desks and files; business machines; telephones; a water
cooler; etc. It would be possible to supply them all, of course, and then
have the actors simply ignore those they did not need to use. But the stage
would look fussy and miscellaneous and would tend to distract attention
from the actors, who would be lost in the mass of detail. And so we reject
the Belasco method.

Yet we want the set to say to the audience, "this is a corporation
office." How can the designer achieve that effect? The modern solution is
to analyze the various elements to be found in the real setting, and then
select just a few of them that are especially characteristic of the locale,
letting them serve as symbols of the full environment. Obviously, our
selection must include those things that are used by the actors. Besides
them, what is especially characteristic of contemporary business offices?
Each designer will of course make a different selection. One design for the
offices in this play included the following items: one large conference
table, four conference chairs, one swivel chair, one typist's chair, one
desk, and one filing cabinet. One further item, of great visual importance,
was added to that list. It is currently the fashion to use open ornamental
screens in office buildings, often of decorated metal; a very large screen of
that type, designed for the set, was used as the major decorative
element.

The Solid Gold Cadillac is not a realistic play; it is identified in the
script as "a fairy tale." Consequently, the designer made a more frankly
symbolic use of the selected elements than would have been suitable for a
less artificial play. The single desk and filing cabinet, in effect, were presented as symbols of office furniture; certainly the set made no pretense
of being a naturalistic reproduction of an actual office, or even a design
that would have been possible for a real office.

The Madwoman of Chaillot is a somewhat more serious play, but
almost equally fantastic. The first act takes place at a sidewalk café in

Paris. With regard to informing the audience about the locale, the primary problem was to identify the city. One designer collected an extensive list of objects and buildings to be found in Paris; only a few of the items on the list were included in the final selection. Some of the items rejected were the Eiffel Tower, the familiar advertising kiosks of Paris, and the unusual subway entrances. Instead, the following items were decided on: the *fleur-de-lis* motif, artificially shaped and trimmed potted bushes, a low platform to represent a sidewalk, an ornamental awning bearing the name of the café, small circular tables with matching chairs, two large sidewalk sunshades, park benches, and a street lamp with the name of the street and a large clock fastened in the center. Most Parisian street lamps look like those of many other cities, but a few bear clocks, which is unusual in the United States. The clock design was selected for the play because it said "Paris," as the commoner type of lamp would not. (See *Figure 8-1.*)

Figure 8-1. Sets for Giraudoux's *The Madwoman of Chaillot.* Act I takes place in a sidewalk café on a Paris street; Act II is set in the basement of a Paris dwelling. (See also *Figures 4-6* and *4-7* for another artist's design for Act I.)

Designers who use the method of selective realism to communicate information about the locale of a play, then, choose from the matching real-life settings a few especially significant details or objects and combine them in their designs, using them essentially symbolically to say to the audience: "This is a seacoast at the southern edge of the Mediterranean, in ancient times" (Plautus's *The Rope*) or "This is an amusement park" (Molnar's *Liliom*) or "This is the living room of a rich, successful, and pompous Englishman" (Barrie's *The Twelve-Pound Look*). Students who are interested in the history of set design may want to check analogous practices in other periods: the medieval mystery plays were designed by this method; it was used on the Elizabethan stage; and it was used to some extent in ancient Greece. It was also used in other periods. Thus, the current approach to the informative function of scenery, although it seems revolutionary as compared with early nineteenth-century styles, is actually harmonious with the practice of a very long stretch of theater history.

The elements that the designer selects may be incorporated into the design in such a way as to reveal their symbolic use frankly and clearly, or they may be disguised to suggest a complete and finished setting, so that they function more subtly. Present practice slightly favors the franker, more theatrical use of scenery, but the basis of choice should not be current fashion but the needs of the script. If the playwright has attempted to create a realistic illusion, as in Ibsen's *Ghosts,* the designer will undoubtedly want to devise a set that will communicate information about the locale unobtrusively, in an apparently realistic fashion; if the play is frankly fantastic, theatrical, and artificial, like Ibsen's *Peer Gynt,* the designer will match the tone of the script.

Selective realism, if carried far enough, approaches fragmentary scenery. Most beginning designers tend to think of scenery in terms of the naturalistic reproduction of settings outside the theater, a method that is so limited as to be crippling, and one that is almost never appropriate. It may at first seem astonishing how little the members of the audience need to see to get the impression of a full setting, so long as what is included is appropriate and expressive and will stimulate their imagination. The examination of the work of any effective set designer will provide scores of examples of that fact. Jo Mielziner praises the revolutionary designer Robert Edmond Jones for his effective use of selectivity, but Mielziner's own work illustrates the same skill. For example, see his front-porch design for *Finian's Rainbow,* the restaurant scene for *Gypsy,* the set for *The Gang's All Here,* and that for *There Was a Little Girl.* For a traveling company for *Abe Lincoln in Illinois,* he made particularly effective use of a carefully lit short flight of steps to suggest a railroad car.[1]

1.　Jo Mielziner, *Designing for the Theatre: A Memoir and a Portfolio* (New York: Bramhall House, 1965).

This discussion is not intended even to hint that minimal scenery is necessarily the best style for any particular production; rather, it is intended to demonstrate a possibility that beginning designers may not be fully aware of, as well as to help free them from their overreliance on literal naturalism, probably the least effective of all styles.

INTEGRATION IN THE GROUND PLAN

After the designer has made his selection of symbolic motifs and structures, he must integrate them with his ground plan to form an organic esthetic whole. He will discover immediately that the ground plan already includes a good deal of data that is relevant to this step: it indicates the placement of all actually functioning units in the set: doors, furniture, stairs, platforms, walls, etc. To a considerable extent, then, the alteration of the design to indicate locale involves only the application of surface decoration, decisions with regard to the style of doors and furniture, etc. The designer may want to add elements not essential to the action, such as a fireplace or pilasters, which will help him indicate time and place. Such additions may even result in alterations in the lines of the ground plan, although in nearly every case such alterations will be minimal.

The designer's decisions in this step may well take the form of quick sketches and written notes. They will, of course, ultimately be recorded in detail in the final perspective and working drawings.

PERIOD DESIGN

Usually, two types of time are relevant to the setting of a play: the date or period in which the action is set and the time of day at which individual scenes occur. Aeschylus's *Agamemnon,* for example, is set in the period just after the Trojan War, approximately a thousand years before the beginning of the Christian era. The opening scene occurs just before sunrise.

The time of day is expressed in the theater primarily through the use of light: golden sunlight streaming at a low angle through the windows suggests late afternoon; lighted floor lamps and chandeliers and darkness beyond the windows obviously picture a night scene. Since the provision of such effects is the responsibility of the person in charge of lighting, and only peripherally concerns the set designer, major attention is given here to the producing of a design that will identify the period or year for the audience, rather than the time of day.

Some plays are only vaguely localized as to time and place: the stories take place at an indefinite once-upon-a-time, and if the setting is "a living room," it might equally well be designed and decorated in any one of fifty different styles. Most plays, however, are more firmly located, and often they are so integrally involved in their setting that only a particular period and style of decor will fit them satisfactorily. Occasionally, very striking productions have been created by frankly and consciously violating the playwright's intentions with regard to setting: Orson Welles's production of *Julius Caesar,* set in Fascist Italy; *Macbeth* transferred to the African jungle; the opera *Carmen* shifted to the twentieth century and retitled *Carmen Jones.* Although such alterations may be successful, to some extent they constitute a rewriting of the playscript and consequently fall outside the scope of our study, which assumes the authority of the script as the playwright created it.

For most plays, then, in order to express the playwright's intentions faithfully, scenic artists will need to design with reference to a particular style of architecture and decor. Since they must normally complete their plans to meet a deadline that usually comes far too soon, they must acquire the ability to master a historic style quickly and to fit their designing to it.

Collecting
Examples

To become familiar with a specific period, the designer must collect as many examples as possible of designs of the period. The artist may want to visit museums to examine actual furniture; but his most useful sources will be books containing pictures. For periods within the last century and a half, it may be possible for him to find copies of magazines contemporary with the action of the play. Paintings are also valuable, especially portraits, which usually contain some furniture in the background. In addition, books on historic styles may be usable, although usually their discussions are disappointingly brief.

The Analysis

Having collected the pictures that will form the material for his study, the designer analyzes them.

The first step consists of simply leafing through the sources, examining the various pictures to get an impression of the general effect of the style. The second step involves reexamining the pictures, carefully analyzing the various elements of design, listed below.

1. *Scale of construction:* whether the objects are massive and overpowering, delicate and fragile, or something in between. In judging scale, the standard of measurement is of course the human body: thus, one period may be

characterized by huge, thick doors that dwarf the people who use them; in another period, designers may have preferred small, plain doors that neatly fit people walking through them.

2. *Three-dimensionality:* whether plane surfaces are generally preferred, as in the case of modern "flush" doors, or whether objects are usually designed with modeling and carving, so that the surfaces are broken into a series of planes.

3. *Methods of construction:* whether openings are spanned by horizontal beams resting on pillars or by stone laid to form semicircular arches; whether furniture is made with exposed pins or with concealed joints; how bracing elements are integrated in the design.

4. *Range of variation:* whether artifacts, buildings, and motifs all seem to be narrowly related to each other, or whether there is a broad range of style, with different designs producing strikingly different visual effects.

5. *Special structures:* the obelisks of ancient Egypt, the skyscrapers and suspension bridges of the twentieth century.

6. *Materials:* the use of marble, wood, cloth, gold leaf, etc.

7. *Color:* the specific colors used and the general type of color: for example, whether the designers prefer delicate pastels or muted greyed colors.

8. *Line:* whether straight lines or curves predominate; whether straight lines are short and broken or continuous; and whether curves are long and sweeping or tightly wound.

9. *Form:* the shapes preferred by the designers (oval, rectangular, triangular, etc.); the degree to which forms match simple geometrical shapes; and the extent to which the underlying shapes are revealed or concealed by decoration.

10. *Symmetry:* where the designs fit on the symmetry-asymmetry continuum.

11. *Influences:* the extent to which the designers use motifs taken from previous periods.

12. *Motifs:* specific decorative designs taken from nature or other sources (animal feet used at the bottom of chair legs, the *fleur-de-lis* design, egg-and-dart molding, etc.).

13. *Degree of decoration:* whether large areas are left unbroken or whether ornamentation is applied to almost all exposed surface.

14. *Taste:* the degree to which decorative design integrates wide variety into an impression of esthetic unity.

In this step, the artist may want to note specific pictures of especially typical designs or motifs; he may even record a few of the motifs in quick sketches or in verbal notes. In the main, however, he will probably prefer to fix his observations in his mind and rely on his memory in using them.

The Spirit of the Period

In the third step in his analysis, the artist focuses on the spiritual elements of design. The use of the term *spiritual* in connection with styles of decoration may seem startling, but each of the historical styles has been profoundly influenced by the spirit of the times in which it was created. In some degree, literature, music, architecture, painting, clothing, furniture design, and interior decoration are all expressive of the beliefs, aspirations, concepts, and values of the people who create them, choose them, buy them, and live with them. Even such an apparently unalterable thing as the shape of the human body is, in appearance at least, varied from period to period to express people's pictures of themselves and their relations to each other, their concepts of ideal human beings, and their likes and dislikes.

Ideally, since the values of a culture are expressed in the whole of its products, the designer should study every aspect of his period. The more he knows of its philosophy, social conditions and relationships, and scheme of values, the more effectively he can achieve a sound empathic integration of the period into his own pattern of thought. However, as has already been remarked, the ideal is never achieved in the theater, and the designer in practice must work within severe limitations of time. Nevertheless, he should make his analysis as broad and deep as he can.

EXAMPLES OF PERIOD STYLES

To clarify the methods of period design, I am including the conclusions resulting from an analysis of three specific periods: Victorian, ancient Egyptian, and American Indian. These periods were chosen as examples so as to illustrate styles of great diversity.

The Victorian Spirit

The nineteenth century was an era in which technological advances were increasing the supply of available goods, and the standard of living was rising steadily. The distribution of the new wealth was extremely uneven, but its continued increase produced a widespread mood of optimism—a feeling that restrictive walls had been broken through, that the opportunities for individual advancement were greater than ever before, and that such opportunities would continue into the future. The apparent tone of the period, then, is that which generally characterizes the *nouveaux riches:* they prided themselves on their obviously remarkable achievements; they took a childlike delight in the display of their new positions; they were headily confident of themselves and the rightness of their systems and methods, a rightness amply demonstrated by their material success. Their scheme of values, including their social and religious beliefs, seemed clearly a sound one; they were determined to consolidate their new social status by carefully adopting the customs and styles of the classes to which they had risen (it was a period of widespread social climbing). Apparent in extreme form among the Victorians was an attitude that a twentieth-century analyst is most likely to overlook: its feeling of modernity. For us, Victorianism is stuffily dowdy, perhaps one of the most old-fashioned of all styles; but for them, it was uniquely modern. They were vividly aware of the tremendous changes that were going on, and they felt the newness of their own period with an intensity that can hardly be matched in previous history, except perhaps in Renaissance England.

But revolutionary as the period now seems, *revolution* is not quite an accurate expression of the way the Victorians saw themselves. They were not, they felt, destroying a culture, but rather improving it; they were the heirs to the ages, but heirs who had brilliantly invested what they had inherited and were far surpassing it. They might have echoed Browning by saying, "The best is yet to be: the last achievement of civilization, for which the first was made." They saw themselves, then, not primarily as innovators but as consolidators.

The expression of the attitudes that we have been describing is clear in almost every detail of the design of the period; we can see it demonstrated by a Victorian inkstand or table or what-not shelf. It may be clearest to define the specific aspects of Victorian design in terms of the list presented earlier in the chapter.

Scale of Construction. Victorian design employed a large scale, but in a very special way. Upholstered furniture was heavily stuffed, often almost bulbous or mushroomlike, and wooden furniture was enormous; yet the basic scale tended to be contradicted and concealed by the wealth of decorative detail covering it. The edges were often shaped in coiled and writhing curves, and the entire surface was broken up into small sections, producing a feeling of delicacy that contrasted with, and concealed, the solidity and size of the unit as a whole.

Line. Straight lines were generally avoided (one picture of a fashionable Victorian living room in New York exhibits not a single straight line, except in some rather unobtrusive horizontal molding). The lines curved constantly, and although gentle curves were occasionally used, the overwhelming practice was to design in small, tight, freely varying curves.

Form.   Shapes were often based on simple geometrical outlines, but the designers regularly destroyed the key points in the shapes, most simply by substituting curves at the corners, either cutting into the figure or projecting out from it. Complex shapes, of the type now called *free form,* were also freely used, but they were usually symmetrical.

Three-dimensionality.   Victorian designers avoided uninterrupted plane surfaces as much as possible. Walls were broken by bays and indentations, and smaller artifacts like furniture and picture frames were carved profusely, with exaggerated emphasis on their thickness.

Symmetry.   Almost all Victorian designs were symmetrical, expressing the solidity and assurance of the period, but outlines were so varied and extravagant that the symmetrical fact is often apparent only after special examination. This peculiar combination of rigidity and flamboyance is perhaps the most striking characteristic of the entire style.

Degree of Decoration.   Everything, including buildings, was profusely ornamented, but the designers typically included sizable plain areas as a contrast to the decoration. Ornament occurred most often at the edges of plain areas and in the supports of furniture. Although plain surfaces were actually larger, the extravagance of the decoration, as well as the complexity of edges, made the ornament dominant in the design.

Influences.   As heirs to the ages, the Victorian designers freely used motifs from other styles: ancient Roman and Greek, medieval, and even Egyptian, Turkish, Moorish, and Chinese. In fact, it is difficult to find a historic style that does not appear in some quantity in Victorian design. The Victorians were conscious of architectural style and appreciatively used other styles, but their exuberance was so overwhelming that their own special tastes tended to dominate any elements picked up from other periods. In most instances, however fully motifs from previous styles were incorporated into the designs, the impression is overwhelmingly Victorian.

Motifs.   Plants and animals, including the human form (discreetly draped), were used as decorative motifs, second only to the abstract curves and shapes that form the commonest decorative elements. Not only were wallpapers and carpets covered boldly with flowers, but iron furniture was molded to simulate twigs, iron grillwork was cast into leaf shapes, picture frames were carved in the shape of shells and foliage, and stained-glass lampshades were designed to look like fruits, flowers, birds, and even spiders in their webs. In fact, one of the striking characteristics of the period was the cheerful acceptance of materials processed so as to imitate other materials. That practice was dismissed with great scorn by later designers as an ultimate example of bad taste, but it was a source of delight for the Victorians, so that designers tended to emphasize the fact of imitation rather than conceal it: imitation twig furniture obviously made from wrought iron pleased by its ingenuity.

Color. Somewhat paradoxically, the Victorians preferred dark colors, including dark woods. Even gold, which was constantly used, was broken and muted by being applied to richly carved areas. A wide range of colors was used, but all of them were enriched by an admixture of black. Brown was particularly favored, and in easel painting the period has been called the "brown-sauce era." It might be expected that the Victorians would have preferred vivid primary colors, but their color schemes generally combined the sobriety and solidity of the darker shades with the exuberance of a vivid and varied spectral range.

Materials. Very little synthetic material was available to Victorian designers. Wrought iron was used, not only for decorative architectural grills, but also in the construction of furniture. Stone, especially marble, was more commonly used than at present, particularly for fireplaces and table tops. Colored glass was common, and was used not only for dishes but also for small statues, lampshades, and windows. Such piled fabrics as velvet and plush were often used for drapes, and a woolen fabric called baize, dyed in a solid color, was used in an unusual way to cover wood surfaces such as doors and the tops of tables.

Methods of Construction. Joints were concealed, and bracing elements were used much less frankly than in the periods before or since the nineteenth century. Often, construction methods were falsified, so that pillars and pilasters in interiors did not actually support the structure placed above them, and flying buttresses and other apparent supports were often added to the outside of buildings as simple ornaments.

Special Structures. One of the most picturesque and characteristically Victorian structures was the *summer house,* a small shelter with roof and floor but no walls. It was often octagonal. Containing chairs and sometimes a swing, it was used as an auxiliary porch or outdoor living room during the summer and was a favorite spot for romance. Incidentally, porches were much larger and more numerous than during the periods before and since, and they were constantly used in place of the rather dark and hot living rooms.

Similar structures, called *bandstands,* were regularly built in public parks to serve as outdoor stages from which local bands could present concerts on summer evenings.

Range of Variation. All of the factors involved in nineteenth-century life and attitudes tended toward great variety in design; but though an analysis of individual artifacts may emphasize the uniqueness of each, the spiritual qualities they share tend to submerge their individuality, so that, to our eyes at least, the general impression is one of similarity rather than difference.

Taste. An assessment of the taste displayed in the design of a historic period is more dependent on our own point of view than the analysis of any other stylistic element; certainly, the people of each period are convinced of the superiority of their own taste. If we define taste in terms of the degree of unity achieved in design, especially in the light of the modern preference for underdecoration, then the Victorian period was characterized by rather bad taste: in some sense, there was more esthetic vulgarity than in almost any other historic period.

The total effect of Victorian design, then, was of a highly individual style expressing self-confidence and optimism by a combination of a basic firmness and solidity with exuberant surface decoration.

The Success of Egypt

The single most remarkable fact about ancient Egypt is its longevity: its story reaches in a nearly unbroken line for longer than that of any other culture in history. Ancient tombs are our major source of information about Egypt, and that fact has led commentators to overemphasize the necrophilia of the Egyptians. The Egyptians believed firmly in an afterlife and spent great labor and money preparing for it, but their picture of it was an almost precise continuation of ordinary life on earth. The tomb paintings and artifacts are solidly grounded in familiar experience, and, far from being gloomy, they depict a round of feasting, drinking, hunting, and social pleasures.

Egypt is relatively treeless, so lumber was precious, and stone was the commoner material for building. That fact alone resulted in a solidity, massiveness, and simplicity of design that strike everyone who examines the Egyptian styles.

In the most ancient times, the dead were buried in the sand, and the tombs were protected by a covering of stone, shaped like a box with slanted sides (the rectangular top was narrower and shorter than the base). Later, in an attempt to make the tombs more impressive, the box was greatly enlarged, and a second was constructed on top of it. A series of three or four such shapes form what is called a step pyramid, and the transition to the familiar Egyptian pyramid consisted simply of filling in the steps so that the outlines formed continuous straight lines. The precedent of that tradition made the sharply slanted wall familiar to the Egyptians, and it was constantly used in their buildings, forming a special characteristic mark of their style.

Egyptian artists were restricted in their use of color by the fact that most modern pigments were not available to them; those that they had were somewhat muted and tended toward the earth colors. However, their delight in life is reflected in their handling of color; they used the full spectrum available with little intermixture, thus achieving the maximum contrast possible. Furthermore, the brilliant Egyptian sunlight heightened the effect of the colors, so that one's general impression of an ancient Egyptian city would have been one of brilliance, just short of gaudiness.

The emphasis on religion, together with the strength of tradition, resulted in the widespread use of pictures of gods as architectural decoration. They were carved and painted according to rigidly codified rules, so that the work of one artist is hardly distinguishable from that of another.

One element of Egyptian art is particularly attractive to people of the twentieth century: it is their stylization and simplification. (See *Figure 8-2*). Perhaps this resulted from their use of stone as an artistic medium, since stone does not readily lend itself to the reproduction of, for example, every individual feather of a bird. The traditional simplicity of religious paintings may also have been a factor. But whatever the reason, Egyptian art is generally characterized by a simplification of outline and detail that reveals rather than distorts the essential appearance of the animal or object portrayed. At first glance, an Egyptian statue of a falcon may seem photographically realistic; but closer inspection demonstrates that the artist has in fact sharply selected, retaining only the most characteristic lines and shapes and smoothing out accidental deviations, so that the statue produces the curious impression of being more falconlike than a real falcon.

The Egyptians learned to handle three-dimensional forms with great effectiveness, and many of the statues of rulers and court officials are remarkably realistic. However, there is an essential peculiarity in their paintings of human beings that immediately strikes the attention: each part of the body is shown in the position that is easiest to draw. Thus, the head is drawn in profile, the shoulders as if seen from the front, the legs, feet, arms, and hands from the side. For contemporary viewers, of course, this conventional posture was so familiar as to be unnoticed, and their attention would have been focused on the essential realism of the drawing of the individual parts.

The Egyptian love of display, color, and luxury is demonstrated in their furniture and smaller artifacts. Makeup was used more freely than at

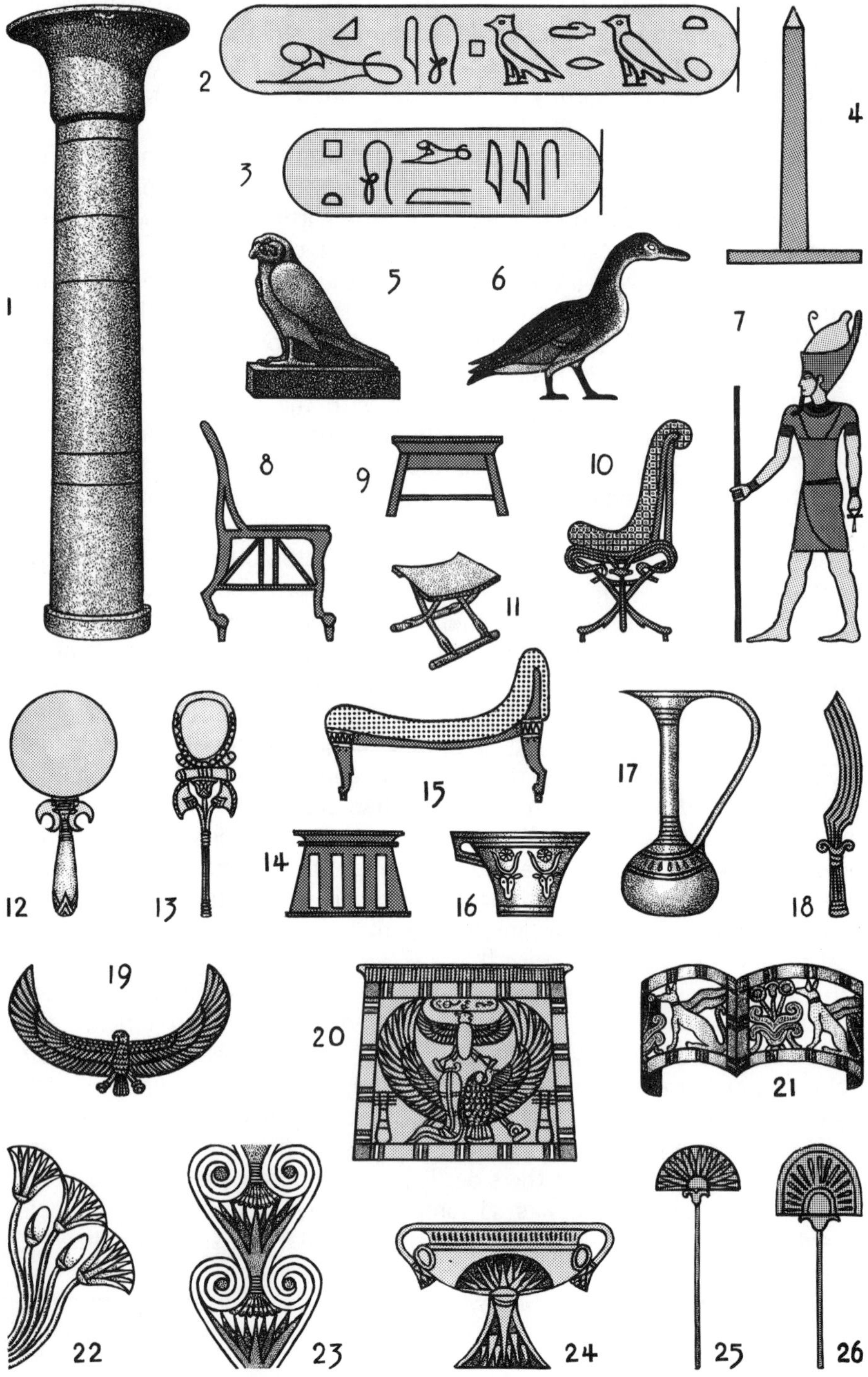

1

2

3

4

5

6

7

8

9

10

11

12

13

14

15

16

17

18

19

20

21

22

23

24

25

26

Figure 8-2. Egyptian design. *Drawings 1 and 4:* the simplicity and monumentality of the larger works. The freer treatment of smaller artifacts is demonstrated by *12* (a mirror), *13* (a cosmetic spoon), and *18* (a dagger). *Drawings 2 and 3:* "Cleopatra" and "Ptolemy" in hieroglyphics; especially interesting is the treatment of the lion representing the letter "L." *Drawings 5 and 6:* abstracted and more naturalistic treatments of animals. *Drawing 7:* the body position typical of Egyptian art. *Drawings 9, 14, and 20:* a table, a window, and jewelry showing the typical four-sided figure with slanted sides. *Drawings 11, 16, 17, 21, and others:* the apparent modernity of much of the design. *Drawings 22-26:* the range of abstraction in Egyptian art, starting with a nearly naturalistic painting of the lotus and moving through different degrees of abstraction until the motif is completely stylized.

any other period, and innumerable paint pots, containers for eyeshadow, and mirrors are to be found in museums. The furniture is elegant, gracefully designed, and beautifully decorated.

And finally, in studying the style of ancient Egypt we must not overlook the many ways in which it matches modern design; in some ways, in fact, it seems more like twentieth-century design than does that of the Victorian period. The use of large, plain surfaces, with a small amount of geometric and simplified naturalistic decoration, seems especially modern. Much of the jewelry could be placed on the counter of a modern store, among contemporary jewelry, without exciting attention; and some of the furniture would also not seem out of place in a modern department store.

Following are the specific aspects of Egyptian design in terms of the checklist.

Scale. Egyptian monumental architecture (temples and tombs, including the pyramids) was on a scale that was hardly matched in any other period; not only were the walls thick and the columns enormous in height and diameter, but no attempt was made to counteract the effect of overwhelming mass. Such structures have a scale of their own, which has almost no relation to that of the human body. The furniture, on the other hand, tended to be delicate rather than massive, and comfortably adapted to the human body, both in scale and shape.

Line. Straight lines predominate; the arch is unknown, and even circular columns, because of their size, lack a clear feeling of roundness. Small artifacts, such as mirrors and jewelry boxes, are freer in form, tending to have curved outlines.

Form.   Rectangles in architecture were less used than in almost any other culture; trapezoids substituted for them.

Three-dimensionality.   The structures achieve thickness by their mass; relief carving is minimal, and in any case the variation in thickness produced by carved decoration tends to be lost in the scale of the structures as a whole. Statues, however, are often of enormous size and fully three-dimensional (for instance, the sphinx).

Symmetry.   Nearly all Egyptian design is symmetrical, although decorative paintings often produce some deviation from total symmetry.

Degree of Decoration.   Applied decoration, painted or carved and painted, was widely used; it tended to be flat and simplified, so that background and decoration were well integrated. Certainly, as compared with those of the Victorian period, Egyptian buildings and furniture seem underdecorated, although the difference is not so much in the ratio between the decorated and undecorated areas as in the relative unobtrusiveness of the decoration.

Influences.   Because of Egypt's long history and its cultural priority, Egyptian designers copied heavily from their own tradition, but hardly at all from the styles of other cultures.

Motifs.   Much of the design and decoration is abstract and geometric, although seldom rigidly so. Plant and animal motifs are used freely, often abstracted in varying degrees: thus the lotus appears in various versions ranging from almost photographically natural to nearly unrecognizably abstract. Almost always, some selection and arrangement is evident, so that even in a naturalistic painting of a fishing scene, the water is likely to be conventionalized and the reeds at its edge carefully combed into a uniform arrangement, broken by only a few that cut across the basic pattern. In general, the intention was to express the underlying natural forms, but to omit minor and accidental variations, with the result that the design combines an impression of abstraction and naturalism.

Color.   Natural pigments were used, generally painted in flat areas and without intermixing, with the intention of providing maximum contrast, which is saved from gaudiness by the greying inherent in the materials.

Materials.   Stone was the major building material for public buildings; private dwellings were made of brick, with minimal use of wood. Wood was generally used for furniture, with inlaid decorations of gold, ivory, and glass.

Methods of Construction.   The stability of buildings was produced primarily by sheer weight; the pyramids are simply heaps of carefully shaped stones, and temples were often in the form of massive colonnades, with the relatively short spaces between the columns covered by stone blocks, resting unfastened on the capitals.

Special Structures.   The pyramid and obelisk are uniquely Egyptian, as are the huge lotiform columns and the slanted walls.

Range of Variation.   Throughout its many centuries, Egyptian design necessarily changed and developed, and the traditions were forcibly interrupted twice, once by pharaonic command, when Akhenaten ordered designers to adopt a new style expressive of the heretical religion he was attempting to force on Egypt, and later under Greek rule, when for a brief time the Egyptian artists copied the style of their conquerors. But in the main, Egyptian design was characterized by its uniformity, so that for the *Antony and Cleopatra* set, for example, the designer could only copy the pictures of the gods, not redesign them, just as an ancient artist would essentially have reproduced their pictures in traditional style, not created a new concept of his own.

American Indian Art

It would be tempting to continue the discussion of historic styles through the entire range of those that have been used for plays, but to do so would expand the book to encyclopedic length. As a kind of footnote, one additional style may be illustrated without detailed analysis.

One way of staging Arthur Kopit's *Indians* is to decorate it in the style of American Indian art. Each tribe established its own traditional styles, but all shared a common feeling. Since the designer's purpose is to create an impression that will be identifiably Indian, rather than construct a lesson in art history, it is sufficient for him to work in a generalized way, not specifically restricted to any single Indian esthetic dialect.

Indian art in general displays two contrasted styles. One, using fluid curves, is related to sand painting. The other, using straight lines, is developed from basket weaving. Painting by modern Indians tends to follow the sand tradition, but the straight-line style seems better suited to the nineteenth century, in which the play is placed. The designs make extensive use of straight lines and zigzags, which are natural to basket weaving. Motifs tend to be isolated, spotted fairly evenly across a surface, each separated from the next by a strip of background—the simplest and perhaps the earliest method of composition. Except for those factors, and the rather restricted color choice, primarily in earth tones, there is little unity in the designs. Motifs that don't seem to belong together esthetically are freely combined, separated by strips of background. There is also a

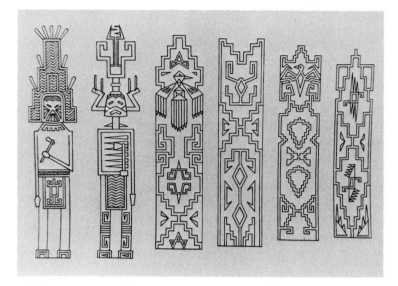

Figure 8-3. Wings for Kopit's *Indians* in the style of American Indian art. The two at the left were part of a false proscenium. The other wings were made in mirror-image pairs (only one of each pair is shown). The differences in size are due to the fact that the wings were designed in forced perspective.

surprising lack of symmetry, which may also result from basketry, since symmetry is less obvious on a curved surface than on a flat. A rectangle, for instance, may have decorative extensions at the top pointing to the sides and then up. We would expect matching extensions at the bottom, pointing to the sides and then down; instead, they are likely to point to the sides and up, like those at the top. Designs for decorative wings for one production of Kopit's *Indians* are shown in Figure 8-3. The motifs have been designed freely, but in the general Indian style.

An Important Resource

These analyses of three greatly differing styles of design are illustrative of the information and conclusions which the scenic artist must develop in mastering a particular style with a view to using it in designing a stage decor, although they are necessarily abbreviated, suggestive rather than exhaustive. The communication of time and place is third in importance among the functions of scenery, but it is nevertheless far from negligible; and since each style of design carries its own implications of spirit, mood, and taste, the use of historic styles, where appropriate, is an important resource for the scenic artist in achieving effects that go beyond the simple temporal, spatial, and cultural location of the action of the play.

9

Designing
for
Esthetics

The designer is now ready to turn to the final aspect of his set, its purely esthetic function.

In its broadest sense, the term *esthetics* applies to all aspects of the arts and consequently includes the entire field of set design. In its narrowest sense, it is restricted to the element of beauty alone. The term is used here to indicate an aspect of design that lies between those two extremes, excluding those functions of scenery that have already been discussed, but including more than simple beauty. Certainly, a design can be visually effective without being pretty or beautiful; it is probably most accurate to say that it should be esthetically interesting.

Every scenic element that is visible to the audience contributes to the esthetic effect of a stage set; the designer's esthetic resources are therefore line, shape, and color. But the total effect is much more than simply the result of adding all of the various elements together: even more important than their individual characteristics are the interrelations among the various elements, which are sensed visually in terms of pattern, balance, and unity.

Nearly all of the decisions the artist has already made in previous steps have esthetic implications, since they have resulted in scenic elements that will be visible to the audience. But even though the artist's attention was focused on other aspects of design, his decisions were not haphazard with regard to esthetics: planning the set as a machine, expressing the mood of the play, and designing in a particular style of decor will all have pushed his plans in the direction of a unified esthetic effect, because all his decisions were carefully made to harmonize with the spirit of the play. The decisions he has already made, then, constitute a kind of framework for the esthetic effect of the final design, and as he turns his full attention to this last element in design, he will be concerned mainly with checking the effects that have already been developed, making fine adjustments, and adding details and surface ornamentation.

Unfortunately, objective principles and procedures are even fewer in the area of esthetics than they are in any other aspect of set design, so that a heavy burden is placed on the designer's own taste. He can cultivate and supplement his taste by developing an understanding of those principles that have been discovered, by constant critical evaluation of his own work as he becomes more experienced, and by the study of the work of other designers.

The principles that underlie all other works of art also apply to the esthetic aspects of scenery: a good design is generally characterized by sensitive handling of a great variety of elements to present meaningful patterns and a clear and unified demonstration of the interrelationships among the various elements. Since the quality of a work of art is represented by the degree of variety, multiplied by the degree of unity, esthetically the designer is interested in increasing both. However, as in theater art as a whole (although to a somewhat smaller degree), the major problem is to achieve unity in the design.

THE SET AS BACKGROUND

In evaluating esthetic effects, the artist must be aware that the actors themselves are the most important part of the stage picture; in fact, since the attention of the audience is focused on them, they are the foreground and accent of the picture: the set itself is background and environment. Consequently, the pattern, as it is represented in the artist's drawings, should be esthetically incomplete. If the set constitutes a complete and satisfying design by itself, it will look busy and overdesigned when the actors appear on it.

Any photographs of sets bare and in use will illustrate this principle. For example, the design for the villain's office in *Our American Cousin (Figure 9-1)* looks unfinished without the actors; the photograph in which they appear displays a finished and satisfying design. Many artists include

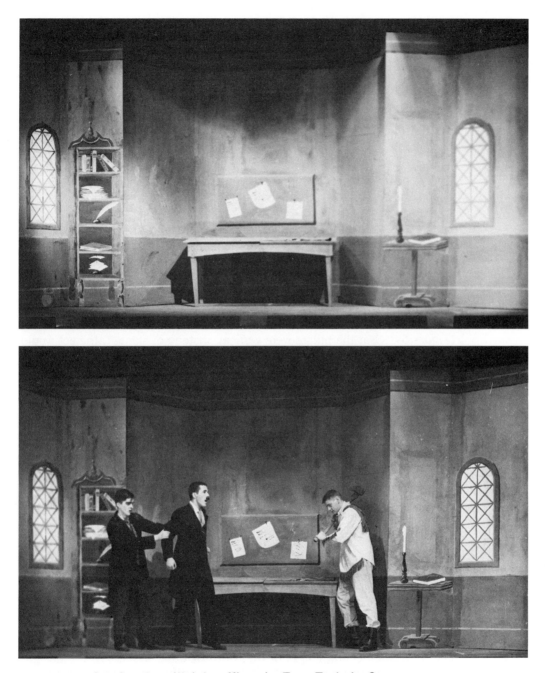

Figure 9-1. Set for the villain's office, in Tom Taylor's *Our American Cousin*. Although the stage picture seems complete when the actors are present, the set alone appears incomplete and underdecorated. [Photographs by Austin Studio.]

pictures of actors in the drawings or paintings of their sets; but in any case the designer must imagine the actors using the set at every point in the design procedure and must evaluate each alternative design as if the set were not bare but peopled by the actors who will use it.

LINE AND SHAPE

Line appears in two forms in scenery; as the edge of a surface, defining its shape and separating it from another, and as a decorative element applied to a surface.

Straight lines in general produce an effect of directness and force; curves suggest grace and lightness. Horizontal lines suggest mass at rest; vertical lines suggest an upward thrust; isolated slanting lines maximally suggest imbalance and tension, although when they form parts of triangles they may become esthetically almost as rigid as triangles in actual construction. In this book, the most extreme illustration of the effect of slanted lines is provided by the picture of the *Antony and Cleopatra* set *(Figure 6-19)*; if the pillars were vertical, instead of slanted, the set would lose the major part of its tension and movement and would become rigid and static.

The most familiar geometrical shape is the rectangle, including its special terminal case, the square. Rectangular shapes are easy to draw and build, and rectangles of various sizes can be readily fitted together; in scenery, as in ordinary life, the rectangle is used more frequently than any other shape.

Rectangles suggest simplicity and rigidity. The square is the least interesting shape in this group, since it is very low in variety, all four sides and angles being identical in size. A rectangle much longer than it is wide supplies more variety but has a disturbing lack of unity. The most abstractly attractive rectangle is one that deviates moderately from the square.

Architects in ancient Greece selected one particular rectangle that conformed to those requirements, naming it the "golden rectangle." It is defined in terms of the proportions between the two sets of sides: the long sides are equal to the diagonal of a square with the same width as the short sides.

In incorporating a rectangle into a design, the designer nearly always determines either the length or the width by other aspects of the design. The following examples indicate the methods of finding the second dimension of a golden rectangle when one side is given.

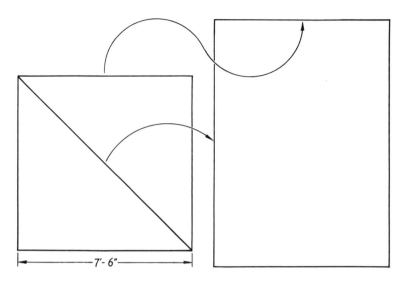

Figure 9-2. Constructing a golden rectangle of given width. The length of the rectangle equals the diagonal of a square the sides of which are the same length as the given width.

1. Suppose that a golden rectangle is needed with a width of 7'-6''. Draw a square 7'-6'' on a side (either full size or to scale), and then measure the diagonal, which will be the same length as the golden rectangle *(Figure 9-2)*.

2. Suppose that the artist wants to construct a golden rectangle with a length of 7'-6''. Draw a line of that length, bisect it, and erect a perpendicular at the center point, drawing it equal to half the length of the original line (in this case, 3'-9''). Then draw a straight line from the end of the perpendicular to one end of the original line; the length of this diagonal line is the same as the width of the golden rectangle needed. (See *Figure 9-3.*)

The length and width of a golden rectangle are incommensurable, which means that they cannot both be expressed in even inches or fractions of an inch. The rectangle described in the first illustration above, for instance, with a width of 7'-6'', would have a length of slightly less than 10'-7⅓''. The designer may specify the length in terms of the golden formula, or he may prefer to round it off to a more convenient even number. In this case, obviously, a rectangle with a length of 10'-7'' or even 10'-6'' would not differ detectably from one of precise golden dimensions.

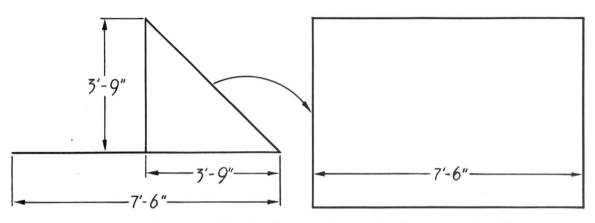

Figure 9-3. Constructing a golden rectangle of given length. The width of the rectangle equals the diagonal of a square the sides of which equal half the given length of the rectangle.

The properties of the golden rectangle are of course not magical. Certainly, the artist will want to use rectangles of widely varying proportions. However, this classic shape is used frequently in design, supplying an easy solution to the need for a figure that will have something of the restfulness and strength of the square without its rigidity and lack of variety.

The circle and ellipse form a pair analogous to the square and rectangle. The circle is extremely high in unity, but has little variety, since it has a single center, and all points in the figure are at an equal distance from it. The ellipse deviates from the circle in a complex and carefully controlled pattern. It has two centers and two major diameters; it can be divided into quarters such that adjacent sections are mirror images of each other, and diagonally opposite sections are identical in shape but with reversed orientation. In the ellipse, unlike in the circle, no two successive points on the outline are at the same distance from either of the centers; however, the sum of the distances between the centers and a point on the circumference is always the same, no matter what point is chosen as the basis for measurement.

If a circle is drawn so that its center matches the center of a square the sides of which are the same length as the diameter of the circle, the circumference will touch the midpoints of the sides of the square. In the same way, if an ellipse is drawn inside a rectangle the length and width of which match the two diameters of the ellipse, the curve will be tangent to the sides of the rectangle at their midpoints. Like the sides of a rectangle, the two diameters of an ellipse may be chosen in any relationship, but the generally most pleasing proportion is that matching a golden rectangle, within which the corresponding ellipse precisely fits.

THE AVOIDANCE OF AMBIGUITY

Although any effect may legitimately be employed by the designer if it is in harmony with the script, in the great majority of cases it is preferable to avoid visual ambiguity. Two elements should be designed as precisely identical or as clearly different; if a line deviates from the vertical, it should slant enough to make it clear that the deviation is intentional; if a curve joins another line, it should be clearly tangential or clearly angled; if two scenic units differ in color, shape, placement, or any other way, the difference should be great enough to prevent any suspicion that it is due to carelessness or a mistake by the designer or the builders.

A designer might well decide that visual ambiguity would be harmonious with the plays of Pirandello, which deal with the ambiguities occurring in ordinary life, or perhaps even with those of Bertolt Brecht, and if so he should use this effect freely, but in most designs it is better to avoid it.

INTERRELATIONSHIPS

The scenic elements that have been discussed so far have been considered in isolation. The stage picture, however, is far more likely to be perceived as a whole in which the interrelationships between the elements are more important than their individual characteristics. The following discussion of the total stage picture will be divided into three major sections, dealing with the texture of the design, the development of a color scheme, and the element of balance.

Texture of the Design

Perhaps the first characteristic of a set design that impresses the audience as the curtains open at the beginning of a play is the texture of the design: the degree to which it seems open and quiet, or busy, decorated, and heavily textured. The impression of texture depends on the number of separate visible areas that have been included in the design and on the degree to which similar motifs are repeated throughout the set. Such repetition may be exact, or it may involve only a few abstract qualities (such as size, color, shape, or type of outline,) while other aspects of the motifs are varied.

The Pattern Effect

The designer should be aware of one particular effect of repetition. As the number of times an element is repeated increases, the interrelationship of the identical elements tends to become more and more obvious, so that finally they seem to join visually to produce an overall pattern, rather than being seen as separate motifs. A single spray of flowers painted in the center of a bare wall would function as an isolated unit; but if the entire wall were covered with regularly spaced identical groups of flowers, the result would be seen as an overall design, supplying a uniform color and texture to the wall, rather than as a mere combination of separate patterns. (See *Figures 3-30* and *3-31.*)

The Color
Scheme

Almost simultaneously with their impression of the visual texture of a set, viewers sense the effect of the pattern of colors that have been used. Color has been mentioned in previous chapters with regard to its effect on attention, its emotional associations, and the fashions in color that are characteristic of historical decorative styles; the principles of color mixing are discussed in Chapter 14.

In addition to those aspects, color is of great esthetic importance; the characteristics of the individual colors are significant, and even more important is the complex set of interrelationships, producing effects of harmony and contrast. What is called a color scheme depends on those interrelationships, and devising the color scheme for the set is one of the designer's major concerns.

Color is one of the most powerful visual elements in design; minute alterations in the colors used in a set can produce surprisingly large changes in its esthetic effect. Many discussions of color emphasize tricks and formulas that are intended to simplify the handling of the complex interrelationships among colors, but the simplification they provide is a false one. Sound color design must take all of the effects of color into account, including the enormous range of hues, greys, shades, and tints that can be distinguished by the human eye, and must balance and manipulate them so as to match as closely as possible the effects the designer has identified in the playscript. The discussion that follows attempts to describe those various factors and their interrelationships, indicating some of the analytical methods by means of which the designer can arrive at satisfactory decisions in his use of color.

The Effect of Light

The apparent color of an object can be altered greatly by careful control of the color of the light that is shown on it. Thus, if a wallpaper with a floral design of red flowers and green leaves on a white background were lit by a pure red light, and all other light carefully excluded, the flowers would become invisible, the background would appear red, and the leaves would turn to black. Such artificial conditions almost never occur in the theater, although the pattern of lighting nevertheless is of great importance in the appearance of a set in actual use. In addition, the principles that control the mixing of colored lights (additive mixture) are different from those that operate in the mixing of pigment (subtractive mixture). The following discussion deals with subtractive mixture, with which the designer is concerned in planning the colors that will be used in painting the flats and other units included in the set.

Color Variables

Any color can be defined in terms of three variables: its hue (a quality that, for example, distinguishes green from orange), the degree to which it contains an admixture of black, and the quantity of white present in the mixture.

The underlying principle for the development of a color scheme is that which applies to all aspects of art: the provision of both variety and unity. The factors that need to be considered are the positions of the colors on the color wheel, the temperature continuum, and the admixtures of black and white. All of these may be varied or restricted to produce different degrees of harmony and contrast (which are in effect synonyms for the terms *unity* and *variety.*

In practical design, the pure colors of the spectrum, without an admixture of black or white, are seldom used. However, our study will be easier if we delay our analysis of the effects of admixture and turn first to the interrelationships of the pure spectral colors.

The Color Wheel. Some spectral colors seem more closely related than others; thus, yellow and orange seem more alike than either yellow and blue or orange and blue. If we were to obtain samples of all of the spectral colors that are clearly distinguishable and arrange them in a sequence so that each color was placed between the two colors to which it seemed most closely related, we would discover that they formed a circular pattern, with all of the colors arranged in a series of regular steps. This familiar arrangement is usually called the *color wheel;* it is diagrammed in *Figure 9-4.*

If the colors in *Figure 9-4* are examined in sequence, it will be noticed that there seems to be a clear shift in feeling at three points in the series, at the colors marked red, blue, and yellow. Although this shift is complex, it can be identified most easily by focusing on the apparent warmth of the colors. Moving from yellow to red, the colors grow progressively warmer; just beyond red, the warmth begins to decrease and continues dropping to blue; on the other side of blue, the feeling is distinctly cool, although the colors gradually warm toward yellow, which functions as a point of balance, with yellow-green clearly (though slightly) cool, and yellow-orange clearly warm.

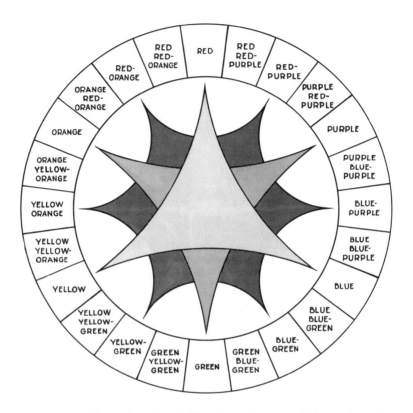

Figure 9-4. The color wheel. The top triangle points to the primary colors, the second triangle indicates the secondary colors. The six-pointed figure marks the colors halfway between the secondaries and primaries, for which familiar names exist. The remaining colors make up the recommended additional steps.

It is easiest to handle the total range of spectral colors if they are organized with reference to the three points where the shift in apparent temperature occurs; thus, the entire wheel can be thought of as made up of an orange group (ranging from an extreme yellow-orange to an extreme red-orange), a purple group, and a green group, with the limits of the groups marked by red, yellow, and blue. Warm colors predominate; there is some disagreement as to the precise points for drawing the lines between the warm and cool sections of the wheel, but the warm area, centered in red, extends for about two-thirds of the entire chart.

For the initial arrangement, the colors were placed so that those most similar stood side by side. Obviously, the farther apart any two colors are on the wheel, the less similar they will be. Inspection will demonstrate that there is a limit to the distance by which two colors can be separated. If, for example, we attempt to identify the color that contrasts most sharply with the blue-green, counting around the circle to the left, the distance between the blue-green and successive colors increases until we reach red-orange, which is twelve steps away. We get the same result if we count to the right. If we count to the red red-orange, however, we discover that while it is thirteen steps away by the path to the left, it is only eleven steps away by the opposite path. The operating measurement is the smallest distance between the two colors, so we must conclude that the blue-green and red red-orange combination results in less contrast than the blue-green and red-orange combination.

For any spectral color, then, the color that will contrast with it most strongly can be identified by drawing a line directly across the color wheel; that is, any two colors in the relationship of maximum contrast lie at opposite ends of the same diameter of the color circle.

A Scheme of Spectral Colors.   The interrelationships among the colors of the wheel that have just been discussed constitute the resources from which a color scheme restricted to spectral colors would inevitably have to be constructed. The artist's procedure would be to use them in making a selection of colors that would combine unity and variety.

Unity (that is, harmony) can easily be achieved by selecting a number of colors from one of the three large segments of the wheel: let us specify the green third of the wheel, extending from blue blue-green through yellow yellow-green. Any colors chosen from this span would be closely related in apparent temperature (all cool). Such a selection would of course be low in variety, and so the effectiveness of the color scheme as a whole could be greatly increased by the addition of one or two colors from outside the basic group.

One possibility would be to shoot a diameter across the wheel from the center of the green segment; it would point to red. Such a combination is possible (of course, any combination of colors is possible); whether it is satisfactory depends on the feeling and effect the designer is trying to produce, so that evaluating it requires an analysis of its effect.

Red and the central green provide maximum contrast (which, of course, is the reason they were originally chosen for traffic lights). Since we are postulating pure colors, the two together can be expected to produce a strident, startling effect, which might well create a sensation of visual vibration; emotionally, they would seem harsh and coarse. If the central green were reduced in area, and the major parts of the design colored in the extreme greens (yellow yellow-green and blue blue-green), the harshness of the contrast with red would be correspondingly reduced, since the red would be 9 steps away from each of the colors rather than the 12 steps that divide it from central green. Obviously, however, the shift of 3 steps would produce only a small change in the basic effect.

If the designer decides that a less harsh combination would be better suited to the effect he wants to produce, he might substitute orange for the red. The new color is 8 steps away from the central green, as compared with the 12 steps separating red and green. Furthermore, if we tabulate the distance between orange and each of the greens (yellow yellow-green, yellow-green, green yellow-green, central green, green blue-green, blue-green, and blue blue-green), and do the same for red, we discover that the orange is on the average 8 steps from all seven of the greens, while the red is an average of 10-2/7 steps away. The results of our computation are supported by visual inspection: the substitution of orange for red very clearly reduces the shrillness of the entire color scheme.

It might be expected that the orange could be replaced with purple without changing the total effect, since mathematically purple, like orange, is an average of 8 steps from the seven greens. However, another factor operates in this case. Of the three major segments of the color wheel, the orange is the warmest and the green the coolest, with purple between them. Consequently, although orange and purple are at the same distance from green on the color wheel, purple is closer to it in apparent temperature, so that the substitution of purple for orange results in a still further decrease in the shrillness of the color scheme.

A color scheme is of course not limited to eight colors. In place of either orange or purple, we might select yellow-orange and red-orange, or red-orange and red-purple, or yellow and blue-purple. Each set, combined with the original seven greens, would produce its own effect, analyzable in terms of their positions on the color wheel and the temperature of the segments from which the colors are taken.

It has already been suggested that the effect of a combination of colors depends in part on the relative amount of each color used in the total design. Obviously, a color scheme made up of equal areas of red, yellow-green, central green, and blue-green would be far more strident than one in which 60% of the area was yellow-green, 20% central green, 10% yellow-green, and the remaining 10% red, scattered in small patches throughout the design. Each color produces its own particular impression, depending on its position in the color wheel, and its special effect is emphasized if a larger area is assigned to it in the scheme. For example, if blue-green and blue-purple appear in the same color scheme, it can be made appreciably warmer by increasing the area of the blue-purple, and appreciably cooler by increasing the area of the blue-green. In this way, the designer can make subtle shifts in the effect of a color scheme even without altering any of the colors chosen.

Pastelling and Greying.   The shrillness of the spectral colors varies considerably, reaching its highest pitch in the red area, and its lowest near blue, but at their quietest the pure colors tend to be unpleasantly strident.

To restrict a color scheme to these colors is analogous to writing a piece of music for brasses and percussion alone: however quietly they played, the music would soon come to seem too loud. Therefore, colors are seldom used in pure forms by artists; nearly always there is some admixture of black or white or both. The pure colors, like the more aggressive musical instruments, are usually saved for climactic accents, rather than being spread broadly throughout a composition.

The emotional effects of admixtures have already been described: the addition of black makes a color seem quieter, more somber, faintly warmer, richer, more opaque, and somewhat more complex and sophisticated; the addition of white makes it seem fresher, lighter (not only literally, but also in terms of emotional effect), airier, somewhat cooler, simpler, and whatever is the opposite of sophisticated. Further, black tends to mute and obscure the color, whereas white alters its fundamental character less sharply; thus, when equal quantities of orange and black are mixed together, the resulting brown is hardly recognizable as related to the original orange, whereas a mixture of equal quantities of blue and white remains clearly blue.

The addition of white to a spectral color is called *pastelling,* and the resulting mixture is said to be *pastelled;* the addition of black to a pure color is referred to as *greying,* although black, not grey, is the actual admixture.

The effects of admixtures of black and white are to some extent contradictory; when both are added to a pure color in equal amounts, the effect of the black somewhat predominates (although this varies with different colors). However, the black and white effects do not necessarily cancel each other; psychologically, the result of the double admixture seems to be partly one of cancellation and partly of addition. Thus, if moderate quantities of black and white are mixed with a pure green, the resulting color combines something of the richness, sobriety, and warmth of the black with the freshness and airiness of the white. The relative influence of the two admixtures can of course be controlled by adding them in different proportions.

An artist designing a color scheme, then, after having first selected the areas of the color wheel that he wants to use, is likely to decide immediately that some of the colors should be heavily muted. If he alters them by adding sizable quantities of black, he will move them in the direction of somberness, sobriety, and richness; if he heavily pastels them, he will make them seem light and delicate. Most often, he is likely to use both black and white to produce still subtler effects, balancing the two admixtures so as to match the mood and style that he has identified in his study of the playscript.

An Example

It may be helpful to describe the development of a color scheme used in an actual set design. *Antony and Cleopatra* is, of course, a great tragedy, but like many other tragedies, in its total impression it seems to energize and uplift rather than depress. It presents a picture of two great cultures and schemes of values in contrast and conflict, but in the main it is set in Egypt, and it is the Egyptian mood and philosophy that dominate the play. Egypt was the most magnificent of the existing cultures, with a history stretching back past human memory and with a highly developed art and technology. In the period in which the play is set, the government had fallen gradually into decay; luxury, self-indulgence, and lack of restraint had rotted its foundations, and the play pictures the slow slipping down of the whole structure as its foundations give way, with, at the end, the Roman soldiers swarming over the ruins.

The designer's intention was to create a set that would combine massiveness with instability, grandeur with neglect, richness with decay. Of course, historical facts such as construction materials, climatic conditions (the brilliance of the Egyptian sun, for example), and the colors traditionally used in ancient Egypt were also influential in devising the color-scheme.

The first decision made with regard to color was to paint the largest area of the set with a color taken from the orange section of the wheel, in order to suggest the warmth of the hot Egyptian sun: yellow-orange was chosen as most likely to produce the effect of sunlit stone. The pure color would have been not only overwhelmingly bright but too fresh and pure to harmonize with the spirit of the play; it was consequently quieted by a considerable admixture of white, and then black was added gradually to produce an effect of somberness and impurity, stopping just short of suggesting actual soiling. As was indicated in Chapter 7, black alters yellow much more sharply than does white; consequently, although much more white was added, it produced little visual effect beyond reducing the glare of the yellow, whereas the quite small amount of black noticeably altered the impression of the mix. Incidentally, the total effect was further emphasized by spattering the entire set heavily with large spots of two colors much lighter and darker than the basic mixture; the result was to produce the appearance of a surface pitted by time and wear.

The design for the stone structures making up the set specified decorations including stripes and rectangles to be painted in colors contrasting with the stone background. Red and blue were finally selected because they provided the sharpest contrast with the basic yellow (if a single color had been chosen, obviously purple would have contrasted still more strongly). Again, it was felt important to reduce the brightness and freshness of the colors. The blue was mixed with a very small amount of red and was then mixed with a sizable quantity of white. The result was much too dark to be called pastel; the effect was rather of a blue that had once been brilliant but had been allowed to fade slightly without being repainted. The red was applied nearly pure, with just a faint addition of black to reduce its vividness.

An integral part of the set was a massive false proscenium, in the shape of two slanted columns and a crosspiece *(Figure 6-19)*. On one column was painted a picture of the Egyptian god Thoth, on the other a picture of Osiris, both larger than lifesize. For the picture of Thoth, the colors already described were used, except that his costume and the symbolic disc-shaped headdress he traditionally wore were painted in a mixture of yellow-orange and white, without the addition of black. Osiris was usually pictured by ancient artists as having skin of normal color, but occasionally he was given a face and body of greyed and pastelled green. This less usual color was chosen for the set, to supply an additional touch of color and to carry some suggestion of decay or of the tarnishing patina of a metal allowed to go unpolished. Finally, large purple drapes were hung at the sides of the set, primarily as masking devices. But instead of a vivid royal purple, a slightly pastelled purple was used, again suggesting dusty neglect.

By far the largest part of the finished set was painted with the greyed and pastelled yellow; the second largest area was blue, and the third red. The green of the Osiris painting occupied perhaps about as much space as the red areas, but because it was less brightly lit, it functioned as a minor accent. The purple of the drapes was relatively insignificant for the same reason.

Just as actors constitute the major focus of the stage picture as a whole, so should their costumes form an essential accentual part of the color scheme. The pattern of colors described was intentionally kept somewhat low-keyed; accents were supplied by the costumes, which were designed in vivid colors, red, blue, gold, green, and purple. In addition, furniture and hand properties were painted to provide sharp contrast, although they were somewhat less vivid than the costumes.

Factors Affecting Relative Sizes of Colored Areas

As the example demonstrates, the relative sizes of the areas occupied by each color in the completed stage picture are an essential part of the color scheme, second only to the selection of the particular colors. What are the factors on which the designer can base his assignment of spatial rank to the various colors he has selected?

Effect of Total Design. The first, and perhaps the most important, of those factors has already been suggested: the contribution each color makes to the particular effect he wants the total design to produce. In music, each note in a chord contributes its own special emotional and esthetic impression, and a composer can greatly alter the effect of a chord by, for example, brassily emphasizing a pair of dissonant notes or, alternatively, concealing them by separating them in different octaves and doubling and otherwise emphasizing the consonant or harmonious notes in the chord. In the same way, each color of the group included in a color scheme produces an individual emotional and esthetic effect, and the artist can alter the total impression by assigning a large area in his design to a particular color or reducing the color to the status of a minor accent. Given a particular selection of colors and a predetermined effect to be developed from them, the designer can thus rank them in order of emphasis, according to the contribution each makes to the total impression.

Spatial Variety.   Nearly all of the principles that apply to other aspects of design are also relevant to the handling of color. Thus, a set painted in a single color would ordinarily be ineffective because, although high in unity, it would lack variety. For the same reason, a color scheme restricted to a few colors close together on the color wheel (especially if they appear in the same temperature segment) would be inadequately varied, even if different degrees of pastelling and greying were used to alter the basic monotony.

Furthermore, even though a varied selection of colors has been made, assigning identical areas to all of the colors in a scheme would violate the principle of emphasis, which requires that a design have a single focus of attention. Usually, then, the designer arranges the colors he has selected in a hierarchy according to the amount of space to be given to each, basing his decisions on the relation between the effect of each color and the impression he intends the total design to produce and assigning different areas to each of the colors in the scheme.

Visual Focus. Another factor involved in this arrangement is *background effect,* according to which the viewer's attention tends to be focused not on the largest area of a design but on the second largest, with other areas attracting attention in the order of their size. (Background effect is discussed further later in this chapter.) The viewer's pattern of attention, however, is also strongly influenced by the fact that individual colors themselves attract attention in different degrees. Furthermore, the distribution of the colors in the design is of great importance in affecting visual focus. Thus, if the set design contains two square feet of pure red-orange, placed in a single spot, the color will attract much more attention than if the same total area was divided into many small spots and spread in the form of a floral wallpaper design over the entire set.

Visual Fatigue.   And finally, one other factor is greatly important in assigning the relative areas to the different colors: the phenomenon of visual fatigue. Just as a single fortissimo strident chord, played in the brasses for a length of time, causes aural fatigue and discomfort, so a very large area of intense color tends to produce a visual feeling of uneasiness, discomfort, and fatigue.

All of the factors discussed, then, suggest that the largest area in a design should generally be assigned to a relatively quiet, muted color that will serve as an effective background without calling great attention to itself and without fatiguing the eye. The smallest area should then be assigned to the most vivid and striking color, which becomes an accent. The other colors, less noticeable than the accent and less quiet than the background, can be assigned rank matching their effects, with the most vivid being given the largest area, and the least vivid the smallest.

Breaking the Rules

Obviously, the effect the designer intends to produce takes precedence over any rules such as those given above; in fact, they should be thought of not as fiats or prohibitions, but as descriptions of the results of different arrangements. It is conceivable that for a particular play (perhaps one by Pirandello or one from the contemporary absurdist school) the designer might find that violating every specific suggestion that has been made would produce precisely the effect he wanted. Here, as in every aspect of art, rules can only be helpful guides: the final and overriding consideration must always be the designer's own purposes, and, the final decision must be made on the basis of his own taste. However, for the majority of sets and for most plays, the specific suggestions that have been made are valid solutions to color problems.

The creation of a color scheme is simply another application of the principles that underlie all artistic decisions; but viewers' response to color is more vivid visually and more intense emotionally than their reaction to many other elements in design, including form, line, and movement. As in the expression of mood by means of color, the designer should develop the habit of consciously noticing and analyzing his response to color in everyday life and should study the work of other set designers, as well as of easel painters, in an attempt to become as fully acquainted as possible with the entire range of color effects.

Balance

Viewers are less likely to be consciously aware of the element of balance in a set than of its texture and color scheme, but balance operates powerfully even if the viewers do not focus their attention on it.

Esthetic balance is always illustrated figuratively in terms of a physical balance involving weights, a bar, and a fulcrum *(Figure 9-5)*. If the supporting fulcrum is in the center of the bar, and the weights are equal and equidistant from the fulcrum, the bar and its weights will be evenly balanced. However, it is possible to balance unequal weights by shifting the heavier weight toward the fulcrum; thus a one-pound weight can be

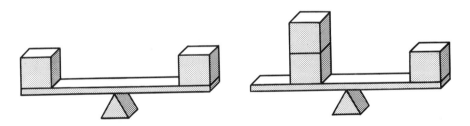

Figure 9-5. Symmetrical and asymmetrical balance. The balancing of unequal weights by adjusting their placement along a bar supported by a fulcrum is analogous to the visual balancing of elements in an asymmetrical set design.

made to balance a two-pound weight if the heavier weight is shifted halfway toward the fulcrum.

The same principle can be applied to visual design, except that psychological weight rather than real weight operates: the figurative visual weight of a design element is the force with which it attracts attention, not simply its size or mass.

Balance is automatically guaranteed in a symmetrical set, since, whatever the psychological weight of the various elements, each is balanced by a duplicate on the opposite side of the stage, at exactly the same distance from the center line. (See *Figure 9-6.*) It is conceivable, of course, that even in an asymmetrical design, elements would be so arranged that the psychological weight of each unit or motif was precisely matched by the weight of another unit opposite it, even though the units did not duplicate each other. More often, each element in an asymmetrical design is placed opposite an element on the other side of the stage that is different in psychological weight; in that case, balance can be achieved only by placing the elements so that the heavier is closer to the center line of the stage and the lighter farther from it.

However, since balance is a quality of the design as a whole, not of individual parts or even pairs of elements, it is the total arrangement of each of the halves that is significant. An objective evaluation of the balance of a design would involve an assessment of all of the factors that influence the force with which a design element attracts the attention of the viewer: color, shape, size, contrast, orientation, etc. Although it is helpful to be aware of such factors, especially when attempting to correct imbalance in a tentative design, our present state of knowledge does not enable us to make an objective analysis of the presence of balance in a design, or the degree to which it deviates from complete balance. In practice, the artist inspects the set as a whole, focusing on the factor of balance and attempting to analyze his response to the design to determine

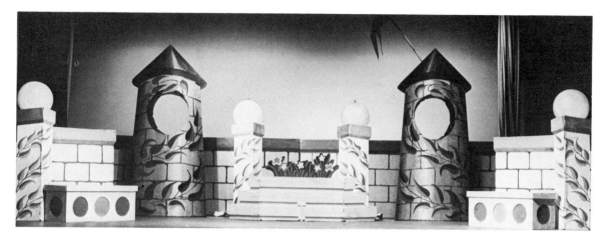

Figure 9-6. Set for Aurand Harris's *Simon Big-Ears* illustrates symmetrical balance. This set, for a children's play, was designed to be transported in a small truck for touring. To save space, the towers were built flat, and thickness suggested by *trompe l'oeil* painting. The benches were constructed so that they could be turned upside down and filled with costumes and properties, and the elaborate planter folded into a compact box shape. [Photograph by Norm Burlingame.]

whether the right and left halves seem to attract his attention equally. This can be done most effectively by using a complete actual set, of course, but practicality requires that the decision be made before the set has been built. The second best basis for evaluation is a colored perspective painting of the set. A perspective outline drawing is less effective, and a ground plan constitutes the minimum drawing that can be used. Whenever anything less than the actual set is used to evaluate balance, the designer must supply the missing elements imaginatively. In particular, it is important that he imagine the set being used by actors; since he is evaluating the relative balance of visual attraction, and since the actors are the most powerfully attractive elements in the stage picture, they are a major factor in judging balance.

If the designer's analysis indicates that the set is not in balance, he can achieve balance only by weakening elements in the half of the design that is too strong or strengthening those in the weak side, using any factor or combination of factors that affect the visual weight of design elements.

This discussion is not intended to imply that visual balance is necessarily desirable. Robert Edmond Jones designed a set for *The Devil's Garden* in which a single small chair appears in the left half of the stage, and all other scenic elements (three chairs, a table, a door, and a large framed wall decoration) are concentrated in the right half. The set was designed for a scene in which an accused postal clerk is being interrogated by a board of inspectors, and the extreme imbalance in the design powerfully emphasizes the isolation of the accused man and the strength of the examiners. Like all other aspects of design, visual balance is one of the artist's resources, which he can use or avoid as seems best for his particular design and play.

Factors Affecting Balance

Unity requires that one element in a design serve as a visual focus, to which all other elements are subordinate. The degrees to which the various elements of a stage picture attract the viewer's attention depend, as has been indicated, on a variety of factors. Some of them are discussed below.

Orientation. The distance between any scenic element and the center line of the stage has already been mentioned as a factor in balance: the farther left or right of that line an element is placed, the more apparent weight it has. Related to that effect is the element of orientation, that is, the angle at which a scenic unit is turned toward the spectators: the more directly a surface faces them, the more striking it is. Thus, if identical doors are placed in the center of each of the three walls composing an interior set, the door in the back wall will be visually much stronger than those in the side walls. Although the old wing-and-drop sets had some serious defects, they had at least the advantage that all scenic elements were placed so as to face the audience directly, giving them maximum visibility.

Height. Height also attracts attention: a door placed at the back of a platform, reached by a flight of stairs, is much more likely to attract attention than if it were placed on the stage floor. In the last act of *Antony and Cleopatra,* the actress playing the queen easily dominated Caesar and a stageful of soldiers, largely because she stood on a platform more than nine feet high, with the other actors only slightly raised above the floor of the stage.

Contrast. As was indicated in the discussion of blocking, contrast is a very strong factor in controlling attention. In the *Antony and Cleopatra* set, the attention is focused on the opening under the final arch, although the other arches are larger and closer to the audience, because each of the first three arches has another behind it, partially filling in the opening with areas of nearly the same color, whereas the fourth arch is backed by sky, and the only interrupter, the beaded screens, contrasts with it and with the openings of the other arches. Contrast may be of any type—color, texture, shape, orientation, size, or height. The intense contrast of an open candle flame with a dimly lit stage is undoubtedly one major reason for its strong visual attractiveness.

Area: The Background Effect. The visual size of a scenic element affects balance. However, the influence of size depends on a paradoxical psychological principle that has already been mentioned: the *background effect.*

It might be supposed that if two areas of different color were combined in a design, one of them occupying 75% of the total area and the other 25%, someone looking at the design would tend to focus on the larger area. Just the opposite is true: it is generally not the largest but the second largest area of design that attracts attention—the eye sees the largest area as background; the second largest area as the figure. That can be demonstrated very easily by taking a sheet of white paper and putting a small black circle near the center. Someone who is shown such a sheet and asked to describe what he sees may even fail to mention the white area entirely and simply reply that he sees a black circle. A circle of white on a black sheet would produce a similar result.

Usually, then, the largest and second largest areas in a stage picture constitute the two extremes of focus, with the viewer focusing primarily on the second largest area, and the largest area attracting the least attention. The other visual areas normally fall in the order that might be expected, with the largest of them receiving the most attention and the smallest the least.

Scale. Related to the area of a scenic element is its scale. Viewers' judgment of scale is determined by two factors: their experience with architectural elements, furniture, and properties in ordinary life and the visual diminution produced by the fact that the viewing distance is greater in the theater than is usual elsewhere. The theatrically normal scale of a scenic element is based on the sizes of similar objects in ordinary life, expanded to achieve effective visual projection.

The use of forced perspective in set design was discussed in Chapter 6. Psychologically, viewers adjust their judgment of the scale of an object according to its apparent distance. Thus, when objects are diminished in forced perspective, viewers see them as if they were full size, so that they have almost the same visual weight as similar objects closer to the viewers. For example, the fourth arch in the *Antony and Cleopatra* set seems to be as large as the other three, so that it has greater weight than its actual share of the stage picture would suggest.

Psychological Gravity.   The mass of scenic elements is a further factor in the degree to which they attract attention, although it is their apparent, rather than their actual, weight that is significant.

The evaluation of the force of gravity in scenery is in effect an imaginative extrapolation from ordinary experience with actual gravity. Normal experience illustrates that mass must be supported either by hanging it from directly overhead or by resting it on a support directly below it. Furthermore, the position of a mass is most stable when the support on which it rests is at least as large as the object being supported. Thus, a pyramid in normal position seems exceptionally stable; a pyramid balanced on its point would seem extremely unstable. These familiar experiences are unconsciously carried over into our reaction to design elements: For his *King Oedipus* set, Michael David set the solid rectangle of his door on a broad base, emphasizing the relationship by painting them the same color. If the various low platforms in front of the door were painted grey to match the walls of the palace, the set would lose a great deal of its apparent solidity: the door would seem to float inexplicably in air.

Such an effect might, of course, fit a particular play; the designer's understanding of esthetic gravity should not restrict him, but should enable him to choose the effect he wants and design a set that will achieve it. Euripides' strange play *The Bacchae* explores the areas of irrationality and madness in human life; in a design for it, Karin McClow made use of psychological gravity to match the distortions and uneasiness of the script. A major part of her design is a flight of steps arranged in a complex curve extending clear across the stage. Although they are structurally solid, from the viewpoint of the audience the stairs seem to lack support and to float in midair. The result is that in use the set gives a dreamlike and irrational quality to the movement of the actors, expressing an element strongly emphasized in the script itself.

Support.   Ordinary life supplies many examples of weights raised high by means of an upward thrust. Such support is part of ordinary direct experience in lifting weights with the hands, particularly in thrusting them above the head. But the same type of support is familiar in our visual experience, supplied by the legs of furniture and by the columns of buildings. Again, this experience unconsciously affects our interpretations of design even though no actual force may be present. We tend to interpret a simple rectangle, for example, as if it were something like the end of a table, with the vertical lines thrusting upward to support the weight of the horizontal top line. Our attention in such a situation is primarily on the vertical force, rather than on the weight being supported.

Ordinary experience suggests that a support should have a particular relationship to the mass supported, not only in height but also in width. Designs that deviate from that expectation impress the viewer as delicate and insecure, if the support is narrower than expected, or as crude and clumsy, if the support is broader than seems necessary. (See *Figure 7-5.*)

Color: Advance-Recession. Besides serving as part of the color scheme of a set, individual colors constitute an important resource in controlling the attention of the audience. Fortunately, the principles governing this aspect of color have been studied.

An optical illusion affects a spectator's judgment of the distance of various colors: if vivid red is placed beside a vivid blue, the red seems closer to the viewer than the blue. In general, this advancing-receding effect matches the apparent warmth of the colors: warm colors seem to advance, and cool colors to recede. The eye tends to focus on the advancing colors, interpreting them as occupying more space, and being more important, in a design than is actually the case. Thus, in a checkerboard design of red and green, the red would seem to predominate slightly. If Michael David's *King Oedipus* design were reversed, with blood-red walls and a grey door, the door would seem much less striking than it does. A similar reduction in the intensity of focus on the door would result if the blue-green wall ornaments were painted red, and the door painted blue-green. Such a change might so increase the attentive strength of the ornament and reduce that of the door that the focus would become ambiguous, almost evenly divided between the two elements.

Of the colors appearing on the color wheel, the secondary color orange and the primary colors red, yellow, and blue most strongly attract attention. However, most people find them garish and raw, so they are seldom used in pure form in the theater. The rawness of a particular color may be counteracted by mixing a small amount of one of the other primaries with it; the resulting mixture will be nearly as striking as the pure primary. Examples of such colors are chinese red (primary red with a small amount of yellow added), blue-green (blue plus a little yellow), and yellow-green (yellow with a little blue).

The addition of white to a pigment noticeably reduces its power to attract attention, and the addition of black produces an extreme reduction. If the designer finds that one of his colors attracts more attention than he intends, he may easily pull it down to its proper position by adding a little black, a somewhat larger amount of white, or a combination of the two.

RECORDING THE COLOR SCHEME

Esthetic decisions will be recorded in final form in the working drawings prepared as guides for the construction crew and perhaps even more clearly, in the designer's perspective painting of the set. Suggestions for recording the color scheme are given in Chapter 14, in connection with making the perspective painting. In making his other decisions, the designer will undoubtedly make many sketches and may even carry them as far as scaled drawings. The form, detail, and accuracy of any drawings he makes in this step are determined by his own preferences and habits of work; if he is uncertain, he should err, as always, on the side of overprecision rather than risk having to redesign an element.

UNITY

The integration of the various visual elements so as to produce an effect of unity has been identified as the most important esthetic element in scenery. An effective design creates an illusion of inevitability; "illusion" because, of course, another designer would produce a different stage picture. Nevertheless, all of the parts of the design should not only seem to belong together, but fit together so precisely that it is difficult for the spectator to imagine an alteration that would not damage the pattern.

In choosing the color scheme, designers often attempt to achieve unity simply by repeating colors; if an upholstery fabric for the set has green, red-brown, and beige as its colors, the designer may assume that any green or brown can safely be used anywhere in the set without affecting the unity of the entire scheme. However, that is a crude and often unsuccessful method. Unity requires a similarity of feeling, not a simple repetition of positions on the color wheel. Thus, if a major color of the set is a clear pastel green, the unity of effect would probably be less disturbed by the addition of a pale violet than a muddy green.

Nevertheless, repetition of visual elements is a very useful device for developing unity in a design. Even pieces of broken glass of various colors, arranged in a random or accidental fashion, can produce a strikingly beautiful pattern when, as in a kaleidoscope, they are repeated so as to form a hexagonal arrangement. In this case, half the images are reversed in mirror-image fashion, another device that is often useful on stage.

It would require hundreds of pages to describe in detail how the impression of unity was achieved in specific set designs. However, a few brief illustrations may be helpful. Shakespeare's *The Tempest* is set on a magic island, imagined as a wild region far from civilization. The basic color chosen for the set for one production was that of a sandy beach or sun-warmed rock, with areas of grass green and faint purple. Since straight lines are rare in nature, only curves were used on the set.[1] (See

1. In an attempt to imitate the audience-actor relationship of Elizabethan times, the director asked the designer to include areas on stage where some members of the audience might be seated, but those areas were not considered part of the scenery. They were painted black, and their offstage edges were bounded by straight lines to separate them from the rest of the stage space.

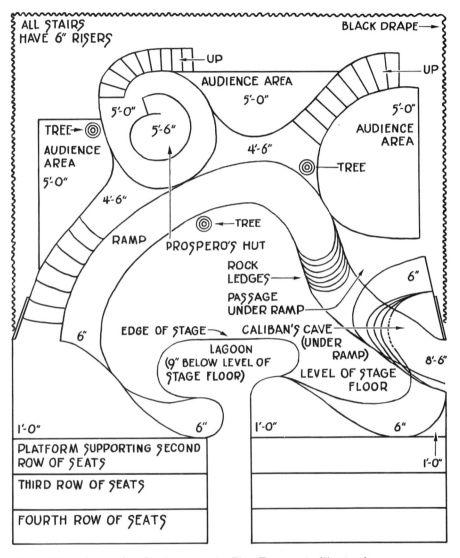

Figure 9-7. A set for Shakespeare's *The Tempest,* illustrating the use of natural curves to unify a complicated design. (See also *Figures 2-14* and *9-8.*)

Figures 9-7 and *9-8.*) Although the set is basically unrepresentational, the shapes and decoration were intended to suggest natural shapes, especially those of rock formations. Three trees were constructed by combining dead branches from actual trees; however, they were treated so as to remove them from ordinary experience. Each was fitted into a specially constructed, obviously artificial base; they were painted pastel green with dry-brushed areas of lavender; and clear glitter was sprinkled for a foot or two

Figure 9-8. *The Tempest.*

on the ends of the branches. They thus became magical and unreal, and at the same time a symbol of trees.

For *We Bombed in New Haven,* as was mentioned earlier, one designer chose the colors and pattern used for camouflage as a symbol of the play, applying it to every area of the set (including floor, furniture, and walls) except a blackboard hanging on one wall. The use of a single pattern produced a strong effect of unity in a set that in fact combined shapes and properties from various sources and of various styles.

The set for Paul Sills's *Story Theater (Figures 1-3, 1-4,* and *1-5)* is an especially clear example of the use of an effect or style (the imitation of pop-up illustrations for children's books) to achieve unity in a set with many vividly contrasting colors—bright clear yellow, vivid red, grass green, black, tan (for the rail fence), green blue-green, blue blue-green, and brown (for the trees and bush).

The set for *The Lark (Figure 6-21)* is unified by the use of a single color, medium grey, for all surfaces except the stained glass; by the multiple use of Gothic arches of identical shape and size (a device that helps tie the window to the rest of the set, in spite of the difference in color); and by the less obvious interrelationship among the platforms, which, although they vary in shape, are fitted together to form easy paths for the actors and a visually integrated base for the set as a whole. A similar platform treatment is illustrated in the set for *The Rimers of Eldritch (Figures 6-23* and *6-24).*

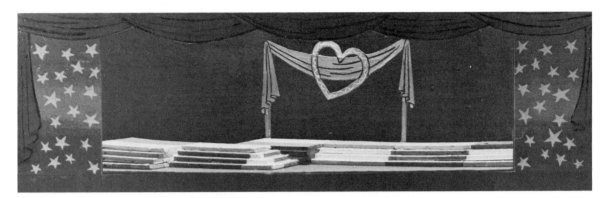

Figure 9-9. *Of Thee I Sing.* A model of the set for the beauty contest scene.

Figure 9-10. *Of Thee I Sing.* The Capitol steps for the inauguration scene (shown in model).

The musical comedy *Of Thee I Sing* takes place in several different locales. The designer for one production, having decided to use a unit set made up of platforms and steps, with a very few properties *(Figures 9-9 and 9-10),* chose to paint the platforms and steps red, white, and blue, colors appropriate to this play, which is a burlesque of American politics. The vivid, unspattered colors also echoed the bright, brash effect of the music and story line. Again, the set was integrated visually by a unity of feeling rather than by the simple repetition of a single color.

If the designer's only concern were the mood of a play, the achievement of unity would be simpler than it is. But most often he will find he must alter his plans to adjust to architectural features of his particular theater or to build in support. He may then be faced with obtrusive braces or masking devices that must be esthetically integrated with the rest of the set so that they seem to the audience to have been chosen intentionally for their appearance, rather than being the result of extraneous necessity.

As an example, see *Figure 1-6.* Because of the shape and size of the offstage area, it was necessary to provide sizable masking devices at the upstage corners of the set. At first the designer simply placed flats there, which masked the areas but had no esthetic relation to the rest of the set. After extended experimentation, the designer made additions to the flats that altered the rectangular shape and related them visually to the platform structure, an effect that was emphasized by painting them in the same colors as those used for the platforms.

The design for *The Taming of the Shrew* shown in *Figure 3-23* did not at first incorporate Gothic arches. The high balcony of the set extended across the forestage from wall to wall of the theater, passing just above the railing of the permanent balcony, which had been condemned as unsafe for use by the audience and was consequently left empty. The weakness of this balcony required that each pillar for the temporary scenic balcony be supported with triangular braces on both sides, producing a visual pattern that was felt to be inharmonious with the play. Again, experiment and the trial of various designs indicated that the obtrusive braces could be neatly concealed by setting open Gothic arches in front of the balcony. These were then worked into the other areas of design, resulting in a unified pattern that produced the impression of inevitability. Probably no one in the audience suspected that the arches were compromises necessitated by an architectural defect, but rather assumed that they had been chosen because of their relation to the period of the play. Far from being exceptional, such compromises must be made in most designs created for actual production.

It is much easier to illustrate the development of unity in a small detail of a design than in a set as a whole. Three examples will be given, one of bad design and two that are more successful.

At one theater, hidden in the corner of the prop room, were found benches built at some forgotten time by some anonymous designer. They were dragged out for use in rehearsals, although they were enough to set on edge the teeth of anyone with good taste. One of them is shown in *Figure 9-11.* Its ugliness is clear at a glance; exactly why it is so badly designed is evident only on closer examination. It is, of course, impossible to judge the unknown artist's ability accurately from a single design. Perhaps the benches were planned and built in an emergency that made it impossible to take time for careful work. Clearly, however, sound design procedures were not followed, whether from lack of time or lack of ability.

The side of the bench establishes the design as strongly asymmetrical; the end, however, is equally strongly symmetrical. The result is a striking lack of harmony. The legs at the end of the bench are 5'' wide *(F*

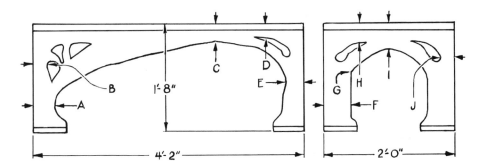

Figure 9-11. An example of bad design: the side and end of a bench.

in *Figure 9-11)*, producing an effect of heaviness; on the side, the legs shrink to a width of only 3″ (at *E*) and 4″ (at *A*). Not only do the various leg widths seem not to belong together, but the heavier legs are put at the ends of the bench, where their width is more emphatically obtrusive than if they had been used at the sides, which are more than twice as wide.

Although 5″ is clearly established as the width of the legs at the end, their structural integrity is violated by cutting presumably ornamental holes (at *H* and *J*) that narrow them to less than 2½″. Similar ornamental cuts also contradict the basic widths of the legs at the side of the bench (*B* and *D*), producing widths of slightly less than 2½″ on the legs, in conflict with the 3″ and 4″ widths defined at *A* and *E*. Similarly, the visual thickness of the supporting apron also varies unesthetically. Omitting the plywood top, the apron is 2″ wide at *C* and 3½″ wide at *I*. Again, the appearance of greatest strength is produced at the end, where it would be least expected, with a resulting clumsiness that conflicts with the apparent delicacy of the side support at *C*.

The ornamental holes are awkwardly shaped and not well related to each other. Three are vaguely commalike; another three (at *B*) form a kind of corner ornament that is not integrated (note in particular the apparently accidental variation in size and shape of the solid strips between the end holes in the group and the center hole). Furthermore, the shape of the three holes as a unit (imagining that the outer edges of the end holes continue across the intervening strips; enclosing the entire unit with a solid outline) is not only ugly in itself, but out of harmony with the curved edge just below it, as well as with the adjacent corner of the bench. At the top, the edge of the shape is almost parallel with the upper edge of the bench; at the side it pulls away in a line shooting down as if to intersect the long curving lower edge at an angle.

The curves that outline the areas between the legs also bear examination. These, as well as the ornamental holes, are notably irregular, but it seems likely that the irregularity is due to poor construction rather than design; in fact, the craftsmanship apparent in the bench is nearly as bad as the esthetic judgment displayed in the design. The curve at the end of the bench joins the right leg smoothly, but joins the left leg at an angle. The edge of each leg curves out at the bottom to suggest a foot, but the terminal curve at the bottom of the right leg includes the added piece of plywood as part of the foot; the foot of the left leg is cut entirely from the vertical piece, so that the added bottom strip lies outside the foot shape. The result is two feet quite different in appearance. A similar conflict in shape appears in the feet at the side of the bench, although it is less noticeable because they are farther apart.

This analysis indicates the major esthetic defects in the design of the bench. However, the structural decisions are also significant. Although in the strictest sense they lie beyond the area of esthetics, one of the most constant marks of a good designer is the care that he gives to questions of practicality and construction.

There is evidence that the method of fastening the parts of the bench together was developed as an afterthought. The normal height for benches is 1'-6", which is how high this design would be if the plywood seat and the blocks at the bottom of the legs were omitted. The bench is 2'-0" wide, an economical measure, since the legs can be cut from a standard sheet of plywood without waste. However, the bench is 4'-2" long, which is uneconomical. The ends and sides of a 4'-0" bench could be cut entirely from a single sheet of plywood, with no waste; the extra 2" makes it necessary to use two sheets, wasting something more than 7 square feet of the sheet most fully utilized. (Even more of the other sheet would be wasted.)

It was decided to miter the leg joints where the sides and ends meet. The advantage of the miter joint is its appearance: the crack between the two pieces of wood coincides with the corner of the joint and is therefore less visible. On the other hand, the miter joint (especially one involving the edges of boards) is difficult to make accurately, and unless it is fitted precisely it is likely to be much weaker than other joints. In fact, the ends and sides of some of the benches had come entirely apart at the corners when they were found in storage. The sturdier butt joint would have been much faster and easier to make and could have been made more accurately. While the crack between the pieces of wood would have been slightly more noticeable, it would have been invisible at theatrical viewing distances.

Apparently the joints were recognized as weak as soon as the benches had been assembled. In an attempt to strengthen them, the designer added triangular plywood blocks at the bottoms of the legs. This is a legitimate device, although in this case a kind of makeshift afterthought. If they were to be used, however, the blocks should have been cut slightly smaller and set inside the legs, rather than beneath them. The design had not taken them into account, so that adding them under the legs thickened the foot motifs, increasing both the general effect of clumsiness and the total height of the bench. Incidentally, the added blocks themselves produced the visible joint line that the miter joint had been intended to avoid.

Extensive as this analysis has been, it has not exhausted the details of this design. Most importantly, it suggests the kind of considerations with which the designer must be concerned. Supposing that a genuine artist had developed this design during his exploration of design possibilities, it is exactly these points that he would observe in testing the sketch and that he would attempt to revise in further versions.

It is with some relief that we can turn to a design prepared by sound methods. The designer's assignment was to develop specifications for the construction of a series of ornamental shutters, vaguely Victorian in style, suggestive of wrought iron although not intended as a *trompe l'oeil* reproduction. In contrast with the designer of the bench shown in *Figure 9-11*, which gives little evidence of having been subjected to any critical analysis, the artist prepared perhaps thirty preliminary sketches for the shutters, steadily refining them until he felt the best available design solution had been achieved. (See *Figure 9-12*.)

Each shutter was made out of two layers of plywood, the major area being cut from a sheet of ¼'' ply, to which was then glued and nailed a rectangular edging and central stiffening cartouche cut from ⅝'' plywood sheathing (chosen because it happened to be the cheapest locally available: notice the concern for practicality). S-shaped curlicues were chosen as the basic motif, and they were twined across the entire space, touching the outline strips of plywood as tangential curves at enough points to make a firm structure. (In fact, the last alteration in the design was the addition of pairs of curves at both the top and the bottom of the shutter to strengthen what were felt to be structural weaknesses caused by too large open spaces.) For further strength, good-sized solid areas of plywood were left inside the ends of the central cartouche, with triangular holes cut to mark their ends.

The pattern was cut in the plywood with a saber saw, and the two layers were fastened together. The entire structure was then painted in a greyed, slightly pastelled blue-green suggestive of the patina of weathered metal, and highlights and shadows were added to shape the fanlike solid areas and to suggest interweaving of the S-curves, producing a somewhat more interestingly varied surface than flat painting.

A comparison of the shutter and the bench will illustrate vividly the difference between good and bad design. That difference consists largely of the presence or absence of analytical, evaluative intelligence. It is obvious that the shutter elements have been painstakingly planned, that their

Figure 9-12.   Successful design: an ornamental shutter.

form has been carefully chosen and precisely adjusted; it is equally obvi-ous that the bench was created without analysis, evaluation, taste, or planning, and that it fails both esthetically and structurally.

The third example involves the creation of what are actually three designs, esthetically integrated as a group because they were intended to be used together. The artist was initially given the outline of a butterfly and asked to develop a wallpaper pattern for a small room, using the but-terfly as the primary motif. It was decided early that the butterflies should be placed evenly across the surface, following a geometric grid, as with most wallpaper designs. But how could they be tied together to form an integrated design?

The designer's first step was to enclose the motif in a line that would simplify the shape while still matching it at key points. Trial sketching demonstrated that such a shape could be made up of four curves (line 1 in *Figure 9-13*). Further experimentation involved enlarging the enclosing shape, resulting in the discovery that the curves tended to approach arcs of circles as the figure increased in size. Continued sketching was guided by an attempt to develop an enclosing four-line figure made up entirely of arcs of circles of the same diameter ("final outlines" in *Figure 9-13*). The radius of these arcs was determined by judging the relation between the butterfly motif and the background area marked off by the curves. At this point, the arcs were extended to form complete circles, and an all-over pattern of overlapping circles developed from them.

It was felt that the resulting design was well unified but lacking in variety, so the circles were broken at the points of intersection to suggest the over-and-under effect of weaving, and it was decided to paint a different pattern of wing markings for each butterfly. Finally, a pure white

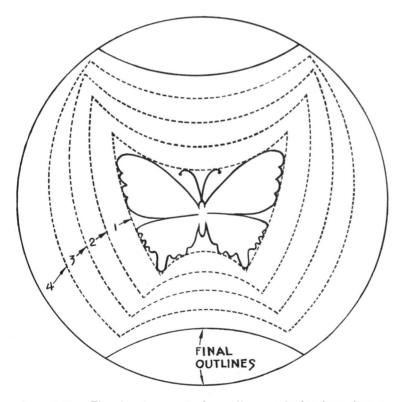

Figure 9-13. The development of a wallpaper design based on a butterfly motif, shown in five stages.

Figure 9-14. A section of the completed wallpaper design.

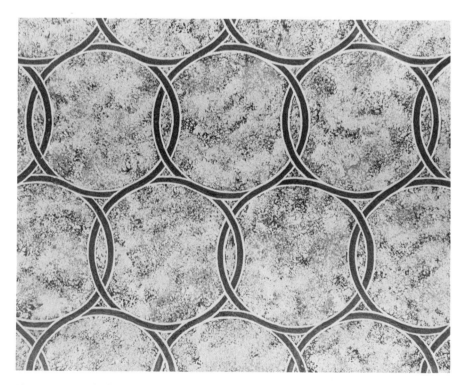

Figure 9-15. A tile pattern designed to harmonize with the butterfly wallpaper.

Figure 9-16. A design for a stained glass window, related to the wallpaper and tile designs.

was chosen for the background, and the entire pattern was painted with gold-colored powder. (See *Figure 9-14.*)

After the working drawings had been completed, the designer was asked to add a small stained-glass window to the room and to prepare a floor-tile pattern. For the floor, the background was painted white and then heavily stippled with dark green and red paint (applied with a sponge) and lightly stippled with gold. The butterflies were omitted, but the circle motif was duplicated as an overall design, the lines painted in gold and edged with white to make them more visible. (See *Figure 9-15.*)

For the window, the area was divided into three panes. A single translucent circle was set in the center of each pane, and a gold butterfly was painted on the glass. The rest of the window was filled with colored shapes radiating from the central circles and crossed by curves that formed transitions in shape between the circles and the rectangular outlines of the panes. (See *Figure 9-16.*)

As design projects, the bench and shutter described above are extremely simple and limited; the development of related wallpaper, tile, and window designs is somewhat more complex. The set designer must, of course, handle a much larger scale of problems, involving all of the elements of the play, including blocking, mood, locale, and architectural conditions, as well as esthetics. However, the methods of analysis described above are typical of the artist's work in developing unity of design, on whatever scale he works.

AN ORDERLY PROCEDURE

Our discussion of the total process of designing a set has been broken into five major steps: the preliminary analysis; designing the machine; designing for mood; designing for locale; and designing for esthetics. To some extent, such a division is artificial; the decisions made at each point in the process affect all later decisions, and there is always the possibility that the designer will find it necessary to return to earlier steps and redesign, or at least adjust, his original plans. Certainly, a designer will be aware of the total design problem at each step in his work. But the point made at the beginning of this discussion should be reemphasized here: at each point in the process, without completely erasing other aspects of the problem from his mind, the skilled professional designer focuses fully on a single aspect of his work; only when he has planned it to the best of his ability does he turn to another part of the work. No other single error could be so destructive of good work as attempting to attack the different aspects of the work of set design in random order or simultaneously. Considered as a whole, set design is unmanageably complex and difficult; but when it is divided into a series of separate problems, and full attention focused on them individually, the work is reduced to manageable size, and each designer is able to handle it at the highest level of effectiveness of which he or she is capable.

PART III

RECORDING THE DESIGNS

10

The Designer's Materials and Instruments

Good quality materials and instruments contribute greatly to the ease and speed with which the designer can prepare his drawings. It is possible to produce good work with the crudest of dime-store instruments and materials, but at a cost of so much greater time and care that the designer should build up a supply of good tools as quickly as his budget will allow.

CARDBOARD

Cardboard is available in a very large range of styles, thicknesses, and sizes. The common size of 22″ × 28″ is a useful one for set work. The board is available with surfaces of varying degrees of roughness, technically referred to as *tooth*. Slick board is annoyingly difficult to use: it gets dirty quickly, and errors are hard to correct because erasures tend to show badly. On the other hand, a heavily toothed board is difficult to draw on accurately, especially with ink. Consequently, the preferred board for theatrical drawings has a very fine, barely perceptible tooth: it should feel smooth but not slick to the touch.

307

TRACING PAPER

Tracing paper is a necessary part of the artist's supplies; it is a tough, thin paper treated so as to make it almost transparent. Like cardboard, it comes in a wide range of qualities and sizes.

The paper is sold in pads and rolls. Not only are the rolls much cheaper in cost per square foot, but they can be used with less waste. The pads are cut in sizes and proportions that are not related to typical theatrical drawings, so it is sound practice to buy the paper by the roll, from which the designer can cut off a section exactly the required size.

CARDBOARD OR TRACING PAPER?

I recommend that students prepare their drawings in ink on cardboard. However, the great majority of designers make their drawings on tracing paper. In educational and community theaters the original drawings are often turned over to the construction crew to be used as a guide in their work; in professional theaters, they are duplicated as blueprints, or by one of the other photographic processes.

The major advantage of the standard, tissue, method is a significant saving in time. The advantages of the more extended, cardboard, method are less clearcut, and for a particular designer may be nonexistent. Primarily, the choice depends on the use of the drawings after the close of the production. The tracing paper originals tend to be fragile and are likely to be worthless after having gone through the hands of the construction crew; consequently, reproducing them as blueprints is to be recommended even in the nonprofessional theater. The more permanent cardboard versions are easier to store than tissues or blueprints are, and they withstand repeated handling better, so if the designer intends to use the drawings as permanent aids, cardboard versions may be worth the extra time needed in preparation. In addition, if cardboard drawings are protected by plastic, they may sometimes be used effectively in lobby or museum displays. And, finally, cardboard drawings form an invaluable, permanent record by means of which the designer can review his own development as an artist. Certainly, even if the drawings provided for the construction crew are made on tracing paper, the designer should attempt to protect them with plastic or to have copies made for his own files.

PENCILS AND LEAD-POINTERS

The designer uses pencils in two ways: for direct sketching and for making outline drawings as guides for inking. Soft pencils are most convenient for sketching, and the ordinary No. 2 wood-encased pencil is entirely satisfactory. As a preliminary to inking, hard lead is preferable; the designer should experiment with different degrees of hardness to find the one that suits him best, but his safest choice is a lead just short of the maximum degree of hardness. Wood-encased drawing pencils are manufactured, but the designer will find mechanical lead-holders much more convenient.

In all but rough sketching, it is very important to have a needle-pointed lead; special lead pointers have been designed for use with lead-holders, and one of them should be included in every designer's equipment. The attempt to maintain a point by using an ordinary pencil sharpener, a block of sandpaper, or a razor blade is much less effective and involves great waste of time and lead.

ERASERS

The artist should have at least two types of erasers, a small, fairly firm eraser for removing pencil lines and a somewhat larger and softer one for cleaning the drawings. Before using a new type of eraser, the artist should rub it vigorously on a discarded sheet of cardboard to make sure it will not discolor the surface.

INKS

Finished drawings are regularly made by retracing the pencil lines with india ink. Although that term is now applied by some manufacturers to various types and colors of ink, it traditionally described a unique ink with special characteristics, and it is used in this book only in the traditional sense. India ink is extremely black; it dries very quickly, producing lines that will not fade and that have a hardness and solidity that make them more like varnish than like ordinary ink. India ink should not be blotted, since it does not sink into the surface of the paper as most inks do, and its effectiveness requires that all of the ink deposited on the surface of the paper be allowed to remain and harden. It is difficult to correct, although it can be chipped and scraped from the surface of the cardboard by careful use of a razor blade.

Because of its greater density and varnishlike characterisitics, india ink must never be allowed to dry on a penpoint or in a brush. Special solvents are manufactured for soaking the ink from penpoints, but a brush filled with dried india ink has been ruined. India ink dries so fast that the artist should train himself never to lay down an instrument containing it, even to speak briefly on the telephone. If he must stop his work and cannot take time to clean the instrument, he should stand it in a container of water until he is able to clear it of the ink. Pens can be cleaned by holding them under the faucet for a moment and then wiping them dry with facial tissue; a little stain may remain, but it will not damage the point if the major part of the ink has been removed. Brushes must be cleaned more thoroughly. Before the ink has dried they should be rinsed and scrubbed gently over a cake of white soap, then both soap and brush should be rinsed again. This process should be repeated until the scrubbing produces no discoloration on the surface of the soap.

Once dry, india ink is no longer soluble in water (a black, water-soluble ink is sometimes sold under the name of india ink, but the comments here refer to the traditional type). Consequently, an india-ink drawing can be used as a basis for a tempera painting, without bleeding or smearing.

Since india ink is difficult to correct, it is important that the artist not smear it while making a drawing. When wet, india ink has a glossy surface that is visible when the drawing is tilted to catch the light. The artist should check the drying in this way before resuming work in an area of the drawing that was recently inked; in particular he should inspect the ends of the ink lines, where there are likely to be minute pools of ink that will dry more slowly than the rest of the line. If the lines seem to have dried, a final check can be made by rolling a roll of ordinary toilet paper across the drawing and then inspecting the surface to see whether any ink has been picked up.

The toilet-paper roll is a useful addition to the artist's materials. Wadded loosely, the paper can be used to brush eraser crumbs from the surface of a drawing. Folded into a pad, it can be used to apply rubbed chalk. It makes an excellent brush- and pen-wiper. And a very effective blotter for picking up a small pool of ink can be made by twisting the corner of a piece of the paper to a fine point, which is then touched to the center of the ink spot; the ink flows up along the paper and can thus be removed without blotting it out over a larger area of the cardboard.

It is good practice when inking a drawing to work in one area as long as it can be done conveniently without brushing inked lines or laying triangles or other instruments over them. Then the designer should shift to another area of the drawing and continue with it as far as convenient. By that time, the first area should have dried, and after checking it he can proceed, giving the second area time to dry. In this way, the designer can work steadily at a drawing without having to wait for sections to dry.

Even when the india ink is dry enough to continue drawing, it may rub up if it is erased; inked lines should be given five or ten minutes of additional drying after the drawing is completed before it is cleaned.

The artist should have a supply of at least two colors of ink in addition to black; red and green are effective choices. Waterproof drawing inks may be used, but the water-soluble inks made for ordinary use are cheaper and more satisfactory.

PAINTS

An important part of the artist's records of each set design is a full-color perspective painting showing the appearance of the completed set, as seen from the audience. For these paintings, the most effective medium is an opaque water-color that is variously known as tempera, gouache, and poster paint (the strictest usage restricts these terms to three slightly different types of paint, but in ordinary use they are interchangeable).

Recommending tempera differs from the more common practice, since most designers use watercolor that, unlike tempera, is transparent. Wherever alternative materials or techniques are available, analysis will reveal that each has its own special advantages and disadvantages. The major advantage of water color is its speed, so it is the preferred medium for perspective sketches. Its great disadvantages are that it is difficult to control with precision and that errors are nearly impossible to correct—in fact, artists in painting usually identify watercolor as the most difficult of all mediums.

The major advantage of tempera is its ready correctability; even if the artist should have the extreme disaster of upsetting a bottle of ink and running a broad splash across a finished tempera painting, it would be possible to correct the painting so that the flaw was completely invisible.

In addition, because the color of the paper or cardboard used for the painting always shows through watercolor, whereas it is completely hidden by tempera, the artist can indicate his intended colors with more precision in tempera. Finally, since scene paint is itself tempera, a painting in that medium is easier for construction workers to match and gives the designer a more accurate report of the appearance of the final set. Watercolor, with its inherent dash and brilliance, may produce a deceptive vibrancy in the designer's painting that does not appear in the finished set.

For all of those reasons, it seems preferable to recommend that students restrict themselves to tempera. As they become more experienced, they may want to experiment with watercolor, and they may want to choose it rather than the tempera medium recommended here, particularly in crisis situations that sometimes occur in the theater, where speed is more important than precision and fast sketching must be substituted for more careful rendering.

Tempera or poster paint is sold in jars of various sizes. The commonest size holds only two ounces; it is much more convenient to buy the paint in quarts. If the paint is bought in single small jars, the designer will find it necessary to buy supplementary jars for almost every set. The pattern of paint use is extremely irregular; one set may require large quantities of blue and another set make no use of blue at all.

With experience, every designer develops a selection of colors that especially fits his or her own tastes, so that ideally a separate list should be made for each artist. However, choices will be suggested for beginning students who have not yet settled on the pattern that is most useful to them.

Designers are likely to use at least twice as much white as any other color. If their budgets are extremely limited, they should buy equal quantities of black and of spectral red, yellow, and blue and a double amount of white.

With a slightly larger budget, green, purple, orange, and brown should be added to the above list.

Assuming still more available funds, it would be wise to add the intermediate colors, yellow-green, blue-green, blue-purple, red-purple, red-orange, and yellow-orange, as well as grey.

Gold and silver may be effectively added to each of the previous lists. They are given separately because they are different in composition from actual tempera paints. Many types of ready-mixed metallic paint are sold, but most of them lack sufficient brilliance. The most satisfactory pigment readily available consists of pure metal, ground to an extremely fine powder. Since it has no binder, it must be mixed with a water-soluble adhesive before it can be used in combination with tempera paints. The metallic powder is available in a range of colors, but a medium yellow gold and a simple silver are the most useful shades.

BRUSHES

Brushes come in a bewildering variety of prices, shapes, and sizes; good brushes make painting easy, bad brushes are an abomination. Unfortunately, it is difficult to distinguish the quality of brushes by eye, so designers should buy only from reputable manufacturers. For scenic design, it is not necessary to buy the most expensive brushes; those in the middle price range should be entirely satisfactory.

Watercolor brushes are used for tempera painting. The most useful shape is pointed, and designers should have a few of the smallest size for painting fine details, as well as larger ones for faster painting of larger areas. For the smaller brushes, designers should choose those with hair length in the range of $7/32''$, $9/32''$, or $11/32''$; for the larger, $13/16''$ or $29/32''$ is recommended. A fully adequate supply consists of one brush for at least each of the colors the artist will be working with at one time; four large and four small brushes is about the practical minimum.

Good brushes are moderately expensive and should be handled carefully. They should not be used for stirring paint, paint should not be allowed to dry in them, and they should not be left standing overnight in water. They should be washed with warm water and soap, smoothed into shape, and laid flat to dry (not stood on end) to prevent their drying at an angle.

COLORED CHALK

The use of rubbed chalk (also called pastel crayons) is described in Chapter 11. For this purpose the colored chalks commonly used for artwork in elementary schools can be used, although artists' pastels are usually available in more brilliant colors and are likely to be more uniformly ground.

PASTEL PENCILS

Pastels are also available in a different form, which designers find especially convenient for certain uses. The chalk itself is identical with that used in ordinary pastels, but it is encased in wood like an ordinary pencil and can consequently be sharpened to a fairly fine point. The black pastel pencils (and similar black charcoal pencils) are particularly useful, although with a liberal budget designers may well prefer to buy a set of the pencils in a full assortment of colors.

STOMPS

For applying rubbed chalk, designers find grey paper stomps extremely useful. They are made of shredded paper and are shaped in pointed cylinders, something like pencils. They come in various sizes; a supply of stomps with diameters of $3/8''$ and $3/16''$ will be adequate. Tortillon stomps are made of strips of paper, wound into pencil shapes; they are useless for designers and should not be bought by mistake.

FIXATIVE

Pastel chalks, whether applied directly or by rubbing, have the defect of not forming a firm bond with the surface to which they are applied, so that they tend to smear or rub off when handled. They can be made more durable by spraying the finished picture with a very dilute solution of varnish or shellac called *fixative*. The simplest and cheapest type of spray consists of two metal tubes fastened at right angles; the end of one is inserted into a container of fixative, and the artist blows through the other tube. Special sprays, operating somewhat like perfume atomizers, are slightly more convenient and produce a more uniformly fine spray.

DRAFTING TAPE

A paper tape, coated with a pressure-sensitive adhesive, is sold under the names *masking tape* and *drafting tape*. The price varies according to width, and the narrow is as useful to the designer as the wide, so that it is better practice to buy the narrowest.

Drafting tape is useful for holding sheets of cardboard to the drawing board, since a T-square and triangles can be moved across it more easily than over the heads of tacks. However, the adhesive tends to bond too tightly with the cardboard, so that the surface is likely to pull off when it is removed. Coating the tape slightly by drawing it through the fingers or pressing it first against a sheet of waste cardboard or the desk so as to pick up small particles of paper or dust will reduce its adhesion slightly. The same kind of tape is also sold with adhesive coating on both sides; although it is more expensive than the single-faced type, it can be used without danger of damaging the working surface of cardboard by placing it under the cardboard, with one surface against the bottom side of the cardboard and the other in contact with the drawing board.

RULERS

Ordinary one-foot rulers are almost useless for the designer. The most generally practical size is a two-foot ruler. The designer's rulers should be as thin as possible and have at least one metal edge so that they can be used for inking.

Most designers prefer to use a special tool called an architect's scale rule. Various scales are provided, including $3/32'' = 1'-0''$, $1/8'' = 1'-0''$, $3/16'' = 1'-0''$, and so on up to $3'' = 1'-0''$. Perhaps the commonest scale used in set drawings is $1/2'' = 1'-0''$.

The major advantage of a scale ruler is that the unit representing a foot is marked into 12 divisions, each indicating a scale inch. It is difficult or impossible to use an ordinary ruler accurately for scales such as $1/2'' =$

1'-0'', or 1'' = 1'-0''; if each inch of the ruler is marked in sixteenths, each space then represents not a scaled inch, but ⅔'' at the larger scale and 1⅓'' at the smaller scale.

Use of the architect's scale thus makes the designer's work easier and makes computation errors less likely. Set construction workers, however, more often work with rulers and tape measures divided in the ordinary way, and though the designer can prepare working drawings easily to such scales as ½'' or 1'' = 1'-0'' with an architect's scale, the construction crew may find it difficult to check parts of the drawing with their own equipment. Consequently, even if an architect's scale is available to the designer, there is some advantage in limiting drawings when possible to such scales as ¾'' = 1'-0'', where a scaled inch equals a space marked on an ordinary ruler (in this case, 1/16'' = 1''). Tables of such scales are given in later chapters.

Even with that limitation, the student may find the architect's ruler preferable. However, with such scales it is perfectly practical to use an ordinary ruler. The architect's scales should not be used as a guide in drawing lines, because the edges are easily damaged; instead, lines should be drawn along a plastic triangle, a T-square, or a metal-edged ordinary ruler.

T-SQUARES AND TRIANGLES

T-squares and triangles are used for drawing uniform angles. The T-square is so called because it has the shape of the letter T, with the stem elongated. Unless the two sections of the square meet at exactly 90°, the instrument is useless; therefore, the T-square should be handled with great care so as not to loosen the joint.

The most useful triangle is the 30-60, which has angles of 90°, 30°, and 60°. The 45° triangle, with one right angle and two of 45°, is only slightly less useful. These triangles are cut from sheets of heavy clear plastic and are available in many sizes; for most uses, 8'' triangles are the most satisfactory size. Triangles are relatively sturdy but can easily be scratched with a razor blade, so they should never be used as guides in cutting cardboard; a triangle with a nicked edge is almost useless.

DRAWING BOARDS

Especially in using T-squares and triangles, the artist must have a support for his cardboard that has straight edges joined by true right angles. Ordinary desks and tables are seldom satisfactory, so it is important to have a good drawing board. A drawing board is simply a large rectangular board, most often made by gluing several smaller boards together, carefully finished so that the edges are true and the surface smooth. Since the accuracy of the edges is critical, many drawing boards have the edges protected by metal strips.

The essential function of a drawing board is to serve as a guide for the head of a T-square. Usually, only the side edges of the board are used in this way, but occasionally it is convenient to place the T-square against the bottom edge of the drawing board and even, though still less often, against the top edge. In these cases, it is important that the edges of the board form precise right angles, and no board should be purchased until the corners have been carefully checked for squareness. Obviously, any board purchased must be larger than the cardboard that is to be used for the drawings; for 22″ × 28″ cardboard, a 2′ × 3′ drawing board is most convenient.

PENS

Ordinary pens may be used in drawing. Cheap penpoints and penholders are readily available and are satisfactory. The artist should have at least two sizes of points, the finest available and a moderate size.

COMPASSES

The bow type of compass is manufactured in three basic styles. One, which is frequently used in grade school, relies on friction to maintain the setting of the legs; it is unsatisfactory and should not be used. The two better grades of compass are designed so that the setting can be controlled by turning a knurled wheel. In one type the wheel is at the side of the compass, and the setting is maintained by a spring; the second type has the wheel centered between the legs of the compass, and the setting is maintained by the threads of the bar on which the wheel is fixed. For ordinary use, a compass with center adjustment is preferable. The size is not critical, but a 6″ compass, which will open to a distance of about 4½″ between the points, is a useful size. The compass should be supplied with a lead holder and a penpoint so that it can be used for drawing in either pencil or ink. Since it is somewhat troublesome to interchange the points, the artist will find it better to have two compasses, one of which he can reserve for pencil use and the other for ink.

Compass penpoints are designed differently from ordinary penpoints; they are made of two separate metal strips, one of which is curved. A knurled knob makes it possible to vary the opening between them, so that the width of the line can be controlled. Like ordinary pens, the points will be ruined if india ink is allowed to dry in them, so the artist should form the habit of rinsing off the point and drying it by running the corner of a blotter through the opening as soon as he has finished using the compass with india ink.

A compass of the type recommended can be used for drawing circles of any radius from nearly zero up to the maximum distance that the points can be spread. However, circles at the two extremes of size are more difficult to draw; consequently, it is convenient to have an additional compass for very small circles. In order to allow the points to come close together, such compasses have the control knob on the outside.

For larger circles, a beam compass should be used. The beam compass is made in three fundamental parts: a metal bar, usually of aluminum, and two points that move horizontally along the bar, their setting being controlled by knurled knobs. Beams of various sizes are available; perhaps the 24'' size is the most useful for the designer. However, the points can be easily slipped off one beam and fastened on another, so that if his budget will allow, the artist can buy a single complete compass and additional beams of different sizes, perhaps 14'' and 36''. The beam compass can be used to draw circles with a radius as small as about 2'', and almost as large as the beam; thus, a 24'' beam compass can be used for circles with diameters ranging from about 4'' to about 46''.

PROTRACTORS

The artist will frequently find it necessary to measure angles that are not provided for by his triangles; consequently, he should have a protractor. One made of clear plastic and showing the entire circle of 360° is most useful.

RAZOR BLADES

Various knives and other cutting devices are manufactured for artists' use, but few are as versatile or generally convenient as the ordinary single-edged razor blade. It can be used to cut cardboard, to chip off india ink, and to produce sharp edges in erasers and stomps. Razor blades sold for shaving have one defect: they are generally coated with oil, which must be somewhat dangerously wiped off before they can be used in art work. However, unoiled blades are available. They are sold in packages of a hundred and are much cheaper than ordinary razor blades.

SHEET PLASTICS

Unless the designer protects his pictures with plastic, they will quickly be damaged or destroyed, especially those used in the scene shop during construction. If the drawings are reproduced by blueprint or other photographic method, the copies can be given to the crew and the originals filed. Even if the originals are used as construction guides, it is not necessary to protect all of them; often, the designer may decide that only his perspective painting has enough permanent value to justify covering it with plastic. Various clear plastics suitable for protecting drawings are sold in rolls; cellulose acetate is satisfactory. The designer should select rolls that are at least 2″ wider than one of the dimensions of his standard cardboard; he can then cut off appropriate lengths and cover his drawings by bringing the edges of the plastic sheet around to the back of the cardboard and fastening it with drafting tape.

ADDITIONAL INSTRUMENTS

The materials and instruments that have been described constitute the minimum that can be considered fully adequate. There are many other products and tools that the designer may want to investigate and add to his equipment as money becomes available, such as a magnifying glass, an elliptical compass, and a mat cutter. Which of such instruments he will find useful enough to buy depends largely on his own habits of work; each designer must make his own selection.

11

Drawing
Techniques

Tools and materials are, of course, worthless unless the designer becomes familiar enough with them to use them easily. Each designer should experiment to discover their range of usefulness. The following discussion describes some of the particular techniques that are of value; additional information is given in later chapters.

APPLYING PASTEL

Pastels can be applied in two ways, which produce different effects. One is to draw with them directly on the paper or cardboard. Although a brilliant line is produced, it is difficult to control and tends to flake off readily. The set designer will find this method useful only for adding small details, particularly for intensifying areas of shadow, as in the folds of drapery. Because the pastel pencils provide much greater control than the larger sticks, in direct application, they are usually used for direct drawing.

The other method of applying pastel, the rubbed chalk method, can be used to produce either a uniform or a graduated smooth wash of color across a surface. The major medium for making colored theatrical pictures is tempera paint, and since an even gradation of color is very difficult to produce with tempera, the addition of pastel to a painting makes the combined medium much more effective and provides the artist with greater control.

To apply a wash of color, the artist first reduces the pastel to a powder by rubbing the stick on a piece of scrap cardboard or paper. Some of the powder is then picked up on the finger, a paper stomp, a wad of cotton, or a pad of cloth or cleansing tissue, which is then rubbed across the area of the drawing or painting that is to be colored.

The choice of transferral device depends on the effect to be produced and the size and shape of the area to be covered. The tip of the finger is especially effective, although this method cannot be easily used for covering large areas. A paper stomp functions almost equally well, except that it makes a still narrower line; that restriction, however, makes it especially valuable for coloring small details. If still greater precision is desired, the stomp can be cut with a razor blade, to produce a sharp edge or point. Cotton or a cloth pad is best for covering large surfaces; cleansing tissue works fairly well, but tends to wear quickly, so that two or three pads may be needed for applying a single wash. The cloth and cleansing tissue should be folded, not wadded, so that a flat surface is available.

The pad or other device is rubbed lightly over the pastel powder, and then the color is tested by rubbing the applicator across a clean area of paper or cardboard. It is difficult to correct errors in rubbed chalk, so it should be applied cautiously, although it can be so easily controlled that once he has learned the technique the artist should seldom have any difficulty.

The chalk should not be applied full strength, because the individual grains produce noticeable streaks; instead, the area of color should be built up in a series of four or five separate applications. The streaks will then tend to blend, and will in any case have been so faint as to be unnoticeable. In testing the pad on a separate sheet of cardboard, then, the artist checks to make sure that the mark is very much lighter than desired for the final color; if it is too heavy, he should rub it across an area of the waste paper until enough of the chalk has been removed to produce a sufficiently faint mark.

The pad is then used to rub the area of the picture to be colored. It should be applied with a circular movement, shifting steadily so that the entire area is covered uniformly. This process is repeated, going over the area several times until the desired heaviness of coating has been obtained. As the chalk wears off the pad, it will be necessary to pick up more of the powder and then return to the picture; each time, however, the mark must be tested again before continuing work.

The method described produces a uniform wash of color. If graduations of color are desired, a uniform wash is first applied to the entire surface, matching the intensity of the lightest area; each successive application is restricted to a smaller and smaller area, so that the amount of color deposited varies smoothly from the lightest to the darkest areas. The application of rubbed chalk is illustrated in *Figure 14-1.*

This method does not provide great control and cannot be used for small areas; even for a large area, it is difficult to control the edges of the colored spaces, so that they may extend into parts that should have been left clean. Various methods can be used for achieving greater control.

Nearly all of a rubbed-chalk surface can be picked up with a soft eraser, although it may not be possible to clean a heavily colored area completely. Where the wash is fairly light, it may be safely run out past its proper outline, and the excess removed by erasing. If a heavily chalked area must have a sharp outline, the space to be kept clean can be protected by a piece of paper or thin cardboard held firmly in place during the application. After the wash has been laid in, highlights can be picked out with a sharp eraser. For example, a chair can be finished with a uniform coating of rubbed chalk, and then the most brightly lit side can be lightened by running over it with a soft eraser. In most such cases, it is preferable to allow some of the chalk to remain, to suggest that the various sides of the chair have the same basic color, so even a very dark rubbing can be treated in this way. Similarly, a wall covered with floral-patterned paper could be given a pure wash of color, and then the flowers individually erased. If desired, the eraser could be sharpened with a razor blade to permit more precise control.

Pastel pencils can be used for intensifying the smaller areas of the design, and they provide maximum deposition of color with much greater control than the larger sticks. For moderate darkening of small areas, paper stomps should be used; they are also useful for blending the marks made by the pencils. Pastel in pencil form is applied directly to the surface; the stomps function indirectly, and are used to pick up the pastel powder, which is then rubbed on the picture. Stomps can also be sharpened with a razor blade. In the wallpaper design described above, a stomp might well be used for darkening the foliage in the design.

The conditions and types of pictures in which pastels are useful to the designer are described in Chapter 14.

ELLIPSES

The noncircular curved figure that the designer has most use for is the ellipse. Several ingenious methods have been devised for laying out ellipses; they involve the measurement of a series of points on the ellipse, which are then joined by a freehand curve.

The ellipse may be thought of as a circle that has been more or less flattened; it thus has two diameters, one longer than the other, and fits into a rectangle. Most often, other elements in the design predetermine the size of this rectangle. Let us suppose that the designer needs to draw an ellipse $1\frac{1}{4}'' \times 2\frac{7}{8}''$. Two methods for drawing it will be described.

The Circle
Method

(See *Figure 11-1.*) Draw a line somewhat longer than the long diameter of the ellipse; cross it with a perpendicular at a point near its center, extending above and below the first line for a total length a little more than the long diameter. Using the point at which the two lines cross as a center, draw two circles, one with a radius equal to the small radius of the ellipse, and the other with a radius the same length as the large radius of the ellipse.

In one quarter of the circles, draw a series of radii, spaced approximately evenly, long enough so that each radius cuts both circles. From the point where the first radius cuts the smaller circle, draw a horizontal line, and from the point where it cuts the larger circle, draw a vertical line; the point where these two lines cross lies on the desired ellipse. Repeat for all of the radii, and connect the points in a smooth curve. This gives a fourth of the ellipse; the diagonally opposite quarter has the same shape, and the other two quarters are mirror images. The entire ellipse may be drawn by this method, although it is usually simpler to draw only a fourth, and to copy it in the proper positions with tracing paper.

The Rectangle
Method

(See *Figure 11-2.*) Draw a rectangle, with the same length and height as the desired ellipse, then draw its vertical and horizontal center lines. Divide the right half of the horizontal center line into a number of equal spaces (say eight); divide the top half of the adjacent end line into the same number of equal spaces. Draw a straight line between the upper end of the vertical center line and each of the division points on the end line of the rectangle. Draw a straight line between the bottom end of the vertical center line and each of the division points on the horizontal center line, extending the lines till they cross the other set. The point where the top diagonal line crosses the left diagonal line falls on the ellipse; the point where the second line in one set crosses the second line of the other also falls on the ellipse, etc. Connect these points freehand with a smooth curve. Complete the ellipse either by repeating this procedure for all four sections of the rectangle or by copying with tracing paper.

This method is especially useful because it can be used for drawing ellipses that are slanted, as in perspective or isometric projections (although for ellipses in perspective, all four quarters must be constructed individually). (See *Figure 11-3.*)

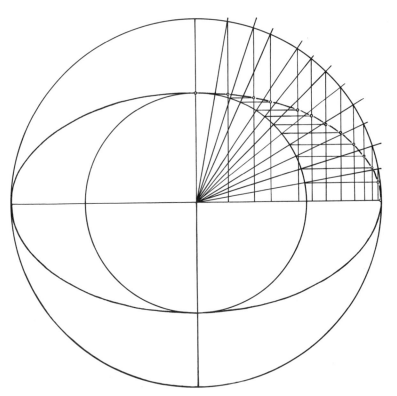

Figure 11-1. The circle method of drawing an ellipse.

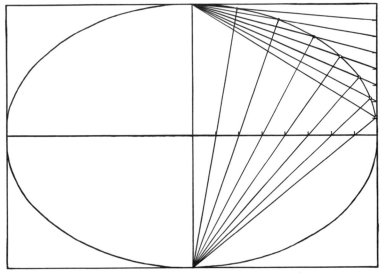

Figure 11-2. The rectangle method of drawing an ellipse.

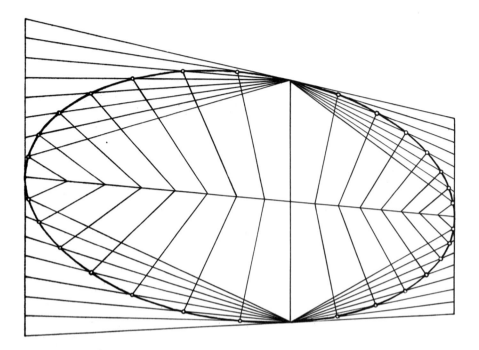

Figure 11-3. Drawing an ellipse in perspective projection. This method is identical with the rectangle method of drawing an ellipse in orthographic projection *(Figure 11-2),* except that the shapes and dimensions vary because of the variations in scale produced by perspective projection. The vertical lines can be divided into a number of equal parts with a ruler, but the line connecting their midpoints must be divided by drawing the diagonals of the perspective rectangle, then the diagonals of its two halves, etc. (these construction diagonals are not shown in the drawing).

TRANSFERRING

Tracing paper is used to transfer a drawing from one sheet to another. Very often it is not possible to make the first drawing neat enough for permanent use; not only may the drawing be damaged by alterations and construction lines, but it may not be possible to determine its exact dimensions until it is drawn, so that it cannot be placed properly on the sheet.

Suppose that the artist has completed a drawing and needs to transfer it to a new sheet to serve as a guide for inking in a permanent fair copy. The first step is to cut a section of tracing paper from the roll, making it somewhat larger than the drawing, but smaller than the sheet of cardboard from which the drawing is to be copied. This is then placed over the original drawing and the edges fastened with short lengths of masking tape. The artist then traces the drawing on the tracing paper, using a fine, hard pencil. He should also identify any helpful guide points (such as the vertical center line of the drawing) and mark them to help him in placing the drawing on the new sheet.

The tracing paper is then turned over, and the drawing is traced again on the other side, this time with a soft pencil (perhaps an ordinary No. 2 pencil), which should also be as sharp as possible; what is wanted is a precise line, but one with a good deal of carbon in it. On this side of the sheet, it is better not to retrace the guidelines or points.

The tracing paper is then turned over and placed on a fresh sheet of cardboard, using the guidelines, and placing it very carefully. The drafting tape is pressed down to hold it in position (using the same drafting tape makes it a little less sticky and consequently less likely to pull up the surface of the good sheet of cardboard when it is removed). Holding the tracing paper with the thumb and forefinger of one hand, spread, the artist rubs uniformly across the surface between them, shifting to a new position and continuing until all the lines have been rubbed. The most effective way to rub the drawing is with the edge of the thumbnail, but for large drawings the artist may prefer to use something else. Probably the best tool is the edge of an ordinary washer, about ¾'' in diameter. The edge of a teaspoon may also be used.

As the tracing paper is rubbed, the soft-lead drawing is transferred to the cardboard below it. If the paper is held firmly, the transfer will be clear and accurate. Naturally, the longer and harder the paper is rubbed, the darker will be the transfer; it is preferable to have it as light as possible, while still being fully legible. The same tracing can be used to rub off several copies; in fact, with great care, as many as twenty or thirty copies can be made from a single tracing. Usually the designer will need to rub off the tracing only once, but occasionally he will spoil a drawing, so it is best to save the tracing until the final drawing is completed.

In order to reproduce the entire tracing, it is necessary to rub the surface of the paper uniformly; the best practice is to rub it fairly lightly all over in one direction, then turn the cardboard and rub in a different direction. If the pieces of masking tape are placed in the center of each edge of the tracing paper, it will be possible to lift the corners and check the rubbing without removing the tape. Even if the rubbing seems to be complete, it is best to pull one piece of tape free at a time, turning the tracing paper back progressively to make sure that no critical points have been missed.

A little practice with this method will enable the designer to use it with maximum efficiency; often, it can be used to speed up drawing by substituting rubbed copying for construction. For example, the drawing of an ellipse is time-consuming; the artist can speed up the work by constructing only a fourth of it and filling in the rest by copying with tracing paper. For a symmetrical stage set, or even one with only a few symmetrical elements, it may save time to draw only half the set and copy it in reverse by rubbing from tracing paper.

When the drawing is to be reversed, and not simply copied, it is traced on only one side of the tracing paper, which is then turned over and rubbed to make the mirror-image copy. In that case, the original tracing should be in soft pencil.

In many cases, the mirror image of a drawing will function as well as the original. For example, an isometric drawing of a rectangular table, to be used as a guide in construction, will be equally accurate and effective in either orientation; in that case, the drawing can be copied on one side of the tracing paper and then rubbed off without retracing on the back.

GRIDDING

A designer frequently finds it necessary to redraw in irregular design to a different scale, in most cases to a larger scale. In ancient Egypt, designs for large paintings were first worked out in miniature and were then enlarged by the method of *gridding;* the same device was used by painters of the Renaissance, and it is valuable for the set designer.

Let us suppose, for instance, that we want to enlarge a small drawing of a floral wallpaper pattern. The first step consists of identifying at least one of the dimensions desired for the final drawing—in this case, say, a height of 6''.

Two grids are necessary; the first is produced as follows. (See *Figure 11-4.*) Horizontal lines are drawn through the top and bottom points of the design to be copied. They are then connected by a vertical line, drawn through the farthest point of the design on the left. This vertical is divided into a number of equal segments (say eight), and a horizontal line is run through each of the division points, clear across the drawing. Let us assume that the segments do not match an even division on the ruler; in that case, a nonce ruler is made by laying a strip of paper along the vertical line and marking the divisions on it. The strip is then placed along the bottom horizontal, with one of the marks at the vertical, and enough divisions are marked on the bottom line so that the right edge of the design is included in the area marked. Verticals are then run through these points, extending entirely across the drawing. Sometimes it is possible to lay out the grid directly on the original drawing. However, if the artist wants to avoid damaging the drawing, it can be covered with tracing paper, and the grid drawn on that.

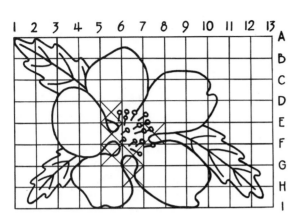

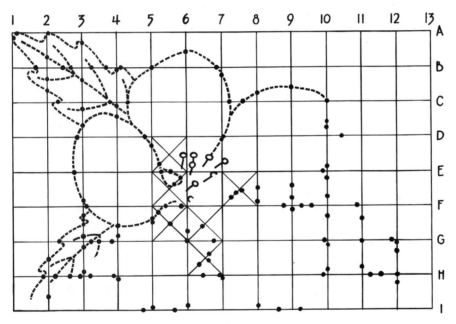

Figure 11-4. The grid method of enlargement. The points copied from the small drawing to the large grid are shown as heavy dots; for half of the picture the full pattern has been drawn in dashed lines. Auxiliary grid lines have been added in six squares, to provide more guide points.

The result of this procedure is a grid of lines covering the drawing and marking it into squares of such size that the motif is exactly eight squares high. The next step is to prepare a similar grid, with the same number of squares, but with the scale enlarged so that eight squares equal the height to which the figure is to be enlarged. In this case, each square will measure ¾''.

Starting with one of the squares (say, the one in the upper left corner), we notice any lines of the design that cross the edges of the square, and we mark similar points on the edges of the matching square of the large grid. The placement of each point is determined by estimating its position relative to the side of the square on which it lies; if it is, let us say, a third of the way down from the top, we copy the point a third of the way down on the matching line of the large grid. This procedure is repeated, square by square, for the entire design.

When this step is finished, we have a series of points marked on the large grid, all of which must fall on the lines of the completed picture. Checking carefully with the small drawing, we connect these points freehand, attempting to maintain the curves, shapes, and angles of the original drawing. When we have finished, we examine the design as a whole, comparing the two drawings, and correct any errors that appear.

How Many Grid Lines?

This method of enlargement, if done with reasonable care, produces a surprisingly accurate reproduction of the original design to the new scale. The original drawings of the gods included in the *Antony and Cleopatra* set were hardly an inch high; for the set itself, they were expanded to almost a hundred times that height, and with no apparent deviation from the small pictures.

The number of grid lines used for a particular drawing depends on its complexity; any number may theoretically be used, although it will usually be necessary to divide the longest dimension of the picture into at least eight units. There is an advantage in a number of divisions taken from the series 8, 16, 32, 64, etc., in which each number is produced by multiplying the preceding number by two; the reason for that recommendation is that the dimensions of the original drawing and the enlarged version are not likely to be simple multiples of each other, and the numbers of divisions in the suggested series can be marked by simply finding a series of center points, a much simpler procedure than attempting to divide two lines of unrelated dimensions into, say, ten or twelve even sections.

The largest possible error in this system is half the distance between grid lines. Enough grid lines should be provided to ensure that none of the major elements in the design are smaller than the resulting squares. Often, the main part of a design to be copied may be relatively large in scale, with small elements concentrated in a few parts of the design. In that case, it is most efficient to draw a grid adjusted to the main lines of the drawing, and then to further subdivide only the squares containing the smaller details; this can be done without further measurement by drawing in the diagonals of the critical squares, which then function as auxiliary grid lines. The artist must, of course, be careful to subdivide the corresponding squares in both grids.

The gridding method of enlargement is faster than might be supposed, but it is irksome, and the time and attention necessary for it are increased in proportion to the number of grid lines used; consequently, the spacing should be as open as possible, while still giving sufficient assistance in reproducing the design.

A major problem, especially with a large number of grid lines, is maintaining accuracy in matching the squares of the small grid with those of the large one. The grid lines are easier to follow if they are drawn in alternating colors, perhaps red and green. Another valuable device is to number the vertical lines and to letter the horizontal lines, marking matching lines on the two grids with the same number and letter. An intersection can then be identified, for example, as G9 and can easily be matched on the other grid.

Special Difficulties

Almost everyone who uses the grid method of enlargement for the first time makes two related errors. One is to focus on the shapes and lines of the picture while marking it; the other is to draw in the lines of the picture while working. These errors nearly always result in serious distortion, usually so extreme as to be uncorrectable. It is essential that the copyist focus only on the points at which the lines of the design cross the grid lines, and copy them as isolated and meaningless points; he must reserve his perception of the design as a whole until all of the points have been laid in.

Gridding has been described in its simplest and most direct form. It is not actually necessary that the grid lines form squares, or that they precisely coincide with the outer limits of the design. Some experience with the method may suggest to the student variations that will somewhat increase its effectiveness for particular designs, but the procedure as described is an entirely practical one. The designer will not only find it of value in his own work, but can also specify it as the method to be followed by construction workers and scene painters for designs that cannot be included full scale in his working drawings.

The method as described results in a reproduction of the original drawing that differs from the original only in size. Occasionally, however, the designer may want to alter the shape of a motif by stretching or compressing it in a particular direction. Suppose, for example, he has prepared a design for a landscape painting three units high and five units wide and finds that to fit it into the available space in the set he must make the painting higher, so that its proportions become four units high and five wide. The alteration can be produced by gridding, without totally redesigning the picture.

Reshaping by Grid

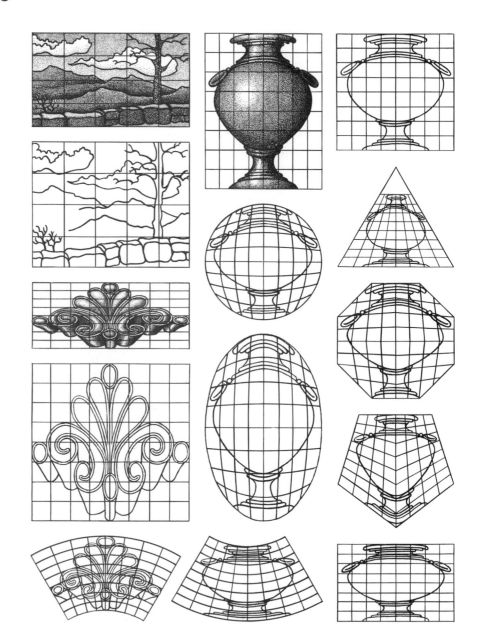

Figure 11-5. The use of grids for reshaping decorative motifs. Three motifs are shown, reshaped to fit various outlines. In each case, the original design is indicated by shading. Each grid has the same number of divisions as the grid applied to the original drawing, although their shapes have been changed so as to fit the new area.

A grid is prepared of the size and proportions to which the picture is to be redrawn, with grid lines dividing it into four squares high and five squares wide. The original drawing is then divided vertically into five equal strips, but instead of being divided horizontally into strips of the same size, they are narrowed so that each one is ¼ of the total height of the picture. The points at which the picture intersects the grid lines are then transferred to the new grid, exactly as described above, except that in this case the grid sections are of different shape in the two drawings.

An extension of this method may be used to produce very great alterations in the shape of motifs, so that, for example, decorations designed in essentially rectangular shape may be adapted to fit into circles, ovals, triangles, or irregular spaces. Such adaptation is not often necessary, but when it is needed, the grid method provides by far the fastest, easiest, and most accurate solution to the problem. (See *Figure 11-5.*)

Figure 11-6 shows an example from actual practice of reshaping a motif by gridding. In this case, a design was prepared for several frames, made from Upson board and string, to hold 8″ × 10″ vertical photographs. However, the wall areas on which the photographs were to be fastened required that some of the pictures be horizontal rather than vertical. The design was altered by gridding to fit the additional pictures.

Figure 11-6. A frame for 8″ x 10″ photographs, as originally designed (*left,* vertical) and as regridded to fit horizontal photographs *(right).*

JAMES GOLDMAN
THE LION IN WINTER

WORKING DRAWING 29
CONSTRUCTION OF TABLE

WAKE FOREST UNIVERSITY
DESIGNED BY DAVID WELKER
NOVEMBER 17, 1978

Figure 11-7.   A typical label for a working drawing.

LABELING

The designer's mind will be so filled with his drawings when he is working with them that he may conclude he will permanently remember every detail. Each new assignment, however, tends to obscure the preceding ones; consequently, each drawing should be properly labeled to facilitate future use of the drawing in teaching, for museum displays, or in later designing. Designers should decide for themselves what identifying information they would like to have, and then plan a uniform label they can add to each drawing. Such a label should certainly indicate the author and title of the play, the theater the set was designed for, the type or purpose of the drawing, and the date at which the work was done. A designer involved in a practical series of productions, who works close to the dates of performance, may prefer to date the designs by the opening nights of the plays; if the designs are prepared long in advance of productions, the designer may decide to record the actual date when each was finished.

Figure 11-7 is an example of a style of label that the designer may adapt to his own needs and preferences.

LETTERING

Aside from accuracy, nothing in a drawing contributes so much to an impressive and professional appearance as well planned and executed lettering. All designers should develop sufficient skill to enable them to letter legibly and attractively.

An enormous number of alphabets have been designed, each with its own character. Like the decorative arts, particular styles of lettering are often associated with historical periods (for example, alphabets with the horizontal lines thicker than the verticals were fashionable during part of the nineteenth century). Lettering is a familiar part of normal surroundings; it appears on monuments, street signs, directional posters, store windows, advertisements, and even the sewing samplers that were often hung in parlors in the last century. Stage sets frequently include lettering matching those and other uses in ordinary life. The study of lettering styles is properly a part of period design. The present discussion is not intended to suggest that only a single type of lettering is acceptable, even for labeling drawings, but rather to describe one simple, effective, and highly legible alphabet. There are many excellent books on lettering, which the designer should consult, particularly when he needs information about the styles fashionable in different periods.

Either capitals alone or capitals combined with small letters may be effectively used in labeling drawings. The following description is restricted to lettering done in full capitals.

The Lettering Grid

Lettering is based on a grid composed of four horizontal lines, forming three spaces. All key points of the letters (with the exception of G and X) fall on one of the four lines of this grid. A, J, P, and R make use of the third line of the grid: the horizontal line of the A runs along it; the tail of the J touches it; and the semicircles of the P and R are fitted into the space between it and the top line. B, E, F, and H similarly use the second line of the grid: the horizontal bars of E, F, and H run along it, and the semicircles that form part of B are fitted into the areas between the top and second lines and the second and bottom lines.

The other letters use the top and bottom lines as their guides, without reference to the two center lines. For the relationship of figures to the grid, see *Figure 11-8*.

Some designers prefer slanted letters; but they are harder to make uniform, and they are more difficult to read. Consequently, it is recommended that the designer use a vertical alphabet. Attractiveness of lettering depends on maintaining uniformity of angle, height, and spacing.

Figure 11-8. An alphabet and figures suggested for working drawings. No letter makes use of all four of the basic grid lines; those that are not significant are shown by dashes. The center group of letters in the middle row uses a line halfway between the two center lines of the grid; this line is not usually included as part of the grid.

Widths   Most of the letters of the alphabet are formed within the limits of a vertical rectangle; normal proportions are produced by a rectangle three units high and two wide. *H* and *N* include both of the vertical sides of this rectangle; other letters of the same width are *A, B, C, D, E, F, G, K, O, P, Q, R, S, U, V, X, Y,* and *Z. I* is the narrowest letter; *L* is narrower than the standard rectangle, and *J* and *T* are slightly narrower. *W* is drawn variously, but the simplest design is made up of two *V*'s drawn together. *M* is essentially a *W* upside down, except that the verticals are slanted less sharply; both of these letters are considerably wider than the basic rectangle.

Not all of the elements of the letters occupy the full width of the space. The bottom semicircle of the *B* touches the right side of the basic rectangle, but the top semicircle is held back slightly. The cross-bars of *E* and *F* also stop short of the right side of the rectangle.

Spacing   Printing should seem to be uniformly spaced, but because most letters are irregularly shaped, mathematically regular spacing seems irregular, and the spacing must be adjusted to compensate for that illusion. Beginning designers most frequently attempt to space letters uniformly either by allowing the same space for each letter or by leaving an equal distance

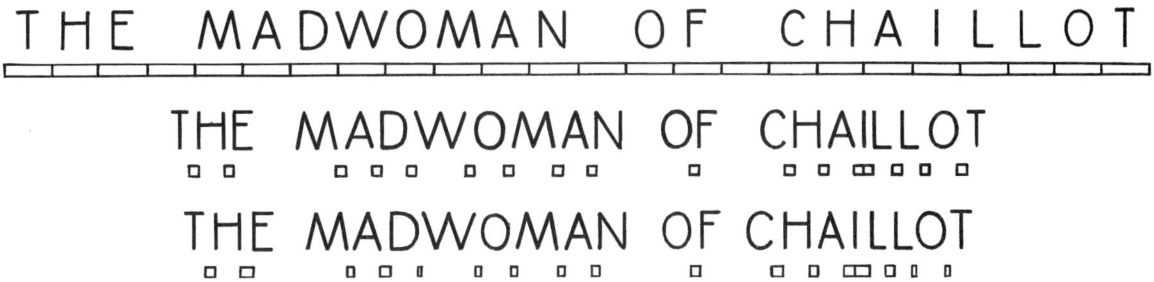

THE MADWOMAN OF CHAILLOT

THE MADWOMAN OF CHAILLOT

THE MADWOMAN OF CHAILLOT

Figure 11-9. Letter spacing. In the two top rows, the letters are spaced evenly, as indicated by the rectangles below the printing. In spite of its actual evenness of spacing, the printing appears to be uneven. The bottom row has been spaced unevenly, but creates the appearance of greater uniformity. *THE* and *CHAILLOT* in particular appear much evener in the third version.

between adjacent edges of each pair of letters, measuring the distance horizontally along the line of printing. Neither method produces the appearance of uniformity, as is demonstrated by the first two examples in *Figure 11-9*. Instead, the letters should be spaced so that there is approximately the same *area* of blank space between each two. Thus, proper spacing is based on square measurement, not linear measurement.

Some combinations of letters are easy to handle; others, like *AM* and *TV,* are difficult to adjust. Often the horizontal size of the letters can be altered slightly so as to close in an unsightly open space: thus, the horizontal bar at the top of *T* may be shortened when it stands beside a letter like *V,* which produces an unusual opening at the bottom of the line; at other times, the letters may be slightly overlapped, so that the horizontal bars of *L* and *T* cross each other, vertically.

Perfect regularity of spacing is not possible without occasionally resorting to extreme distortion of the forms of letters. For example, the *LA* combination produces a large open area that could be corrected only by destroying the familiar shapes of the two letters. In such cases, it is better to preserve the essential shapes, even at the expense of some unevenness in spacing. With *LA,* for example, the horizontal line of the *L* should be shortened slightly, and the remaining open space accepted as inevitable.

Skilled letterers first draw a two- or four-line grid and then sketch the letters in lightly with pencil, check their placement, and make adjustments as necessary. Finally, they ink the letters and erase the pencil lines.

Where the printing extends beyond a single line, the grids for successive lines should be spaced two units apart. The grids can be laid out by measuring with a ruler, although special gridding instruments, such as the Ames Lettering Guide, are faster and more convenient.

DEVELOPING SKILL

Good craftsmanship requires that the designer have so much experience with his tools and materials that he is able to use them readily, easily, and automatically. Each instrument and material has its own qualities and peculiarities, its own strengths and weaknesses. The beginning designer should be alert to those qualities, experimenting with his tools and materials to discover how to use them most effectively, what their total range of possibilities is, and what functions they perform most effectively. As his familiarity with them grows, he will come to use them automatically, and his experience with them will gradually free him from mechanical limitations, making his work seem easier and more natural.

12

Ground Plan
and Elevations

The designer's decisions must be recorded in a form that will enable the construction crew to build and assemble a set that will precisely match his intention. The drawings that are normally made can be divided into four groups:

1. The ground plan (also called floor plan), showing the outline of the set in position on the floor of the stage
2. Elevations, showing the appearance of the front of the flats and other scenic units
3. A perspective painting, showing the appearance of the completed set as seen from the audience, or a carefully prepared scale model
4. Working drawings, including an indication of the materials and methods of construction to be used, dimensions, and directions for painting

The perspective contains the same information given in the first two types of drawing, but it is difficult to use in determining dimensions; consequently, the ground plan and the elevations constitute the minimal drawings that can serve as records of the design. The working drawings are of great practical value but are esthetically secondary, being simply an implementation of the designer's decisions. The ground plan and elevations are discussed in this chapter. Perspective paintings are described in Chapters 13 and 14, set models in Chapter 15, and working drawings in Chapter 16.

GRAPHIC PROJECTION

All theatrical drawing is described in terms of a *picture plane*—that is, the plane surface (the sheet of paper or cardboard) on which the picture is drawn—and lines of projection. It is assumed that the picture plane is placed in a special relationship (in front and upright, or above and horizontal, etc.) to the scenic element to be drawn, and that imaginary straight lines are then extended (projected) from each part of the scenic element to the picture plane. The points at which these lines strike the picture plane are then marked, the result being a representation of the object.

Three types of drawings, or projections, are commonly used by the set designer: orthographic, perspective, and isometric. The type of drawing depends on the angles between the picture plane and the lines of projection.

To draw the ground plan and elevations the designer uses the simplest type: orthographic. (Perspective and isometric projections will be discussed later.) This is a kind with which everyone is familiar, though not everyone knows the technical term for it. Ordinary street maps are produced this way. A detailed street map shows the outlines of houses in much the same way as the ground plan of a set shows the units of the furniture and scenery.

The word *orthographic* comes from the Greek *orthos,* meaning "straight" or "right-angled," and *graphia,* meaning "drawing." An orthographic drawing is one produced by setting up the picture plane parallel with the main surface of an object and projecting lines at right angles to the picture plane from one to the other.[1]

---

1. According to the strictest definition, the object shown in an orthographic projection need not be parallel with the picture plane, but other positions are so rare in theatrical drawing that the abbreviated definition given here seems of more practical value than a fuller one expanded to include all possible cases.

THE GROUND PLAN

A scaled drawing of the ground plan on tracing paper was part of the design step described in Chapter 6. Since this version is likely to involve some experimentation resulting in erasures or unwanted construction lines, it will probably be necessary to copy it more neatly. If the drawing is to be photocopied, the new version will also be done on tracing paper; if the drawing is to be used in the scene shop, it should be done on cardboard, which will stand up much longer under rough handling.

It is a great convenience to include in the permanent drawing a two-color grid identical with that described in Chapter 6. Many designers find the preparation of the grid irksome, and it is possible to use a ground plan without it, but it is so much help in setting up the scenery on stage that it seems to justify the extra trouble. It provides an automatic guide in measuring points on the stage floor, largely dispensing with time-consuming measurements of the drawing during the set assembly.

Most directors, however, prefer to work with an ungridded ground plan, since they do not need such precise dimensioning, and since it is easier to plan the blocking on an uncluttered drawing. For this reason, it is desirable to prepare two copies of the ground plan in final form, one with grid for use by the designer in preparing working drawings and by the crew in assembling the scenery on stage, the other for use by the director in planning the blocking. If the ground plan is transferred from the original tracing paper version by retracing and rubbing, it takes only a very little extra time to make the director's copy, and it is much more convenient to have two copies, since the director can design the blocking and the set designer can prepare working drawings simultaneously without having to pass a single copy back and forth a dozen times.

The first step in making the final ground plan drawing, then, is to copy the full grid diagram on a fresh sheet of cardboard. The ground plan is then redrawn on the new grid or transferred from the tracing paper by rubbing. Finally, the pencil lines are traced in india ink, the drawing labeled, and the surface cleaned with a soft eraser.

Careful color coding throughout the drawing greatly facilitates its use. The grid should be drawn in diluted red and green ink; the labels and the lines of the scenery in india ink. All other information or instructions should be printed in full-strength red ink. Often such material can be printed in the margins of the sheet, with arrows drawn to the relevant points on the ground plan, as needed. If lettering must be placed on the grid itself, care should be taken to arrange it so that it does not touch the horizontal lines of the grid or cross any of the lines of the scenery. A height of $3/32''$ is suggested for lettering working drawings, with successive lines $1/16''$ apart.

Guide Points

It is usually desirable to make one addition to the permanent ground plan. It was suggested in Chapter 6 that, where possible, key points in the scenery be aligned with easily identifiable points on the grid. Even when that has been done, such guide points are not always immediately evident from the drawing. They should be marked for the convenience of the crew by drawing a small red circle around each guide point.

In some cases, the guide points will fall outside the areas representing the scenery. For example, the side wall of a set may have been placed so that its downstage corner stands on the outside line of the grid, 1'-0'' back from the corner of the proscenium, and the wall lies along a line drawn from that point to the back line of the grid, 4'-6'' in from the outside corner. Such a wall is not likely to extend all the way to the back of the stage, so that the point at the back of the grid that determines how the wall must be placed lies well beyond the end of the unit. In that case, the line of the wall should be extended in red (again, using full-strength ink), all the way to the guide point, which should then be circled. (See *Figure 12-1.*)

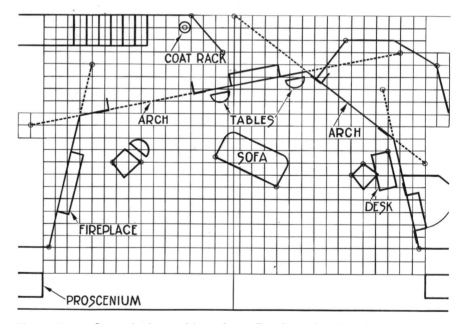

Figure 12-1. Ground plan guide points. Furniture is placed so that at least one leg of each unit falls on an easily identifiable guide point on the stage floor. Four walls are designed so that they point toward key grid points. The guide points are indicated by small circles for the convenience of the assembly crew; when they lie beyond the ends of the walls, the lines are extended by dashes to help the crew identify them.

Marking the critical guide points on the floor plan in this way is not likely to take more than five or ten minutes and may save an hour's work in assembling the set at rehearsal and performance time.

Sometimes the drawing as described above may be entirely adequate. Usually, however, the designer will find it desirable to add other information or instructions.

Additional Information

Each flat should be identified by a code letter; it is most convenient to assign the letters in the order in which the flats will stand, starting at the down-left corner of the stage and moving around the set to the opposite corner. These letters should be printed behind the walls, each one centered behind the flat to which it refers.

The heights of platforms and stairs should be indicated, as this information is often helpful in assembling the set. Usually, the heights can be printed inside the outlines of platforms, either in the center of the space, or in one corner. All heights should be shown as measured from the floor of the stage, not from adjacent platforms. If a small 1'-0" platform is placed on top of a larger platform 2'-6" high, which itself rests on the stage floor, the height of the large platform should be indicated as 2'-6" and the height of the small platform as 3'-6". It is usually unnecessary to indicate the height of individual steps of a flight of stairs if the heights of the two levels that they join are clear; however, if the stairs are irregular and, for example, include large landings, the designer may find it desirable to mark the heights of the landings.

Furniture and other stage properties may not be readily identifiable from a ground plan, so it is good practice to label each piece.

The dimensions of individual scenic units are given on drawings other than the ground plan. Since the grid itself constitutes a two-dimensional ruler, it is usually unnecessary to add any dimensions besides those already described.

ELEVATIONS

As has been said, both elevations and ground plans are produced by orthographic projection; they differ in the position of their picture planes. For the ground plan, the picture plane is horizontal; for the elevation, it is vertical. Furthermore, an elevation picture plane is usually placed so that it is parallel with a major surface of the scenic unit, so that elevations of standard flats show them as rectangles. A simple way to think of this kind of projection is to imagine that the picture plane (the paper or cardboard used for the drawing) is as large as the scenic element and is placed flat against it. The outlines are then traced directly onto the sheet, and the drawing is finally scaled down.

Scenic units like furniture may of course be shown in elevation, but the term is usually used in the theater to apply only to drawings of flats or other elements with large plane surfaces.

It was indicated at the beginning of the chapter that the appearance of a set can be completely described by ground plan and elevations alone. The plan shows the arrangement of the flats and other units on the stage floor, but does not show their shapes, except for the bottom edges; the elevations supply the remaining information. If students were to prepare working drawings to serve as a guide in the construction of a set that had already been fully represented in elevations, they would discover that their construction drawings repeated much of the information already given in the elevations. Such duplication is unnecessary and uneconomic. In some cases, it is preferable to make the construction drawings complete and omit from the elevations any information that will appear in the later drawings. Often, therefore, the number of elevations that must be drawn can be greatly reduced, and it may occasionally be possible to dispense with them altogether.

Continued experience will help students predict what elevations can safely be omitted. For any sets they are designing as part of their study, it is suggested that full elevations be prepared; after the working drawings are completed, the students can then profitably examine the two groups and identify the duplication that might have been avoided.

Shape   In preparing his design, the artist will have already made numerous sketches and verbal notes, including tentative descriptions of the color scheme. It is now necessary to plan the precise shapes of the scenic units, as well as of designs to be painted on them. Not only must the sketches be refined so as to create exactly the effects intended, but clear instructions must be supplied to the crew to enable them to cut, build, and paint the scenery to match the designer's intentions.

The refinement of the sketches consists primarily of redrawing them precisely, so that the decorative motifs are effectively integrated, repeated elements are identical, and the halves of symmetrical designs accurately match. The designer should make the instructions for the builders as simple as possible. As in other aspects of design, an esthetic effect should not be cheapened merely to make the construction easier, but as the artist works over his designs he should consciously focus on any structural simplification that will still achieve the desired effect. Very often he may find that such simplification strengthens, clarifies, and generally improves his design.

Simplifying an Arch

Take the example of the moorish arch shown in *Figure 3-9.* First the arch was sketched freehand. Since it was intended to be built as a header placed between two standard flats, it seemed desirable to carry the side framing all the way to the bottom of the header unit; consequently, it was necessary to incorporate the end of the 2'' stile into the design. The arch was resketched several times to improve the interrelationships among the various elements—for example, to relate the size of the columns to the curved section and to make an attractive total design. Each sketch was more carefully drawn than the preceding one, so that the final version was about as regular as the designer could make it freehand.

The last sketch was then analyzed for elements of regularity, in order to discover the simplest way to construct it. The height of the flats was 12'-0''. Using the flat height as shown in the sketch, the designer constructed a temporary ruler by dividing the height into 12 units, each representing a foot, and one of the sections was divided by 12, to provide for inch measurements. Using this ruler, the designer found that the space between the side flats was 7'-6'', the distance from the floor to the center of the curved section was 10'-9'', and the bottom of the header stiles was 5'-10½'' from the bottom of the flats.

Inspection of the large curved section suggested that it might be closely approximated by three curves, the center one with a large radius and the two side curves with a much smaller radius. Since the arch is symmetrical, the center of the large curve obviously lies on the vertical center line of the unit. This center line was marked, and a number of trial curves drawn with a compass, adjusting the position of the point and the opening of the legs until the curve seemed to match the sketch as closely as was possible. Measurement demonstrated this center was 5'-1½'' below the top of the flat. The point at which the arc seemed to pull away from the sketched curve was then marked by eye—at 2'-7½'' below the top of the flat. A matching point was then marked on the opposite side of the central curve.

In order for the two side curves to flow smoothly into the center one, they had to be drawn as tangents to it; that meant that the centers of the short-radius curves must lie on radii of the large curve, drawn to the points of tangency. The next step, then, was to connect the two points already marked at 2'-7½'' below the top of the unit with the center of the large curve.

The position of the center of one of the small curves was then found by the same procedure that had been used for the middle curve: the point of the compass was placed at different positions on the center-curve radius, the legs opened so that the pencil point touched the end of the central curve, and the small curve drawn. After a series of trials, the position that seemed to produce an arc most closely approximating the sketched curve was identified; the resulting radius was 1'-6''. The curve was then drawn firmly, and a matching curve added at the other side of the arch. The radius of the small curves at the bottom of the header was determined in the same way; it turned out to be 11''.

The description of this procedure has necessarily been long, but the analysis itself took very little time. Obviously, the dimensions as stated would enable a construction worker to reproduce the unit easily. It may seem that the discovery of this simple means of drawing a complex arch was due to a series of happy accidents; but such accidents happen more frequently than not to a careful artist who is on the lookout for them. Every set illustrated in this book contains at least one example. One more instance will be described.

Directions for Slanting

For the *Antony and Cleopatra* set *(Figure 6-19),* the first step in adapting the design to Egyptian architecture and decoration was to collect and analyze pictures of the period, as described in Chapter 8. The slanted pillars, with their crosspiece, were then drawn freehand and resketched until their shape and proportions seemed to produce the right effect. Up to this point no angles or dimensions had been measured. Having developed an acceptable sketch, the designer then analyzed it to discover the simplest way to describe it.

The false proscenium above was chosen for analysis, as it faced the audience directly. The height from the floor to the underside of the horizontal crosspiece was determined by the proscenium opening, since the entire unit was intended to fit into and around the proscenium. Allowing a comfortable space for fitting, the designer set this height at 13'-0'' and constructed a temporary ruler as long as this distance in the sketch, divided into 13 sections, each representing a foot. Experiment demonstrated that the outside edge of the pillars matched the diagonal of a rectangle 13'-0'' × 3'-0'', that the inside edge matched the diagonal of a rectangle 13'-0'' × 2'-0'', and that the bottom edge of the pillar was 3'-0'' wide. The lines of the sketch were not drawn with absolute precision, but their deviation from those measurements was so slight that it was undetectable. Again, such a simple description of a complex shape may seem to be due to an unusual group of fortunate accidents, but such accidents occur regularly.

The arch was redrawn carefully with a ruler, to those measurements, and the effect of the scaled drawing checked with that of the sketch; the designer was unable to discover any difference, so this extremely simple dimensioning was adopted for the design. (See *Figure 12-2.*) The widths of the thickness piece and the horizontal beam, which were determined by the same method, turned out to be 2'-6'' and 2'-0'': two more surprising

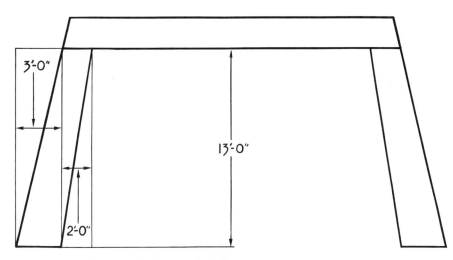

Figure 12-2. Dimensioning angled lines.

accidents. Incidentally, when the design was later checked with books on Egyptian architecture, it was discovered that the two angles used in the pillars were within a hairsbreadth of angles commonly used by ancient architects. That fact, however, is not due to accident, but is a demonstration that the designer had absorbed the spirit and detail of Egyptian design prior to making his sketches. As he made his trial sketches for the design, those angles looked right to him, as they would have looked right to an ancient designer; their later confirmation simply proved the soundness of his method.

Even with the greatest care and the highest degree of serendipity, of course, not all irregular units will be describable in such simple terms. Often, major elements may be indicated simply, with a few lines left to be drawn freehand. But when major motifs cannot be simply described, they must be carefully drawn and gridded, so that the builders can copy them point by point. If at all possible, it is preferable to show such elements full-sized in the drawings, even if it is necessary to break them into parts and separate them on three or four sheets. In that case, matching guidelines should be included in the drawings, so that the separate sections can be easily assembled during construction. If full-size drawing is not possible, it is better to use the largest scale that will make it possible to show the entire unit on a single sheet; enlargement from half-size to full-size is only slightly easier, for example, than enlargement from quarter-size to full-size, and the advantage of being able to see the entire drawing at once is more important than an increase in scale short of full size.

Irreducible
Irregularities

Painting
Elevations

Having refined, regularized, and analyzed all of the structural and decorative patterns of his flats and other scenic elements, the designer is ready to record them in the form of elevations. For the great majority of sets, only flats need be shown in the elevations, so our discussion will be limited to this commonest type.

The most complex elevations are those that give the construction crew the information they need in painting the flats. The scale chosen will depend on the complexity of the design and on the space needed for indicating dimensions and other necessary information. There is considerable advantage in including elevations of all the flats to be used in a set on the same drawing. Even if the largest scale making that possible does not provide enough space for the required instructions, it is probably better to make a single omnibus drawing and then supplement it with drawings to a larger scale showing individual flats or decorative motifs. (See *Figure 12-3.*)

If the scale of ¾″ = 1′-0″ is used, it is possible to draw two rows of 12′-0″ flats on a sheet of standard-sized cardboard, for a total width of 74′-0″, which would nearly always be adequate for representing an entire set. The flats should be arranged in the order in which they will appear in the set, starting at the down-right corner of the stage. Flats that are to be joined side by side in the same plane should be drawn together; where flats are joined at an angle, they should be separated by a small gap of perhaps half an inch (actual, not scaled). The code letter of each flat should be indicated, preferably centered under the outline of the flat; these letters should match those given in the ground plan. The widths of the individual flats and of continuous wall sections may be added if this is desired.

The flats should be shown from the front, with all decorative elements drawn. For repeated motifs, or flats that are mirror images, it may be possible to draw the decorative patterns only once and add a note indicating where they are to be duplicated, although an inexperienced crew may find it difficult to reverse a design.

A method of assigning code names and numbers to the colors to be used in painting a set is discussed in Chapter 14; the code designations should be added to the elevations. The designer may prefer to place all of the color coding outside the edges of the flats, perhaps in one or two lists, drawing arrows even for the larger areas. If sections or individual motifs will be shown in auxiliary drawings to a larger scale, the color designations may be omitted from the small-scale elevations and given only on the larger drawings.

Assembly
Elevations

Usually, the ground plan, painting elevations, and working drawings supply all of the information needed for constructing and assembling a set.

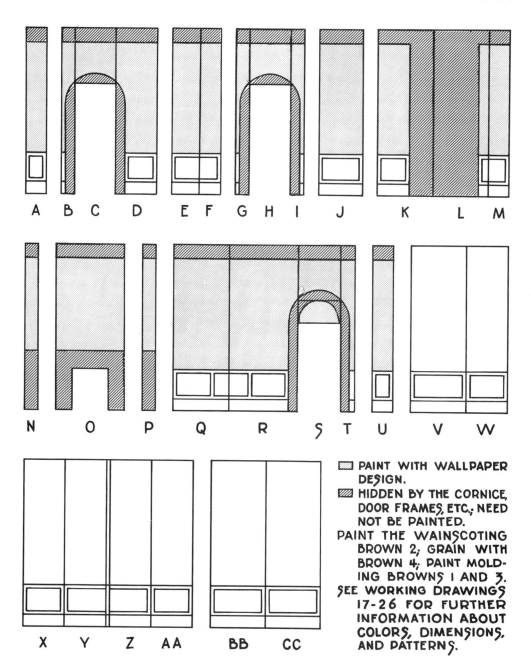

A B C D E F G H I J K L M

N O P Q R S T U V W

X Y Z AA BB CC

☐ PAINT WITH WALLPAPER
DESIGN.
▨ HIDDEN BY THE CORNICE,
DOOR FRAMES, ETC.; NEED
NOT BE PAINTED.
PAINT THE WAINSCOTING
BROWN 2; GRAIN WITH
BROWN 4; PAINT MOLD-
ING BROWNS 1 AND 3.
SEE WORKING DRAWINGS
17-26 FOR FURTHER
INFORMATION ABOUT
COLORS, DIMENSIONS,
AND PATTERNS.

Figure 12-3. A simple painting elevation: Ibsen's *Hedda Gabler.* This drawing gives only general information about the larger areas; specific motifs and dimensions were given on other working drawings, prepared to a larger scale.

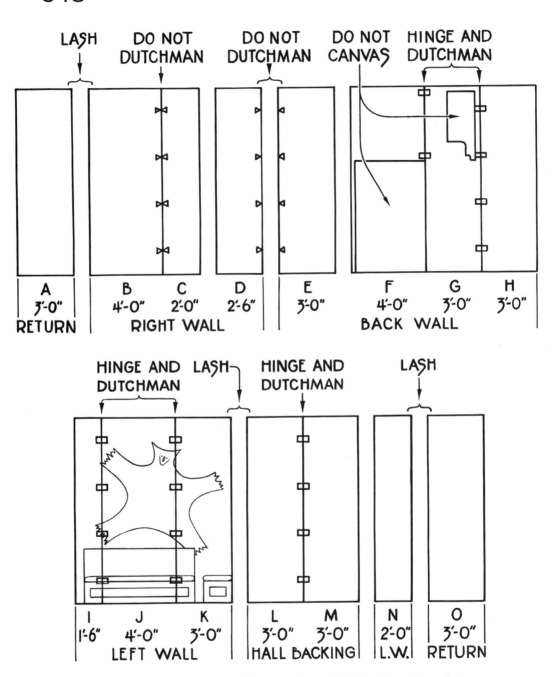

Figure 12-4. An assembly elevation: Wilder's *The Skin of Our Teeth*. Because the placement of the animal skin on flats *I-J-K* depends on the position of the sofa and footstool, they are shown in place; other furniture is omitted.

Occasionally, however, it may be desirable to make an additional set of elevations to assist in fastening the scenic elements together on stage. These drawings need not show how the flats are to be painted, but they should show their outlines, including any openings (for example, for doors and windows). Their primary value is in indicating the pattern of hinging and dutchmanning and the assembly of three-dimensional units to be fastened to the flats. Examples of such units are three-dimensional cornices, pilasters, fireplaces, drapes, and pictures hung on the walls. Some designers include in their assembly elevations pieces of furniture that stand close to, and parallel with, the flats. Since the positions of these pieces are already indicated by the ground plan, it is usually more convenient to omit them, but if, for example, the arrangement of pictures hung on a wall is determined by the placement of a davenport, the assembly crew may find it easier to hang them properly if the furniture is also shown.

The most convenient arrangement for the assembly elevations is the same as that for the painters' drawings; they are shown from the front and should be joined or separated in the drawing as described in the preceding section. The drawing should show not only where hinges are to be placed, but also whether they go on the front (canvassed) or back side of the flats. Where flats stand side by side in the same plane, hinges on the front should be drawn in the form of small rectangles, 2″ × 4″ (to scale), centered on the joint; each half of such a rectangle represents one leaf of the hinge. A special symbol is conventionally used to indicate hinges to be fastened to the backs of the flats. It is formed by drawing only the diagonals and verticals of the rectangle described, the horizontals being omitted; the result is two triangles, pointing toward each other. Flats that will stand at an angle to each other are separated in the drawing; their hinging is shown by drawing half a hinge on each flat, using a (scaled) 2″ square for a hinge on the face and using a matching triangle, pointing toward the edge of the flat, for a hinge on the back. Dutchmanning must be indicated by a verbal note. Often it may be possible simply to print "Dutchman all joints hinged on the face"; however, it may be necessary to provide a special note for each joint to be covered.

13

THE
PERSPECTIVE
DRAWING

No member of the audience ever sees the set as it appears in the ground plan or elevations. Since the set is designed and built for the audience, a design cannot be evaluated with complete confidence except on the basis of a drawing that represents it as the viewers will see it. For that drawing, perspective projection must be used.

The word *perspective* comes from the Latin *per,* meaning "through," and *specere* meaning "to look." A perspective drawing is one that represents what a stationary viewer would see if she or he were looking not at the picture plane, but through it at the set beyond.

The basic theory of perspective projection is simple; its practical application is considerably more complicated. The set designer need not master all of the types or aspects of perspective, since his use of it is usually restricted to a special set of conditions. However, he should become familiar enough with theatrical perspective to use it easily and to prepare accurate perspective drawings quickly. His study of perspective can be divided into two parts, both equally important: first, he must achieve a clear understanding of the fundamental theory and principles; and second, he must master the specific skills that he needs to use in practice.

351

SELECTING THE VIEWPOINT

Obviously, no two people in an audience have exactly the same view of the stage; in fact, if a single member of the audience moves in his seat, or stands up without otherwise moving, his view of the stage changes slightly; even the distance between the eyes results in each eye's seeing a slightly different picture. To represent the appearance of a set from every possible position in the theater would require an enormous number of perspective drawings. To reduce the amount of work, the designer chooses a position that represents the most typical view of the stage and draws a single perspective from that position. The usual one chosen is on the center line of the auditorium, facing the stage directly, in the center seat of the row about half or two-thirds of the way back. It is desirable for a designer who is to work regularly in a particular theater to select such a key seat and record the critical measurements, so that perspectives of various sets will be comparable and can be prepared without remeasuring. The essential measurements are as follows:

1. The distance from the viewer's eye to the front edge of the acting area. Usually, it is most convenient to consider the nearest edge of the acting area as coinciding with the line where the back of the proscenium wall joins the stage floor. Occasionally, a director may instruct actors to use the area in front of this line, but except for sets involving false prosceniums, all of the scenery will nearly always start behind this line.

2. The height of the viewer's eye above the level of the stage floor. This height will vary greatly for different theaters. The actual height for a particular theater may be used, although many designers prefer to set it arbitrarily at 3' or 4' above the stage floor. The 3' distance is convenient because in many cases the upper edge of wainscoting is at this height, as well as doorknobs and the backs of chairs; furthermore, chair seats are usually a foot and a half above the floor, so that their height can easily be found by marking a point halfway between the eye-level line and the floor of the stage. On the other hand, 4' is a convenient height because a vertical line can be dropped from it to the stage floor, that line can be cut in half, then each segment can again be halved, thus marking it off at 1' intervals.

THE PANE-OF-GLASS METHOD

Let us assume that a viewer is sitting in our chosen seat, and that his eye is 3'-0'' above the floor of the stage and 40'-0'' from the front edge of the scenery. Let us suppose the set is 12'-0'' high and extremely simple in design, formed of three straight walls, with a door in the center of each. Now imagine that there is a large pane of glass standing vertically on the floor just in front of the viewer, at arm's length, and that he has a felt pen with which he can mark on the glass. (See *Figure 13-1.*) Looking through the glass, he sees the stage set; taking his felt pen, he traces its outline on the glass exactly as he sees it. Since he will have separate views with each eye, and since his view would change if he moved, he must close one eye

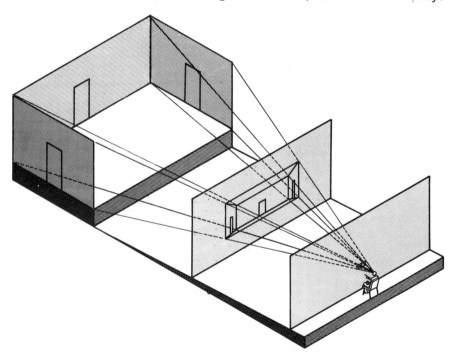

Figure 13-1. The pane-of-glass method of making perspective drawings. A simple stage set is shown, with walls at right angles. Two picture planes are included, in the form of vertical sheets of glass, and the projection of the stage set is shown on each. The scale of the projection is much smaller for the picture plane closest to the spectator.

and hold his head perfectly still while he makes his drawing. The result would be an accurate perspective drawing of the set.

Theoretically, that method of making perspective drawings is perfectly sound. It is never actually used in the theater because it has two serious practical defects. One is the extreme difficulty of holding the eye absolutely immobile. The other is that this method can be used to draw pictures only of sets in existence. Nevertheless, the methods that are used are all indirect ways of duplicating the pane-of-glass method, and students of perspective will understand the various processes much better if they constantly refer back to the basic method described here.

PLACEMENT OF THE PICTURE PLANE

As has been explained, the surface that receives the drawing constitutes the picture plane. In our imaginary example, we described the picture plane as a pane of glass placed at arm's length in front of the viewer. Imagination, or experiment, will demonstrate that if the picture plane is moved closer to the viewer, the drawing becomes smaller; if it is moved farther away, the drawing becomes larger. However, the proportions and shape of the drawing remain the same, regardless of the distance of the picture plane from the viewer: if the back wall of the set is three times as long as it is high, those proportions will be identical wherever the picture plane is placed. If the *spectator* moves toward or away from the set, his view changes, not only in size but in proportions; but the movement of the picture plane changes only the *size* of the picture. (The pictures in *Figure 6-9* illustrate the great difference in appearance of the same room produced by changing the distance from which it is viewed.)

This information gives us two important principles of perspective: (1) the distance between the viewer and the set is visually significant, so that the appearance of the set depends on it; and (2) the distance between the picture plane and the viewer, or the picture plane and the set, has no visual significance, and can consequently be determined on the basis of convenience.

Our purpose is to prepare a perspective view of a set without actually having to construct it: in other words, to deal with it in two-dimensional terms. To do that we must handle it in two separate steps; the first involves the ground plan.

It would be possible to draw a full-scale ground plan, having the same dimensions as the actual set. However, the two principles given above enable us to work with the set on a more convenient scale; by applying them we can produce a perspective drawing of any desired size, using a ground plan of manageable scale.

Later in the chapter a special method of preparing perspective drawings of stage sets is discussed, the primary advantage of which is that it can be done much faster than the traditional method. Before turning to it, however, it seems desirable to describe briefly the method more commonly used.

TRADITIONAL METHOD OF PREPARING PERSPECTIVE DRAWINGS

In practice, the designer proceeds as follows. He first selects the width he prefers for the finished picture. He then draws his ground plan to a scale such that the proscenium opening is of the selected width. One of the scales already recommended will be most convenient, although if the designer wants to produce a picture requiring an odd scale (for example, $^{15}/_{16}'' = 1'-0''$) the resulting awkwardness is less serious than it would be for other types of theatrical drawings. If the designer happens to have selected the same scale that he has already used in drawing the ground plan of his set, then that part of his new drawing will be identical (and, in fact, he can, if he prefers, use the original drawing). However, his new ground plan must include extra information: it must show the position of the viewer and the placement of the picture plane. (The position of the viewer is technically called the *sight point*.)

For illustrating the method, let us assume a proscenium opening 30'-0" wide and 24'-0" deep, a set 12'-0" high, and a sight point 40'-0'' from the front edge of the set and 3'-0'' above the level of the stage floor. Since the sight point is in front of the stage, the center line of the ground plan should be extended and a point marked on it representing 40'-0'' from the front line of the set (if the scale of ¾'' =1'-0'' is being used, then the point will of course be 30'' in front of the set).

The picture plane chosen is a vertical one, parallel to the proscenium. If it is placed close to the sight point, a small drawing will result; as we move it closer to the ground plan of the set, the size of the drawing gradually increases. If we place it flat against the front of the set, extending clear across the proscenium opening, the resulting picture will be exactly as wide as the opening itself. Since we have drawn the ground plan to a scale having the proscenium opening the same width as that chosen for our picture, this is the proper position for the picture plane. It then appears on our drawing as a straight line, extending right across the front of the stage.

So far, the construction has been relatively straightforward and based upon familiar methods. The next step requires some clarity of imagination.

Horizontal Positions

Imagine the spectator, sitting with his eye at the point we have marked as the sight point. Imagine him looking at the back corner of the set on the left side of the stage, as he faces it. He would see the corner by means of a beam of light traveling in a straight line from the corner to his eye. If we were to draw this beam of light on the ground plan, it would appear as a straight line connecting the corner of the set with the sight point and, consequently, crossing the picture plane at an angle. Let us imagine for a moment that instead of working with a ground plan we are in a real theater, with a pane of glass extending clear across the stage where we have imagined our picture plane to be. Our viewer could not himself mark the glass, but if he had an assistant on stage with a felt pen, the viewer could tell his assistant to mark the point on the glass where the corner of the set was visible from his seat. If the assistant drew a vertical line through that point, extending from the top to the bottom of the glass, the vertical corner between the back and side walls would lie along that line.

Let us now return to our small-scale ground plan. The point at which the picture-plane line is crossed by the sight line represents the position, in ground plan, that the corner of the set will occupy in our finished perspective drawing. (See *Figure 13-2*.) Let us say that we measure the point at which the sight line crosses the picture plane and discover that it is exactly 2½'' from the left edge of the set. Let us take a new piece of cardboard and draw on it a rectangle 22½'' wide and 9'' high; at the scale we have chosen, that represents an area 30'-0'' × 12'-0'', the dimensions of the front of our stage set. On the lower edge, we measure in 2½'' from the corner of this rectangle and mark the point; we do the same at the top edge of the rectangle. Then we connect those two points with a vertical line. That line, at the scale we are using, matches exactly the vertical line drawn on the imaginary full-sized sheet of glass. In other words, in our final perspective drawing, that line will be where the back and left side walls of the set meet. Since our set is symmetrical, the same measurements can be used to mark the matching line for the right back corner of the set. Once we have located the top and bottom of the line, we will have produced an accurate perspective projection of the corner.

Obviously, the same step must be repeated for every element in the set; in each case, a sight line is drawn connecting the element with the sight point. The positions of the various points where sight lines cross the picture plane are transferred to the top and bottom edges of the rectangle that defines the edges of our finished picture, and vertical lines are drawn to connect each pair. In each case, the scenic element that we have projected will appear at some level on its matching vertical line.

Vertical Positions

The next step is to determine the vertical position of the various elements in the set. The ground plan we may imagine as a sheet of cardboard

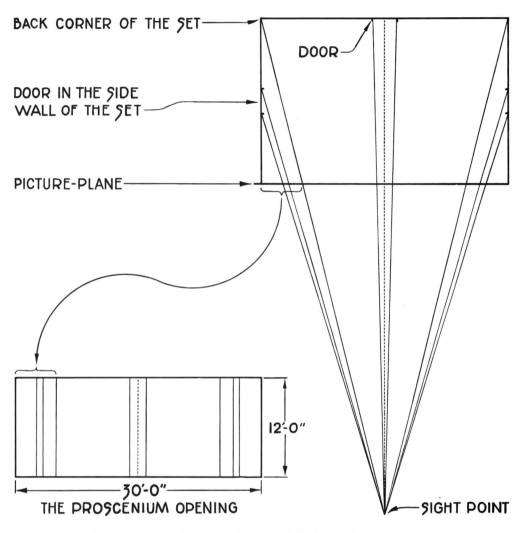

BACK CORNER OF THE SET

DOOR

DOOR IN THE SIDE
WALL OF THE SET

PICTURE-PLANE

12'-0"

30'-0"

THE PROSCENIUM OPENING

SIGHT POINT

Figure 13-2. Perspective projection of horizontal dimensions. *Right:* a ground plan of the stage, with the center line (dashed) extended and the sight point marked at a distance of 40'-0'' from the front edge. Sight lines are drawn from the back corners and from the doors in the center of the walls. *Lower left:* a rectangle as high as a standard flat represents the picture plane. It is drawn to the same scale as the ground plan. The points at which the sight lines cross the picture plane in the ground plan are transferred to the picture plane rectangle, and vertical lines are run through them. The vertical edges of the walls and doors lie along these lines, although they are shorter. The method of determining their tops and bottoms is shown in *Figure 13-3.*

placed flat under the set, with the scenery resting on it. The ground plan gives complete information about the arrangement of the set on the floor of the stage; it does not give any information about height (for example, the height of the flats or the height of a door opening). To present such information, we must use something like the ground plan, but differently oriented. A new picture plane has to be visualized. It is simplest to think of drawing on a new plane standing vertically along the center line of the stage, extending from the sight point all the way to the back wall of the stage.

In our first drawing, we imagined in effect that we were a member of the audience looking at the set from a center seat. From that position, we would see only the edge of our new plane of projection, extending vertically in a straight line. To see this new plane fully, we must move around to the side and look at it from right angles. (See *Figure 13-3.*) In this position, the plane on which we drew the ground plan appears simply as a horizontal line; and the old picture plane is a vertical line. This view no longer tells us very much about the shape of the bottom edge of the set, but it gives us full information about the heights of the various elements. We must draw the set in this new position; and since the distance of an object from the sight point affects its projection, we must carefully maintain the proper dimensions both vertically and horizontally. The sight point itself, as we originally assumed it, must be drawn 3'-0'' above the floor of the stage and 40'-0'' in front of it. The picture plane again appears at the front of the set, beginning at the stage level, 3'-0'' below the sight point, and extending 9'-0'' above it. Of course, it is exactly the same length as the height of the rectangle to which we transferred the points obtained in step 1.

The rest of the procedure matches that for step 1: sight lines are drawn from the points that are critical in determining the heights of the scenic elements (the top and bottom of each unit); then the positions of the points at which they cross the picture plane are transferred to the vertical lines in the picture-plane rectangle. For example, sight lines are drawn from the top and bottom of the back wall, and the points at which they cross the picture plane are transferred to the vertical line along which the corner of the set runs. The part of the line between these two points then constitutes the perspective drawing of the corner; it is redrawn to make it identifiably darker. The opposite corner of the set can be marked in the same way. Since the top edge of the back wall forms a straight line between the top of the two verticals, we can determine its position in the picture by connecting them with a ruler; the same procedure is followed for the bottom edge of the wall.

The front edges of the side walls were assumed to be in contact with the picture plane; they will consequently appear full size (to our scale). Since they are 30'-0" apart and 12'-0" high, they will obviously match

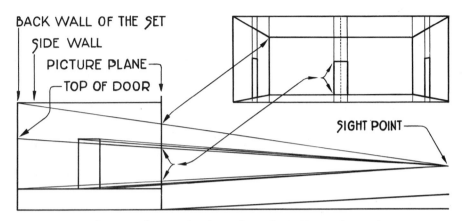

Figure 13-3. Perspective projection of vertical dimensions. At the left and bottom a cross section of the stage and auditorium is shown, with sight lines drawn from the top and bottom of the back wall and the tops and bottoms of the doors. In the upper right corner, a reproduction of the picture plane from *Figure 13-2* is shown. The points where the sight lines cross the picture plane in the cross-section view are copied on the corresponding lines in the upper drawing, and the matching points are connected with straight lines.

the side edges of our picture rectangle. The top of the left wall can then be placed by drawing a straight line from the upper left corner of the rectangle to the upper left corner of the back wall, which we have now outlined completely. The bottom edge is drawn similarly, and the edges of the right side wall are marked in the same way. The result is a perspective outline of the walls of our stage set. The doors can be drawn by the same process.

Before proceeding to the next step, the student must thoroughly understand this method of producing a perspective drawing, so a brief repetition may be of value. The method requires the use of three separate drawings, all made to the same scale: (1) a rectangle with the same width as the proscenium opening and the same height as the set; (2) a ground plan showing the stage set, the picture plane, and the sight point; and (3) a vertical elevation, showing the stage set, the picture plane, and the sight point. On the ground plan and the vertical elevation, the artist draws sight lines extending from key points in the set to the sight point. The points where the sight lines cross the picture plane are transferred to the rectangle and connected with lines that match the edges of the set units.

The Method Summarized

Transferring Measurements by Paper Strips

In the description of this method, a ruler was used to transfer the first point from the ground plan to the rectangle. Because the sight lines cross the picture plane at a variety of angles, the distances marked off seldom match even divisions on the ruler. It is easier and more accurate to transfer them by laying a strip of paper along the picture-plane line, marking the end of the picture plane and the position of the point to be transferred, and then moving the paper to the edge of the rectangle and copying the measurement on that line. Students should train themselves to use this method of transferring measurements not only in making perspective drawings, but also for any other drawings where the measurements do not match divisions on a ruler.

GRID METHOD OF PREPARING PERSPECTIVE DRAWINGS

The method of preparing a perspective projection that has been described is a sound one; however, a method has been devised that reduces the amount of measuring and marking, and makes it possible to produce full perspective drawings much faster.[1]

This simpler method uses as its basic tool a perspective drawing of an imaginary generalized stage set, the dimensions of which are adapted to a particular theater. Unlike actual sets, its angles are all 90°. It consists of a box the width of the proscenium opening, with a depth equal to the depth of the stage and with a height matching the standard height of flats in this theater. In addition, the floor, ceiling, and side walls of the box are covered with a grid of squares produced by vertical and horizontal lines drawn a foot apart. Before preparing his first set design, the designer should make a drawing of the perspective projection of this generalized set, adjusted to the dimensions of his own theater, which he can then use as a permanent tool in preparing perspective drawings of his future sets. Because this drawing is of primary importance, its construction will be described in detail.

Constructing the Grid

First Steps

Let us assume the same dimensions as those used previously in this chapter: proscenium opening 30'-0''; depth of stage 24'-0''; height of

---

1. The grid method of making perspective drawings, described on this and the following pages, was developed by the author in 1943.

scenery 12'-0''; distance from the front edge of the set to the sight point 40'-0''; sight point 3'-0'' above the floor of the stage; scale to be used ¾'' = 1'-0''. (The following procedure is illustrated in *Figure 13-4.*)

1. First draw a line a little longer than 48'' (at our scale, representing 64'-0'', or the distance from the sight point to the back wall of the stage).

2. On this line, mark points dividing the line into two sections, 18'' (=24'-0'') and 30'' (=40'-0''). The 18'' section of the line represents the depth of the stage and constitutes the center line of the stage, and the 30'' section represents the distance between the front edge of the acting area and the sight point.

3. Draw a rectangle 11¼'' wide (=15'-0'') and 18'' deep, using the 18'' section of the long line as one side of the rectangle. This rectangle represents half of the stage floor; since our imaginary set is symmetrical, we need measure only one side of it, so it is unnecessary to draw the full stage.

4. Mark off the side edge of the rectangle at intervals of ¾'' (=1'-0''). (By "side edge" is meant the free side, which does not form part of the long line.)

5. Supply a straight edge long enough to reach from the sight point to the outside back corner of the rectangle. It is possible to use a long wooden slat as the straight edge, but it is preferable to prepare one from cardboard. Cut strips of cardboard about an inch and a half wide; lay them end to end so that they total the necessary length. Lay shorter sections along the strips, covering the joints, and tape them securely so as to form a single long strip. At the end of the strip, a square extension should be left at the side, approximately doubling the width of the strip. Draw a line across this extension, continuing the edge of the strip. Push a thumbtack through this line approximately in the center of the square extension, and fasten the tack firmly in place at the sight point on the original line (probably this will have to be done on the floor). The strip will then lie on top of the drawing, with one end held firmly at the sight point, so that the entire strip can be moved back and forth with the sight point as a center. The sight point will then coincide with one edge of the long strip of cardboard; this is the operating edge, which should be used in all future measurements.

6. Keeping the long strip firmly in place at the sight point, move the strip so that the operating edge touches the outside back corner of the rectangle, that is, the corner that does not touch the long center line. Where the strip

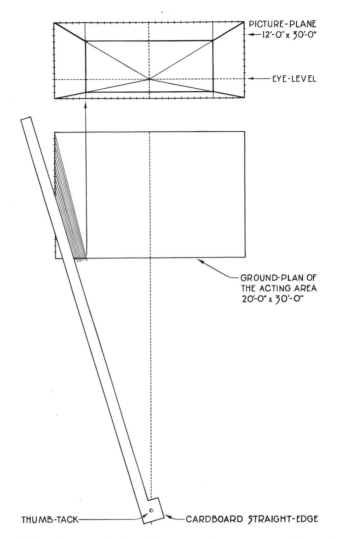

Figure 13-4. A ground plan for preparing a perspective grid. *Bottom:* a ground plan, with a cardboard straightedge fastened on the center line of the stage, 40'-0'' from the edge of the acting area. The side of the acting area has been marked at 1'-0'' intervals. *Top:* the edges of the picture plane (same scale) are marked off at 1'-0'' intervals, and the vertical center line and the eye-level line have been drawn. Lines have been run from each corner to the vanishing point. The points at which the back corners of the acting area project across the stage's front edge have been copied from the ground plan, and vertical lines drawn through them. The sections of these lines that lie between the vanishing lines represent the vertical edges of the back wall.

crosses the front edge of the rectangle, draw a short line along the edge of the strip, marking the point of crossing.

7. Move the strip so that its edge lies on the point ¾'' (=1'-0'') in front of the back corner of the rectangle. Mark the point at which it crosses the front of the rectangle, by drawing a short line along the edge of the strip.

8. Continue in this way until all of the points on the side of the rectangle have been projected across the front edge. When that has been done, the thumbtack may be taken up and the unit disassembled.

9. On a fresh sheet of cardboard draw a rectangle 9'' high and 22½'' wide (=12'-0'' × 30'-0''); this rectangle represents the front of the stage (or acting area) and, consequently, the picture plane.

10. Mark off the side edges of this rectangle at ¾'' intervals (=1'-0''). Also mark the center points of the top and bottom edges, and connect these points with a vertical line. Find the points on the side edges that mark the distance of the eye above the bottom edge of the rectangle (3', 4', or the actual distance measured from the theater itself), and draw a horizontal line connecting these two points.

Vanishing Points

At this point it is necessary to make use of a principle of perspective that has not yet been discussed. This principle can be demonstrated most easily in an actual architectural situation. Find a fairly long rectangular hall. Take a ruler or yardstick and stand at one end of the hall, exactly in the center of the end wall, facing the wall at the opposite end of the hall. Point with the ruler at the bottom edge of the right side wall beside you. Your ruler will be parallel to the wall that is behind you and at a right angle to the straight line where side wall and floor meet. Now move the ruler so that it points toward the bottom edge of the wall four or five feet in front of you, and check the angle again. Two lines (the ruler and the edge of the wall) of course form a double angle, in this case one obtuse and one acute; it is simpler if you focus your attention only on the acute. Moving the ruler so that it points toward the edge of the wall farther and farther from you, you will see that the angle becomes steadily more acute. When you have moved it so that it points to the edge of the wall at the far end of the hall, the angle will have become so small that ruler and edge will be almost parallel. Try to imagine the hall extended into the distance, and continue to move the ruler along its imagined edge; the two lines will steadily approach each other, until they are actually parallel (this would theoretically happen only at an infinite distance). When the ruler has been moved to where it is parallel with the edge of the wall, it will be pointing at a spot in the center of the wall at the far end of the hall; this spot is technically referred to as the *vanishing point*. Try to remember the position of this spot on the far wall. Then, without moving from your position, check the top edge of the right wall and the top and bottom edges of the left wall: you will discover that they all point toward the same vanishing point. So far, the experiment in the hall has illustrated a fundamental principle: any group of receding parallel lines seem to meet at a common vanishing point when represented in linear perspective.

Now try to focus on all four lines (the edges of the side walls) as parts of a single system, and watch them as you squat down on the floor; you will discover, as you move down, that the vanishing point moves down also, with the angles of the lines shifting so that they still point toward it for every position of the eye. Climb on a chair, and you will discover that the vanishing point rises so as to stay level with your eye, the angles of the lines again shifting with it. This illustrates another fundamental principle of perspective: the vanishing point of any horizontal line appears at the level of the viewer's eye.

With these two principles, we can now return to the drawing. Compare the imaginary stage set with the hall used in the experiment: both are rectangular, with the edges of the walls, ceiling, and floor horizontal and parallel; in both cases the viewer is facing the center of the back wall.

In drawing the stage set, it has been decided to place the spectator so that his eye is 3'-0" above the stage floor; the vanishing point for the entire system of lines must lie, therefore, on the horizontal line drawn at that (scaled) distance above the bottom edge of the rectangle. The sight point is assumed to be on the center line of the stage, which is marked as a vertical line; consequently the vanishing point for the stage set must be the point at which those two lines cross.

In the drawing *(Figure 13-4),* the left edge of the rectangle matches the front edge of the side wall of the set, so the corners of that wall will also appear at the same points as the corners of the rectangle. Since the top edge will point, or vanish, toward the vanishing point already identified, it can be partially located by drawing a straight line from the top corner of the rectangle to the vanishing point. Repeat for the other three corners of the rectangle.

Marking the Back Corners

The two side walls will lie in the areas drawn, but they will not fill them. Since the top and bottom edges have been drawn all the way to the vanishing point, they are represented as if the walls extended to infinity. To find the positions of the back vertical edges of the side walls, refer again to the original drawing. The position of the back corner of the side wall is shown by the point where the sight line intersected with the picture plane. Laying a strip of paper along the picture plane line, mark three points: the free corner of the rectangle, the corner that lies on the center line, and the point of intersection between the picture plane line and the sight line drawn from the back corner of the side wall. Then place the strip of paper at the bottom of the new drawing, so that the point marking the center line lies on the center line and the point marking the free corner of the rectangle coincides with the corner of our new rectangle. The point marked between these two extremes is then transferred to the new drawing. Moving the strip of paper to the top of the rectangle, repeat this step.

Draw a vertical line connecting those two points, but do not extend it all the way: draw only the portion that falls between the top and bottom edges of the side wall. Use the same strip of paper to mark matching measurements on the other half of the rectangle (which will involve turning the strip around, in order to make the points marking the center line and the corner fall in the right position). With this step the outline of the side walls is completed. The back wall can be completed by connecting the corners of the two side walls with horizontal lines. The lines extending beyond the side walls, to the vanishing point, should then be erased.

Place the slip of paper in the same position on the original drawing and transfer all of the points where sight lines were marked across the picture plane. Transfer these to the top and bottom edges of the new rectangle, being careful to turn the slip so that the points marking the center line and the corner of the rectangle are placed properly. Then connect each pair of points with a vertical line, drawing it only where it falls on the surface of one of the side walls. These vertical lines will divide the top and bottom edges of the two side walls at a series of matching points. Connect each pair of points with a horizontal line.

Earlier in the procedure, all four sides of the large rectangle were marked off at ¾'' intervals (=1'-0''); now connect each of those points with the vanishing point, starting each line at the edge of the rectangle, but drawing it only to the point where it touches the edge of the back wall.

The perspective drawing (Figure 13-5) now shows an imaginary set in the form of a rectangular box, having width, height, and depth that match the width of the proscenium opening, the height of standard scenery, and the depth of the stage. The floor, ceiling, and side walls of the set have been marked off in 1'-0" squares (drawn in perspective).

Checking the Grid

One of the basic principles of perspective is that if two objects or areas of the same size are at different distances from the viewer, the closer object looks larger. The designer should apply this principle in checking the

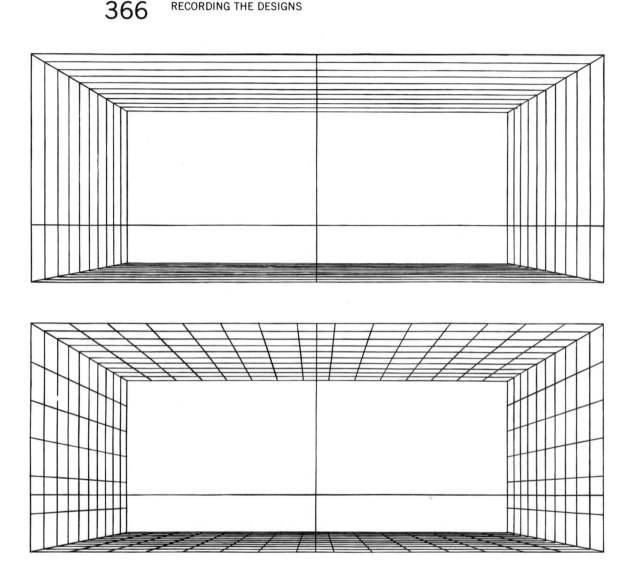

Figure 13-5. Completing the perspective grid. The drawing at the top reproduces the top drawing from *Figure 13-4,* on a larger scale. In addition to the sight line projecting the corner of the back wall, the points at which the other sight lines cross the picture plane have been copied, and verticals and horizontals run along the floor, ceiling, and side walls of the set. However, to improve legibility, only even-numbered lines have been copied. In the bottom drawing, the edges of the picture plane have been marked off at 2'-0'' intervals, and a line has been drawn through each point toward the central vanishing point, although they are stopped when they reach the back wall.

accuracy of his drawing: if he has drawn correctly, the space between each two vertical or horizontal lines should be larger than the space between the next two lines; that is, as the lines move toward the center of the rectangle they should get steadily closer and closer together. If the lines have been made uniformly dark, an error in spacing will show up as a special dark or light streak across the drawing.

Inking and Labeling

The entire drawing should now be inked. In effect, it will be used as a complex perspective ruler for measuring drawings that are made over it; it will be easier to use if it is drawn with the same diluted ink used in drawing the ground-plan grid. Furthermore, since the perspective grid is used by transferring information from the ground plan, it is important that the same color coding be used, and that matching lines be drawn in the same color. It is suggested that the center line be drawn in red and the other lines in alternating colors. (The center line and the horizontal line at eye level should both be drawn clear across the rectangle, but the other lines should be restricted to the side walls, floor, and ceiling, leaving the back wall blank.)

Finally, the drawing should be carefully labeled. Following is a sample label (which, however, was used for a stage with different dimensions from those given in the preceding example).

PERSPECTIVE GRID
The Albion College Theater
Stage: 19'-0'' × 23'-0''
Scenery Height: 12'-0''
Sight Point: 40'-0'' from the
  acting area, 3'-0'' above
  the floor of the stage
Scale in the Picture Plane:
  ¾'' = 1'-0''

Notice that the scale is specified only for the picture plane. Because areas get perspectively smaller as they move away from the viewer, a different scale applies for different distances behind the picture plane. The purpose of the perspective squares drawn on the walls of the set is to furnish a readily usable indication of the scale at each distance in the stage space.

Using the Grid

Since the perspective grid will be used repeatedly, it should be considered at least a semipermanent part of the designer's tools. No drawing should be done on it directly; instead, whenever it is used, the drawing should be done on tracing paper.

Before any drawing is begun, the designer should mark the corners of the grid on the tracing paper and lightly draw in the center line and 3'-0" (eye level) horizontal. Without those points of reference, it might be difficult to transfer the drawing when it is finished.

Students should construct a grid adjusted to the measurements of their own theater. Let us assume that you have a grid completed, that it is covered with tracing paper, and that the points of reference have been marked.

Units on the Stage Floor

Suppose that your ground plan shows a stage property (a box), the bottom of which measures 4'-0" × 6'-0". The box is to be 2'-0" high and is placed with the long side facing the audience, parallel with the edge of the stage, with the front edge 4'-0" back from the front of the acting area and with one end 1'-0" left of the center line, the other end being 5'-0" right of the center line. The following description indicates how the grid can be used to produce a perspective drawing of the box. (The procedure is illustrated in *Figure 13-6.*)

Using as a measuring ruler the horizontal lines on the floor of the stage, as shown in the grid, move up along the center line 4'-0", and mark this point lightly. On the horizontal grid line that passes through this point, mark a point 1'-0" left of the center line, using the diagonal lines pointing toward the vanishing point as a measuring ruler; make a similar mark 5'-0" right of the center line. Connect these two points with a straight line. That line indicates the position of the front edge of the box, where it rests on the stage floor. The back edge of it should then be drawn in the same way; it will be 4'-0" behind the front edge, and will extend 1'-0" to the left of the center line, and 5'-0" to the right. The left edge of the box can then be drawn by connecting the left ends of the two lines, and the right edge of the box is drawn similarly; the result is a ground plan of the box, in perspective.

The next step is to draw one vertical corner, say the front right corner. Using a T-square and triangle, run a light line up from this point, extending about an inch and a half. The corner of the box will run along this line. The height of the corner is dependent on its distance from the front of the stage. The box has been specified as 2'-0" high; the perspective projection of that height is shown by the grid drawn on the side wall. Move to the lower right corner of the outside rectangle. Count back along the edge of the side wall to the point 4'-0" from the front edge of the wall (that is, the same distance as that between the front edge of the box and the front of the area shown in the grid). Taking a slip of paper, measure

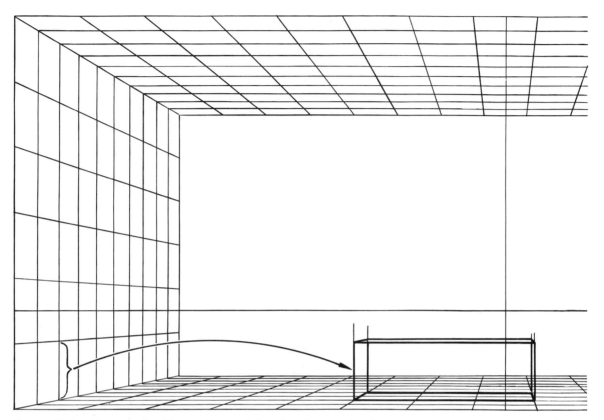

Figure 13-6. The perspective grid used for drawing a simple three-dimensional form. To provide a larger scale, only slightly more than half the full grid is shown; in addition, the squares are 2'-0'' rather than 1'-0''. The procedure for drawing the box is described in the text.

2'-0'' on the vertical scale at this point, using the grid drawn on the side wall. Transfer this measurement to the vertical line drawn from the corner of the box. The resulting point indicates the top of that corner. Since the left front corner of the box is the same distance from the front of the stage, it will project as the same height, so it can be drawn by running a vertical line up from the corner point and marking the same measurement on the line.

The back corners of the box will project to a different scale, since they are 4'-0'' farther from the front of the stage. Their height is determined in the same way, using the scale on the side wall 8'-0'' from the front edge. When the two back edges have been drawn, the top edges of the box can be produced by connecting adjacent corners with straight lines.

This simple drawing illustrates some of the principles of perspective. The top and bottom lines of the ends of the box vanish toward the same vanishing point that was used in setting up the perspective grid, because they are parallel with the lines of the grid; if the box were slanted, they would vanish toward a different point.

Some parts of the box lie behind others in such a way as to be hidden; lines defining those parts should be erased. If the box were open on top, the view would be slightly different than if it were closed; for this drawing, assume that it is closed.

The drawing described is one of the simplest possible; but the same methods work for all perspective drawings, however complicated. Even a set with complexly angled walls, filled with ornate furniture, is drawn by the same method.

Units Above the Stage Floor

The grid can be used equally well for scenic elements that do not rest on the floor, so long as the necessary dimensions are known. Let us suppose that a set has as one of its elements a triangular pennant (Figure 13-7). Its size and position are as follows:

1. The top edge is 2'-0'' wide.
2. The length is 4'-0''.
3. The top edge is hung horizontal, 7'-6'' above the stage floor.
4. The pennant is parallel with the front edge of the stage; one corner is 8'-0'' right of the center line, the other 10'-0'' from the center line.
5. It is 11'-0'' from the front of the stage.

The simplest way to draw the pennant would be to draw first an enclosing rectangle, 2'-0'' × 4'-0'', and then connect the two upper corners to the center of the lower edge. Not all scenic elements can be handled in this way, however, and to make the illustration more generally meaningful, we will describe the method of drawing it by itself.

The parts of the pennant can be drawn in any convenient order; let us begin with the top edge. It is 11'-0'' back from the front edge of the stage floor. First find that position by counting back 11 of the spaces marked on the stage floor, starting at the bottom of the grid. The two ends of the top of the pennant are 8'-0'' and 10'-0'' from the center line; those two points are located on the 11'-0'' line, and marked. The top edge of the pennant is 7'-6'' above the stage floor, so the next problem is to

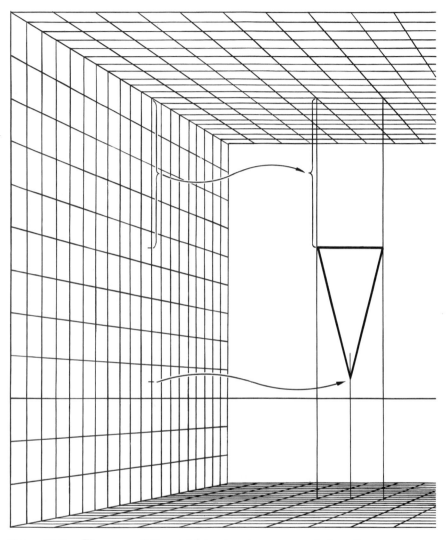

Figure 13-7. The use of the grid in drawing suspended units. The braces and arrows indicate the transfer of measurements from the side wall to the scenic lines. (In this grid, the squares are 1'-0'' on a side.)

locate two points at that height, directly above the points already marked on the floor of the stage.

One method would be to run vertical lines from the two points on the floor, using a T-square and triangle, and then measure up the specified distance. Another method would be to locate the matching points on the ceiling grid and then connect them with the two points on the floor. Since a point 7'-6'' above the stage floor is also 4'-6'' from the ceiling of our grid (assuming the grid has been drawn 12'-0'' high), the distance could equally well be measured down rather than up from the stage floor. Each of the methods described would produce the same result; the choice is determined by convenience.

The matching points on the stage ceiling are marked next. In this case the front edge of the ceiling is at the top of the drawing, so count down 11'-0''. Having located the two ceiling positions, verticals should be drawn between the pairs of points, connecting each of the two ceiling points with the point on the floor directly below it.

Now, moving to the side wall, count back to the vertical line 11'-0'' from the front of the stage. Laying a strip of paper along this line, mark on the paper the bottom edge of the line, and put a second mark at the 7'-6'' height. This height is not directly shown on the grid, but it will lie halfway between the 7'-0'' and 8'-0'' points, which are shown. Often, the division can be made by eye; if the artist wants to be certain to measure accurately, he can use a ruler to find the midpoint.

When the 7'-6'' height has been marked on the strip of paper, move the strip to one of the vertical lines drawn for the pennant, place one point on the point already marked on the floor, and mark the 7'-6'' height above it. The same height is then marked on the other vertical line, and the two points connected; the resulting line indicates the position of the top edge of the pennant, hanging in space.

The bottom point of the pennant is placed in the same way: it is 11'-0'' back from the front of the stage floor, 9'-0'' left of the center line, and 3'-6'' above the stage floor. When this point has been marked, straight lines are drawn connecting it with the ends of the top line, and the drawing of the pennant has been completed.

This second exercise is only slightly more difficult than the box, but it illustrates even more clearly that the repeated application of the same principles and methods will make it possible to draw any stage set, however complicated, on the grid.

Minimum Measurements

These examples have further demonstrated that not every point on a set need be measured in laying out a perspective projection. For any straight line, it is necessary only to find the two points at the ends of the line; they can be connected directly with a straight edge, without further work. The designer should select only the key points in his set for measurement.

Lines that are parallel to the surfaces of the imaginary box shown in the perspective grid are easiest to locate; the lines of most stage sets, however, are slanted in relation to the grid. These lines are easier to define if the original ground plan was designed with reference to its own grid (of which the perspective is a reproduction). Suppose, for example, that the side wall of a set rests on a line running from the front corner of the stage to a point on the back wall 7'-0'' left of the center line, but that the wall extends only 10'-0'' back along that line. Locate the point specified, on the far edge of the floor, 7'-0'' left of the center line, and also mark the matching point on the ceiling. Draw straight lines joining them to the top and bottom left corners of the outside rectangle, thus defining a plane along which the side wall extends. The ground plan indicates that the far end of the side wall falls inside one of the grid squares, at a point that is difficult to describe. It is just slightly more than 3'-2'' from the left edge of the grid, and just a little more than 9'-6'' from the front line of the grid. Since it falls on the diagonal line that has already been drawn, on the basis of precise measurements, either of the two dimensions just given will locate it; probably the 9'-6+'' will be the easiest to approximate. Counting back from the front edge of the ceiling in the perspective grid, identify the two lines that are 9'-0'' and 10'-0'' from the front of the grid; judging by eye, faintly mark the left-to-right center line of the square. If greater accuracy is desirable, you can find the precise perspective center by drawing the diagonals of the square. Mark a second line just a hairline back of this center, and extend it to cross the diagonal. This point marks the far corner of the wall at ceiling height. Dropping a perpendicular from it to the floor then marks the back edge of the wall.

Irregular Shapes

The most difficult scenic elements to draw in perspective are irregular ones, especially those composed of curved lines. The simplest method is essentially the same as that used for enlarging drawings, described in Chapter 11; in this case, however, the redrawing will probably be to a smaller scale than the elevation, and it will be altered according to the principles of perspective.

Suppose that the curved pattern to be drawn lies on a flat surface: the abstract trees in Michael David's set for *Oedipus at Colonus* are an excellent example *(Figure 6-5)*. First the elevation is enclosed in a grid. In this case, it is convenient if the grid is related to the perspective grid, so the basic squares should be marked at 12'' intervals, even though the top and bottom edges of the grid, as well as the side lines, extend beyond the figure. If the grid width does not match one of the numbers in the 4, 8, 16 sequence, it is usually easiest to extend it by adding 12'' squares beyond the pattern to be copied until the total width equals one of the recommended numbers *(Figure 13-8)*.

It is usually best to set the bottom line of the grid at floor level, even if the pattern appears only above floor level. Suppose, for example, that the figure to be copied consists of a large ornamental carving above a

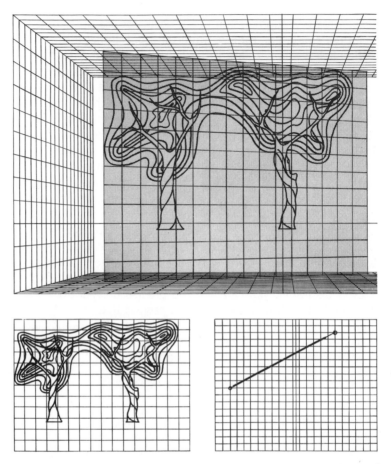

Figure 13-8. The perspective projection of curves on a plane. A drawing of two trees in silhouette, raised above the stage floor, is shown. At the lower left the trees are drawn in orthographic projection, gridded for redrawing in perspective. The lower right drawing shows a ground plan of the stage, with the position of the trees indicated by a heavy line. Since the ends of the unit do not coincide with easily measurable points on the ground-plan grid, they are extended by light lines, and the measuring points marked with circles. The drawing at the top of the page shows the grid enclosing the trees redrawn in perspective; to make it more clearly visible, the rectangular area has been shaded. The grid has been extended one square farther to the right than was necessary for enclosing the trees; that was done so that the width of the grid would be 16 units, greatly facilitating the division of the perspective rectangle, as the squares can be marked by finding a series of midpoints. The height, however, was divided into 12 squares, so the divisions could be copied from the scales on the side wall.

fireplace, and that the lowest point in the figure is 3'-4½'' above the floor. The grid should be drawn as though resting on the floor, and then extended up until it encloses the entire design, in which case the three bottom rows of the grid will be blank, and the design will start in the fourth.

Having completed the first grid, the artist then redraws it in perspective on the perspective grid. The vertical lines will remain vertical, and the horizontal line at eye level will remain horizontal; all other lines will slant, according to the principles of perspective. In effect, this method consists of enclosing the motif in an imaginary wall, with the grid painted on it. The wall is then drawn in perspective exactly as if it were part of the set.

The drawing is then transferred from the elevation to the perspective grid, using exactly the same methods used for gridded enlargements. When the transfer has been completed, the perspective grid lines can be erased, and the design will appear in its proper position in the set.

Three-Dimensional Shapes

Irregular three-dimensional objects are drawn in perspective by an extension of this method. The object is enclosed in a temporary rectangular gridded box. It is most convenient if the box is drawn in dimensions of even feet, although the squares may be subdivided to any extent desired. The box is then redrawn in perspective, using the perspective grid, the irregular object is drawn within it, and the edges and gridding of the temporary box are erased.

The designer will probably need to draw chairs more frequently than any other irregular three-dimensional shapes. Let us assume a simple chair has to be drawn with a seat 1'-6'' high and a back 3'-0'' high. Suppose that the back is slightly slanted, the front legs straight, and the back legs slightly slanted back. Suppose further that the front edge of the seat is wider than the back edge, but that the average of the two dimensions is 1'-6'', with the seat padded and 2'' thick. Let us assume that the legs and back supports are of metal rods about an inch in diameter, with the back rest about 6'' deep, and padded like the seat. (See *Figure 13-9.*)

The precise method by which a perspective drawing of such a chair is made depends somewhat on the degree of accuracy the artist feels is required. Let us suppose that he decides he can dispense with total accuracy, and that all he needs is a convincing picture with dimensions close to those of the actual chair. In that case, it is possible to work directly on the perspective grid, without first preparing elaborate elevations of the chair from different angles. (See *Figure 13-10.*)

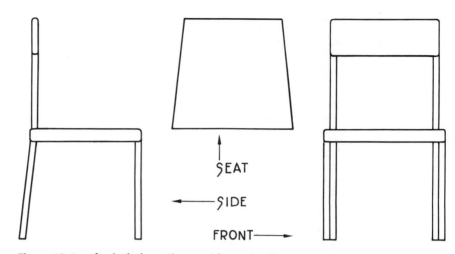

Figure 13-9.   A chair in orthographic projection.

The first step is to make a perspective drawing of a rectangular box, placed on the perspective grid as prescribed by the ground plan. This box will have the same dimensions as the chair: it will be 3'-0'' high and 1'-6'' wide and deep. (Notice that if the eye level has been set at 3'-0'', the top surface of the box will not be visible.)

The box is then divided by a horizontal plane. First, the center point of each of the vertical lines at the corners of the box is marked, using a ruler to measure it; these four points are then connected by straight lines, thus defining the plane.

Next the seat is sketched in. First, points should be marked on the back edge of the center plane, just a little inside the corners of the box; then the front edge is extended beyond the corners of the box, and points are marked just a little outside the corners. These four new points are then connected, producing a flared shape corresponding to the seat of the chair. A short vertical is dropped from each corner of this trapezoid, and each vertical is marked off at 2'' below the corner. It will probably be accurate enough to mark these by eye. The new points are then connected, except that one or two of the lines (depending on how the chair is placed) will be hidden by the seat.

The front legs can be drawn by running two parallel lines straight down from each of the front corners of the seat, spacing the parallels an inch apart, again judging by eye. For the two back legs, a single vertical is dropped to the floor as a guide. If the legs are imagined as slanted straight back, the bottom of each leg is marked slightly behind the vertical line, at the floor level. If the designer intends to show the legs flared not only back but to the side, then the points marking the ends of the legs must be placed not only back of the verticals, but shifted to the sides, away from

Figure 13-10. The box method of drawing a chair in perspective.

the basic box. When these points have been determined, they are connected to the back corners of the seat with straight lines, spaced to suggest a thickness of 1''.

The ends of the metal rods forming the framework of the back are marked in the same way and connected to the top back corners of the seat with straight lines. Either measuring or judging by eye the artist then marks a strip 6'' wide across the back, at the top, and the proper thickness is added.

Since it was assumed that the seat and back are padded, the outlines of these units are redrawn more heavily, with curves substituted for the square corners, the box lines are erased, and the drawing of the chair is finished.

One of the simplest types of chairs has been used as illustration, but obviously the same methods could be used for representing shapes of any degree of complexity. If the back, for instance, has an outline shaped in irregular curves, they can usually be sketched on the rectangular shape that was developed as one of the later steps in the procedure just described. In the most extreme cases, it would be possible to further grid the back (with squares of 6'', 3'', or even smaller dimensions) and lay in the shape with any degree of accuracy desired.

At the beginning of the chapter, it was said that perspective drawing is simple in theory but complicated in practice. If the artist has the basic theory firmly in mind, he can solve many problems by thinking back over their relation to the fundamental method.

Visual Checking

The student will have discovered by this time that perspective drawing, especially in the areas toward the back of the stage, sometimes involves the use of very small scales (notice, for example, the distance representing 1'-0'' at the back end of the center line). At such scales, even the width of an ink line occupies significant space on the drawing, and completely accurate measurement becomes difficult. The necessity for thinking in three dimensions and for measuring to constantly varying scales also produces many more errors than will occur in an orthographic projection of the same units. Consequently, the artist should train himself to stop frequently while preparing a perspective drawing and check it visually to catch any mistakes. The simplest check, and usually a sound one, is to decide whether the drawing as a whole looks right; in doing this, of course, the artist should imagine as vividly as possible how the finished set should look, checking his imagined view with the drawing. A valuable further check is to apply some principles of perspective.

SOME PERSPECTIVE PRINCIPLES

Horizontal Planes
Below Eye Level
Slant Up; Those
Above, Slant
Down

The perspective grid is in itself a simple drawing, in perspective, of an open box. Notice that the floor of the box, as drawn, seems to slant up, while the ceiling slants down. The horizontal lines at the top of the side walls slant down, while those at the bottom slant up, as the eye moves from the front of the walls to the back. However, they slant at different angles: as we move down from the top of the side wall, it is evident that the lines slant less and less until finally we reach one that is horizontal; below it; the lines slant in the opposite direction (up), with the most extreme slant at the bottom edge of the wall. Checking the height of the horizontal line, we find it is at 3'-0", which was selected as the eye level of the imaginary spectator.

This check reveals some fundamental perspective principles. Horizontal planes below eye level seem to slant up, so that we see the top of the surfaces; horizontal planes above eye level slant down, and we see the underside of the surfaces. To illustrate this principle in somewhat different terms: if two identical areas are marked on the floor (let us say two small throw rugs of the same size), placed so that one area is farther from the viewer than the other, the most distant one will appear in a perspective drawing *above* the other. If two objects appear in a plane overhead, at different distances from the viewer (say, for instance, two chandeliers hanging from the ceiling), the farthest one will appear *lower* than the other in a perspective drawing.[2]

A corollary of that principle is also valuable to the artist. On the perspective grid, locate the lines representing a foot-wide vertical strip of the left wall; the easiest to examine is the strip next to the front of the stage, which will be marked by the outside edge of the drawing and the vertical line next to it. This strip is divided by horizontal lines a foot apart, most of which slant in the perspective drawing. Draw a light horizontal line (not in perspective: parallel with the bottom edge of the picture plane) from the bottom of the second vertical line back to the edge of the picture. The distance from the bottom corner to the point where this line crosses the edge of the picture represents the size of slant of the bottom edge in that strip. Repeat the same procedure for the line a foot above the stage floor, noting the vertical distance between its front and back; do the same for the horizontal lines at the 2'-0" and 3'-0" levels. The experiment demonstrates that, just as the slant decreases as we move up the drawing toward eye level, the vertical distance through which parallel lines of the same length rise also decreases; furthermore, at eye level, the rise, like

2. For absolute accuracy, the term *picture plane* should be substituted for *viewer* in this paragraph.

the slant, ceases altogether. If we continue the measurements above eye level, we will see that the slant reappears above eye level, and continues to increase the farther we go, although the relationship between the two ends of the lines is reversed, with the farther end below the nearer.

This principle is of great value in judging a drawing's accuracy. For example, if a set includes a flight of stairs running down from the back of the stage toward the audience, the bottom step would, in perspective, apparently have the greatest depth, and the depth of the tread of every higher step would be progressively narrower until eye level is reached, where it would be zero. Steps above eye level would successively display wider and wider treads, although if there is facing at the front of the steps, the treads themselves would be concealed.

All Points at Eye Level Fall on the Horizon

Even more important is that all points at eye level on the set appear in a perspective drawing on a straight line, drawn horizontally across the picture plane. Let us imagine that there are ten chairs on a stage, arranged irregularly around the floor, at varying distances from the spectator. Assume that the back of each chair is 3'-0" high, and that the viewer's eye is also 3'-0" above the stage floor. The chair legs and seats would appear at different levels, depending on their distances from the spectator, but the top lines of all the chair backs would run in a horizontal line across the picture at the (scaled) distance of 3'-0" above the floor of the stage. In the same way, if the bottom part of the walls is covered with paneling 3'-0" high, its top edge will form a straight line at that level, no matter what the shape of the room—whether it is rectangular with slanted side walls; complexly composed of nooks, jogs, and other irregularities; or even built with curved walls.

Three feet is a convenient eye level to use in making theatrical perspective drawings, since key lines of scenic elements often fall at this height. Knobs of doors, backs of chairs, paneling, and mantels are frequently set at this level. Furthermore, the normal height of a chair seat is 1'-6", so it is easy to determine the position of the seat by simply marking the halfway point between eye level and the floor.

Lines Parallel with the Picture Plane Do Not Vanish

Often the back wall of a set is parallel with the front edge of the stage (that is, parallel with the picture plane). Shapes, designs, or other scenic elements appearing on such a surface will vary in size, according to their distance from the viewer; but in a perspective drawing their shapes will appear identical with their real shapes. A square will appear as a square, a circle will appear as a circle (not an oval), and irregular figures will retain their natural shapes.

On the other hand, figures placed on planes that are not parallel with the picture plane have both their sizes and shapes altered in perspective projection. Circles on such planes project as ovals; squares and rectangles appear with sides slanted and angles altered. Spheres project as circles, however, no matter how they are located in the set, since a sphere always presents a circular outline parallel with the picture plane.[3]

The angles and lengths of straight lines may be altered by perspective, but their shape is not changed: a straight line always projects as a straight line, no matter how it is placed in relation to the picture plane.[4] Knowing this can be particularly useful in checking perspective drawings. Often, a series of isolated scenic elements are arranged so that key points lie in a straight line, even if the line does not appear in the set. For instance, the steps of most stairs are designed so that a straight line drawn from one corner of the top step to the matching corner of the bottom step would touch the corresponding corner of each step in between. The accuracy of a perspective drawing of such a flight of steps can be checked by drawing a light line in that position. In the same way, if a row of identical columns appears in the set, it will be possible to draw a straight line through matching points for the entire series.

Straight Lines Project Straight

Another application of the straight-line principle provides a method for finding the center lines of perspective squares or rectangles. Assume that a square element appears in a drawing in such a position that the sides are vertical and the top and bottom slant at different angles. The horizontal center line of the square can be found by marking the center points of the two vertical sides and connecting them with a line. But the vertical center line cannot be found in that way, since it will be closer to the far side of the square than to the near side (because the perspective scale gets steadily smaller as it moves away from the viewer). However, the two diagonals of a square cross at the center of the square, and since we know the corners of the square, and since the diagonals, being straight lines, will appear in perspective as straight lines no matter how the square is oriented, we can find the location of the center point by connecting opposite corners of the perspective square with straight lines. A vertical line drawn through the point at which the two diagonals intersect will mark the

Finding the Centers of Rectangles

3.   Theoretically, the perspective of a sphere is not precisely circular; however, under theatrical conditions the deviation is likely to be less than the width of a pencil line and is consequently negligible.

4.   The single exception to this statement is a straight line pointing directly at the viewer's eye: it would project as a point.

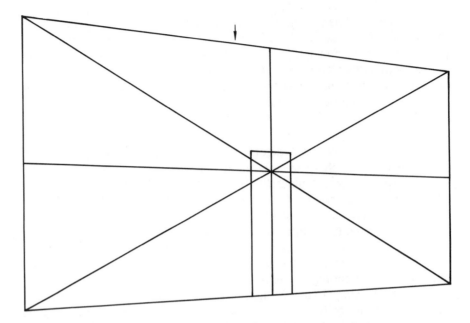

Figure 13-11. Finding the center of rectangles in perspective. This can be done quickly by drawing the diagonals; the point at which they cross is the center. Because of the shift in scale throughout a perspective drawing, the perspective center of a rectangle not parallel with the picture plane is always some distance beyond the actual center. The arrow indicates the center line of the rectangular wall shown, as measured by a ruler; the door has been drawn at the perspective center.

vertical center line of the square, in perspective. (See *Figure 13-11*.) The same method may be used in finding the centers of rectangles and other figures.

This method would have been helpful, for example, in locating the point of the pennant described at the beginning of the chapter, if the pennant had been slanted at an angle to the picture plane.

REDUCING CONSTRUCTION TIME

A few final points may be useful to students. As they develop assurance in handling perspective projection, they will find that they can reduce the amount of time and work they must do in a number of ways. Even when a set is highly asymmetrical, it may contain a number of symmetrical elements. For example, Michael David's set for *Oedipus at Colonus (Figure 6-5)* seems at first glance almost completely asymmetrical; but the semicircular colonnade surrounding it is symmetrical. For such units, it is a waste of time to draw both halves of the set independently; only one half should be drawn according to the procedures discussed in this chapter; it can then be copied on a separate sheet of tracing paper, which is turned over to transfer the design to the original sheet.

Even for asymmetrical elements, however, experience may enable the designer to reduce the number of points he must identify by the rather laborious mechanical method; familiarity with perspective should make it possible for him to draw an accurate projection with only a few key points marked. So long as his freehand lines coincide with the carefully measured points, and so long as he checks the final drawing carefully, he may be able to work much more quickly, without significant loss of accuracy.

ACCIDENTAL JUXTAPOSITIONS

Beginning designers are sometimes disturbed to discover odd accidental juxtapositions and patterning in perspectives: the line of a column may be accidentally continued by the edge of a table leg; the end of a wall may fall exactly on the center line of a door or some other scenic feature in the hall behind it; the front corner leg of a chair may exactly hide the leg at the back corner, producing an impression of a three-legged structure. These unintended visual relationships could be prevented by shifting the scenic units in various ways, but such shifts would result in other similar juxtapositions for members of the audience sitting in seats elsewhere in the theater. As a matter of fact, the same kind of juxtapositions occur constantly in ordinary life; we do not notice them unless they happen to fall at the focus of attention. The designer should simply accept the fact of their existence and complete his drawing according to the sound principles of perspective. Especially he should avoid altering the drawing arbitrarily so as to disentangle such patterns. If the drawing is to have any value, it must be an honest and accurate representation of the appearance of the set from the chosen position. Obviously, if the drawing indicates a serious error (if, for instance, an entrance that must be prominently visible to the entire audience is almost hidden), then he must redesign, but if the previous steps have been soundly done, such an error is impossible.

UNNECESSARY PRECISION

Beginning designers are also sometimes disturbed at their inability to measure with precision in the areas of the drawing where the scale is smallest. By definition, however, a perspective drawing reproduces what the audience actually sees (and that, of course, is its major value). Consequently, if two positions (representing points perhaps 6″ apart on the stage floor) are so close together in the drawing that the artist is unable to distinguish between them, then a member of the audience, sitting in the specified seat, would have equal difficulty. The artist, therefore, can safely ignore any error that is too small for him to be able to correct.

Incidentally, an examination of the perspective grid with this in mind will reveal some useful facts about the audience's ability to distinguish positions and dimensions of scenery. Especially toward the back of the stage, members of the audience find it difficult to evaluate dimensions measured perpendicular to the back wall. Suppose a three-shelf bookcase was set into the back wall, and that one shelf was 1′-0″ deep, another 1′6″ deep, and the third ⅞″ deep. It is likely that no member of the audience would notice they were not the same depth.

On the other hand, a slight left-right deviation is readily noticeable from the audience. A pilaster attached to the back wall that leaned forward as much as an inch and a half might look perfectly straight to the audience, but if it leaned a half inch to the side, the difference would be immediately noticeable.

DRAWING FURNITURE

When drawing a very complicated or crowded set, one technique may be of value. Since the furniture cuts across so many of the basic lines of the set, drawing it over the set itself can be confusing; furthermore, the final lines and construction lines of the set may obscure some of the lines of the grid. The solution to this problem is to remove the sheet of tracing paper on which the set has been drawn, replace it with a fresh sheet, and draw the furniture independently. In conformity with what should be the designer's standard practice, he should mark the corners of the drawing, as well as the vertical center line and the horizontal eye level line, before he begins drawing the furniture.

If the two sheets of tracing paper are placed on top of one another with those guide points and lines fitted together, the furniture may be transferred to the set drawing and will be in its correct position.

A FINAL VISUAL CHECK

As a final check on the accuracy of the drawing, the designer should place his ground plan and elevations beside his perspective, imagine the completed set as accurately as possible, and check the perspective drawing to make sure that it matches his conception.

THE PERMANENT COPIES

The construction of the perspective drawing of the stage set is now completed. Two steps remain: reproducing the drawing in more permanent form and preparing a full-color painting showing the appearance of the set when painted and lit.

In making the permanent copies, the artist takes two fresh sheets of cardboard and draws on each a rectangle of the same dimensions as that used for the outside edge of the perspective grid. Space is provided in the bottom margin for an identifying label.

The artist then turns the tracing paper drawing over and redraws the lines of the set, omitting guidelines and construction lines. The drawing is transferred by rubbing to each of the fresh sheets.

The two drawings are then carefully inked, using india ink. The first is used in the scene shop to guide the construction crew and may also be useful in setting up the scenery on stage. The margins of the second drawing are extended at least two or three inches beyond the corners of the rectangle (the reason for this treatment will be discussed in the next chapter). This second drawing serves as the basis for the finished painting.

14

Finishing the Perspective

The outline perspective drawing will give a great deal of information about the appearance of the finished set, but it omits the color scheme and the effect of lighting. Normally, the drawing at this point will be completed by painting it in full color. Some directors, however, cannot evaluate the appearance of a set from ground plans and elevations and may be unwilling to give more than a tentative approval until they have seen a perspective rendering. If the director has not approved the set at the ground plan or elevation stage, the designer may prefer to submit the perspective drawing in outline, so any changes the director may specify can be made before the final painting.

Although the inked perspective may be adequate for that purpose, it is possible to indicate the effect of lighting on the set, and to produce an appearance of much greater finish, by shading with rubbed pastel crayon. This procedure is extremely fast, requiring something like an hour for a full drawing, and is also a useful technique to be familiar with when working to very tight schedules.

LIGHTING

A preliminary step to any shading is the development of a lighting design. The basic theory of lighting was discussed in Chapters 4 and 6. Since the lighting pattern is usually in constant change throughout a performance of a play, the perspective can show only one momentary setting. The designer will want to select a lighting pattern that is fairly typical of the play and that reveals the set clearly. Since at best the painting can portray only one of the many light settings, the set designer need not feel that the lighting shown must conform rigidly to the pattern that will be used for the set; however, it should certainly present a possible and effective pattern of lighting.

The designer has already analyzed the relative importance of the various areas and levels in his set. Usually, the most important areas will be the ones most brilliantly lit.

The designer must imagine the pattern of light desirable. If he wishes to check the practicality of this lighting pattern, and if he wishes to show the pattern on his set painting in a way clearly recognizable to the director and lighting technician, he should visualize not only the effect required but also the way in which it might be produced.

Most stage lighting comes from spotlights. The designer should imagine the shape of the light as it passes from the spotlights to the set. If the stage were filled with smoke or fog, the shapes of the beams would be visible, but usually the light can be seen only where it strikes part of the set or an actor.

A spotlight beam nearly always assumes the shape of a cone, with the light bulb at the point and the light spreading out as it moves away from the source. If this cone is pointed toward a surface at right angles, it produces a circle of light, but nearly all spotlights are directed at about 45° to the stage floor; cutting the beam diagonally at that angle produces an oval rather than a circle.

But the critical area of the beam is not the floor level but the level of the actors' heads, with the upper half of the body slightly less important. When an acting area is lit, the beams are generally adjusted to light the area between 3' and 7' above the stage floor. The light in this space is visible only when actors are using the area, and even then the cone of light continues past them to fall on the stage some distance behind. For this reason the actors are likely to stand just within the edge of the oval area as it is defined on the stage floor.

In noting the position of beams of light on the ground plan, the designer first decides where he wishes the light to fall on the actors. He then imagines the position of the source of light and the final position of the beam on the stage floor. If the source of the light is to be a spotlight, then he generally calculates the center of the beam as passing through the acting area at about 4' above the stage floor. The beam will then fall on the stage floor at an angle of 45° behind the area, in an oval shape. Having identified the position of this oval, the designer should sketch it on the ground plan. Normally, two spotlights are directed toward each acting area, but their outlines on the floor are nearly identical, and for the purpose of preparing the perspective a single oval is usually sufficient.

For an acting area toward the back of the stage, the beam of light may be cut by the back wall, so that part of it falls on the set itself. The part falling on the floor will have the usual oval shape, the rest—also a partial oval—will appear vertically at the bottom of the flats.

Light Cut by Two or More Surfaces

More complex shapes result when spotlights point toward the corner of a platform or a pair of flats jutting into the acting area. The shape of light falling on such surfaces can be determined by complex diagrammatic analysis of the scenery and lighting, but it can be handled more practically by vividly imagining the light as a three-dimensional shape, noting its position at the key points, especially on the edges of the structure, and then connecting them with essentially circular curves. If the designer makes a practice of checking his paintings against the finished sets after they have been lit, he will improve his skill in imaginatively constructing such light patterns.

The size of each pool of light at the level of the stage floor varies according to the type of light source and its adjustment, but in producing his demonstration of possible lighting for his set, the designer can approximate sizes by remembering the set is usually lit so that actors do not pass through dark patches in moving from one acting area to another. The lights are usually adjusted so that the pools overlap in the critical areas above waist height; the pools of light the designer draws on the floor should, then, overlap somewhat more.

Shadows are extremely important in expressing the shape of scenery; where furniture or other scenic elements interrupt a beam of light, they will cast shadows on the floor or scenery behind them. Such shadows are defined by invisible lines that connect the source of light with the interrupting unit and continue until they strike the floor or scenery behind it.

Gradations in lighting on a set may be divided into six types:

Variations in Brightness

1. The spotlights that are directed toward the different acting areas will be of various degrees of brightness, those aimed at the most important area being brightest of all.

2. The edge of a cone of light is almost never sharp; it is likely to be out of focus, so that the characteristic shape of a pool of light cast by a spotlight is a small central oval of maximum brightness, around which is a ring, perhaps 2′ to 3′ wide, that gradually fades from moderate brightness at the center edge to no light at the outside.

3. Some areas of the set, especially the upper sections of the walls, have no direct lights trained on them; these areas are much darker than those that directly reflect spotlights.

4. The brightness of a scenic surface varies according to the angle between the surface and the beam of light, with maximum brightness when the angle is 90° (an unusual situation). Even when the corner of a platform juts directly into the cone of a spotlight, it may be so arranged that one surface is more directly turned toward the source of light than the other, with a marked difference in brightness.

5. One scenic element may cast a shadow on another.

6. The brightness of scenic areas is also strongly affected by the reflectivity of the surfaces on which the light falls, controlled mainly by the colors used in painting them.

A RUBBED-CHALK RENDERING

Having outlined on the ground plan the pools of light cast by the various spots, the designer turns to one of his perspective outlines and sketches the appearance of the light in perspective. It is easiest to begin by drawing each pool of light on the stage floor and then to sketch the position of light on the flats and other scenic elements that extend above the floor. For a rubbed-chalk rendering, this should be done very lightly.

For the moment, let us ignore the sixth factor listed above (the variations in reflectivity of the colors used on the set) and assume that all areas reflect the light equally. The finished picture will have five fundamental shades, but the extreme dark will be added last, and throughout most of his work the artist should think of the set in terms of two shades. One of these, which we might call the base shade, represents the major color of the set, neither directly lit by a spotlight nor sharply shadowed.

The designer's first step is to cover all such areas with this base shade. It must be carefully kept off the areas of brightest light, but can be run across the darkest areas as well as those where it will remain as the final coat. The procedure, then, is to rub a base coat over the entire picture, except for the areas showing the positions of pools of direct light. Black chalk is the most effective for this type of rendering, although any dark color may be used. It is undesirable to attempt to match the actual colors of the set, since to do that successfully would require more time than preparing a full painting, and to do it inaccurately might be misleading.

The next step is to shade all areas that are darker than the basic coat. Some of these will have sharp outlines (for example, the side of a platform turned away from the light). Almost equally important is the representation of the areas that will receive little light, although they are not in direct shadow. Imagine the pools of light greatly enlarged to perhaps three times the diameter drawn; the areas outside these imagined outlines would be darker than the basic shade. Often there is a steady darkening toward the tops of the flats, combined with slightly darker areas at the front edges of the side walls.

When these two colors, the base and the shade, have been laid in, the outlines of the pools of light should be erased. This may leave sharp edges, which should be blended so as to be unobtrusive. The entire surface should be smoothed and blended and the darkest areas reinforced so as to produce a smooth progression of shade.

The pools of light should then be given a very light coating of chalk, leaving them clearly lighter than the base coat. The brightest area, in the center of each pool, should be cleared with an eraser, and the edges should be blended into the tone of the rest of the light.

Finally, the artist should take the chalk (a pastel pencil is most manageable for this step) and fill in the darkest areas by drawing directly on the cardboard. These areas may be smoothed by rubbing and blended into the surrounding shades as required.

In describing this process, we ignored the different reflectivity of the scenery's colors. In practice, they must be taken into account. In effect, a separate four-step series of shades is developed for each of the colors. Suppose, for example, that a spotlight cuts across the wall area so that part of the pool of light falls on a dark wood paneling and part of it on light-colored plaster. Both the paneling and the plaster would be represented exactly as described above, except that the base shade for the paneling would be much darker than that used for the plaster; in fact, the lightest shade used for the paneling might well be darker than the darkest one used for the plaster.

Usually the color of the cardboard is used for the brightest highlight, but, if desired, white chalk or even white paint may be used for exceptionally bright highlights. The work can be done even more quickly if a very light grey cardboard is used instead of white. The color of the cardboard can then be left untouched for the major basic shade of the set, and only the shadows and highlights added; in that case, white pastel must be used for areas lighter than the cardboard.

Figure 14-1 illustrates the various steps in preparing a rubbed-chalk version of a perspective drawing.

Figure 14-1. The rubbed-chalk method of finishing perspective drawings: a set for Sheridan's *The Critic.* The picture is shown in five stages of development, starting with the inked outline and proceeding through the application of the base coat, the shadows, and the extreme shadows, with reinforcement of the highlights completing the picture.

THE FULL-COLOR PAINTING

The preparation of a full-color painting of a stage set requires much more time and care than a rubbed-chalk version, but the essential techniques are similar, and the painting is so much more effective a representation that the designer should consider it a normal part of his work.

The most effective medium for preparing set paintings is tempera, or poster paint. Water is used as the vehicle in tempera paint; it differs from ordinary water color in being opaque, so that one coat can be hidden by a second, and errors can be easily corrected.

The first step in preparing a tempera painting of the set is to draw the outlines of the pools of light; since the paint is opaque, these lines need not be erased, and can be drawn firmly. The next step is to mix the colors. Since the artist must thoroughly understand the principles of color mixing, we will discuss these principles before continuing the discussion of the procedures involved in the full-color painting.

COLOR MIXING

Various aspects of color have already been discussed in previous chapters. In handling paint, the artist must in addition master the principles of color mixing; fortunately they are simple in theory and only slightly more complex in application. One of the problems involved in the mastery of color mixing is the great variation in paints offered for sale. A color labeled *sage green* by one manufacturer may be very different from the *sage green* sold by another. Even paints identified by such theoretically precise names as *red-orange* may vary noticeably from brand to brand.

If the designer could use the colors exactly as they are supplied by the manufacturer, no problems would arise; that sometimes happens, but very rarely. In the great majority of cases, when the artist sits down to prepare his painting and to produce color samples that can be used by the construction workers in mixing the scene paint, he must work from a selection of paints every one of which must be altered.

The final colors will precisely match those the artist has chosen for the set only if the available commercial paints are analyzed and mixed according to the basic principles of color mixing. The discussion of color mixing that follows is, therefore, divided into two main sections: the first deals with the theoretical principles, in terms of pure colors, however rare such colors may be in actual practice; the second describes the application of those principles to the handling of ordinary commercial pigments.

(Color variables were discussed in Chapter 9, and the color wheel illustrated in *Figure 9-4*.)

The Primaries

The color wheel is divided at three points of special significance, where the red, yellow, and blue appear. These colors are fundamental to the theory of mixing, because they cannot be produced by mixing pigments of any other colors; conversely, all other colors (except white) can be produced by mixing these three in various proportions. For that reason they are called *primaries,* a word indicating that they are theoretically the first points from which color mixing must proceed.

Mixing Pure Colors

The Secondaries

If any two of the primaries are mixed in equal quantities, a color is produced that lies halfway between them on the color wheel; thus, red and yellow mixed in equal quantities produce orange, yellow and blue produce green, and blue and red produce purple. These mixtures are called *secondaries.*

In most discussions of color, the term *secondaries* is limited to the three colors just described, that is, to colors produced by equal mixtures of pairs of the primaries. In ordinary speech, however, the names of the secondaries are commonly used much more broadly, so that the term *green* is applied not simply to a half-and-half mixture of blue and yellow, but also to mixtures of the two primaries in varying proportions. When one of the two primaries clearly predominates, its name is customarily added to the secondary as an adjective, producing the terms *yellow-green* and *blue-green*. This pattern of nomenclature provides names for all the colors in a 12-step color wheel. There are no familiar terms for the additional steps in the 24-step color wheel that is recommended in this text; names are suggested that are a clear, though somewhat clumsy, extension of the familiar practice: the closest primary or secondary is added as an adjective to the standard terms, producing *yellow yellow-green, green yellow-green,* etc.

Throughout the rest of our discussion, the term *secondaries* will be used in the broader sense, to indicate the colors produced by mixing two primaries in any proportions; the half-and-half mixtures to which the term is usually restricted will be identified by the term *central*: thus, any mixture of red and yellow will be considered to be one of the oranges, but a half-and-half mixture will be designated *central orange*.

Color nomenclature is a vexing problem, because there is great variety in the way terms are used. Many writers, for example, prefer the term *violet* to *purple*. Both terms come from natural objects (ultimately, a flower and a shellfish), and in neither case does the object uniformly match the color that its name is used to describe. Obviously, the particular terms chosen, and their definitions, are subject to individual taste and convenience, but so long as it is clear what is meant by them in the present discussion, the student should have little difficulty following the analysis.

Any mixture of two primaries results in a color that lies between them on the color wheel; its precise position depends on the relative proportions. Thus, if 1 quart of pure yellow paint is mixed with 3 quarts of pure red, the resulting color is a redder orange than that produced by the half-and-half mixture, so it appears on the color wheel halfway between central orange and red (and is called red-orange). A color wheel can thus be produced with any desired number of steps, the colors being prepared by mixing pairs of primaries in different proportions. Experience suggests that a 24-step color wheel is most practical.

Complementaries

The second phenomenon of importance is that if all three of the primaries are mixed in equal quantities, the result is black. If the student has read widely in the literature on color, that statement may seem surprising, since nearly all discussions state that the mixture of the three primary pigments in equal quantities produces not black but grey; only a very small percentage identify it as black. Experimental mixing of the paints sold by various manufacturers as primaries will demonstrate that the resulting colors match the theoretical discussions: in the great majority of cases, the mixture appears grey, and only very rarely will it seem to be a true black. Furthermore, the greys vary over a wide range, from near black to a grey so light as to be almost central. However, grey rather than black is produced only because in nearly all sets of paint sold as primaries one or more of the colors contain some contaminating white paint; this is especially likely in paint identifed as "primary yellow."

If commercial pigments all contained white contamination in equal proportions, it might be possible to state the principles of color mixing to allow for it. Since they vary significantly, it is more effective to analyze mixtures in two steps, in the first ignoring any possible contamination of white and focusing only on the effects of combinations of the pure primaries, and then afterward adjusting for the degree of white contamination.

Some theorists insist that black must not be called a color, using arguments based on the principles of physics. From the viewpoint of the artist, however, both black and white are used in the main exactly like the pigments shown on the color wheel, and it seems much more convenient to refer to all of them by the same term.

Each central secondary color is made up of equal quantities of two of the primaries. If the remaining primary is added, black is produced, although two parts of the secondary must be used to one part of the primary. Pairs of colors that mix to black are called *complementaries*. Three sets of such colors appear on the color wheel: red and green, blue and orange, and yellow and purple.

The Analysis of Mixtures

In practical color mixing, the pure primaries are used less often than complex colors, but the principles just described operate even though the primaries are not present in pure form in the mixtures, so that at every point the artist must analyze his work in terms of primaries.

Let us imagine that a quart of primary blue paint is added to a quart of central orange; by definition, the orange is a mixture of 1 pint of red and 1 pint of yellow. Expressed in terms of the same unit, then, the total mixture will have the following formula:

1 pint of red
1 pint of yellow
2 pints of blue

According to the second principle cited, the 2 pints of red and yellow will combine with 1 pint of the blue to produce 3 pints of black. The formula for the mixture can therefore be restated as follows:

3 pints of black
1 pint of blue

The result, then, will be a very dark blue.

That example illustrates the basic method of predicting the effect of mixing any two quantities of pigment together: each is analyzed for the percentage of the different primaries contained in it, and all quantities are stated in terms of the lowest common denominator. The figure representing the pigment that appears in the smallest quantity in the total mixture is subtracted from the total quantity of each primary color (leaving a remainder of zero for one or more of the computations); the quantities subtracted are then added together and identified as black. If the subtraction produces no remainders, then the total mixture will be black. If a remainder appears for only one of the primary pigments, then the total mixture will be of the same color, darkened by the addition of black in the quantity determined. If remainders appear for two primaries, the total mixture will fall on the color wheel between those primaries, its precise position being determined by the relative amounts of the two colors, and it will be darkened by the addition of the quantity of black indicated by the computation. (This analysis does not account for quantities of white that may be present in the mixture; that is discussed in a later section.)

Following are analyses of illustrative mixtures.

It may be helpful to consider first three mixtures so simple that computation would not be necessary in ordinary practice.

Suppose that 2 quarts of primary blue are mixed together; obviously, there will be no change in the color. Mathematically, such a mixture would be expressed as follows:

2 quarts of blue
0 red
0 yellow

The smallest quantity of pigment is 0. Subtracting that from each figure leaves the same formula. Zero red and 0 yellow then combine with 0 blue to produce 0 black, and the resulting mixture is consequently pure blue.

Suppose that 1 quart of primary yellow is added to 1 quart of central orange (made up of 1 pint of yellow and 1 of red). The combined pigments will be as follows:

1 pint of red
3 pints of yellow
0 blue

Again, computation demonstrates that no black will appear in the mixture, and that the resulting color will be orange, but much closer to the yellow end of the orange section of the color wheel than to the red end.

Imagine the combination of 1 quart of primary yellow with 2 quarts of central purple. By definition, the purple is composed of equal parts of red and blue; consequently, the formula for the mixture will be as follows:

1 quart of yellow
1 quart of red
1 quart of blue

Following the method of computation described, the figure representing the smallest quantity of pigment (1 quart) is subtracted from each item in the formula, and the quantities subtracted are added together and identified as black. Since the remainders in this case are 0, the resulting mixture will be pure black. Incidentally, this is perhaps the most startling application of the principles of color mixing: since the yellow appears much lighter than the purple, it is astonishing to see a quantity of purple paint turned black as yellow is added to it.

If the quantities in the previous mixture are reversed, a different result is obtained. Suppose that a quart of purple is mixed with 2 quarts of yellow. Analysis will reveal the following proportions:

1 pint of red
1 pint of blue
4 pints of yellow

Subtraction leaves 0 red, 0 blue, but 3 pints of yellow. If the quantities subtracted (1 pint of red, 1 pint of blue, and 1 pint of yellow) are added together, the final mixture will contain 3 pints of black, so that the color will be made up half of yellow and half of black.

White

The primaries were defined as those steps on the wheel that could not be mixed from other colors. Obviously, black is not one of them, since it can be produced by mixing the primaries themselves. White is like black in that it does not fit on the color wheel, but it is like the primaries in that it cannot be produced by mixing other colors. To obtain paint in white or the primaries, it is necessary to find materials in nature that already have those colors and process them so they can be used in painting. White can be mixed with all of the other colors, contributing its own visual and emotional characteristics to the resulting tints.

Any color can be analyzed in terms of the four unmixable pigments: red, yellow, blue, and white. In practice, it is simpler to add black to the analytical formula, describing the particular color in terms of the relative proportions of black, white, and two of the primaries it contains. (The reason only two primaries appear in the description is that the third, if present at all, is entirely included in the figure indicating the quantity of black present.) Of course, for a particular color, one or more of the items may be present in 0 quantity. If we ignore the black and white content of a mix, the remaining part of the formula describes a primary or secondary color with an identifiable position on the color wheel. If we like, we can describe any color in three terms: its position on the color wheel and the proportions of black and white pigments it contains.

Tints and Shades

Obviously the black and white admixtures have great importance in the effect of the total mixture, especially if they appear in large quantities. Given a particular color-wheel position, it is thus possible to produce a very great number of tints and shades, all of which will fall at the same point on the color wheel, but which will vary because of the amounts of black and white added.

In order to visualize this range of color possibilities, let us choose yellow-green for our basic color-wheel hue. Black and white themselves may be mixed in a very great number of distinguishable proportions; for convenience let us restrict our discussion to nine mixtures, with the following formulas:

Black 0
White 8

Black 1
White 7

Black 2
White 6

Black 3
White 5

Black 4
White 4

Black 5
White 3

Black 6
White 2

Black 7
White 1

Black 8
White 0

The figures refer to the number of parts of each pigment included in the mixtures. The first mixture is pure white, since it is made up of eight parts of white and no black; the last mixture is pure black. All the other mixtures are varying shades of grey.

Each of these mixtures could be added to our basic hue (yellow-green), and the quantities could be varied in any proportions desired. Identical formulas can be used, except that the two elementary pigments mixed are the selected hue (yellow-green) and one of the shades of grey (including of course the pure black and white).

Let us consider, for example, the effect of such a series of mixtures prepared with the 4-4 grey, the medium grey lying halfway between black and white.

The first step in the series would be the pure yellow-green (yellow-green 8, grey 0). The second step would show a very slight admixture of the grey (yellow-green 7, grey 1). The series would continue by even steps, with the last being pure grey (yellow-green 0, grey 8).

If such a series were prepared for all of the greys shown, including black and white, it would display the total range of colors that can be mixed from yellow-green without altering its position on the color wheel. Of course, it would be possible to fit other steps between those shown on the chart, and further subdivision could be carried out as far as desired. However, experience has suggested that the nine-step division is the most convenient in designing scenery, since the scale becomes more cumbersome as the number of steps is increased. The artist is, of course, not restricted to the particular mixes shown; rather, such a chart functions like a ruler. Just as he may occasionally want to specify a length that falls between subdivisions marked on the ruler, he may frequently choose a mix not shown on the color chart. Nevertheless, the chart is useful as a device for measuring and describing.

Practical Mixing

The principles of color mixing that have been discussed will guide the designer in preparing pigments that match the colors he has selected or imagined. The illustrations that have been given have been especially selected for their simplicity; practice is somewhat more complicated. Let us now consider an example that is more representative of the conditions the artist is likely to meet.

Producing Imagined Colors

Suppose that his problem is to produce a color suitable for a section of a groundrow showing rolling, grassy hills. Suppose he decides he wants a predominantly cool effect, lightened to suggest aerial perspective. Referring to the color wheel, he quickly rejects the orange and purple segments and decides to use a green; the choices are essentially central green, yellow-green, or blue-green. Yellow-green is more characteristic of foliage, but let us assume that he prefers the greater coolness of the blue-green, and that he finally selects green blue-green as the color most closely matching the effect he has in mind.

Turning to his supply of tempera paint, he may discover that the closest color has too little blue in it. Cautiously he adds blue to a small quantity of it until he produces the color-wheel mix that seems correct. Since he wants to suggest the pastelling effect of distance, he puts a quantity of white into a new mixing pan and adds the green blue-green a few drops at a time until the mixture seems to match the color as he imagines it. The color is likely to look somewhat too simple, plain, and thin, so he may decide to add a little black to deepen and sophisticate it. This change can be made by adding either black pigment or orange red-orange; each drop of the orange color, however, will combine with a part of the blue blue-green to produce more than a drop of black. If he decides to alter the color in this way he must proceed cautiously.

Constant imaginative analysis of the mixtures is required at each stage, and some of the decisions will probably prove unsound. Many may be correctable (for instance, if he adds too much blue in the first step, he can restore the mixture by adding more green or yellow). Occasionally, a mixture will be so far off that it will be simpler to wash out the pans and start fresh. In altering a mixture, it is important not only to notice the direction of change, but also the speed. It is best always to begin by adding less of a new pigment than will be needed; if the resulting alteration is only a fourth of the total change that is desired, then a second addition of twice as much pigment can be made. As the mixture comes closer and closer to the intended color, the additions should become steadily more cautious.

When the artist feels that he is very close to the correct color, he force-dries a sample over a candle flame, being careful not to burn it, and then makes whatever final adjustments are necessary.

Duplicating Colors

Sometimes the artist will want to duplicate a color he can see, rather than one simply imagined. Let us suppose that he is preparing a wallpaper design, and that for one of the colors he wants to match a wine-red drapery fabric. His first step in this case, as in the previous instance, is to identify the position of the basic hue on the color wheel. In doing that, he must in imagination subtract any black or white admixture present in the color and focus only on the free primaries. This is a somewhat difficult procedure, but the designer can expect that his skill will increase steadily as he becomes more experienced. He is likely in this case to conclude that the fabric is basically an extremely red red-purple, perhaps lying between two of the divisions on his color wheel. Having made this identification, he then focuses on the black content of the color and, let us say, concludes that it contains a fairly heavy amount of black, perhaps a fifth or a fourth of the entire quantity of pigment. The white content is likely to be more difficult to identify, since wine red usually contains very little of it; let us suppose the color contains a trace of white, too slight to express in easy units.

The process of mixing is essentially identical with that discussed in the first example. Since the purple is a relatively minor part of the mixture, the artist begins with pure red and adds purple to it in very small quantities; he constantly checks it against a sample of the fabric, although in each instance it is necessary to subtract the black and white content of the fabric and focus only on the pure color-wheel hue.

When satisfied with the mixture, he slowly adds black until the color seems correct and then finally mixes in the white. Since only a trace of white was identified in the original color, he might not want to add even a whole drop to his mixture; the white can be diluted with water or with some of the basic mix, and the resulting mixture can be added a drop at a time.

Standards of Accuracy

By these methods, with care and experience, it is possible to duplicate colors exactly. For example, the experienced designer can match a color of paint so precisely that if half of an area is painted with the original mix and half with the duplicate, it is impossible to detect the difference. Such precision is hardly ever necessary in theater practice. However, color is such an important resource for the designer that he should hold himself to high standards of color mixing and should not be satisfied with any colors that do not create the effects he has designed.

Contamination

So far, all of the principles and examples given have assumed that the artist works with pure colors (for example, that pure red is available to him, without any admixture of yellow, blue, white, or black). In practice, pure primary colors are almost unobtainable; even if two jars of paint are labeled by their manufacturers as primary red (or spectrum red—a term often used synonymously), the chances are overwhelming that they contain at least traces of other colors. The artist may not be able to detect any difference between the colors of the paint in the two jars, yet one may be contaminated by a trace of yellow and the other by a trace of blue.

It might seem that a trace of contamination that is invisible to the artist can safely be ignored. Suppose, however, that a jar of presumably primary yellow paint contains a single drop of red, and that such contamination is not visible. If the designer needs to mix a quantity of leaf-green paint (that is, yellow-green), he will probably prepare it from central green by adding what he assumes to be primary yellow. The single drop of red will combine with one drop of the yellow and one drop of the blue (present in the green paint) to produce *three* drops of black. A contamination that originally could not be seen might thus become strikingly visible, and the mixture prove useless for preparing a pure, clear yellow-green.

Contaminations of the secondary colors are relatively unimportant, since each is a mixture to begin with. Thus, if a red-orange contains either a red or an orange contamination (that is, if it contains slightly more of either color than the theoretical formula would prescribe), it is still readily usable. Not only is it unlikely that the designer would want to use it without further mixture, even if it were theoretically pure, but he can easily correct any deviation by adding a little of the color that is short. Furthermore, if the pigment contains any contamination of the third primary (in this case blue), the blue will already have entered into combination with the other colors to form black and consequently will have been neutralized. No matter what other color is added to the basic pigment, there will be no sudden multiplication of the contamination. The effect of any contamination is already maximally present, and if it is invisible to the designer, further mixing can only reduce its effect by diluting it further.

Testing for Contamination. Since one cannot safely rely on the appearance of the paint as supplied by the manufacturer, the following test has been devised for demonstrating the type of admixture present in primary colors.[1]

Take two white containers (saucers work nicely) and put a few drops of the paint to be tested in each one. To one of the dishes, add a single drop of one of the secondary paints adjacent to the primary on the color wheel; to the other dish, add a single drop of the other secondary adjacent to the primary. Stir the paint to blend well. If both samples of paint remain clear, the paint being tested is a true primary. If one of the samples becomes muddy and greyed, the paint being tested contains a con-

---

1.   This test for contamination was developed by the author in 1947.

tamination of the *other* secondary (or, in terms of primaries, it contains a contamination of the primary lying at the end of the color-wheel segment of which the other secondary is a part).

Let us suppose the designer wants to check a new jar of yellow paint for possible contamination with red or blue. A drop of orange is mixed with a few drops of the yellow, and a drop of green mixed with another small sample. If both remain clear, the yellow has no red or blue contamination. If the sample mixed with orange becomes muddy, then the yellow contains blue contamination; if the sample mixed with green becomes muddy, the yellow contains red contamination.

This test operates by tripling any contamination present in one of the two mixes. It does not guarantee chemical purity, but if contamination exists so minute that it is invisible when multiplied by three, the designer can confidently rely on its remaining invisible however the paint is used.

Black and White Contamination.   Besides admixture with traces of another primary, any paint may contain contamination with white or black, or both. Blue is often contaminated with black, and yellow with white. Such admixtures may occasionally cause difficulties, although they are far less serious than those described above. They do not multiply when mixed, and if they are unnoticeable in the original paint are likely to be equally unobtrusive in mixtures.

Black and white contaminations cause trouble in two special situations. Since yellow is similar in appearance to white, it may contain a good deal of unnoticed white admixture. If the yellow is then mixed with a color very dissimilar to white, such as blue-green, the white may produce clearly visible contamination of the new mix. In the same way, a black-contaminated blue, when mixed with yellow, may produce a greyed green, rather than a clear one.

The second circumstance in which white contamination becomes objectionable is when a color so contaminated is used in an attempt to mix black. Since much yellow contains some white admixture, the combination of yellow and purple seldom produces the absolute black that would result from a mixture of pure colors; instead, the white present in the yellow pigment mixes with the black produced by the yellow-purple combination to form a distinct grey, which in the case of heavy contamination may be almost as light as medium grey. For that reason, artists seldom attempt to mix pure black from primaries, although the yellow-purple combination can readily be used to darken a color that has some grey in it.

Substituting for Pure Primaries.   Since pure primaries are almost unobtainable, it is suggested that the designer buy instead paints that are intentionally selected to match a particular pattern of contamination. For each primary, he should select two jars of paint, one contaminated with one of the other two primaries and the other contaminated with the third primary. These colors should be as close as possible to the theoretically pure primary. Thus, his substitutes for the primaries would be a very red red-orange and a very red red-purple, an extreme yellow-orange and an extreme yellow-green, and a blue-green and blue-purple as close to primary blue as possible.

From those six colors, it will be possible to mix the entire color wheel, except for the tiny space separating each pair. Thus, the extreme red-purple and blue-purple can be used to mix the entire range of purples, and the extreme red-orange and yellow-orange will produce the entire range of oranges. Pure primary red will be unobtainable from this selection; the red-purple and the red-orange can be mixed so that the blue and yellow admixtures cancel, leaving a red at the primary position on the color wheel, but there will be a considerable black admixture. This limitation, while a real one, is less serious than it might seem. Primaries are extremely useful as a basis for mixing, but they are almost never used in pure form in design. Even if a very vivid red were needed for a set, the designer would probably choose an extreme red-orange or red-purple, rather than the pure primary.

Psychologically, colors seem to vary more clearly in temperature than in any other way, so that the terms *warm* and *cool* are sometimes used to describe the direction of alteration. The following table matches the terms of psychological temperature with the real contaminations.

Warm red is primary red contaminated with *yellow.*
Cool red is primary red contaminated with *blue.*
Warm blue is primary blue contaminated with *red.*
Cool blue is primary blue contaminated with *yellow.*
Warm yellow is primary yellow contaminated with *red.*
Cool yellow is primary yellow contaminated with *blue.*

The Theory Summarized   As has already been indicated, the theory of color mixing is simple. It may be reduced to the following principles:

Red, yellow, blue, and white cannot be mixed from other colors, but must be obtained from natural products having those colors.

The first three colors listed are *primaries.*

Any two primaries mixed together produce what are called *sec-*

ondaries; if they are mixed in equal quantities, the resulting color will stand halfway between them on the color wheel, and in this discussion is identified as *central.*

The primaries divide the color wheel into thirds; all other colors on the color wheel are secondaries.

The position of any secondary color on the color wheel depends on the proportions of the two primary colors that are mixed to produce it.

The three primaries, mixed in equal quantities, produce black, provided all three colors are pure.

Each primary, when mixed with the secondary opposite to it on the color wheel in the proportions of one to two, produces black, provided both colors are pure.

When a color is made from a mixture of all three primaries in different quantities, the primary present in the smallest quantity combines with equal quantities of each of the other primaries to form a total quantity of black equal to three times the quantity of the smallest primary. The position of the total combination on the color wheel is determined by the proportions of the primary or primaries remaining after the quantities in the black combination have been subtracted from the original supplies of primaries.

Any color can be definitively described by stating its position on the color wheel, and the degree of admixture with black and white.

COMPLETING THE PERSPECTIVE PAINTING

Having explored the principles of color mixing, we are ready to return to the practical task of completing our perspective painting.

Before the artist begins painting, he should prepare a series of mixes for each of the colors to be used. Such a series should include at least five mixes: the base color, a highlight, a dark, an extreme highlight, and an extreme dark. It is simplest to mix the base color first and then prepare the other mixes as variations of it. The designer should mix enough of his base to enable him to divide it into three parts.

Preparing the Mixes

    Let us suppose that the walls of his set are to be a somewhat greyed leaf-green, that is, a spectrum green with a considerable amount of added yellow, a small amount of white, and a somewhat greater amount of black. He begins by mixing these colors together in what seem to him to be the right proportions. Since tempera paint changes color considerably when it dries, it is necessary to dry a sample to check its final appearance. The easiest way to prepare a sample is to paint a small area at the edge of a piece of paper and dry it by holding it over a candle flame. If the color when dried does not match the artist's imagined effect, he must change the proportions of the colors. The second mixture is then painted beside the first; it will be easiest to compare them if the second sample is lapped over the first, so that the two mixes appear side by side. This sample is force-dried and checked for effectiveness. This process continues until the desired color has been produced.

The artist should then pour part of the paint into two additional containers, so that he has about a third of it in each. One of the containers is set aside to use for the base mix; the other two are used for the highlights and shades.

The shade is produced by adding more black to the base mix. Since green is composed of yellow and blue, a somewhat clearer and more interesting color can be produced by also slightly increasing the amount of blue in the mixture. This can be done by adding pure blue or, in this case, since the base color is yellower than spectrum green, by adding ordinary green. Again, a sample is dried for testing. Since this mix represents not a new color but the effect of the base color slightly shadowed, the two must be clearly related. It is easiest to check this relationship if the proposed shade is painted beside a sample of the base color. The two mixes should be clearly distinguishable, but not separated any farther than necessary.

When the correct mix has been produced, about a third of it is poured into another container; it is then altered further in the same direction with the addition of more black and blue (or green). It is tested against the second mix in the same way that the second was tested against the base; again, the colors should be as close together as possible, while still being clearly distinguishable.

The finished mixes are then set aside, and the second container of base mix is used for producing the lighter tints. In this case, the percentage of the various pigments is altered by adding more white and yellow. This mix is tested against the base color. When a satisfactory mix has been achieved, a third of the paint is poured into a final container and further lightened by adding still more white and yellow.

When the five mixes have been produced, they should be arranged on the desk in order, from the lightest to the darkest. They should form a smooth series of related colors, spaced at approximately even intervals. Since the painting is likely to require more of the base color than any other mix, the largest amount of paint should be in the middle container; usually the artist will need least of the lightest and darkest mixes. It is most convenient to make up mixes for all of the colors before starting the actual painting. At least, each base color should be prepared, so that the entire group can be checked to make sure they form an effective scheme.

Scene painters cannot be asked to mix their pigments from the perspective painting, since it represents the appearance of the set under lights; consequently they should be given samples to guide them in preparing the scene paint. Almost always, the proper color to paint the scenery is the base mixture that stands at the midpoint of each tint-shade series. As soon as the artist has completed his series, he should take a small card, perhaps 3″ × 4″, and paint the lower half of it with the base color; one such card should be prepared for each series. At the top of the card the name of the play should be typed, with a code designation for the color. It is most convenient to use the names of the primary and secondary colors and to assign a different number to each version of a color; thus, if six greens are used in the set, they should be labeled "Green 1," "Green 2," etc. The same code designations are used in preparing the painting guides in the elevations or working drawings.

If a hole is punched in the top corner of each card, and the cards are fastened together with a pronged paper fastener, each one can be swung out individually and used to test the mixtures of scene paint as they are prepared (Figure 14-2).

If the spatter colors are simple variations of the base coats, it may be possible to describe them in verbal notes. If the designer decides to use less closely related colors for spattering, he will probably find it desirable to supply sample cards for them also.

The order in which the various areas of the picture are painted depends primarily on their shapes and is determined by convenience and ease of painting. Often the artist may prefer to paint a background first and then lay in the details; that is the usual practice when painting a wallpaper design, for instance. (Sometimes, however, it is easier to paint a detail first, for example a narrow molding, and then paint the background beside it.) Pointed shapes are difficult to paint, whereas circular shapes are easy. Such shapes frequently occur together, as, for instance, at the edge of a tree or bush; often the artist will find it easier to paint the background first, and then add the leaves of the tree.

The artist's general practice should be to paint the first of two areas slightly larger than its outline and then lay in the edge of the second area on exactly the right line, so that this area slightly overlaps the first. In doing so, he must take care not to lose the outline. If the painter is in doubt about the placement of an edge, he can find it again by cautiously scraping with a razor blade until the line reappears.

Painting Lighting

Variations in lighting follow the same pattern as those shown in any rubbed-chalk picture of the set. The major difference in technique is that areas must be painted solid, with the blending done as a separate step. Usually it is easiest to begin with the base color, laying in all of the areas to be painted with that mix first. Then the shade, the extreme shade, the highlight, and the extreme highlight can be added in order. The artist may find the placement of the different mixes easier if he will add auxiliary outlines defining their edges; this can be done in pencil.

The edges of the various areas will have hard outlines, and for accuracy's sake these must be destroyed by blending, which requires that the paint be moist. It is usually most convenient to paint all of the various shades of one color first and then remoisten especially for blending. The artist runs a brush slightly moistened in water across the edge between two areas to be blended, in an irregular circular pattern; the brush picks up a little of both mixes, blending them so that an intermediate shade is produced. New edges appear at the outside of the blended area, although the contrast between the blended area and the untouched areas will be

WAITING FOR GODOT
COLOR SAMPLE   GREEN I

Figure 14-2.   A color-sample book.

lower than that between the two original areas. The artist then repeats the process at the edges of the blended area and continues until the line between the blend and the untouched area is dim enough to be indistinguishable.

The artist then takes up the series of mixes of the next color and applies it to the painting in the same way, finally blending where desired.

It is possible to blend tempera painting so smoothly that no irregularities are visible. However, to achieve this effect requires not only a high degree of skill but also a great deal of time. If the blending is moderately even, it can be smoothed greatly by going over it with rubbed chalk, after the tempera is completely dry.

In this case, colored chalk should be used. Colors should be selected that match fairly closely the areas where the blending is to be reinforced; it is possible to mix the chalk after it has been reduced to powder. Each area of the painting is rubbed lightly with chalk powder of a matching color, the chalk being carried past the edge into the adjacent area with which it is to be blended. The result is a smooth, even progression that effectively represents the appearance of light on the finished scenery and produces a handsome painting of the set. (See *Figure 14-3.*)

Figure 14-3.   Steps in painting: a set for Noel Coward's *Blithe Spirit. From left to right:* (1) the drawing has been inked, and the edge of a spotlight indicated (shown here by dashed lines); (2) the areas have been painted in without blending; (3) adjacent shades have been blended; and (4) additional blending has been achieved by rubbed chalk and spatter, and extreme highlights and shadows have been added.

Since the rubbed chalk tends to reduce contrasts slightly, the designer should make a final check of the painting. He may find it desirable to pick up the highlights here and there by erasing some of the rubbed chalk, or he may add accents with his extreme highlight and shade. He may even make two additional mixes by adding a small quantity of his extreme colors to white and black, so that the areas of greatest light and shadow can be sharpened by mixes that, while related to his base colors, are essentially off-white and off-black.

Protecting   As the final step, the painting should be sprayed lightly with fixative, to preserve the chalk blending. The painting should then be covered with clear plastic, fitted with a mat, and, if desired, framed for display. Matting can be done much more neatly and easily if the areas at the edges of the picture are painted out well past the border. It was suggested that the ink lines marking the edges of the picture used as a basis for the painting be extended 2'' or 3'' beyond the corners; these extensions serve as guidelines in cutting and placing the mat, making it possible to paint beyond the edge of the picture without obscuring its position on the cardboard.

THE USE OF THE PAINTING

The perspective painting is of great practical value in the theater. Together with the ground plan, it gives the director clear information about the appearance and practicality of a set. Apprentice members of construction crews often have difficulty reading working drawings; the perspective painting, by showing exactly what a unit of scenery should look like when completed, helps them greatly. And, finally, the painting serves as the clearest, most legible, and most complete record of the designer's artistry, a permanent work of art in itself that is useful for teaching, for public display, and for personal satisfaction long after the actual set has been disassembled and stored in unrecognizable form in the scene shop.

15

SET
Models

Every designer should develop the ability to make an accurate perspective drawing and painting of a stage set; however, it will occasionally be desirable to prepare a model instead.

Some excellent directors have great difficulty in visualizing in three dimensions and consequently may not be able to read ground plans, or even perspective paintings, effectively. They are likely to find a model much easier to interpret, especially if the set makes significant use of platforms, stairs, or ramps. Complex curves take much longer to draw in perspective than straight lines, so that even a skilled draftsman may be able to build a model of a set involving many curves more quickly than he can prepare a perspective drawing of it. Assisting the director in evaluating the set is the most important reason for preferring a model to a painting; saving time is less significant, but when time is short it may be a persuasive reason.

There are several reasons for preferring perspective paintings. They are easier to preserve and store; models are nearly always damaged within a few months of construction, while paintings can be protected with plastic and filed with the working drawings when they are no longer needed by the director or the construction crew. Although it is possible to rig miniature lights for a model in an attempt to imitate stage lighting, the approximation is likely to be extremely rough. It is actually easier to show the

411

effect of stage lighting accurately in a perspective painting than in the most elaborately electrified model.

Furthermore, the painting will have been prepared to show the set as it will appear to a member of the audience sitting close to the center of the auditorium. A model is more likely to be viewed and assessed from angles that do not match the position of any member of the audience, most often from above, that is (in the real theater) from the flies or the ceiling of the auditorium.

Whether a designer chooses to prepare a perspective painting or a model, then, will depend on his or her particular circumstances. Nevertheless, the ability to make an accurate model is a useful skill, only less important than the ability to make an accurate perspective painting. Indeed, it might be wise for students to prepare both a painting and a model of the major design projects they develop during their study.

CONSTRUCTION MATERIALS

It may be clearest to discuss models of two extreme types; other sets will constitute combinations of the two types in varying degrees. The first is a standard box set, without platforms or stairs; the second is a set made up entirely of platforms and stairs, without flats.

Various materials are used in building models, including balsa wood, but generally the most useful are two weights of cardboard. The first is fairly firm and about $1/16''$ thick: heavy drawing board works very well. The second is heavy cardboard, preferably ⅛'' or ¼'' thick: ⅛'' Upson board is excellent. An adhesive will be needed. The fastest is rubber cement, but it must not be used because it rots within a fairly short time, with the result that the pieces of cardboard fall apart at a touch. White glue, sold in small squeeze bottles, is permanent, although it takes longer to set. It can be bought much more economically in gallon containers that are readily available in any hardware store. From these containers it can be poured into the clear plastic bottles with button tops in which kitchen detergent is sold.

THE STAGE WALLS AND FLOOR

The first step in preparing either type of model is to decide on the scale to be used. It is most convenient to use the same scale as that of the ground plan, although a different scale may be chosen if desired. The outline of the stage is then drawn on the heavy cardboard, extending out to the permanent walls of the stage. A second silhouette of the stage floor is marked on the cardboard, turned at right angles to the first. They are then cut out and glued together. Using two layers makes the unit stiffer, and turning the layers at different angles helps prevent warping. The glued layers are laid on a flat surface such as the floor or a desk top, covered with plywood, and weighted with books until the glue has dried. After the weights have been removed, the ground plan of the set is drawn in position on the stage floor.

The outside wall of the stage is then drawn on a sheet of the lighter cardboard, in the form of a long strip, with the corners of the wall marked by lines drawn across the strip, and with the outline of the proscenium opening indicated. The strip, including the proscenium opening, is cut out, and the corners are scored by holding a ruler in place and drawing along it heavily with a nail or other metal point. The strip can then be carefully bent along the scored lines. If that is difficult, the strip can be made more bendable by turning it over and cutting through the back along the same lines, about halfway through the cardboard.

The width of the strip, representing the height of the walls, can be drawn equal (at scale) to the height of the actual walls; usually it is more convenient to run it only a couple of feet higher than the flat height that is standard in the theater where the set is to be used. When the wall strip has been cut and bent, the edges of the laminated base are covered with glue, and the strip is wrapped around them and held in place by pushing pins through it into the base or by setting books outside it to press it against the base until the glue has set.

MODELS OF BOX SETS

The construction or painting elevation showed the walls of the set in a row, with gaps where the walls met at an angle. This elevation is copied on the lighter cardboard, except that the walls are fitted together in a single strip, without gaps. Walls that are not part of the basic structure (for instance, masking walls) will have to be drawn as separate units. (*Figure 15-1* and *15-2* show the ground plan and elevation for the same set.)

Decorative details are included in the drawings, matching those of the painting elevation. Tempera paint is then used to finish the walls. The representation can be made as detailed as desired, with panels, hanging pictures, wallpaper, and drapes indicated. Even if actual fabric is to be used in the set itself, it is difficult and unnecessary to reproduce it in the model; instead, the drapery can be painted on the cardboard representing the flats. If desired, the walls can be finished by spattering them. At this scale, the easiest way to spatter is to dip the bristles of a cheap toothbrush

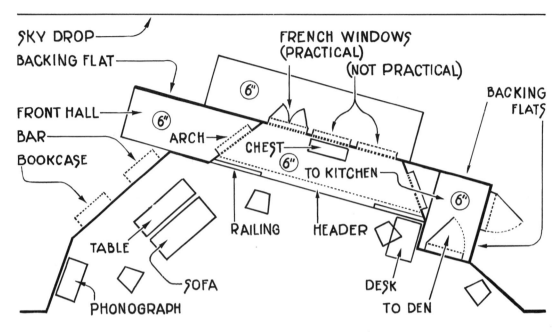

SKY DROP
BACKING FLAT
FRONT HALL
BAR
BOOKCASE
ARCH
TABLE
SOFA
PHONOGRAPH
FRENCH WINDOWS
(PRACTICAL)
(NOT PRACTICAL)
CHEST
TO KITCHEN
RAILING
HEADER
DESK
TO DEN
BACKING
FLATS

Figure 15-1. Ground plan of a set for *The Gazebo*.

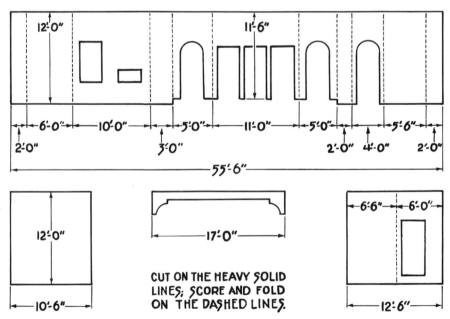

12'-0"
11'-6"
6'-0"
10'-0"
5'-0"
11'-0"
5'-0"
5'-6"
2'-0"
3'-0"
2'-0"
4'-0"
2'-0"
55'-6"

12'-0"
10'-6"

17'-0"

CUT ON THE HEAVY SOLID
LINES; SCORE AND FOLD
ON THE DASHED LINES.

6'-6"
6'-0"
12'-6"

Figure 15-2. Elevation of walls for a model of *The Gazebo* set.

into thinned tempera paint and draw the side of a nail across them. The paint flies out at a fairly sharp angle, so that it is deposited some distance beyond where the brush is held. The brush should not be held directly over the cardboard, so that if some of the paint drips from it the design will not be spoiled. After the spattering is completed, generally in two colors, the cardboard is set aside to dry thoroughly.

Next, the joints between wall areas that meet at an angle are marked and scored, as was done with the walls of the stage, and door and window openings are cut out. A line is drawn parallel with the bottom edge of the wall strip an actual quarter or half inch below it. The entire bottom edge of the wall is scored, and the wall strip is cut out, using the new line for the bottom edge rather than the line representing the bottom of the flats. The bottom strip is cut through up to the bottom of the flats at each corner of the set. The wall strip is then folded at the vertical scorings, where the walls of the actual set meet at an angle, and the narrow strip at the bottom is folded back; it forms a tab along the bottom of each wall, which is used to glue it to the stage floor. At some corners, these tabs may cross; at these points, they are cut away at an angle so that they will fit against the stage floor without lapping over each other.

The underside of the tabs is then glued, and the walls are carefully fitted against the ground plan that has been drawn on the floor, with the tabs behind the walls (on the offstage side). It is more convenient if two people can work together at this point. The tabs can be temporarily fastened with map tacks or pins. After all of the walls have been set in place, laying a book across their top will help hold them steady until the glue has dried.

Meanwhile, strips of cardboard about a quarter of an inch wide are cut and glued together in layers until they equal (to scale) the size of the thickness pieces to be used in the actual set. These are then cut in lengths matching the heights and widths of door and window openings. Doors and windows are cut and painted like the walls, except that quarter-inch tabs should be left on the edges so that they will extend out beyond the openings in the walls. When the glue holding the walls to the floor has thoroughly set, the weight is removed and the thickness lengths are glued to the back of the flats, edging the openings. The tab edges of the doors and windows are then glued and pressed against the back of the thickness pieces. Of course, the same method can be used for other openings, such as fireplaces and bookcases that are built into the wall. For arches, it will be necessary to cut the cardboard in matching curves and then laminate it to the desired thickness.

Finally, the short cardboard strips representing masking flats are cut out. If any of their edges touch the back of the set walls, vertical tabs should be left on those edges, in addition to the tabs at the bottom of the flats. Most often, masking flats are in the form of two-folds. After they

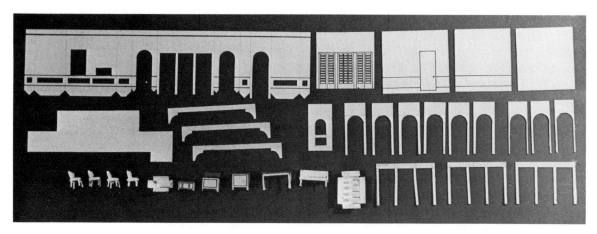

Figure 15-3. Units for the *Gazebo* model, before assembly. *Top row,* walls; *center row, left to right,* platform, header (three layers to provide thickness), door to den, arch thicknesses; *bottom row,* furniture, wall cabinet, and French window thicknesses.

Figure 15-4. The model of the *Gazebo* set assembled.

have been scored and bent, and the tabs bent back, they should be glued and set in place. The outer walls of the stage should be painted on both sides, black or dark grey, and the stage floor should be painted to match the appearance of the floor of the finished set. (*Figures 15-3* and *15-4* show all the units for one model before and after assembly.)

Cardboard Jacks

Often long walls will warp slightly, or unsupported edges of flats may lean rather than standing up straight. They can be supported from the back, out of sight, by blocks of wood glued to the stage floor and the walls. Another possibility is to cut a strip of cardboard, perhaps an inch or so shorter than the walls themselves and about twelve (scaled) feet wide. It is

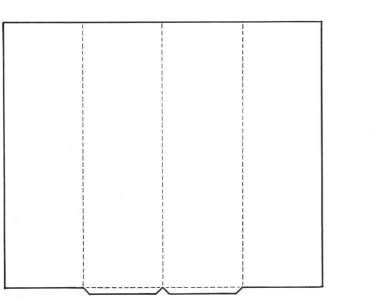

SCORE ON DASHED LINES

Figure 15-5.   A cardboard jack.

scored vertically three times, so as to divide it into four equal rectangles. When it is cut out, tab strips should be left under the two center rectangles. (See *Figure 15-5*.)

The strip is then folded on the scored lines, the bottom tabs folded back, and the two end sections lapped and glued together. When the glue has set, the tabs and the outside of the double section are covered with glue and pressed tight to the stage floor. This triangular structure serves the same purpose as a jack behind an actual wall of flats, holding the wall straight.

Model Furniture

It will usually be necessary to provide furniture for the set. Indicating the size and approximate shape is more important than reproducing minute details of carving or upholstery. Furniture may be constructed out of any materials that seem suitable. Balsa wood can be easily carved, and it may be possible to make tables, bookcases, and chests of drawers out of balsa, plastic, or cardboard. Details can be painted on if desired. It is more convenient to glue the furniture to the stage floor, rather than simply standing it in position.

PLATFORM SETS

At the opposite extreme from a set made up entirely of flats is one using only three-dimensional structures, platforms, ramps, and stairs. (See *Figures 15-6* and *15-7*.) Because the height of units is especially important in this type of set, the scale should be chosen so that the various heights can easily be built up accurately by laminating layers of cardboard. Assuming that steps and platform heights are multiples of 6'', and that ⅛'' Upson board is used for the model, ½'' = 1'-0'' will generally be found the most convenient scale. Two layers of the cardboard will then equal 6'', and four layers will equal a foot.

For this model, as for a model of a box set, the designer constructs a base representing the stage floor, traces the ground plan in position, and wraps the stage walls around the base.

The outline of all raised areas appearing in the set (that is, all areas 6'' or higher above the stage floor) is then drawn on Upson board; however, the edges distinguishing between raised areas of different heights

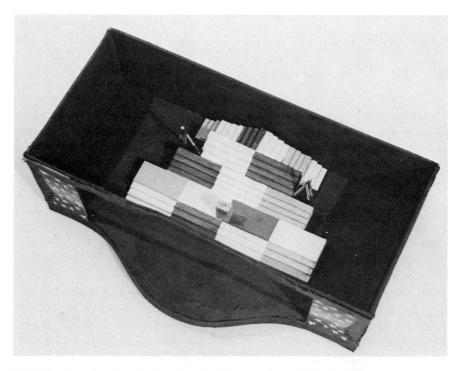

Figure 15-6. Model of the inauguration set for *Of Thee I Sing*. (See *Figure 9-10* for a picture of the set from the audience's viewpoint.)

Figure 15-7. Model of the beauty contest set for *Of Thee I Sing*. (See *Figure 9-9* for the audience's view of the set.)

may be omitted. At the scales suggested, this shape is drawn twice, with the grain of the cardboard running in opposite directions. The two patterns are then cut out and glued together under pressure. This area is glued in place on the stage floor. Next, similar tracings are made of all areas 1'-0'' or higher, and they are cut out and laminated. These shapes are glued in place on top of the first glued area. The 1'-6'' areas are next cut and fastened in place, then the 2'-0'' areas, and so on until the highest level has been reached. (See *Figures 15-8* and *15-9*.)

Most sets, even if they are made up primarily of platforms, ramps, and stairs, will also contain some decorative or two-dimensional details, even perhaps some flats or arches (See *Figures 15-10* and *15-11*). These should be cut out and fastened in place, using either Upson board or somewhat lighter cardboard. When the structure is fully assembled, it should then be painted with poster paint, including the stage floor and the outer stage walls. If furniture is used, it can be constructed in miniature as for a box set. Small twigs can be combined to form trees or bushes, and held in place by forcing their glue-covered ends into holes punched with a nail in the Upson board.

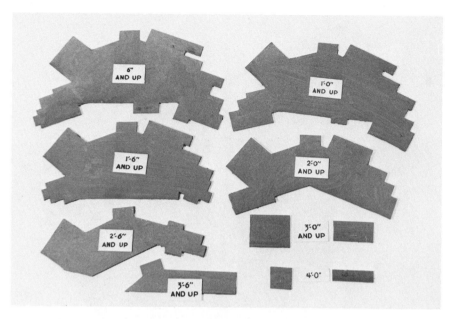

Figure 15-8. Platform silhouettes for a model of *The Rimers of Eldritch* set. Only one of each pattern is shown; for the model, two of each were necessary. (See *Figure 6-23* for a ground plan of the set, and *Figure 15-9* for completed model.)

Figure 15-9. Model of the set for *The Rimers of Eldritch.* (See *Figure 6-24* for a photograph of the actual set.)

Figure 15-10. Model showing the outside of the castle for *Once Upon a Mattress*. (See *Figure 4-13* for the audience's view of the set.)

Figure 15-11. Model showing the throne room set for *Once Upon a Mattress*. (See *Figure 4-14* for a view of the set from the audience.)

As with models of box sets, the model of three-dimensional scenery can be finished in any degree of detail desired. If it is to be used for public display, as part of a television broadcast or an advertising exhibit, a fully decorated model will be most effective; if it is intended for the use only of the director and the construction crew, an undecorated model that accurately shows the shapes of the various units may be adequate.

Especially if the raised areas have curved edges, it may be possible to construct a model in a third or half the time that would be required for a finished perspective painting. When time is short, this may be a decisive factor in choosing which method of presentation to use, and many directors may prefer the three-dimensional mock-up even when there is time to prepare a painting.

16

The
Working
Drawings

A stage set, however beautiful, that exists only in the designer's imagination can have no function on the stage itself; and even if it were recorded in the form of a carefully prepared ground plan and perspective painting, it would be essentially a proposal, rather than a set. It is only when the designer's decisions have been translated into cloth and wood, the colors of paint, and the magic of light that they become a real set. The working drawings constitute the dictionary by means of which the construction workers, painters, and erection crew make that translation.

Set design is both an art and a craft. When the designer is selecting from his resources and organizing them to produce a new and esthetically significant pattern, he is functioning as an artist; when he is preparing the instructions for the technical crew, he is functioning as a craftsman.

The two functions can be separated, both in theory and in practice; certainly, many theater workers are excellent craftsmen but mediocre artists, and it is at least conceivable that a set designer might be a great artist, while neglecting the mastery of the related craft. Such an artist, however, would be most unusual, and designers who express contempt for craftsmanship are almost always far short of top rank.

Robert Edmond Jones spoke to a group of theater students at the University of Minnesota shortly before his death. At the time he was an almost legendary figure in the history of American set design. Except for one moment in the speech, he showed a uniform modesty. The single time he expressed obvious pride in his own work was when he pointed not to one of his revolutionary designs, his position as designer-laureate to Eugene O'Neill, or his sets for Broadway hits, but to his skill in making working drawings. Far from being unusual, pride in craftsmanship is one of the commonest characteristics of first-rank artists, and in the practical theater the ability to prepare good-quality working drawings is one of the designer's most important skills. There is no precise formula for determining just what information should be included in the working drawings; all that can be said is that they should include everything necessary.

The designer should attempt to establish an easy working relationship with the construction supervisor so that each can adjust to the other's preferences and habits of thinking. While avoiding unnecessary work, he must provide all the guidance needed. Continued experience in working with a particular construction staff will help the designer in deciding what he must specify in his instructions and what he can leave to their good judgment. With a skilled supervisor in the scene shop, the designer may not need to draw the exact placement of corner blocks and braces; in fact, he may be able to dispense altogether with construction drawings of standard flats, supplying only a list showing the number of such flats of various widths required. Usually, he will not need to specify grades of materials or types of lumber, although if a scene shop regularly uses two different weights of canvas, he might occasionally want to indicate the weight preferred for a particular unit. Certainly, for inexperienced set builders, or for crews with which a designer has not worked previously, it is far safer to supply the fullest information. Adding corner blocks to the working drawing of a flat takes only a few minutes; if the set builders attached the corner blocks of a flat incorrectly because the designer failed to specify their placement, the necessity for rebuilding the flat after the deadline had arrived for erecting the scenery on stage might prove disastrous. The working drawings described in this chapter are relatively complete, somewhat more detailed than will probably be necessary in a theater where the designer has established a smooth working relationship with the construction crew, but slightly short of the absolute maximum of elaboration.

SCALES AND CATEGORIES OF DRAWINGS

The scales used for working drawings are more variable than those used for the drawings already discussed; in practice, they range generally from

⅜″ = 1′-0″ to full scale. Aside from the limitation imposed by the size of the cardboard used, the choice of scale is determined by the information the drawing is intended to communicate; often small sections of a unit are shown beside the basic drawing at a much larger scale, to reveal such details as the placement of hinges.

There is some advantage in organizing the drawings around the probable work assignments, so that crew members working on different projects will not have to share the same drawing. Drawings that could have been crowded on a single sheet are sometimes drawn on two or three, to facilitate their use in the scene shop.

Working drawings can be divided into two major categories: one type explains the method of construction, and the other indicates exactly how the units are to be painted.

The construction drawings can be further organized in three groups: those describing the construction of flats; those dealing with essentially three-dimensional units such as doors, windows, fireplaces, pillars, trees, and rocks; and those dealing with pieces of furniture.

The great majority of working drawings of all types are drawn in orthographic projection, but a considerable number make use of isometric projection, a method of drawing that is discussed later in the chapter.

CONSTRUCTION DRAWINGS FOR FLATS

Even if the construction supervisor has agreed that drawings of standard flats may be omitted, the designer is likely to find himself preparing more construction drawings for flats than for any other single type of unit. Any deviation from standard procedure must be indicated: flats with specially shaped edges; with openings for fireplaces, arches, doors, and windows; or with other alterations always require special instructions, even for a skilled construction crew.

The commonest such deviation is the omission of canvas from openings in the flats, which should be indicated by printing "do not canvas" in the opening itself or near the opening, with an arrow pointing to the opening. Where flats are to be hinged together, the positions of the hinges must be drawn with the proper symbol to show whether they are to go on the front or back, and indicating wherever the joint is to be dutchmanned. Where a series of identical flats are to be built, only one need be drawn, with a note of the number to be built. When one flat is a mirror image of another, often one of the drawings can also be omitted (with the omission indicated by an appropriate note), although inexperienced workers may' have difficulty in reversing a pattern as they build it.

Although flats are approximately an inch thick, they function essentially as two-dimensional surfaces; consequently, in most cases the third dimension can be safely ignored in preparing the drawings. By far the most effective way to represent a plane surface is by the use of orthographic projection.

Since, during most of the construction, builders work with the flats placed face down, construction drawings should show the appearance of the flats from the back. From that side, all of the framing, the diagonal braces, and the plywood fasteners can be clearly seen.

DIMENSIONING

All critical dimensions must be indicated. The first requirement of dimensioning is that it be accurate and unambiguous, but it is also of great practical importance that it be easily legible. The following recommendations are designed to fulfill all of those requirements.

All printing on a drawing should be identically oriented, so that any figures or verbal instructions can be read without turning the sheet. As a general practice, all dimensions and instructions should be printed outside the drawing, although in some cases ease of reading may be increased by a different placement: for example, the words "do not canvas" are usually printed inside the section to be left open. The lines of the scenery should be drawn in india ink. If desired, the standardized label may also be printed in black. All other lines, as well as all figures and printing, should be in red ink (although for gridding it is occasionally desirable to make some of the lines red and some green). Printing should be large enough to be easily legible: $3/16''$ is recommended for the height of letters, with successive lines of printing $1/8''$ apart.

Arrows are used to indicate the space to which a set of dimension figures refers. Their simplest form can be illustrated by describing the method of marking the dimensions of a plain flat. (See *Figure 16-1*.) The top and bottom edges are extended to one side (say the right) for $9/16''$. A light pencil mark is made on each of these lines, $1/2''$ from the vertical edge of the flat. These two marks are joined lightly in pencil. Four points are then marked at the center of this vertical line, the top two $1/16''$ apart, the second and third $3/16''$ apart, and the third and fourth $1/16''$ apart, placed so that the midpoint of the vertical line falls halfway between the second and third marks. A pencil mark is also placed at the top and bottom of the vertical line, $3/16''$ from the ends. Horizontal lines are drawn through the second and third of the marks at the center of the vertical line, extending a little more than a quarter of an inch on each side of the vertical; these lines mark the top and bottom of the space for the figures.

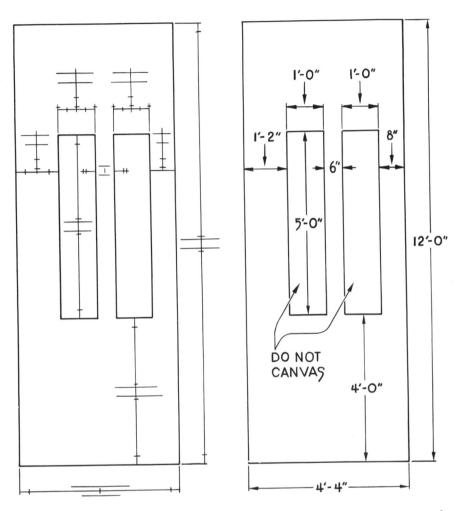

Figure 16-1. Dimensioning. The flat shown has two openings. The drawing at the left includes the guide lines for the arrowheads, dimension figures, and extension lines. The drawing at the right shows the dimensioning completed, with construction lines erased.

In this space, the actual height of the flat is printed lightly in pencil. When properly arranged, the dimension is inked in red, then the horizontal extensions of the rails of the flat are inked, and finally the vertical line, with a gap left for the printing, is inked. The vertical line extends down to the first of the centered pencil marks, just above the figures, begins again at the fourth mark, and continues to the bottom of the flat. A vertical arrowhead is then drawn at each end of the vertical line; the arrowheads should be narrow and 3/16'' long (that is, extending to the points already marked).

The width of the flat is indicated similarly. The outside edges of the rails are extended either up or down (for illustration, let us say below the flat) a distance of $9/16''$; a point is marked on each, $\frac{1}{2}''$ below the corner of the flat, and these two points are connected with a horizontal pencil line. Marking the space for the dimension figures comes next. First the center point of the horizontal line is marked, then points are marked $3/32''$ above and below it. A short horizontal line is drawn through each of these two points, extending a little more than $\frac{1}{4}''$ to the left and right of the center point. The dimension is printed between these two lines. When this spacing has been adjusted satisfactorily, a point is marked on the horizontal line on each side of the dimension figures, $1/16''$ from them. At the same time the lengths of the arrowheads are marked, $3/16''$ from each end of the horizontal. The lines and figures are then inked in.

The dimensions of slanted lines are indicated similarly. However, the short extenders are drawn at right angles to the slanted lines, while the dimensioning grid is always drawn horizontally, so that all of the printing can be read from the same position.

It is customary to express dimensions shorter than a foot in inches alone; dimensions of a foot or more should be expressed in feet and inches, and to make misreading less likely, a hyphen should be placed between the two. Even for dimensions in whole feet, the inches should be indicated: $12'-0''$, not simply $12'$.

The method described requires that the extender lines be at least $\frac{3}{4}''$ apart. Dimensions for slightly smaller spaces can be given by moving the figures to one side and drawing a two-headed arrow without any gap in its shaft. A second shaft is then drawn from the figures to the center of the dimensional arrow, and a single head is added, pointing to the dimension line. This arrow should be at least $\frac{3}{8}''$ long (including the arrowhead), and it should not touch either the figures or the dimension line: leave a gap of $1/16''$ at each end.

Even this device cannot be used for spaces much smaller than $\frac{5}{8}''$. A special method has been devised for indicating the dimensions of such spaces. The dimensional arrowheads, instead of being drawn inside the space to be marked, are placed outside it, pointing in the opposite direction, that is, toward the space. The vertical lines representing the shafts of the arrows should be extended $1/16''$ beyond the arrowheads, for a total length of $\frac{1}{4}''$. The dimension figures are placed as in the previous example, and a similar arrow is drawn toward the center of the space, except that in this case a gap is left only at the end next to the figures: the point of the arrowhead is placed directly between the points of the dimensional arrows.

It is often necessary to mark segments, as well as the total dimension. For example, if three flats are shown side by side in an elevation, it may be desirable to indicate not only the total dimensions of the wall they form, but also the widths of the individual flats. In such cases, the arrows, lines, and figures should be arranged so that they do not overlap confusingly. The widths of the individual flats should be indicated by the first method described above; for the total width, the outside lines of the wall should be extended down an additional half inch, the dimension printed in the proper place, and a single arrow run across (of course with a gap to provide space for the figures), extending the entire distance.

Usually, the dimension figures are placed at the center of the arrow. However, if a line of the drawing happens to run close to that point, the figures should be shifted to the most legible position.

In drawing a circle, a builder sets the points of his compass so that the distance between them is equal to the radius of the circle; consequently, circles or arcs should be dimensioned by radius rather than diameter. In this case, a double-headed dimensional arrow is drawn from the center of the circle to some point on the circumference, and the length of the radius is given in figures placed in a gap left in the center of the arrow. The radius may be drawn in any direction, although a horizontal, vertical, or 45° angle is most attractive. If the circle is not complete, the radius should be drawn to a point inside the arc, rather than to either end, to improve legibility.

Most often, only the dimensions of actual scenic units need be given. Occasionally, however, construction depends on points that lie outside the unit. The pillars for the *Antony and Cleopatra* set *(Figure 6-19)* are examples of this. Still more common are arches of complex shape, where the centers of the arcs often fall outside the structure. The location of such points must be indicated for the builders, sometimes by drawing extensions of the lines of the unit in red and supplying the necessary dimensions.

COLOR

The drawings of complex structures can often be made more easily legible by the addition of color. For example, it was essential that the different parts of the high platform in the *Antony and Cleopatra* set be assembled in the correct order; this was indicated on the drawing by using one color for those that were set in position first, a second color for the next group, etc. Ink, water color, or tempera paint may be used, although the fastest medium is rubbed chalk. The significance of each color should be indicated by adding an explanatory table, showing a small square of the color with an explanation of its use.

The practice of drawing grid lines in two colors was mentioned above. One of the special difficulties of enlargement by gridding is keeping track of the individual squares; especially complicated grids are much easier to follow if selected lines are drawn in a different color. Thus, if the grid divisons are 2'' apart, the lines marking the ends of feet might be drawn in red, with the lines between them in green.

Color may also be used in other circumstances, wherever it seems genuinely helpful. In drawing the squares of the screen in *The Solid Gold Cadillac (Figure 3-33),* the designer distinguished between the pieces to be discarded and those to be used in the design by laying a light green wash of rubbed chalk over the sections to be saved.

One cautionary note: if plans are later to be blueprinted, color coding will prove almost useless. An alternative method of coding should therefore be employed from the start.

PAINTING INSTRUCTIONS

In Chapter 12 it was suggested that it may sometimes be preferable to include information such as painting guides on the construction drawings, rather than in separate elevations. That is particularly true when the painted motifs partly or entirely match the edges of units that must be especially shaped in construction. Such a combination is most likely to occur in working drawings for furniture, picture frames, or similar items, since painted motifs would not show on construction drawings for flats. The decision to combine the painting guides with the construction drawings, or to present them separately, should be based on the convenience of the builders. If they are included in the working drawings, they should conform to the specifications given in Chapter 12.

VERBAL NOTES

Usually, it is necessary to add printed notes. Such notes should be placed well clear of the construction and dimension lines, but preferably associated with the parts of the drawings to which they refer. An arrow may be run from the note to the corresponding point in the drawing, placed so as to miss other lines; if necessary, they may be specially shaped. The most attractive treatment is to draw them as straight lines, joined by arcs of tangent circles.

ISOMETRIC PROJECTION

Three-dimensional units such as furniture, platforms, and stairs may be recorded in orthographic projection by making three drawings, showing the front, top, and side of the unit separately. Often, such drawings will clearly show the shape and construction of the unit; sometimes, however, it is difficult to read them, and a projection has been developed that generally expresses the shape of such units more clearly than any number of orthographic views. This is called *isometric projection.* The word *isometric* comes from the Greek *isos* "equal" and *metron* "measure." The reason for this name will become evident during the description of the projection.

Isometric projection is of value only for representing three-dimensional units. Since it is more troublesome to draw and read than orthographic, orthographic is the preferred type even for three-dimensional units when their shapes can be indicated clearly that way. Often individual sections of a structure can be drawn the simpler way, and a single isometric view added to show how they fit together.

Isometric projection can be described and defined in various ways, but the easiest approach is to imagine first how orthographic views of the same object would appear. *Figure 16-2* shows the orthographic projection

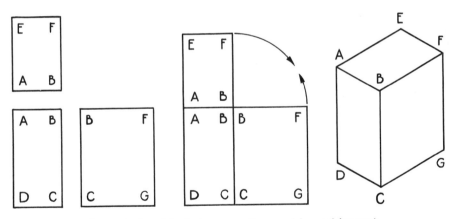

Figure 16-2. The relationship between orthographic and isometric projection. A simple box is shown in three views. In the first, three sides appear in orthographic projection, artificially separated. In the second, the edges have been joined to conform to their actual positions on the box, except for the *BF* edge, which still appears as two lines. The final drawing shows the box in isometric projection, with each edge represented by a single line of true dimension, but with angles no longer 90°.

of the top, side, and front of a plain closed box, with a top 2′ × 3′, a front 2′ × 4′, and a side 3′ × 4′. Although all the dimensions are given accurately, it is somewhat difficult to imagine the completed box, and the drawing omits or falsifies certain facts. For example, the edges lettered *AB* are not separate, as shown, but are in fact the same line, where the top and side surfaces join. The three rectangles can be redrawn in contact with each other. That arrangement, however, still leaves the *BF* edge shown as two lines at right angles to each other, whereas in the object *BF* is a single line.

Imagine that the lines of the drawing are made of thin, rigid metal rods, joined so that the angles may be shifted. Then imagine that the upper right corners of the top and side (marked *F*) are pulled together. As they come toward each other, all three rectangles of the orthographic drawing are pulled out of shape. Their edges get no longer or shorter and they remain parallelograms, but all the angles inside are changed. The corners are no longer 90°: some are smaller, some larger.

The new figure will have certain advantages as well as disadvantages over the original orthographic projections:

1. The length, height and width of the parallelograms remain the same and can be measured directly. Furthermore, experiment will show that measurements remain accurate anywhere in the drawing for lines parallel with the original rectangles (i.e., for lines parallel with the axes *AB*, *BC*, and *BF*).

2. The lengths of the diagonals have been altered, so one diagonal is longer than the other; experiment will show that all measurements along lines *not* parallel with the three axes have been changed and are no longer of any use for determining true dimensions.

3. All angles have been shifted, so they no longer correspond to the angles in the object itself.

4. The continuity of surfaces is expressed and no two planes are artificially divided, as in orthographic projections.

An isometric projection, then, combines some of the measurability of an orthographic drawing, with some of the apparent solidity of a perspective drawing.

Differences between Isometric Projection and Perspective Drawings

It may be helpful at this point to describe the ways in which it deviates from a true perspective. In perspective the scale alters steadily as areas move away from the viewer. A perspective drawing shows the far side of a box smaller than the near side. An isometric drawing uses the same scale throughout the drawing for lines parallel with the axes; for that reason, in an isometric drawing the far end of a box may seem too large, since— being more used to perspective drawings—we expect that end to look smaller than the front. It is this uniformity of scale that explains the term *isometric,* since all measurements along lines parallel with the axes can be made with a single scale.

The second major deviation from perspective drawing is in the angle at which the object is turned to the viewer. A perspective may be drawn with the object shown at any angle. In an isometric projection the object must be turned in a special way: the viewer is supposed to be looking directly at one corner; the three sides are shown at identical angles with the line of sight. For example, after pulling together the two corners marked *F* in *Figure 16-2,* the designer would find that he was looking directly at corner *B,* and that the angles between the axes *AB, BC,* and *BF* were all equal.

Isometric views are always drawn with reference to an imaginary right-angled solid turned as described. An isometric drawing, then, is based on a group of three lines (axes) that meet at actual angles of 120°, representing the corner where three planes meet in the real object at angles of 90°.

Occasionally, a designer may want to show an object that is tipped, with none of the axes vertical. But generally speaking his drawings will show one of the axes in the vertical position. Four basic arrangements or interpretations of the three planes are then possible (see *Figure 16-3*):

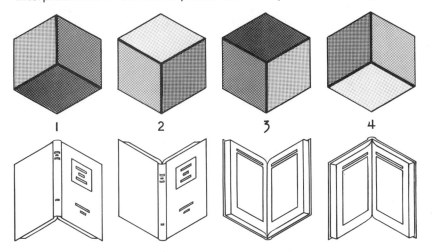

Figure 16-3. The orientation of objects in isometric projection. In isometric drawings objects are nearly always shown in one of the four positions illustrated. Each position is shown in two drawings, the top one showing a simple box, the bottom one showing an open book placed so as to fit against one corner of the box above it. The three-line grid has been drawn with heavy lines in the top pictures. *Drawing 1:* the outside of a box above eye level. *Drawing 2:* the same box below eye level. *Drawings 3 and 4:* the inside of a box above and below eye level.

1. If the vertical line is above the others, the point of meeting may be interpreted as the near bottom corner of a box, above eye level, viewed from the outside.
2. If the vertical line is below the others, the point of meeting may be interpreted as the near top corner of a box, below eye level.
3. With the vertical line below the others, the drawing may be interpreted as showing the inside of a box, above eye level.
4. With the vertical line above the others, the drawing may be interpreted as showing the inside of a box, below eye level.

Which of those four arrangements and interpretations is selected for a particular drawing depends on which position will reveal the construction of the scenic unit most clearly. For example, *Figure 16-4* shows a small table, drawn in positions 1 and 2. Since we most often look at tables from a point above them, position 2 seems more natural in appearance, but raising the table above eye level, as indicated in position 1, reveals the construction much more clearly, showing the design of the legs, the supporting horizontals under the top, and the use of metal corner braces, details obscured or completely hidden in the first drawing.

The most important factor in preparing isometric drawings is a psychological one: the artist must learn to think in terms of the basic lines, along which he measures, and in terms of the special angles, which, whether they are 120° or 60°, represent angles of 90° in the object. He must remember that direct measurements can be made parallel with the basic lines, but not in any other direction.

In making isometric drawings, one simple instrument is invaluable: the 30-60 plastic triangle, made with angles of 30°, 60°, and 90°. Place a T-square across a sheet of cardboard, parallel with the edge, and then place the 30-60 triangle against the T-square so that the short side of the right angle is vertical, and draw along that edge. Then move the triangle along the edge of the T-square so that the hypotenuse of the triangle cuts across the vertical line, extending up and to the left from the top of the vertical, and draw that edge. Now turn the triangle over, from left to right, and place it against the T-square so that the hypotenuse coincides with the point at which the two lines meet, and draw along the hypotenuse again, up and to the right of the vertical. The result is a three-line figure with the lines meeting at angles of 120°, which will be recognized as the figure forming the center of the isometric cubes in positions 2 and 3. All of the lines for all positions of the isometric cubes can be made similarly with the T-square and the 30-60 triangle. The T-square may be placed

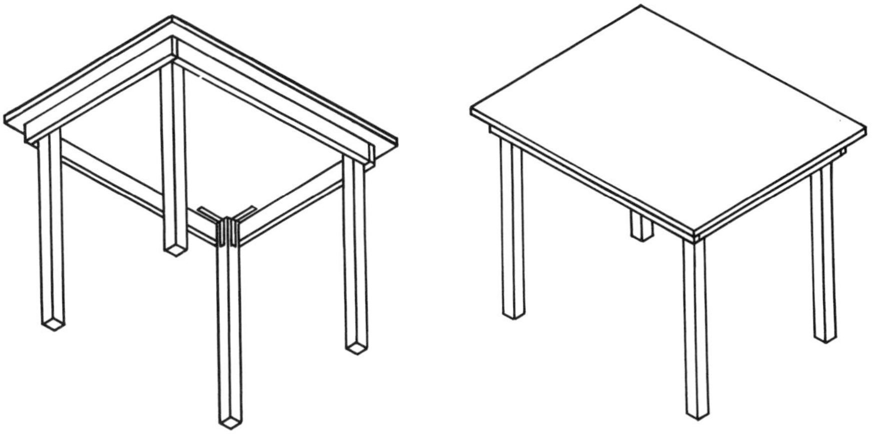

Figure 16-4. Isometric views of a table in two positions. Although position 2 (*right*) matches the view usually seen in ordinary experience, position 1, which raises the table above eye level, reveals its construction much more clearly.

horizontally, in which case the 30° and 90° angles of the triangle are used, or it may be placed vertically, with the 60° and 90° angles used. A little experience with isometric construction will soon make the use of the triangle almost automatic.

So far, the shapes used to illustrate isometric drawing have been very simple. A plain rectangular bench will serve as an example of a more complicated shape. Assume the following dimensions: height, 1'-6''; length, 4'-0''; width, 2'-0''; legs, 2'' square, set back 1'' from the edges of the top; seat, 1'' thick; the legs connected by stretchers fastened inside them, raised 3'' off the ground, and with height and thickness of 2'' and 1''. *Figure 16-5* shows the bench in orthographic projections of the top, side, and end.

More Complex Shapes

In preparing the isometric drawing (*Figure 16-6*), we must first select the view; in this case, let us use position 2. The next step is to draw the three basic lines that, in this position, represent the near corner of a box, below eye level. Since the bench is essentially boxlike in shape, next draw a box of the same dimensions, into which it would precisely fit (that is, 1'-6'' × 2'-0'' × 4'-0'').

Starting at the point where the three basic lines meet, measure down on the vertical line 1'-6'', at the scale selected for the drawing; this represents the near corner of the box. The bench could be placed so that this near corner was on either our right or our left; let us assume it is on the left, so that the front of the bench extends to the right. Measuring from

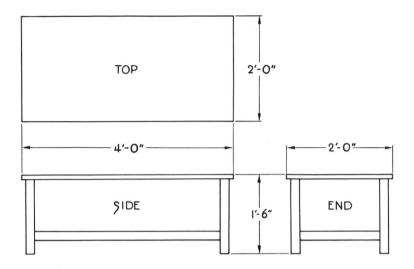

Figure 16-5. An orthographic drawing of a bench. The same bench is shown in isometric projection in *Figure 16-6.*

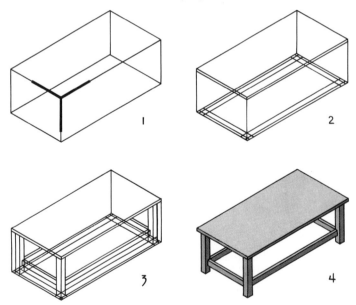

Figure 16-6. Drawing a bench in isometric. The first drawing shows the basic box, with the isometric grid marked with heavy lines. In the second drawing the thickness of the top has been drawn, as well as the lines marking the edges of the legs, where they rest on the floor. In the third drawing the legs have been extended up to meet the top, and the stretchers have been drawn.

the point where the basic lines meet, mark a point 4'-0'' away on the basic line extending up and to the right; this represents the front edge of the bench (or box). On the line extending up and to the left, mark a point 2'-0'' from the central point of intersection.

Using the T-square and triangle, next drop verticals from each of the last two points marked. From the bottom point marked on the basic vertical, run lines left and right parallel with the other two basic lines, so as to cross the new verticals. The resulting figure represents one end and one side of the box. From the point marked on the left slanted basic line, draw a line parallel with the other slanted basic line, extending to the right, and a similar line from the point marked on the right basic line, this new line extending up and left, parallel with the left slanted basic line. These two lines are drawn long enough to cross. The top of the box (or bench) has now been outlined.

Since the sides of the bench are not solid, we will be able to see through them; we should therefore complete our basic box shape by dropping an additional vertical from the upper corner of the top and by extending lines up from the outside corners of the end and side that have already been drawn. These lines will cross the vertical at the same point.

The top of the bench is 1'' thick. At the three front corners, we measure down 1'', and mark the points; these are then connected, to define the bottom edge of the seat. Lines drawn through the mark on the front corner of the box parallel with the basic lines pass through the 1'' marks at the other corners; consequently, in practical drawing, it is only necessary to measure one of these points.

The legs were specified as set back from the edges of the box by 1''. At the bottom of the box, measure one inch from the front corner along each of the lines marking the bottom edge of the side and end of the box; repeat this measurement at the back corner, and, using the T-square and triangle, draw lines through all four of these points parallel with the edges of the bottom of the box. The resulting (isometric) rectangle marks the outside edges of the legs.

The legs are 2'' square, so that the inside edge of each is 3'' from the corresponding edge of the box. Mark these points in the same way as in the previous step, and draw lines through the marks parallel with the edges of the bottom of the box. It will be seen that these last eight lines, defining the inside and outside edges of the legs where they rest on the floor, cross to form four small (isometric) squares, representing the ends of the legs. From the corners of these squares, extend verticals up to the bottom edges of the seat.

The drawing of the bench is now completed, except for the addition of the stretchers. Although these are drawn by applying the principles that have already been used, they are somewhat more difficult because they are not in contact with any of the surfaces of our basic box.

The stretchers were described as being 2″ high and raised 3″ off the ground; their top edges will thus be 5″ above the ends of the legs. Since the stretchers are fastened between the legs, our measuring must be done on the lines representing the inside corners of the legs; for the legs at the extreme left and right, they will be the edges nearest the center of the drawing. Since the stretchers are horizontal, we need measure them only on these two legs; their positions at the other two corners of the bench will be determined automatically by drawing the lines parallel with the basic lines.

Starting at the bottom of the inside edge of the leg farthest to the left, we measure up 5″; this measurement is repeated on the right leg. Through these points, we draw lines parallel with the two basic slanted lines, to form an (isometric) rectangle. These lines should be extended on into the adjacent faces of the legs.

The stretchers are 1″ thick. Measuring along the lines just drawn, mark points 1″ from the inside corner of each leg, on the faces of the legs. Draw lines through these points parallel with the slanted basic lines. The result is an outline of the top edges of the stretchers.

The stretchers are 2″ wide. The inside of the stretchers is visible at the far corner of the bench. Measure 2″ down from the point where the top edges of the stretchers meet the corner of the back leg, and through that point draw lines parallel with the upper edges of the stretchers. On the near end and side of the bench, the inside of the stretchers will be hidden, but the outside will be visible. Where the top front edge of the stretcher meets the corner of the front leg, measure down 2″ (on each side of the leg) and draw the usual lines. From the previously measured points on the faces of the legs at the extreme left and right of the drawing, marking the corners of the stretchers where they meet the legs, drop verticals to meet the bottom edges of the stretchers.

In preparing the picture, we drew some guidelines that are not part of the bench; other lines represent actual parts of the bench, but would be hidden when it was viewed from the angle represented. Retrace the drawing so as to darken the lines representing actual and visible parts of the bench. If desired, the drawing can now be inked and the extraneous lines erased.

The procedure that has just been described is much simpler than it seems, and a little practice should enable the designer to handle this extremely useful projection easily.

Simple Nonisometric Shapes

Isometric projection is best adapted to representing straight-lined objects formed with right angles, since only such objects can be directly measured in isometric. Occasionally, however, it may be desirable to make isometric drawings of objects that have decorative details or other elements that involve curves, or angles other than 90°, so the designer should be familiar with the methods for drawing them.

Drawing an octagonal prism in isometric is, for instance, only slightly more difficult than drawing a cube. (See *Figure 16-7*.)

Let us assume a prism 3'-0'' high, with an octagonal cross section made by cutting the corners from a 2'-0'' square. First draw the square with true angles (in orthographic projection), to whatever scale is convenient. The corners of the octagon can be found by using the following method: Draw the square's diagonals. Open the compass to half the length of one diagonal and use the corners as centers to mark points on the edges. Then connect each point to the other closest to it by a straight line, thus forming an octagon.

Next draw a 2'-0'' square in isometric (to the same scale used for the orthographic drawing). By means of a strip of paper, copy the measurements from the orthographic square and transfer them to the sides of the isometric square, and add the lines necessary to complete the isomet-

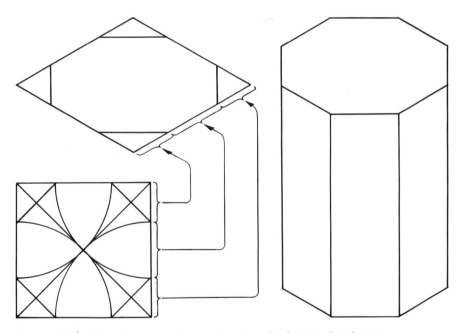

Figure 16-7. Drawing an octagonal prism in isometric. *Lower left:* a square of the specified size is drawn in orthographic projection, and an octagon constructed within it. Above it is an isometric square of the same size; the points at which the corners of the octagon touch the basic square are transferred from the orthographic to the isometric drawing. *Right:* verticals of the specified length have been dropped from the corners, their bottom ends joined, and construction lines erased.

ric projection of the octagon (the lines that cut across the corners of the square are horizontal and vertical in isometric projection). Extend vertical lines down from the corners of the octagon. Only four of the edges of the prism would be visible in this position; omit those that would be hidden. From the corners of the isometric octagon, measure down 3'-0'' along the verticals, mark the points, and connect with straight lines; the result will be an isometric projection of the prism.

For a somewhat more difficult construction, let us draw a pyramid with six identical sides. (See *Figure 16-8.*)

As in the case of the octagon, the first step is to draw the hexagonal base in orthographic projection. A hexagon is most easily constructed by first drawing a circle; let us assume a hexagon fitted into a circle with a radius of 1'-0''. Having drawn the circle to scale, place the point of the compass on the circumference and make a mark cutting the circumference at the same distance as the radius; then place the point on the mark and make a new mark at the same distance beyond it. Stepping around the circle in this way divides it into six equal arcs; connecting the dividing points by straight lines forms a hexagon.

Unlike the octagon, the hexagon is not related to a square. Before it can be projected in isometric, it must be enclosed in a straight-line figure

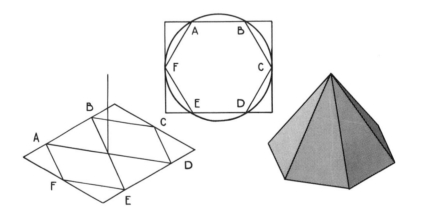

Figure 16-8. Drawing a hexagonal pyramid in isometric. At the top center, a hexagon is drawn inside a true circle (in orthographic projection); it is then enclosed in a rectangle the ends of which run through opposite corners of the hexagon, and the sides of which coincide for part of their length with two sides of the hexagon. This rectangle is redrawn in isometric (*bottom left*), and the corners of the hexagon are copied on it from the orthographic construction. The center of the hexagon is found by drawing two of its diagonals, and from that point a vertical is erected of the height specified for the pyramid. That point is then connected to each corner of the hexagon.

with the sides meeting at right angles. Any square or rectangle larger than the hexagon could be used, and the hexagon could be placed in any position with reference to the sides of the enclosing figure. The simplest construction method, however, is to use a rectangle the same length as the distance between opposite corners of the hexagon and the same width as the distance between opposite sides, with the hexagon placed so that two of its sides lie on the sides of the rectangle. For a hexagon based on a circle with a 1'-0'' radius, the enclosing rectangle will be 2'-0'' long; its width is incommensurable, that is, it cannot be expressed in feet and inches, so it must be transferred by a paper strip from the orthographic to the isometric projection.

The next step, then, is to enclose the orthographic hexagon in a rectangle by extending two of its sides and drawing lines vertical to them through the remaining corners of the hexagon.

The basic isometric lines are then drawn; in this case it is most convenient to draw only the slanted lines and to add the vertical later. Let us choose position 1 for the basic lines, since that position will reveal the shape of the pyramid most clearly.

The length and width of the rectangle are than laid out on the basic lines, and parallels are drawn to complete the rectangle in isometric. The points where the corners of the hexagon fall on the edges of the rectangle are transferred from the orthographic drawing by strips of paper. Connecting adjacent points will complete the drawing of the hexagon in isometric projection.

The specifications indicated a hexagonal pyramid, with equal sides; its point will consequently stand directly over the center of the figure. Let us assume that the pyramid is 3'-0" high. The center can be found either by drawing the diagonals of the enclosing rectangle or by connecting two sets of opposite corners of the hexagon. Next, a vertical line is run up from the center point where the diagonals cross, and a point is marked 3'-0" above it. This new point is then connected by a straight line with each of the corners of the hexagon; all but one of these edges will be visible. Guide lines and hidden edges are erased, and the construction is completed.

It is not necessary that the nonisometric figure touch the edges of the enclosing square or rectangle. In *Figure 16-9,* a box is shown with an equilateral triangle drawn in the center of each face. The drawing illustrates the method for determining the position of one of these triangles. The position of the top point of the triangle is determined by measuring its distance from the top of the rectangle and from one side edge. These measurements are transferred to the edges of the rectangle in isometric, and lines projected across parallel with the basic lines. Where the lines cross indicates the point of the triangle. The other points are identified in the same way, and the drawing is completed by connecting all three with straight lines. Any straight-line figure, however complicated, can be projected in isometric by using the same method to determine the key points.

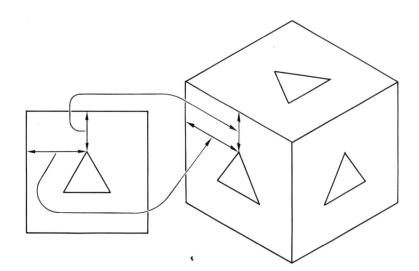

Figure 16-9. Nonisometric lines in isometric projection. A cube is shown in isometric, with an equilateral triangle drawn on each face. The drawing shows how to determine the position of the top point of one triangle. On an orthographic drawing *(left),* the distance of the point from the top of the enclosing square is determined, as well as its distance from one side edge. These dimensions are then transferred to the isometric projection of the square.

If the figure is not enclosed in an isometric shape (rectangle or square) in the actual scenery, then a rectangle can be drawn around it and erased after the projection is finished. Three-dimensional nonisometric shapes can be drawn in the same way, by enclosing them in an imaginary cube or rectangular prism, which can then easily be reproduced isometrically, and which serves as a temporary basis for measurement.

Isometric Curves and Circles

Projecting curved figures, especially if they are nongeometric and complicated, is somewhat more difficult; the simplest method is a slight modification of the familiar gridding procedure. The orthographic drawing is first gridded, using as many divisions as seems desirable. A matching grid is then drawn in isometric, the points where the design crosses the grid lines are marked, and the drawing is completed by joining them with freehand lines. This method is illustrated in *Figure 16-10.*

The nonisometric form that occurs most frequently in isometric drawings is the circle. In isometric projection, a circle appears as an ellipse, and consequently cannot be drawn accurately with a compass. If absolute

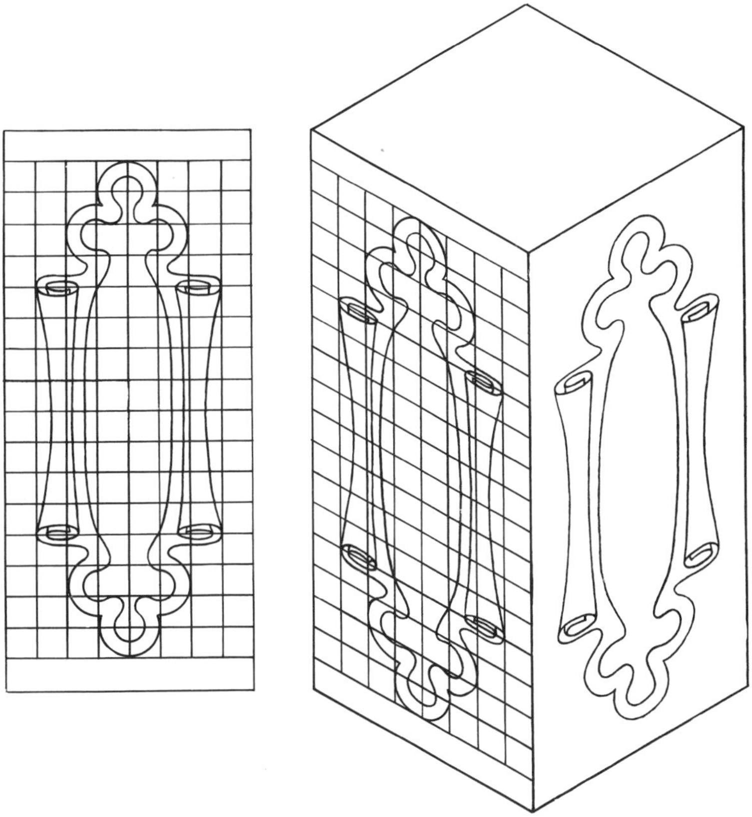

Figure 16-10. The grid method of drawing curves in isometric. A curved figure of any complexity can be transferred from orthographic to isometric projection by the familiar gridding process.

accuracy is necessary, the circle must be projected as a series of points, like any other nonisometric shape, and the points connected freehand; in that case, the familiar gridding procedure must be followed.

However, a method has been devised for using a compass to draw an approximation of an isometric projection of a circle close enough to be used in most cases without drawing attention to its deviation from a true projection. This approximation involves using four centers and two settings of the compass. (See *Figure 16-11.*)

Examination of an ellipse will demonstrate that the two ends approximate arcs of a small circle, and the two sides arcs of a larger circle. If the ellipse is enclosed in an isometric square, the midpoints of the sides of the square cut the ellipse into four sections, matching the areas that seem to be controlled by the two radii. The problem in using arcs of a circle to

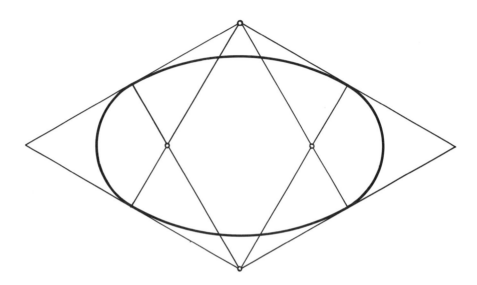

Figure 16-11. The compass approximation of circles in isometric projection. An enclosing square is drawn in isometric projection, and straight lines drawn from each 120° angle to the midpoints of the opposite sides. The four points at which these lines cross (marked here by small circles) are used as centers for drawing circular arcs tangent to the sides, which join to produce an approximation of an isometric projection of a circle.

approximate the ellipse is to find the centers from which these four sections can be drawn.

For each adjacent pair of arcs to join smoothly, their centers must lie on the same line, and the line must form right angles with the edges of the enclosing parallelogram. Construction, then, is as follows.

From the midpoint of each side of the isometric square, draw a line at right angles to the edge, across the square; in this case a true right angle must be used, not an isometric right angle. It will be discovered that the lines intersect at four points, two of them inside the square and the other two at the corners of the square. These four points are used as the centers for drawing arcs of circles connecting the midpoints of the sides of the square; each of the two points matching the corners of the square is used to draw the arc on the far side of the ellipse, and the two points inside the square are used to draw arcs connecting the two closest midpoints.

Occasionally, such an approximation may be unacceptable, but in most instances it is entirely adequate for a working drawing, and it has the advantages of being much faster to construct, and easier to make neatly, than the theoretically more accurate gridding method. *Figure 16-12* indicates the degree of error involved in this approximation.

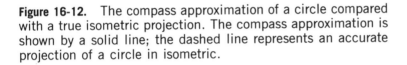

Figure 16-12. The compass approximation of a circle compared with a true isometric projection. The compass approximation is shown by a solid line; the dashed line represents an accurate projection of a circle in isometric.

Although an isometric projection often expresses the shape and construction of a scenic unit much more clearly than could be done in any number of orthographic views, essential details may be hidden even in an isometric drawing. Because there are only a few positions in which an object may be placed for an isometric drawing, the designer may discover that critical joints or other parts of the object are hidden, no matter how it is placed. Even more commonly, he may want to reveal the interior construction of an object that, when completed, has a facing hiding the supporting frame. A common solution to that problem is to draw what is called an *exploded isometric.* In such a drawing, parts of the unit are shown as if they had been moved aside, thus revealing the hidden details. (See *Figure 16-13.*)

Two principles should guide the designer in preparing an exploded isometric: one is to leave as much of the unit as possible intact; the other is to draw the parts removed as if they had been shifted in directions at right angles to the surfaces of the object (right angles, of course, in terms of the isometric projection). Arrows should then be drawn from key points on the displaced parts to the positions on the central structure where they will be placed when it is reassembled. An exploded isometric is somewhat more difficult to read than a standard isometric drawing, but is useful for showing structural relationships that cannot be indicated so clearly in any other way. (Isometric drawings appearing in other chapters include *Figures*

The Exploded
Isometric

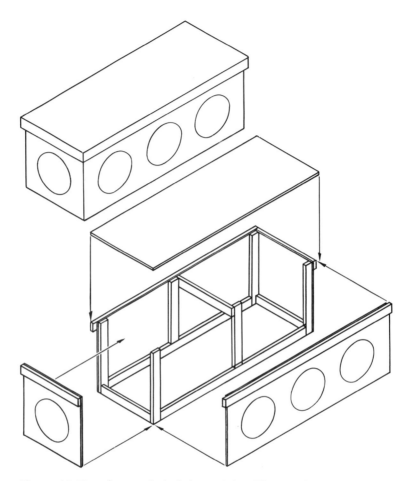

Figure 16-13. An exploded isometric. The exploded drawing shows the top raised and the near end and side moved forward to reveal the internal bracing. For comparison, a straight isometric drawing of the bench is shown at top left.

3-3, 3-4, 3-5, 3-6, 3-7, 3-10, 3-11, 3-15, 3-16, 3-17, 3-18, 3-19, 3-20, 3-21, 3-22, 3-24, 3-25, 3-26, 3-42, 3-44, 3-45, 3-46, 3-47, 3-48, 3-49, 3-50, 3-51, 3-52, 3-53, 6-6, 6-7, 7-5, and 13-1; see also 16-14 and 16-15.)

Dimensioning in Isometric

The basic methods for indicating the dimensions of objects shown in isometric projection are the same as those used in orthographic drawings; the essential difference is that the short extender lines must be drawn at isometric right angles, rather than at true right angles. Only the arrows indicating heights will appear vertical in isometric drawings; arrows showing widths and lengths will be slanted. As in orthographic drawings, the figures giving the length of slanted arrows must be oriented with relation to the edges of the cardboard, rather than to the angles of the arrows; that is, all figures and letters must be printed so that the construction workers can read them without turning the drawings.

Often, a scenic unit is shown in both isometric and orthographic projections on the same sheet of cardboard. Since dimensions are slightly easier to indicate and read on an orthographic drawing, it is preferable, where possible, to include them in the orthographic drawing and omit them from the isometric.

The scales used in making working drawings of three-dimensional units vary more than in any other type of theatrical graphics, since the sizes of the structures may vary from a wastebasket a foot high to an enormous platform structure rising 30' into the air. Where possible, full-scale drawings are most convenient for the builders. Smaller scales are much easier to use if they are selected so that an inch is represented by a unit already marked on the standard tape or yardstick. Following is a table of such scales, showing the maximum size of structure that can be drawn to each scale on a standard 22'' × 28'' sheet of cardboard (these figures make no allowance for margins).

Scaling in Three-Dimensional Units

½'' = 1''	(6'' = 1'-0''):	3'-8'' × 4'-8''
¼'' = 1''	(3'' = 1'-0''):	7'-4'' × 9'-4''
⅛'' = 1''	(1½'' = 1'-0''):	14'-8'' × 18'-8''
$^1/_{16}$'' = 1''	(¾'' = 1'-0''):	29'-4'' × 37'-4''
$^1/_{16}$'' = 2''	(⅜'' = 1'-0''):	58'-8'' × 74'-8''
$^1/_{16}$'' = 4''	($^3/_{16}$'' = 1'-0''):	117'-4'' × 149'-4''

OBLIQUE PROJECTION

One further type of drawing needs to be illustrated; it is called *oblique projection,* and it stands between isometric and orthographic.

At first glance, an oblique drawing looks somewhat like isometric. (See *Figure 16-14*.) The primary difference is that in isometric projection all three visible surfaces are equally distorted; in oblique, one surface is drawn without distortion, in orthographic projection. From key points on the corners of this drawing, slanted lines are drawn at any convenient angle, up or down, to indicate planes on which the thickness of the object

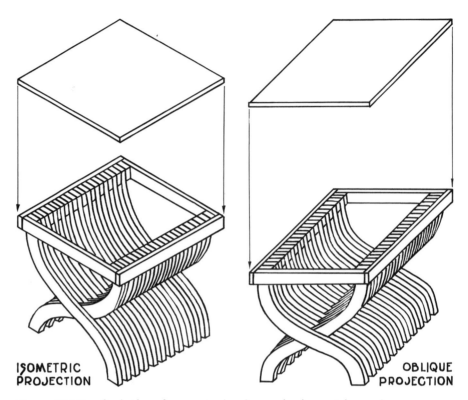

Figure 16-14. A design for a stool, shown in isometric and oblique projection (both drawings to the same scale).

can be measured. The surface chosen for representation in orthographic should be the most significant face of the object, and the one that displays the most complicated curves. If the back of the object has the same shape, its outline will appear at the ends of the slanted lines.

Isometric projection creates an effect of three-dimensionality similar to that of a perspective drawing, but with greater measurability. Oblique drawings seem almost equally solid, but since the crucial face is shown in orthographic projection, it is completely measurable in all directions, not simply parallel with the axes of the prism. This is especially useful for complicated curves, since they would be distinctly distorted by either perspective or isometric projections, and critical measurements would be impossible. Oblique drawings can be made almost as fast as orthographic. Although they are rarely used by set designers, they are extremely useful for representing such structures as elaborate cornices or furniture with complexly shaped front surfaces. (Oblique projection is also illustrated in *Figures 3-12* and *9-5*.)

ARRANGING WORKING DRAWINGS

Typically, each sheet contains a number of related working drawings, together with printed instructions and a label. Complicated views, especially in isometric, are usually drawn first on scratch cardboard or paper and then transferred to a clean sheet before inking. When several drawings are to be combined on one sheet (see *Figure 16-15*), the height and width

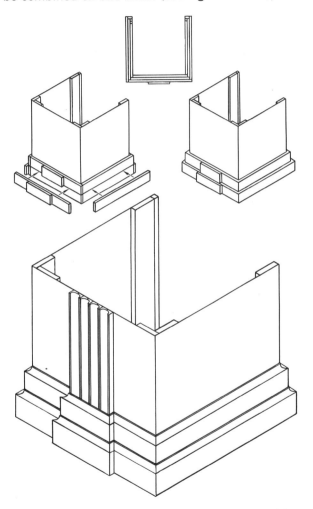

Figure 16-15. The base of a pillar. *Top:* in orthographic ground plan. *Center left:* partly assembled, with three sections removed to reveal the boards beneath. *Right:* the boards in position. *Bottom:* the unit drawn to a larger scale with cove molding added.

of each (actual, not scaled) should be recorded on a piece of note paper to facilitate arrangement of the drawings. Shifting the sketches or drawings around on the desk will enable the designer to identify the most effective arrangement. Ideally, the outline of the combined group should be similar to the shape of the cardboard, except that the vertical measurement should be proportionately shorter. Right and left margins should be equal, and the bottom margin should be distinctly larger than the top. Usually the label is centered at the bottom of the sheet, but since it does not extend entirely across the drawing, the visual margin runs through it rather than at its bottom edge.

Even with irregular drawings, it is usually possible to arrange the outer edges so as to coincide with the edges of an imaginary rectangle. Having set up what seems to be the best arrangement, the designer should total the width of all of the drawings placed side by side in a single row across the sheet. This figure is then subtracted from the total width of the cardboard. The remainder indicates the space available for margins, for printed instructions, and for separating the drawings. The vertical arrangement can be worked out by the same method.

THE DESIGNER AS ARTIST

Figures 16-16 through *16-27* constitute a brief portfolio illustrating the range of designer's drawings, from ground plans through working drawings and ending with the perspective.

The magic of theater is more than a familiar phrase. Drama is an experience—a happening. But it transcends ordinary life in that it presents experience analyzed, organized, and understood, clarified and made vivid.

As the most complex of arts, theater not only incorporates or borrows from all of the other arts, it includes numerous sub-arts, of which set design is an important one.

It is possible to approach design simply as a series of technical problems, but to do so is to reduce the designer from artist to craftsman. Designers who focus their attention on the total experience that theater is intended to provide for the audience (without neglecting the essential technical concerns) will find that their skill will increase, their imagination will broaden, and they can look forward confidently to a steady rise in their stature as artist. They will also deepen their understanding not only of set design and the art of the theater as a whole, but also of life outside the theater.

DESIGNER'S
PORTFOLIO

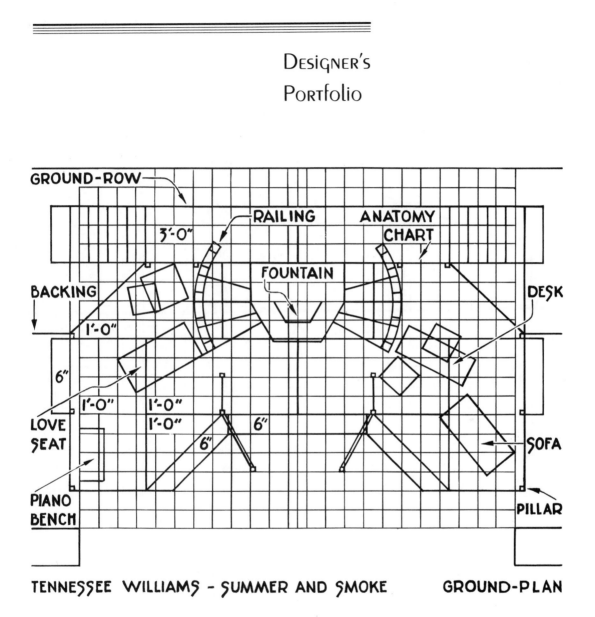

TENNESSEE WILLIAMS - SUMMER AND SMOKE   GROUND-PLAN

Figure 16-16.   A ground plan showing simultaneous staging. The design combines three separate settings, all in place throughout the performance: a living room *(stage right)*, the corner of a park, with an ornamental fountain *(center)*, and a doctor's office *(left)*.

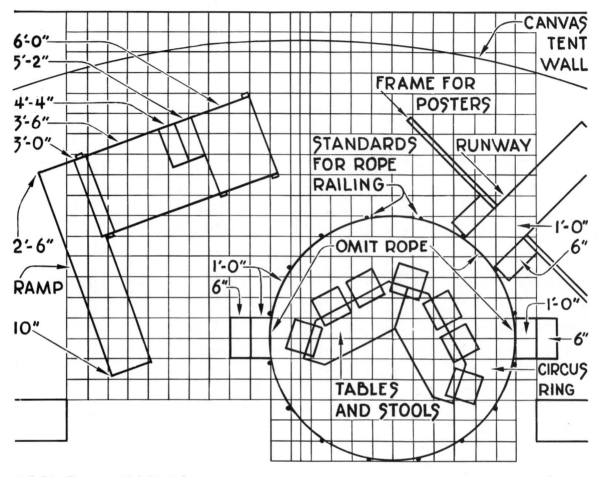

ARCHIBALD MACLEISH - J. B.   GROUND-PLAN

Figure 16-17. A set for *J. B.* Although the play is identified as occurring in a circus tent, it is only vaguely localized. The circus ring, the 3'-6'' platform, and the 4'-4'' platform constitute major acting areas, closely associated with different characters in the play. Notice that the circus ring extends well out beyond the proscenium wall, indicating that the act curtain was not used in this production.

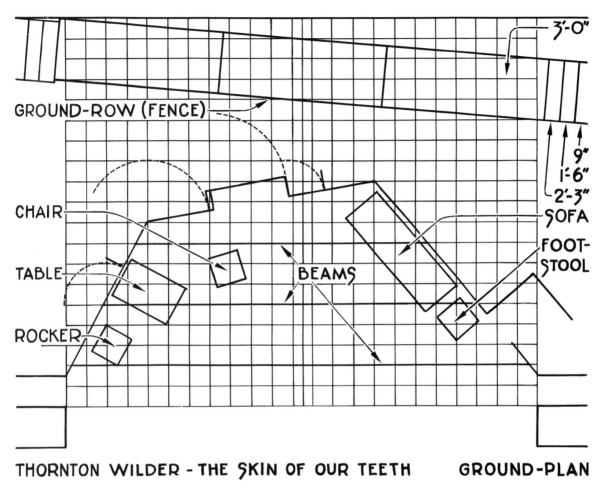

GROUND-ROW (FENCE)

3'-0"

9"
1'-6"
2'-3"
SOFA

CHAIR

FOOT-
STOOL

TABLE

BEAMS

ROCKER

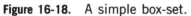

THORNTON WILDER - THE SKIN OF OUR TEETH   GROUND-PLAN

Figure 16-18. A simple box-set.

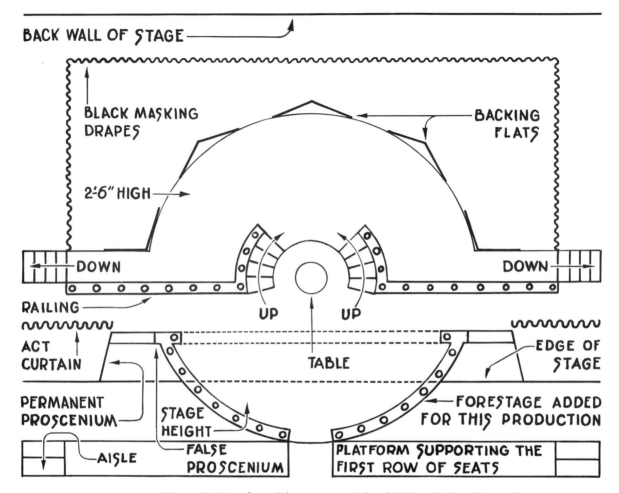

BACK WALL OF STAGE

BLACK MASKING DRAPES

BACKING FLATS

2'-6" HIGH

DOWN   **DOWN**

RAILING

UP   **UP**

ACT CURTAIN

TABLE

EDGE OF STAGE

PERMANENT PROSCENIUM

STAGE HEIGHT

FORESTAGE ADDED FOR THIS PRODUCTION

AISLE   **FALSE PROSCENIUM**

PLATFORM SUPPORTING THE FIRST ROW OF SEATS

Figure 16-19. A multipurpose set for Chekhov's *The Three Sisters* (see also *Figures 2-16* and *2-17*).

Figure 16-20. Painting and assembly elevations: Sheridan's *The Critic.* The top drawing shows slightly more than half of the back wall of the set; the center is indicated by a dashed line. Only general information about the pattern of the painting is shown here; dimensions and details were given on additional working drawings, one of which is reproduced in *Figure 16-21.* *Center:* the stage left section of the wall, from the back. *Bottom:* the center section from the front and back. At the end of the play, these units opened to reveal a spectacular sea-battle scene.

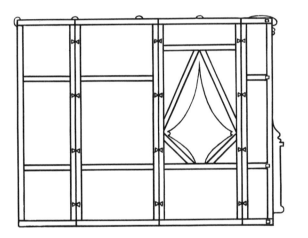

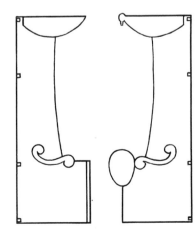
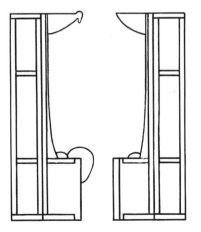

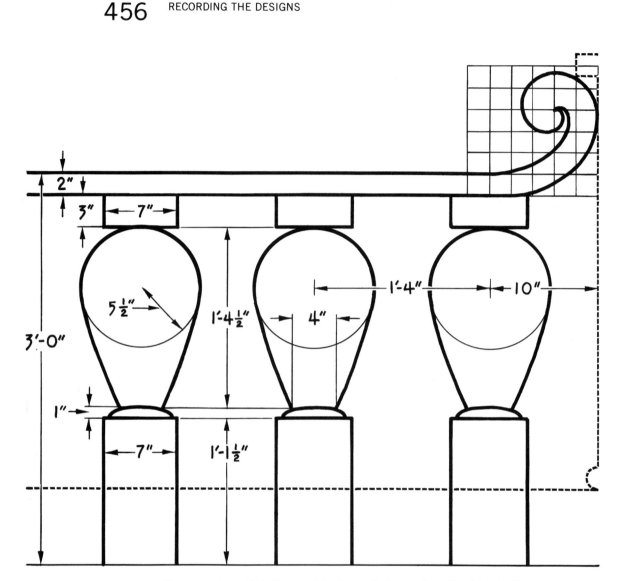

Figure 16-21. Painting guide for a balustrade: Sheridan's *The Critic*. This drawing shows part of the railing from *Figure 16-20*, at a scale making it possible to supply dimensions. The bottom curves of the balusters and the spiral section are drawn freehand; all other parts of the design are mechanically defined. The balustrade fits against the base of a pillar, and a platform stands in front of the flats, concealing the lower part; the edges of these units are indicated by dashed lines.

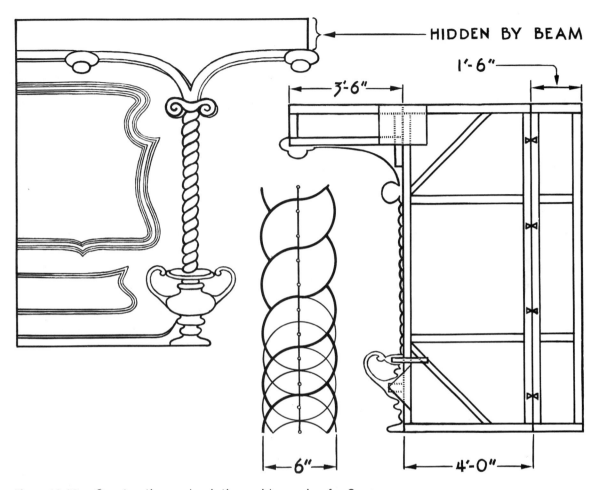

Figure 16-22. Construction and painting guide: a wing for Oscar Wilde's *The Importance of Being Earnest,* Act III. The construction is shown at the right. The pattern of the twisted section of the column is made up of arcs of overlapping circles, with radii of 3″ and centers spaced along a straight line at 2″ intervals. The center drawing shows the pattern, with the construction circles drawn full at the bottom and the lines appearing in the pattern drawn heavy; at the top, only the pattern lines are shown. Additional information about construction and painting was given on other drawings to a larger scale. (See *Figure 6-14* for a photograph of the finished set.)

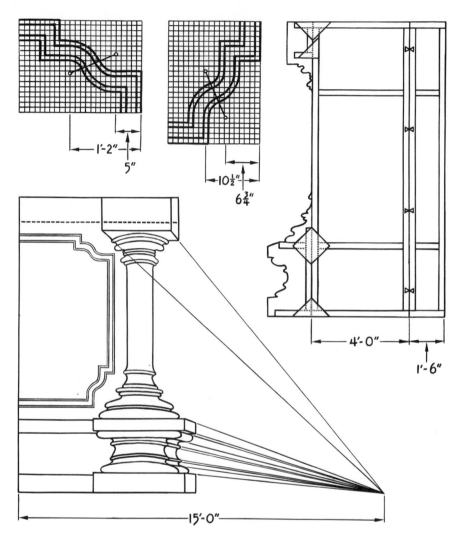

Figure 16-23. Construction and painting guide: a wing for *The Importance of Being Earnest,* Act I. As shown in the top right drawing, the wing is made of two stock flats, with shaped pieces of plywood fastened to one edge. Thickness is simulated with paint, the edges aligned with an artificial vanishing point *(lower left).* The area above the dashed line was hidden by a beam. The pattern for the molding, which was painted on the flat, is shown *(top left)* superimposed on a grid of 1″ squares. The curved sections are identical in pattern, although placed differently. The curves in each unit are drawn from two centers and meet at a line drawn between the centers. The precise shaping of the pillar was given on other drawings. (See *Figure 2-18* for a photograph of the finished set.)

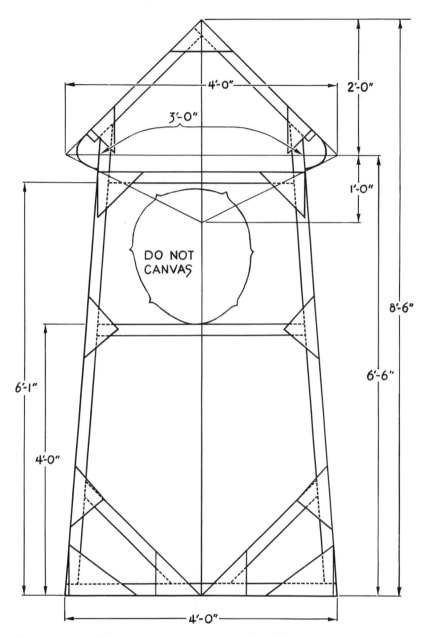

DO NOT
CANVAS

Figure 16-24. Dimensioning nonrectangular flats: construction guide for towers for *Simon Big-Ears.* This drawing illustrates the design of an irregularly shaped flat so as to provide easy measurement. The curves at the sides of the roof are free-handed, as is the opening in the canvas (shown full scale on a different working drawing). All other dimensions are simple. (See also *Figures 9-6* and *16-25.*)

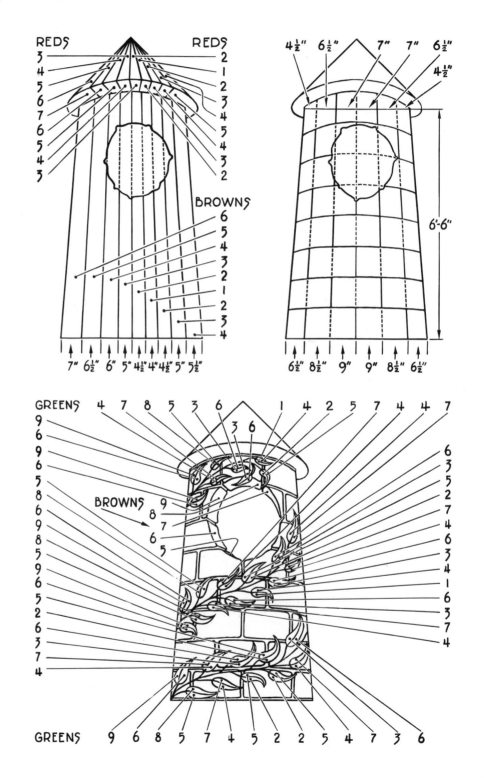

Figure 16-25. Painting guide for the *Simon Big-Ears* towers. The two towers were mirror images; only the stage right one is shown. The tower was first painted in nine vertical stripes (top left); the edges of the stripes were then blended, and the blending reinforced by spattering. Mortar lines were added *(upper right)*: the mortar lines are shown solid, construction lines are shown by dashes. All the colors used in the towers were arranged to suggest three dimensions, so that even the leaves at the edges of the tower are shown darker than those in the center. As a result, an unusually large number of colors, and of separate areas, are specified. The color numbers corresponded to the code designations appearing in the designer's color-sample book. (*Figure 9-6* shows a photograph of the completed set.)

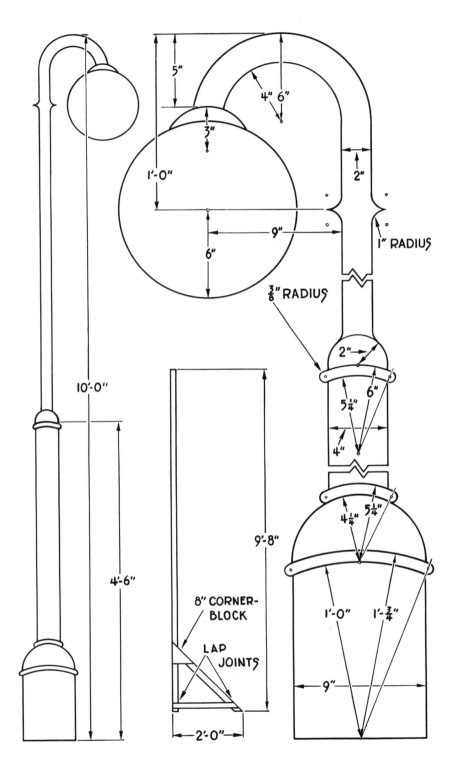

Figure 16-26. Construction and painting guide for a lamp post for Thornton Wilder's *The Skin of Our Teeth*. This drawing illustrates the dimensioning of a fairly complex structure; all curves are arcs of circles. The lamp post was cut from plywood, with thickness suggested by painting. It was supported by a jack attached to the back, shown in the center bottom drawing.

Figure 16-27. A multipurpose set for Goethe's *Faust*. Architectural forms combine to define acting areas and provide a flexible machine for organizing the actors' movements. [Designed by David Moore.].

INDEX

The page numbers of illustrations are given in italics.